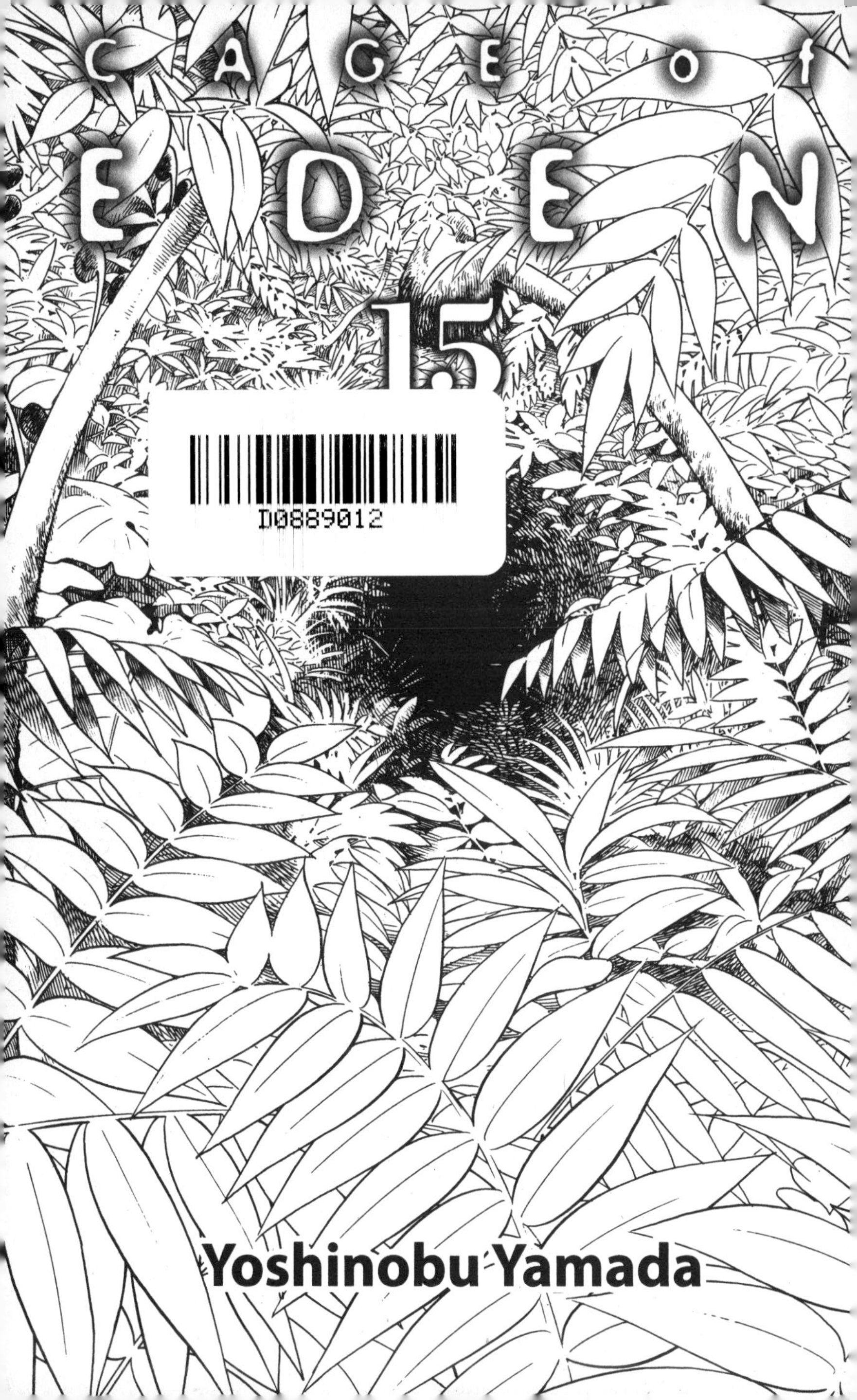
CAGE of EDEN
15
Yoshinobu Yamada

CAGE of EDEN

CONTENTS

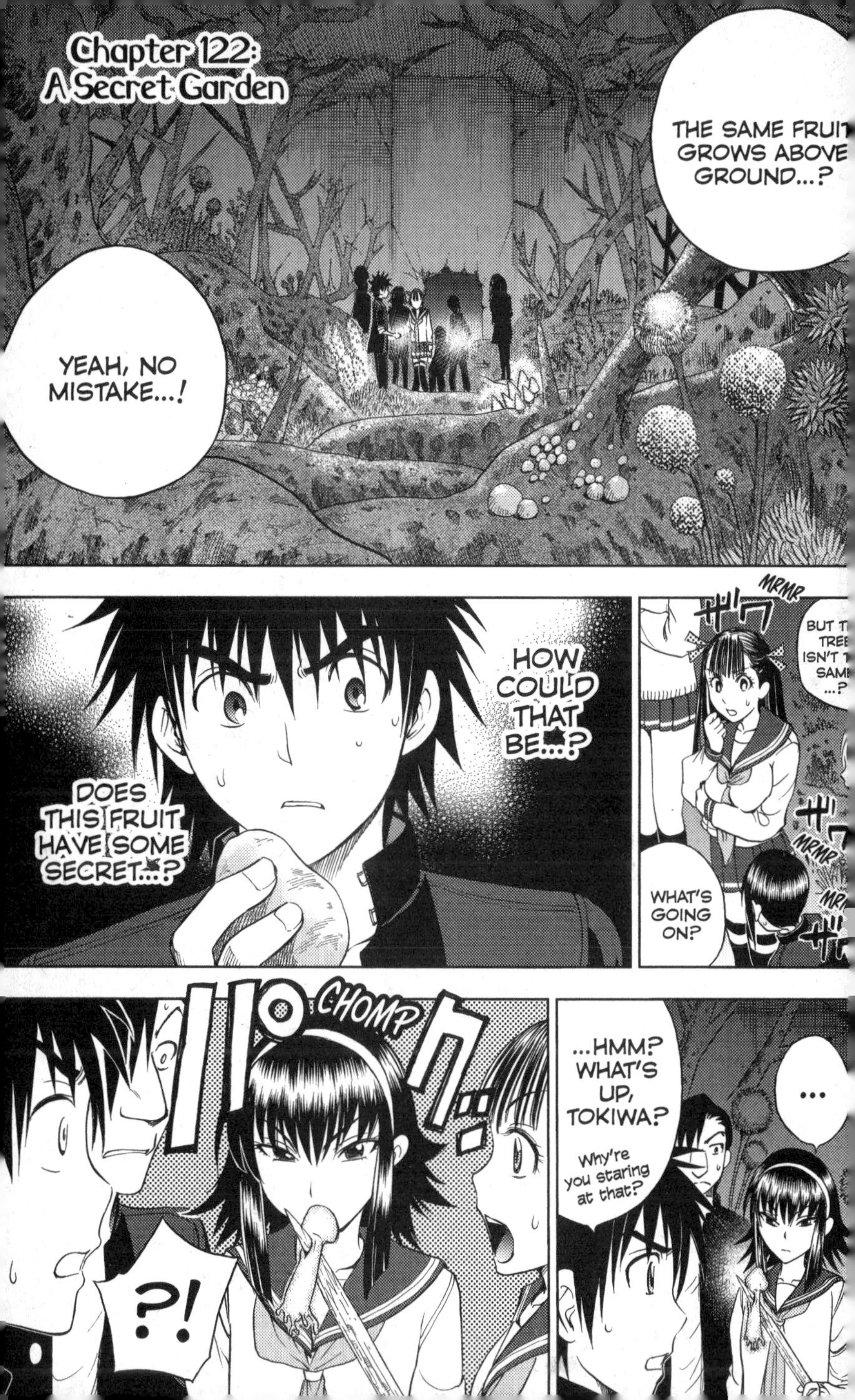
Chapter 122: A Secret Garden
THE SAME FRUIT GROWS ABOVE GROUND...?
YEAH, NO MISTAKE...!
MRMR
BUT T TREE ISN'T T SAM ...?
MRMR
WHAT'S GOING ON?
HOW COULD THAT BE...?
DOES THIS FRUIT HAVE SOME SECRET...?
...HMM? WHAT'S UP, TOKIWA?
Why're you staring at that?
...
CHOMP
?!

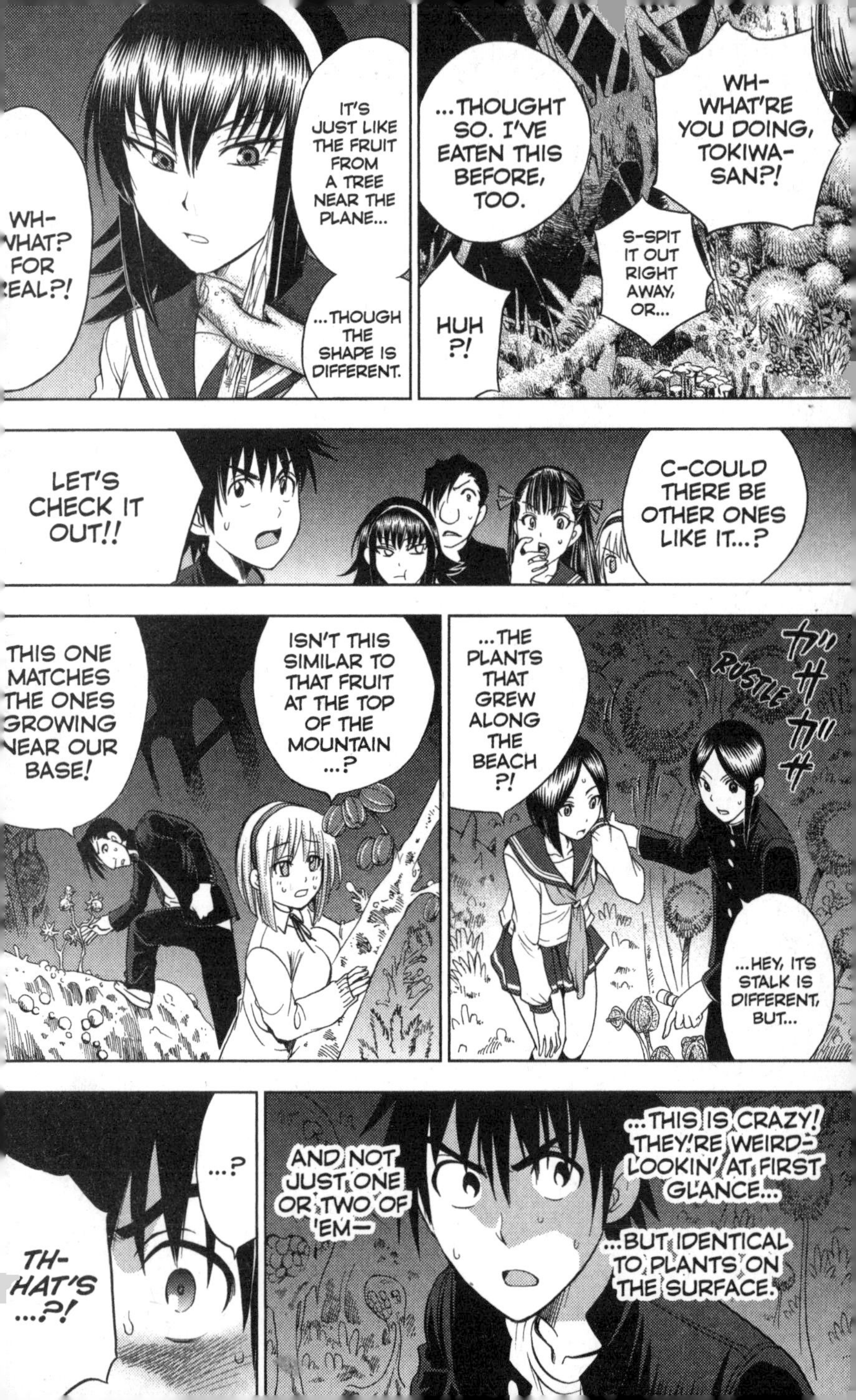
WH- WHAT'RE YOU DOING, TOKIWA-SAN?!
...THOUGHT SO. I'VE EATEN THIS BEFORE, TOO.
S-SPIT IT OUT RIGHT AWAY, OR...
HUH ?!
IT'S JUST LIKE THE FRUIT FROM A TREE NEAR THE PLANE...
...THOUGH THE SHAPE IS DIFFERENT.
WH- HAT? FOR EAL?!
C-COULD THERE BE OTHER ONES LIKE IT...?
LET'S CHECK IT OUT!!
RUSTLE
...THE PLANTS THAT GREW ALONG THE BEACH ?!
...HEY, ITS STALK IS DIFFERENT, BUT...
ISN'T THIS SIMILAR TO THAT FRUIT AT THE TOP OF THE MOUNTAIN ...?
THIS ONE MATCHES THE ONES GROWING EAR OUR BASE!
...THIS IS CRAZY! THEY'RE WEIRD-LOOKIN' AT FIRST GLANCE...
...BUT IDENTICAL TO PLANTS ON THE SURFACE.
AND NOT JUST ONE OR TWO OF 'EM—
...?
TH-HAT'S ...?!

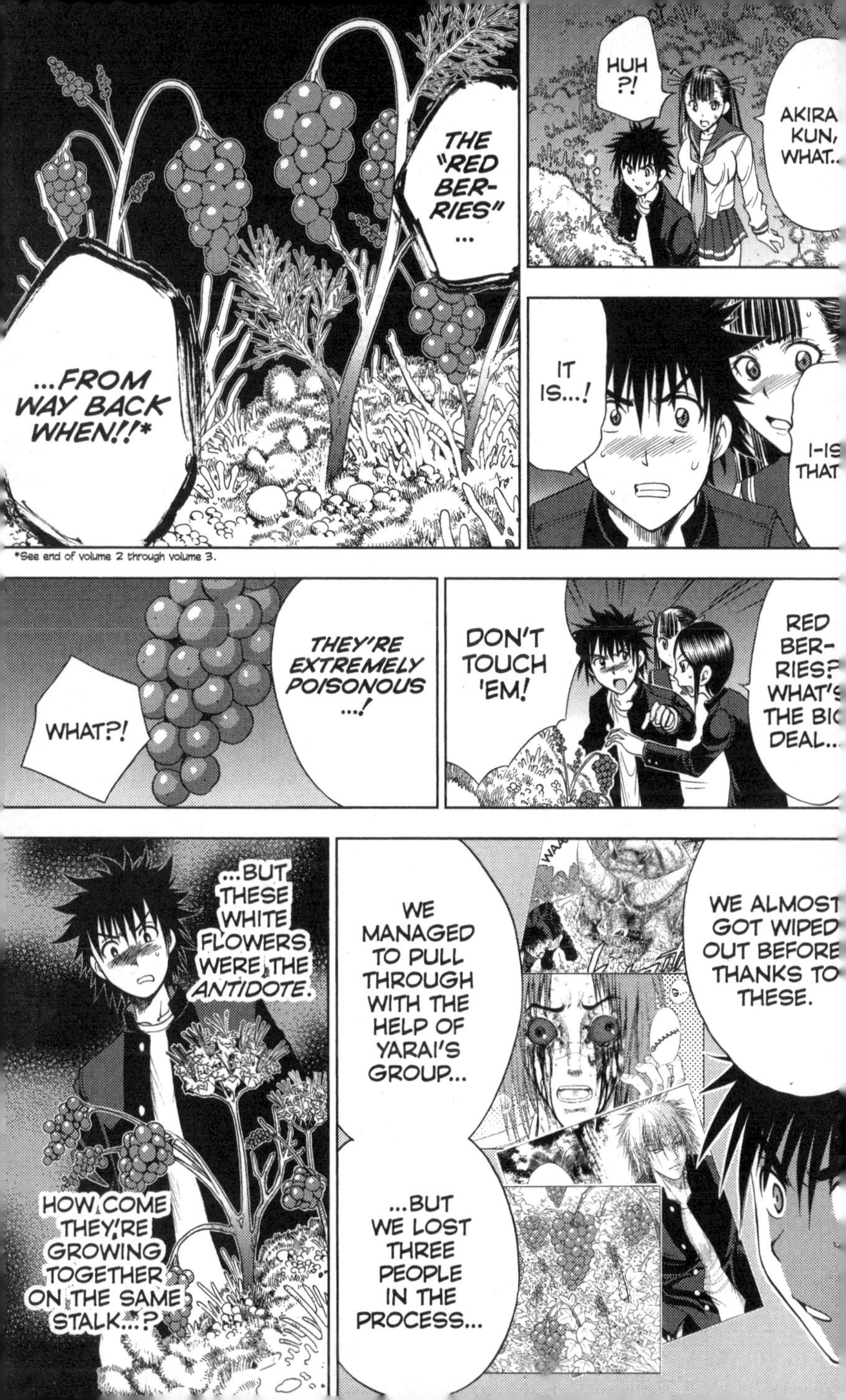
AKIRA KUN, WHAT..
HUH?!
I-IS THAT
IT IS...!
THE "RED BERRIES"...
...FROM WAY BACK WHEN!!*
RED BERRIES? WHAT'S THE BIG DEAL...
DON'T TOUCH 'EM!
THEY'RE EXTREMELY POISONOUS...!
WHAT?!
WE ALMOST GOT WIPED OUT BEFORE THANKS TO THESE.
WE MANAGED TO PULL THROUGH WITH THE HELP OF YARAI'S GROUP...
...BUT WE LOST THREE PEOPLE IN THE PROCESS...
...BUT THESE WHITE FLOWERS WERE THE ANTIDOTE.
HOW COME THEY'RE GROWING TOGETHER ON THE SAME STALK...?

*See end of volume 2 through volume 3.

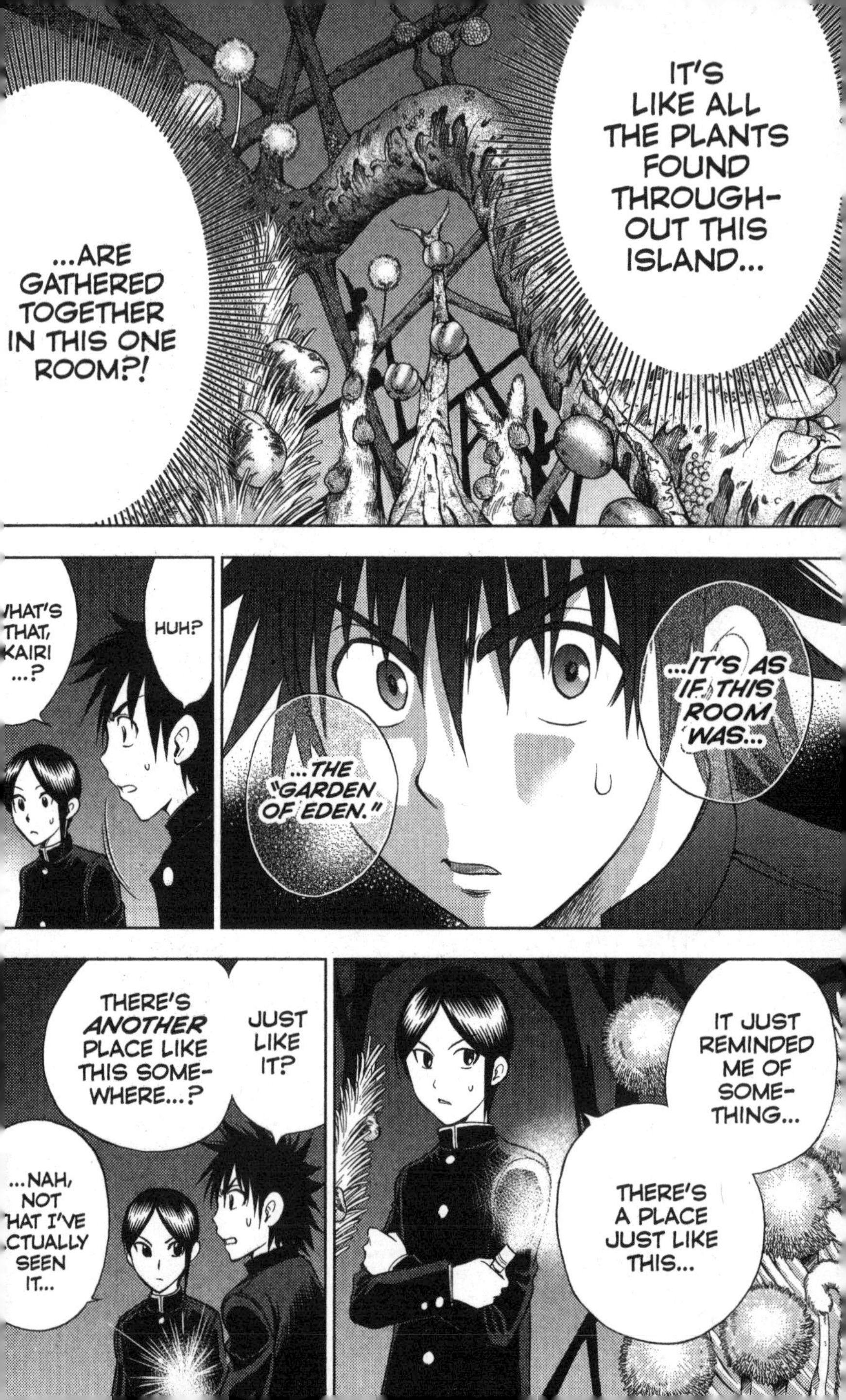

IT'S LIKE ALL THE PLANTS FOUND THROUGH-OUT THIS ISLAND...
...ARE GATHERED TOGETHER IN THIS ONE ROOM?!
...IT'S AS IF THIS ROOM WAS...
...THE "GARDEN OF EDEN."
HUH?
HAT'S THAT, KAIRI ...?
IT JUST REMINDED ME OF SOME-THING...
THERE'S A PLACE JUST LIKE THIS...
JUST LIKE IT?
THERE'S *ANOTHER* PLACE LIKE THIS SOME-WHERE...?
...NAH, NOT HAT I'VE CTUALLY SEEN IT...

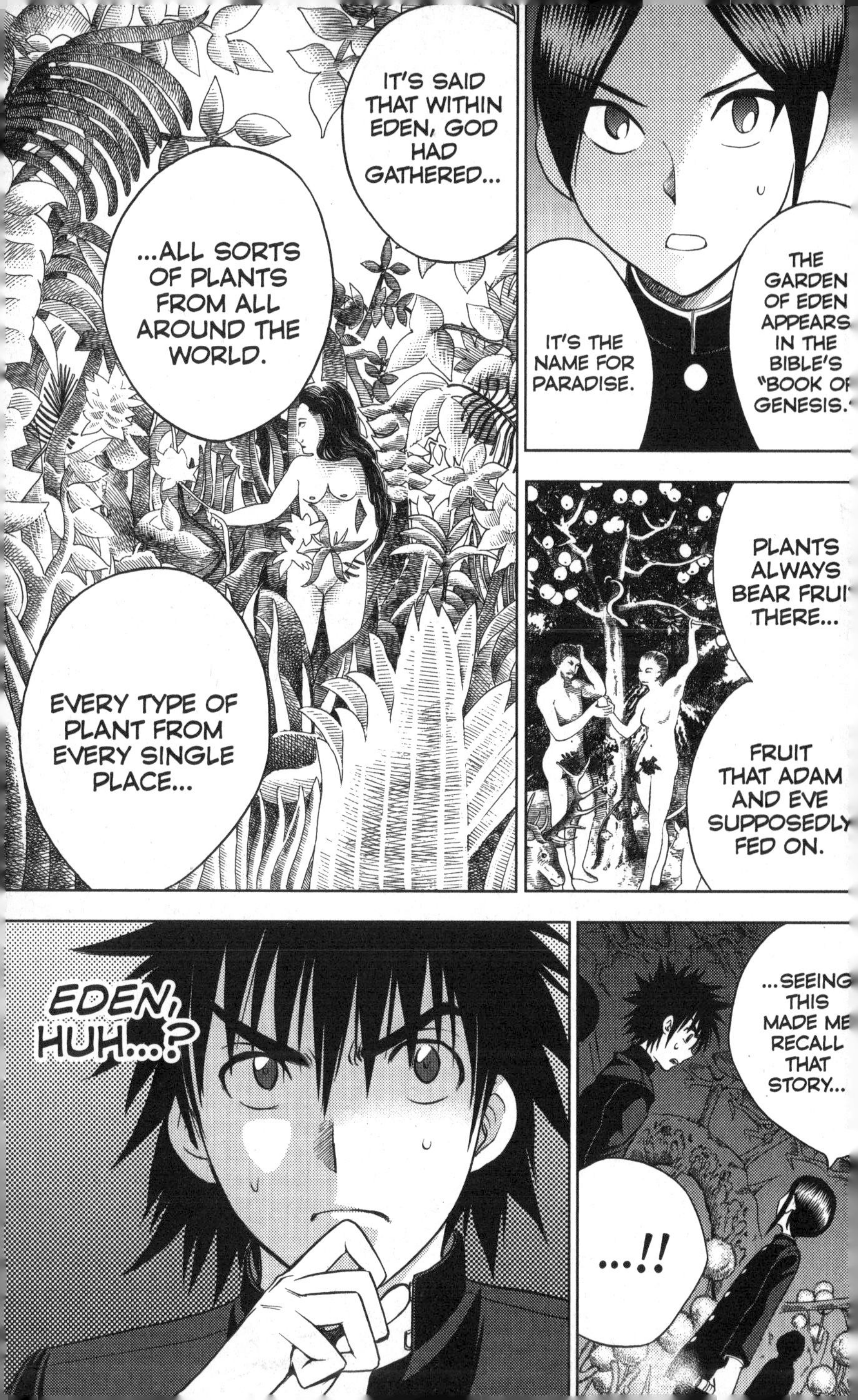
THE GARDEN OF EDEN APPEARS IN THE BIBLE'S "BOOK OF GENESIS."
IT'S THE NAME FOR PARADISE.
PLANTS ALWAYS BEAR FRUIT THERE...
FRUIT THAT ADAM AND EVE SUPPOSEDLY FED ON.
IT'S SAID THAT WITHIN EDEN, GOD HAD GATHERED...
...ALL SORTS OF PLANTS FROM ALL AROUND THE WORLD.
EVERY TYPE OF PLANT FROM EVERY SINGLE PLACE...
...SEEING THIS MADE ME RECALL THAT STORY...
...!!
EDEN, HUH...?

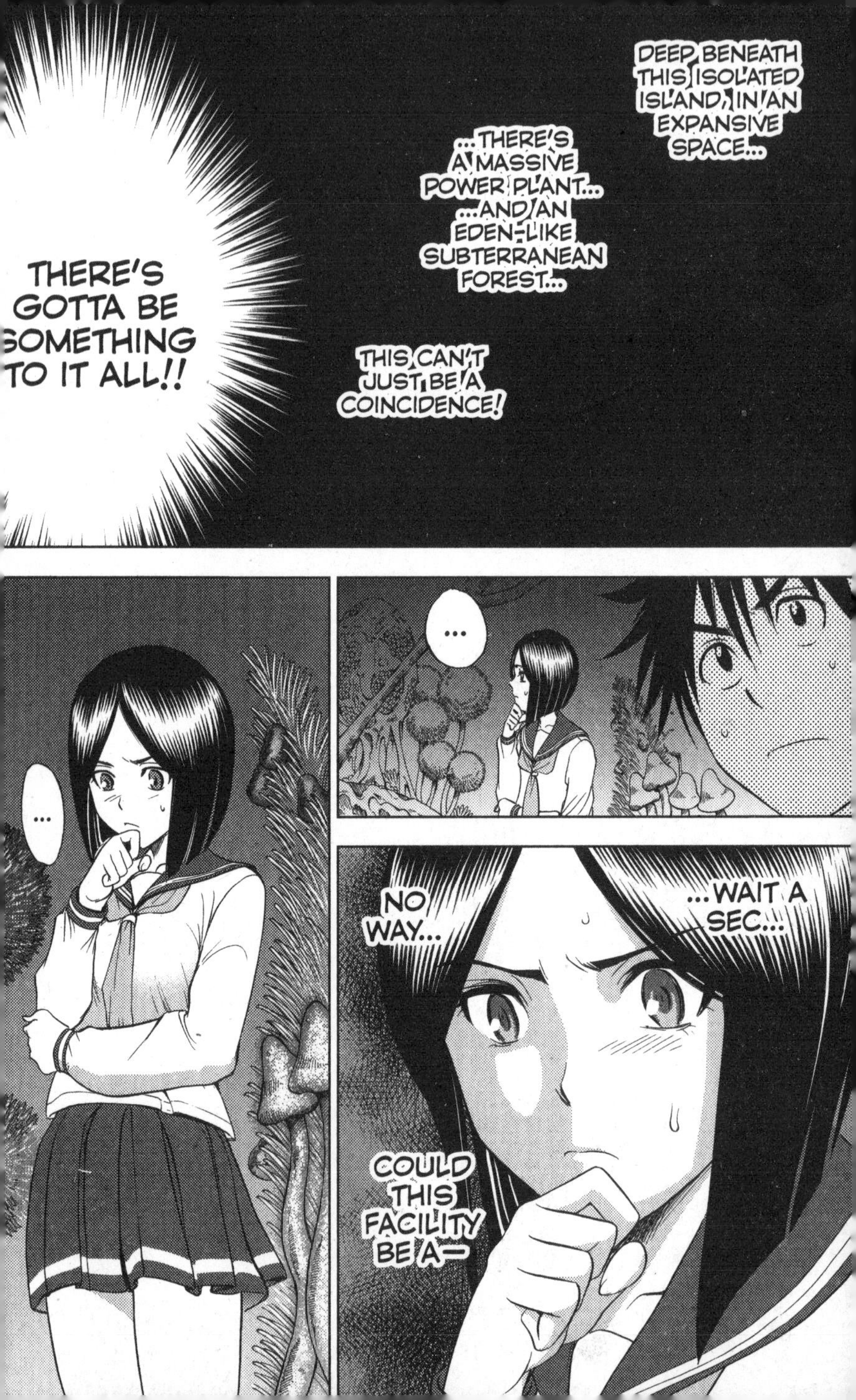
DEEP BENEATH THIS ISOLATED ISLAND, IN AN EXPANSIVE SPACE...
...THERE'S A MASSIVE POWER PLANT... ...AND AN EDEN-LIKE SUBTERRANEAN FOREST...
THIS CAN'T JUST BE A COINCIDENCE!
THERE'S GOTTA BE SOMETHING TO IT ALL!!
...
...WAIT A SEC...
NO WAY...
COULD THIS FACILITY BE A—
...

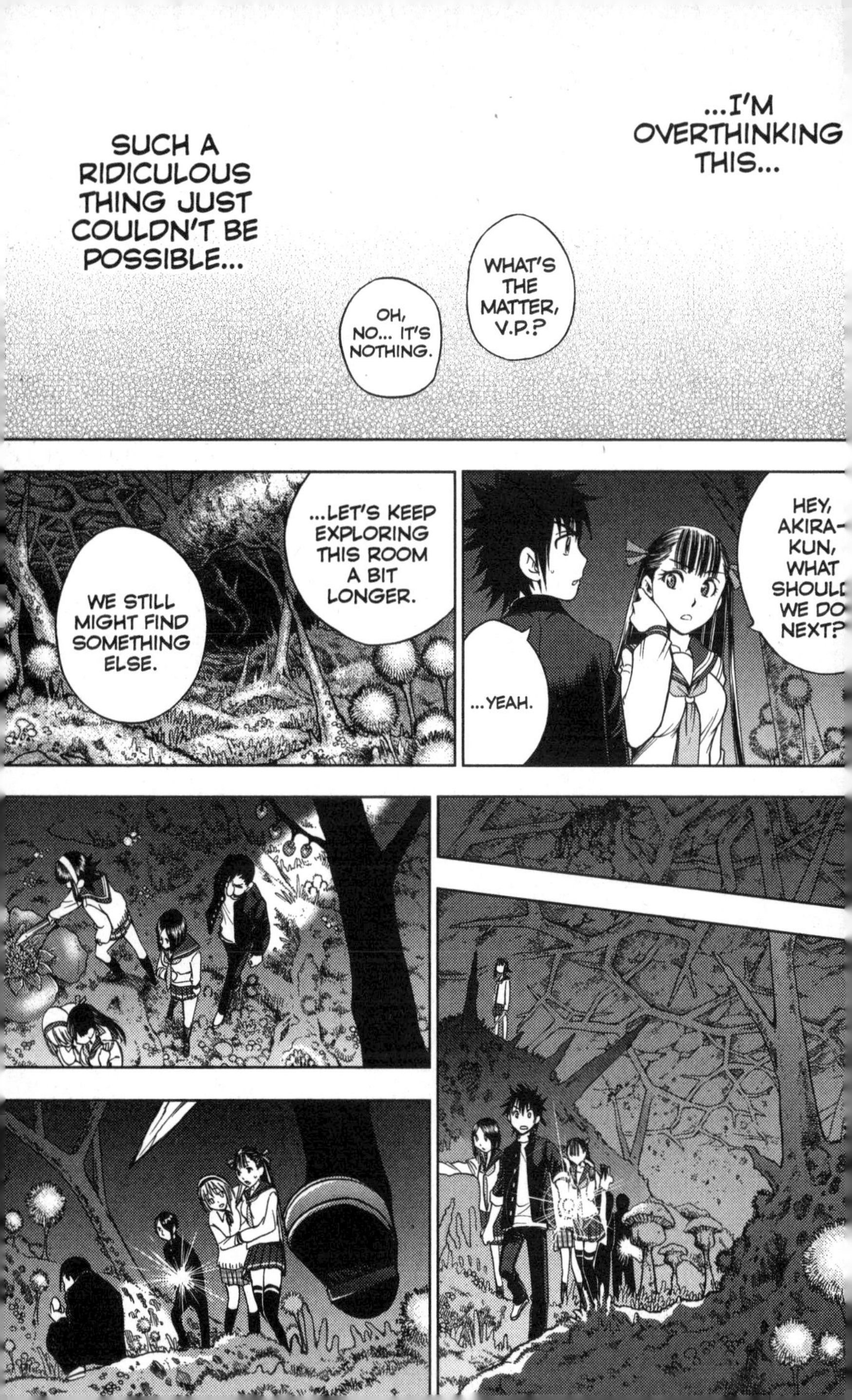
...I'M OVERTHINKING THIS...
SUCH A RIDICULOUS THING JUST COULDN'T BE POSSIBLE...
WHAT'S THE MATTER, V.P.?
OH, NO... IT'S NOTHING.
HEY, AKIRA-KUN, WHAT SHOULD WE DO NEXT?
...YEAH.
...LET'S KEEP EXPLORING THIS ROOM A BIT LONGER.
WE STILL MIGHT FIND SOMETHING ELSE.

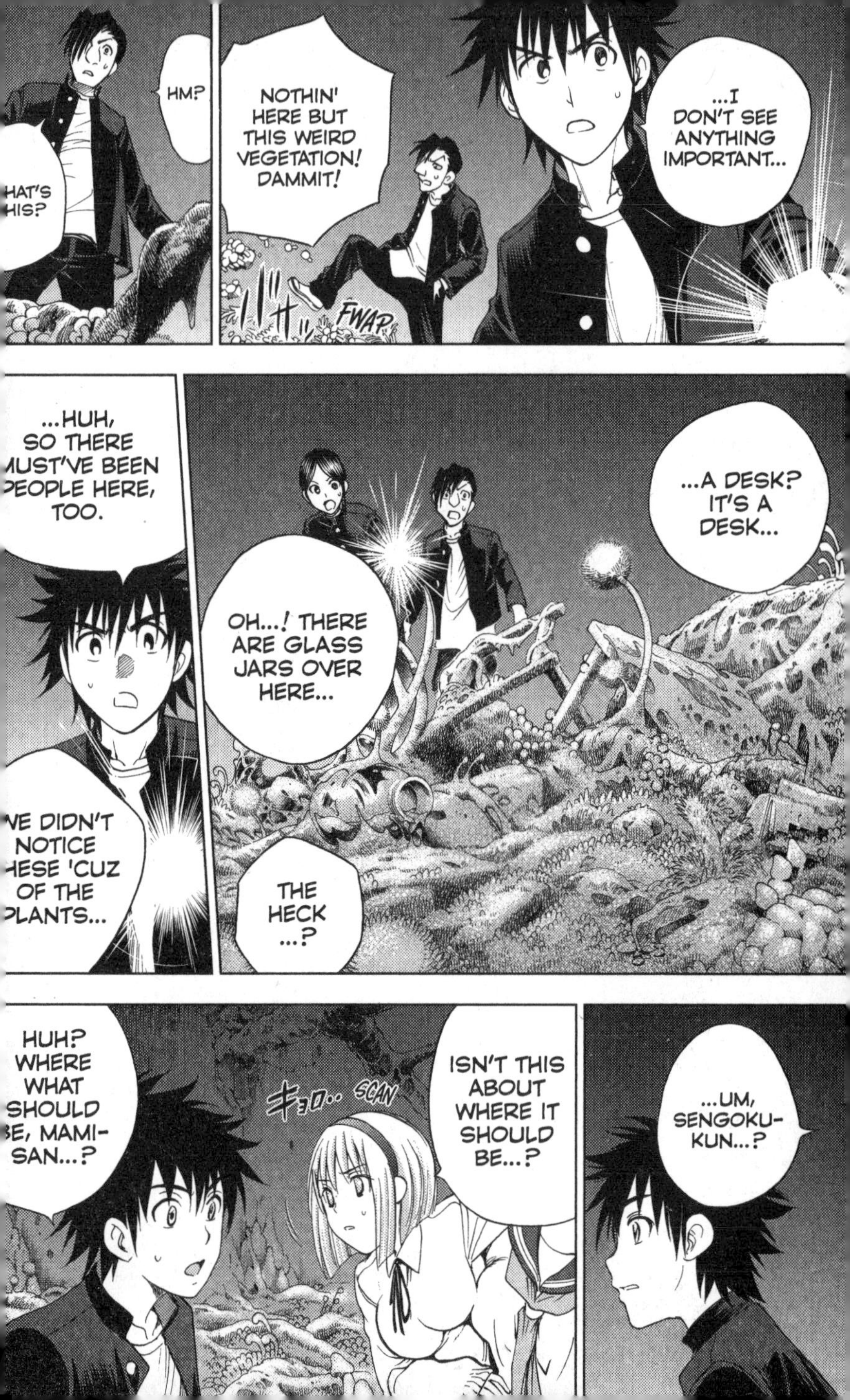
...I DON'T SEE ANYTHING IMPORTANT...
NOTHIN' HERE BUT THIS WEIRD VEGETATION! DAMMIT!
FWAP
HM?
HAT'S HIS?
...A DESK? IT'S A DESK...
OH...! THERE ARE GLASS JARS OVER HERE...
THE HECK ...?
...HUH, SO THERE MUST'VE BEEN PEOPLE HERE, TOO.
WE DIDN'T NOTICE THESE 'CUZ OF THE PLANTS...
...UM, SENGOKU-KUN...?
ISN'T THIS ABOUT WHERE IT SHOULD BE...?
キョロ‥ SCAN
HUH? WHERE WHAT SHOULD BE, MAMI-SAN...?

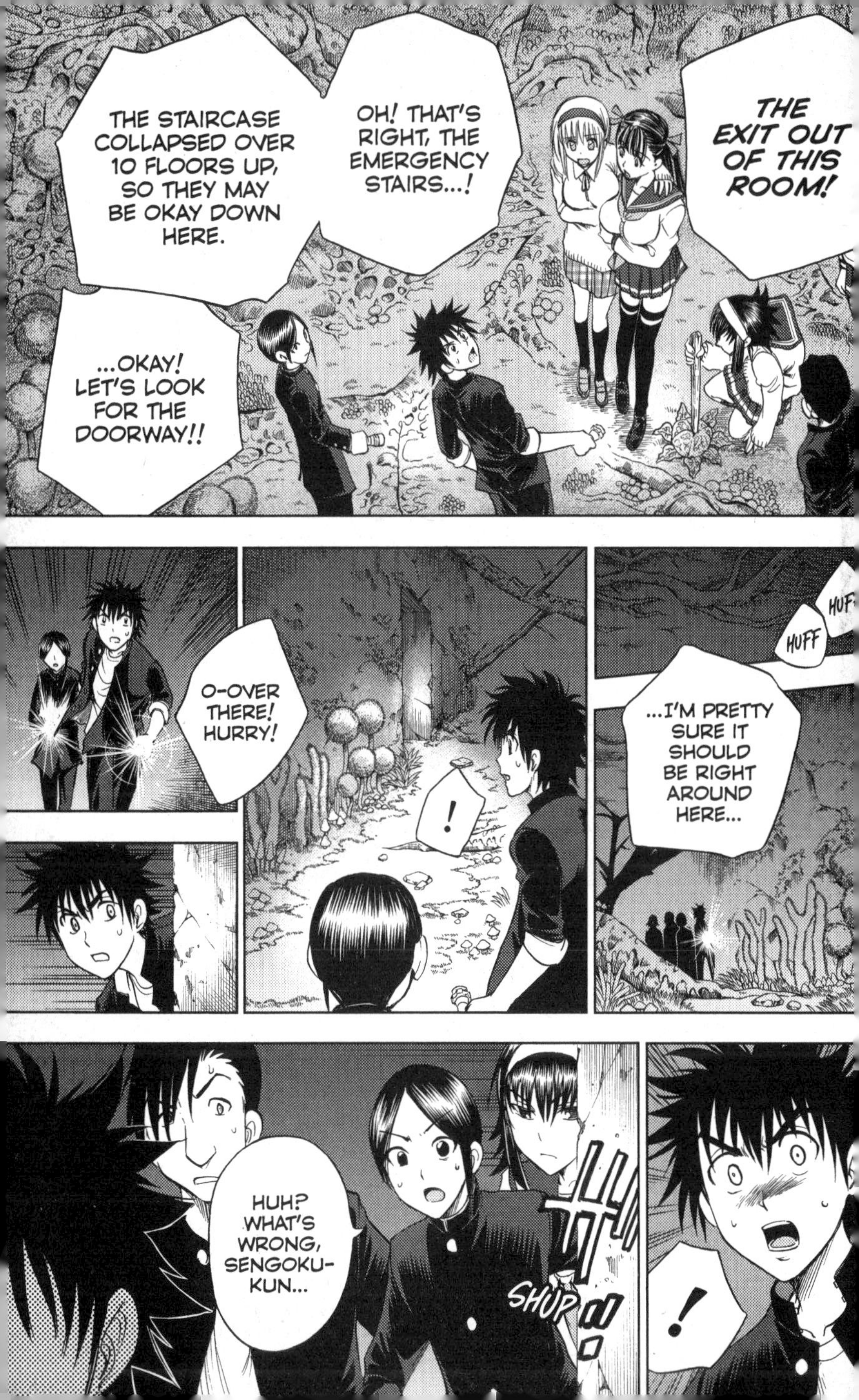
THE EXIT OUT OF THIS ROOM!
OH! THAT'S RIGHT, THE EMERGENCY STAIRS...!
THE STAIRCASE COLLAPSED OVER 10 FLOORS UP, SO THEY MAY BE OKAY DOWN HERE.
...OKAY! LET'S LOOK FOR THE DOORWAY!!
HUFF
HUFF
...I'M PRETTY SURE IT SHOULD BE RIGHT AROUND HERE...
!
O-OVER THERE! HURRY!
!
SHUP
HUH? WHAT'S WRONG, SENGOKU-KUN...

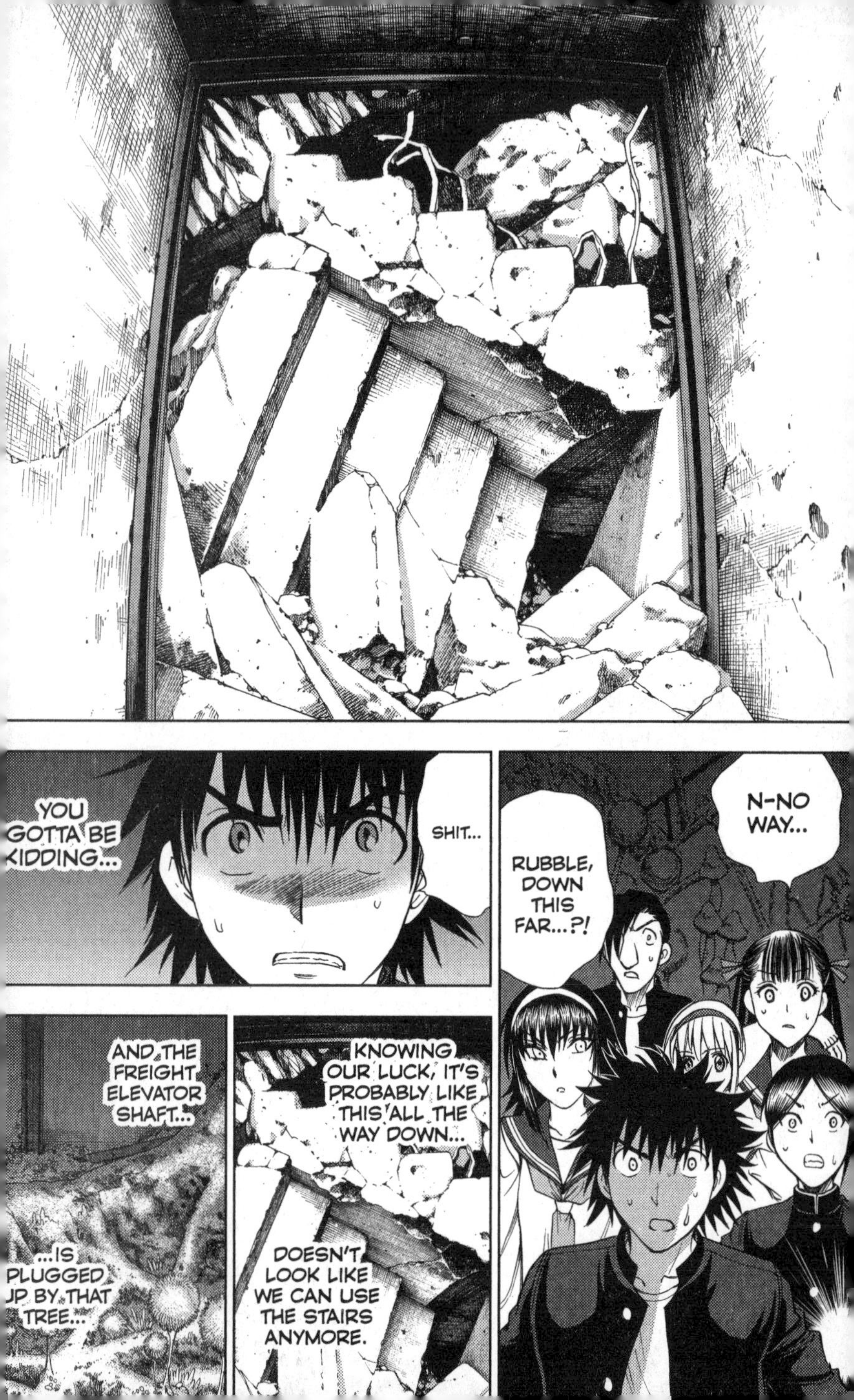
N-NO WAY...
RUBBLE, DOWN THIS FAR...?!
SHIT...
YOU GOTTA BE KIDDING...
KNOWING OUR LUCK, IT'S PROBABLY LIKE THIS ALL THE WAY DOWN...
DOESN'T LOOK LIKE WE CAN USE THE STAIRS ANYMORE.
AND THE FREIGHT ELEVATOR SHAFT...
...IS PLUGGED UP BY THAT TREE...

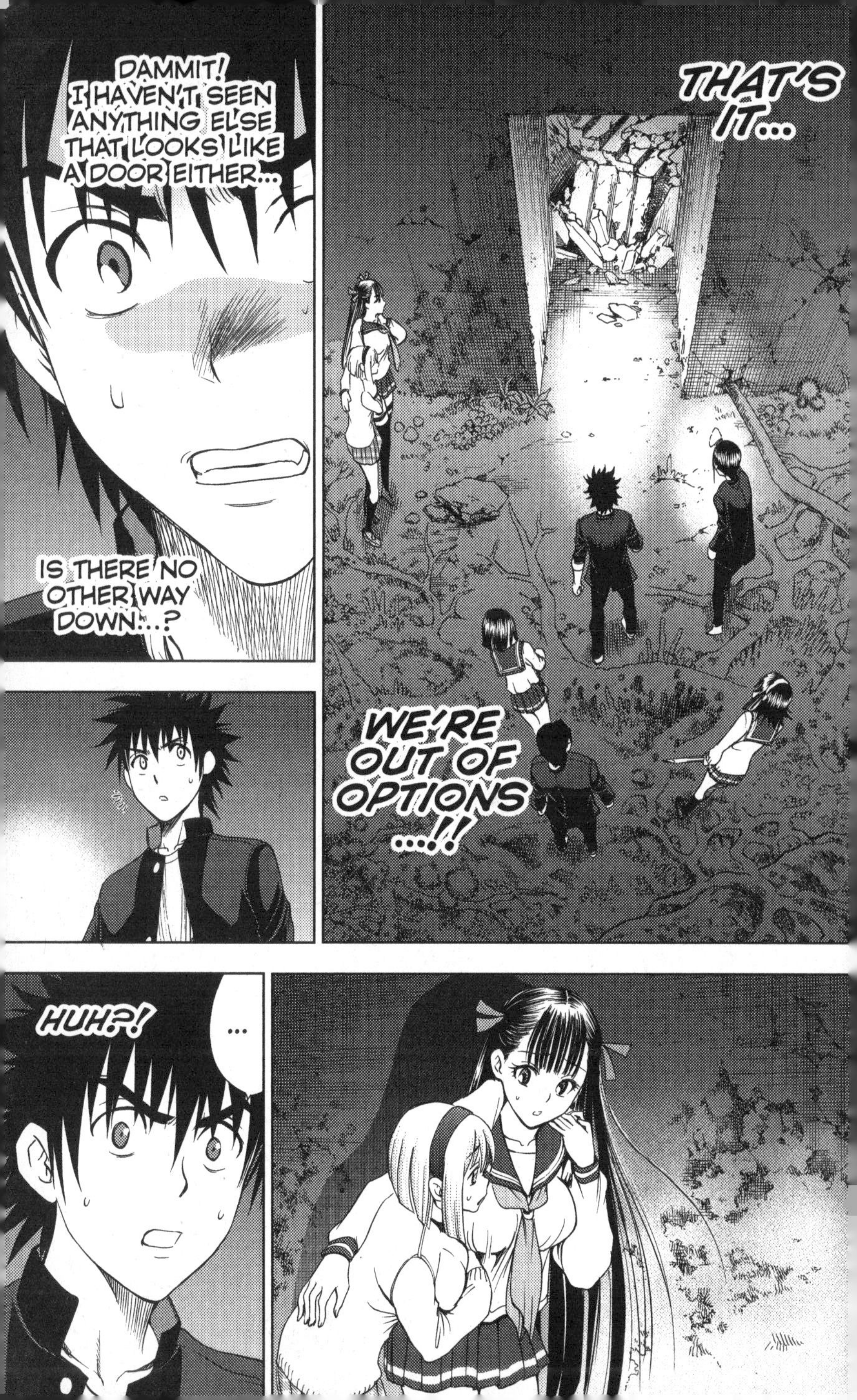
THAT'S IT...
WE'RE OUT OF OPTIONS ...!!
DAMMIT! I HAVEN'T SEEN ANYTHING ELSE THAT LOOKS LIKE A DOOR EITHER...
IS THERE NO OTHER WAY DOWN...?
...
HUH?!

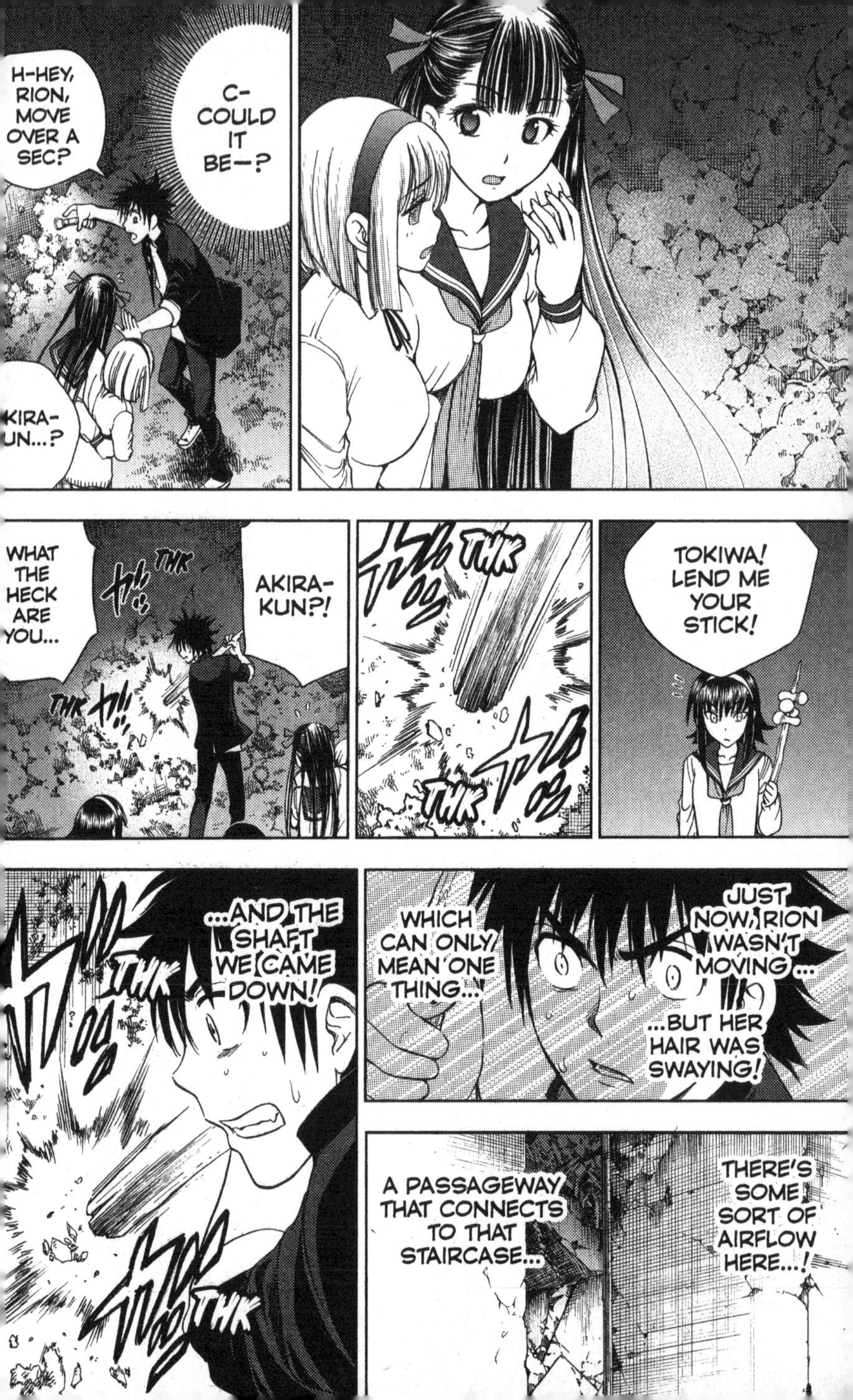
C-COULD IT BE—?
H-HEY, RION, MOVE OVER A SEC?
KIRA-UN...?
TOKIWA! LEND ME YOUR STICK!
THK
THK
AKIRA-KUN?!
THK
WHAT THE HECK ARE YOU...
THK
JUST NOW, RION WASN'T MOVING...
...BUT HER HAIR WAS SWAYING!
WHICH CAN ONLY MEAN ONE THING...
THERE'S SOME SORT OF AIRFLOW HERE...!
A PASSAGEWAY THAT CONNECTS TO THAT STAIRCASE...
...AND THE SHAFT WE CAME DOWN!
THK
THK

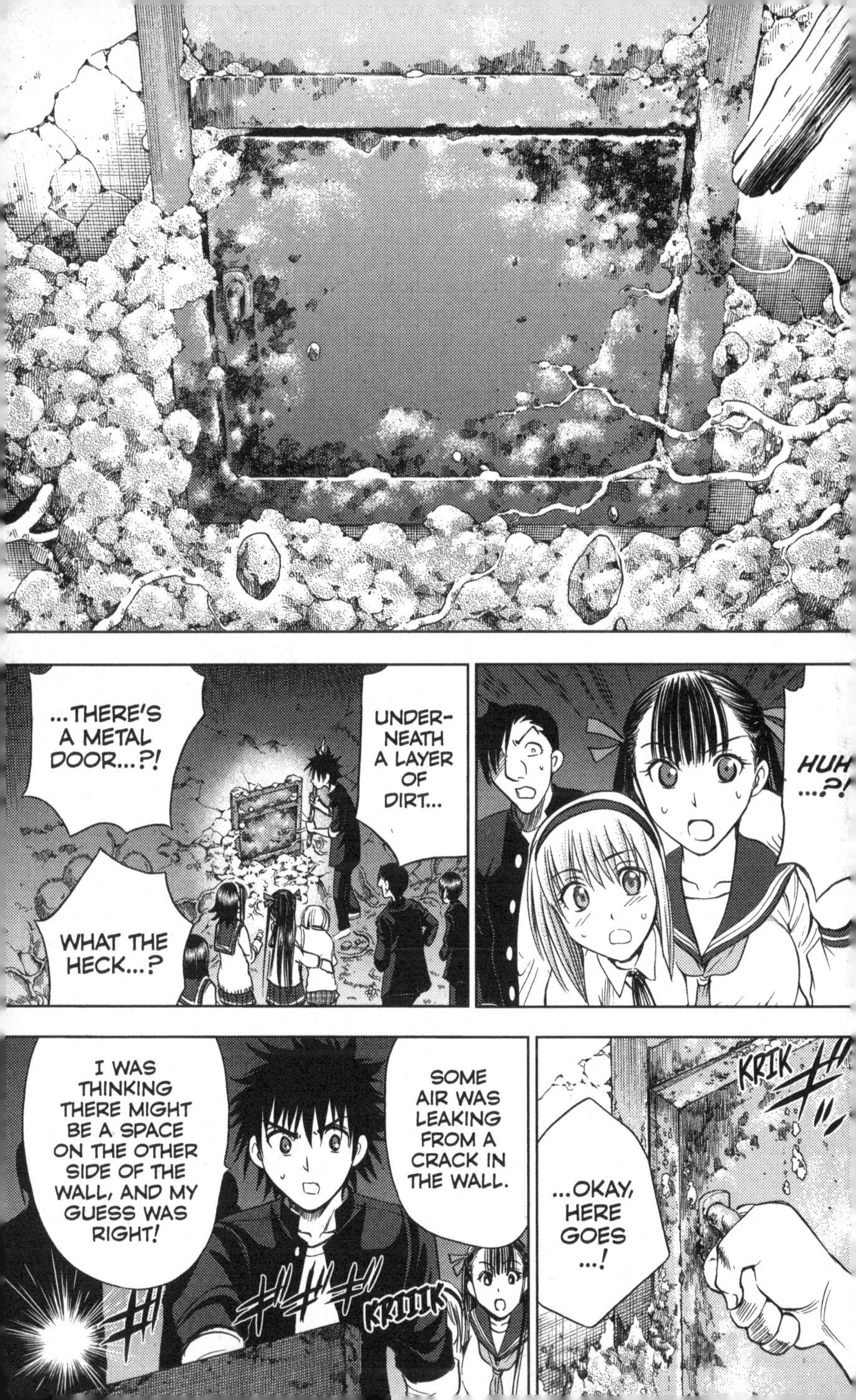
HUH ...?!
UNDER-NEATH A LAYER OF DIRT...
...THERE'S A METAL DOOR...?!
WHAT THE HECK...?
KRIK
...OKAY, HERE GOES ...!
SOME AIR WAS LEAKING FROM A CRACK IN THE WALL.
I WAS THINKING THERE MIGHT BE A SPACE ON THE OTHER SIDE OF THE WALL, AND MY GUESS WAS RIGHT!
KRIIIK

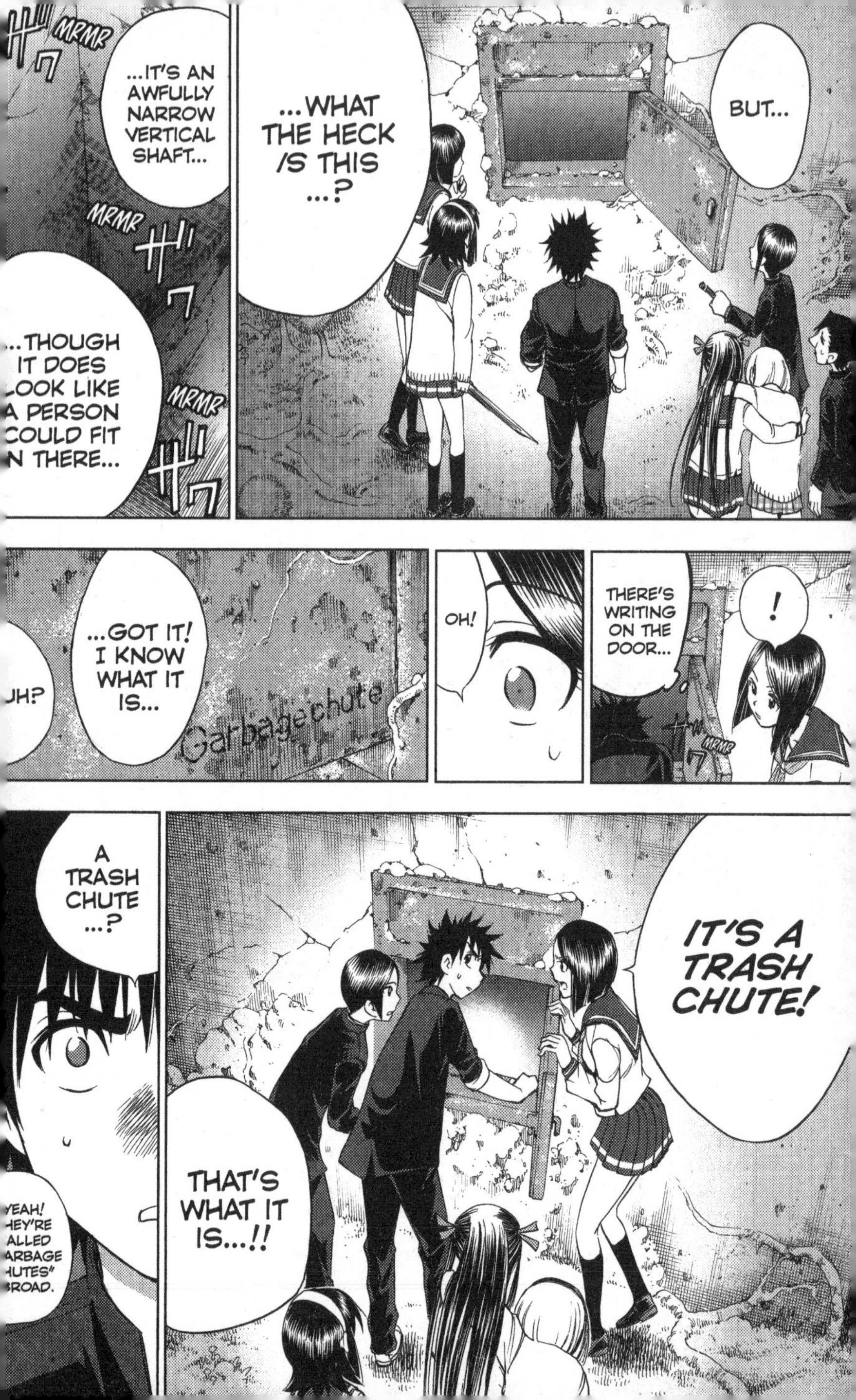
BUT...
...WHAT THE HECK IS THIS ...?
...IT'S AN AWFULLY NARROW VERTICAL SHAFT...
MRMR
MRMR
...THOUGH IT DOES LOOK LIKE A PERSON COULD FIT IN THERE...
MRMR
!
THERE'S WRITING ON THE DOOR...
MRMR
OH!
...GOT IT! I KNOW WHAT IT IS...
UH?
Garbagechute
IT'S A TRASH CHUTE!
THAT'S WHAT IT IS...!!
A TRASH CHUTE ...?
YEAH! HEY'RE ALLED ARBAGE HUTES" BROAD.

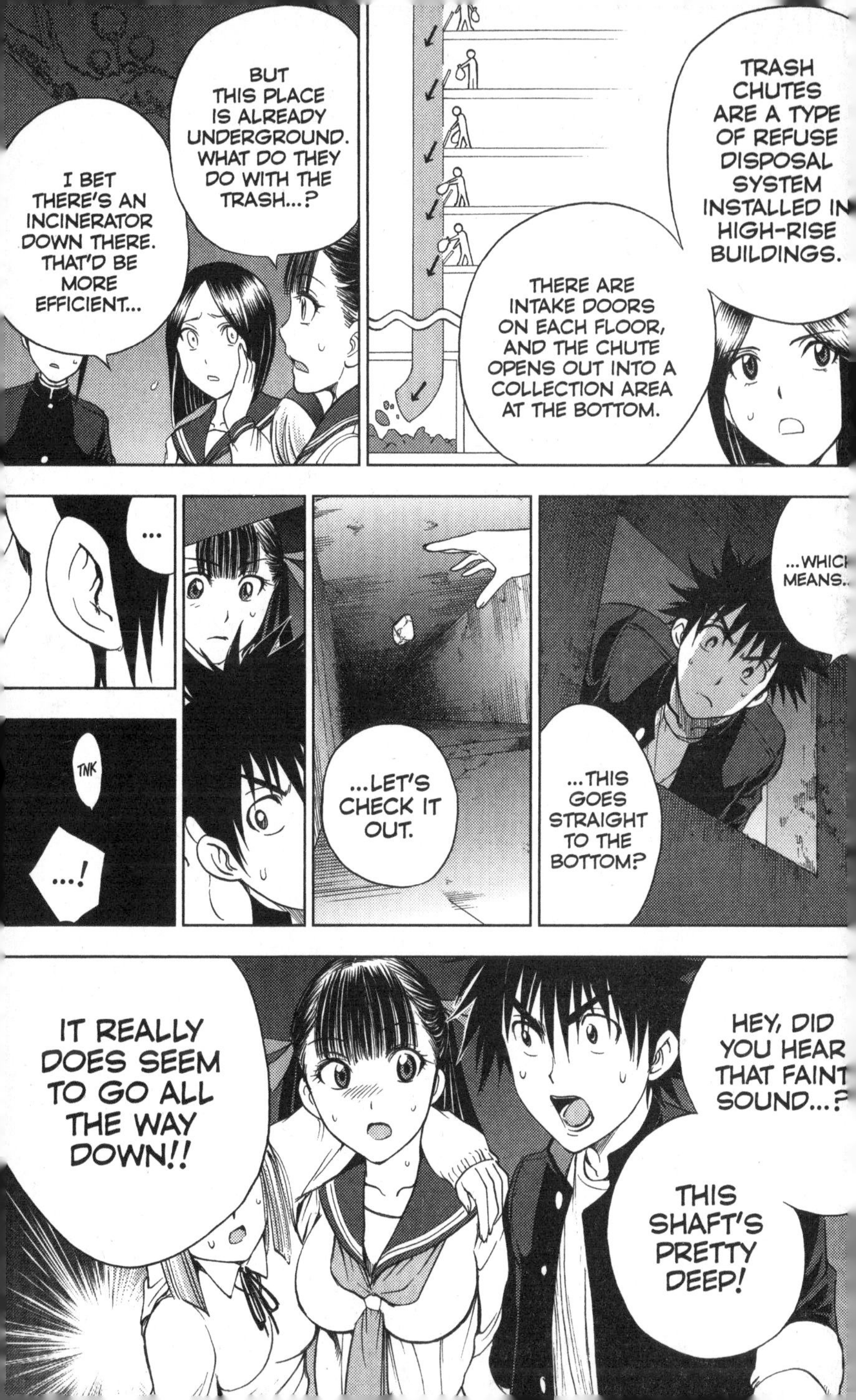
TRASH CHUTES ARE A TYPE OF REFUSE DISPOSAL SYSTEM INSTALLED IN HIGH-RISE BUILDINGS.
THERE ARE INTAKE DOORS ON EACH FLOOR, AND THE CHUTE OPENS OUT INTO A COLLECTION AREA AT THE BOTTOM.
BUT THIS PLACE IS ALREADY UNDERGROUND. WHAT DO THEY DO WITH THE TRASH...?
I BET THERE'S AN INCINERATOR DOWN THERE. THAT'D BE MORE EFFICIENT...
...WHIC MEANS..
...THIS GOES STRAIGHT TO THE BOTTOM?
...LET'S CHECK IT OUT.
...
TNK
...!
HEY, DID YOU HEAR THAT FAINT SOUND...?
THIS SHAFT'S PRETTY DEEP!
IT REALLY DOES SEEM TO GO ALL THE WAY DOWN!!

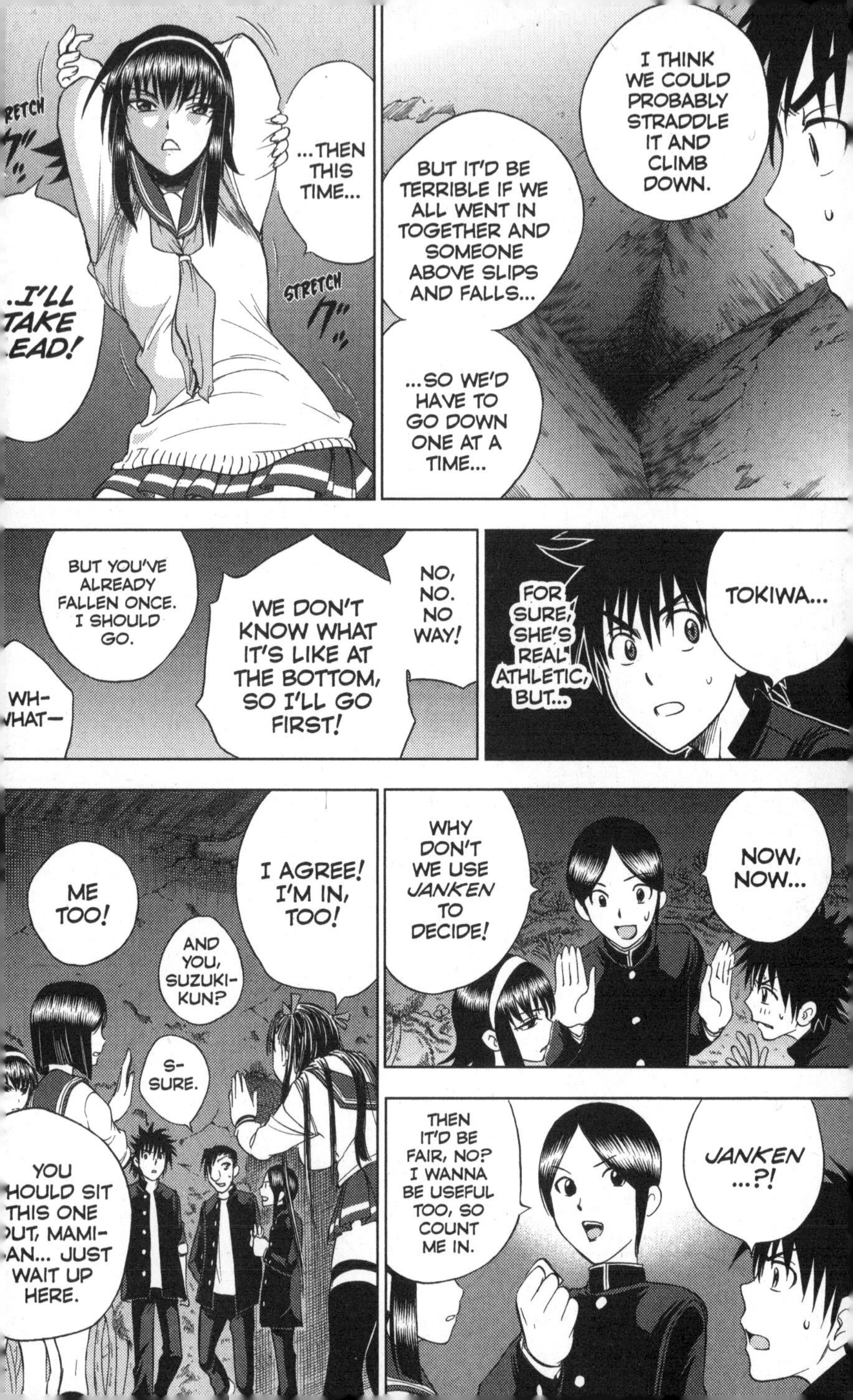
I THINK WE COULD PROBABLY STRADDLE IT AND CLIMB DOWN.
BUT IT'D BE TERRIBLE IF WE ALL WENT IN TOGETHER AND SOMEONE ABOVE SLIPS AND FALLS...
...SO WE'D HAVE TO GO DOWN ONE AT A TIME...
STRETCH
...THEN THIS TIME...
RETCH
..I'LL TAKE EAD!
TOKIWA...
FOR SURE, SHE'S REAL ATHLETIC, BUT...
NO, NO. NO WAY!
WE DON'T KNOW WHAT IT'S LIKE AT THE BOTTOM, SO I'LL GO FIRST!
BUT YOU'VE ALREADY FALLEN ONCE. I SHOULD GO.
WH- HAT—
NOW, NOW...
WHY DON'T WE USE JANKEN TO DECIDE!
JANKEN ...?!
THEN IT'D BE FAIR, NO? I WANNA BE USEFUL TOO, SO COUNT ME IN.
I AGREE! I'M IN, TOO!
ME TOO!
AND YOU, SUZUKI-KUN?
S- SURE.
YOU HOULD SIT THIS ONE UT, MAMI- AN... JUST WAIT UP HERE.

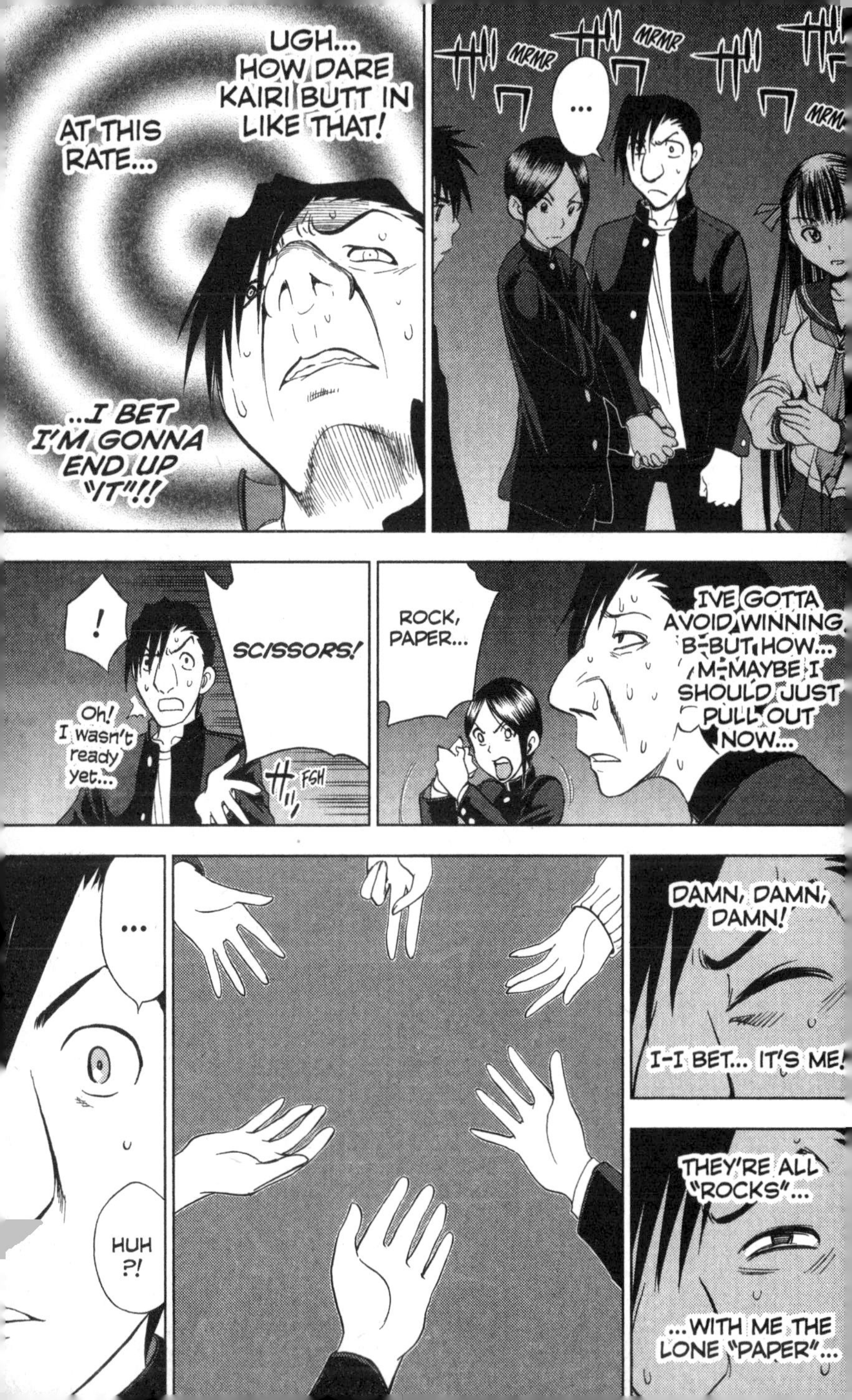
MRMR
MRMR
MRMR
...
UGH... HOW DARE KAIRI BUTT IN LIKE THAT!
AT THIS RATE...
...I BET I'M GONNA END UP "IT"!!
IVE GOTTA AVOID WINNING B-BUT HOW... M-MAYBE I SHOULD JUST PULL OUT NOW...
ROCK, PAPER...
SCISSORS!
!
Oh! I wasn't ready yet...
FSH
DAMN, DAMN, DAMN!
I-I BET... IT'S ME!
THEY'RE ALL "ROCKS"...
...WITH ME THE LONE "PAPER"...
...
HUH?!

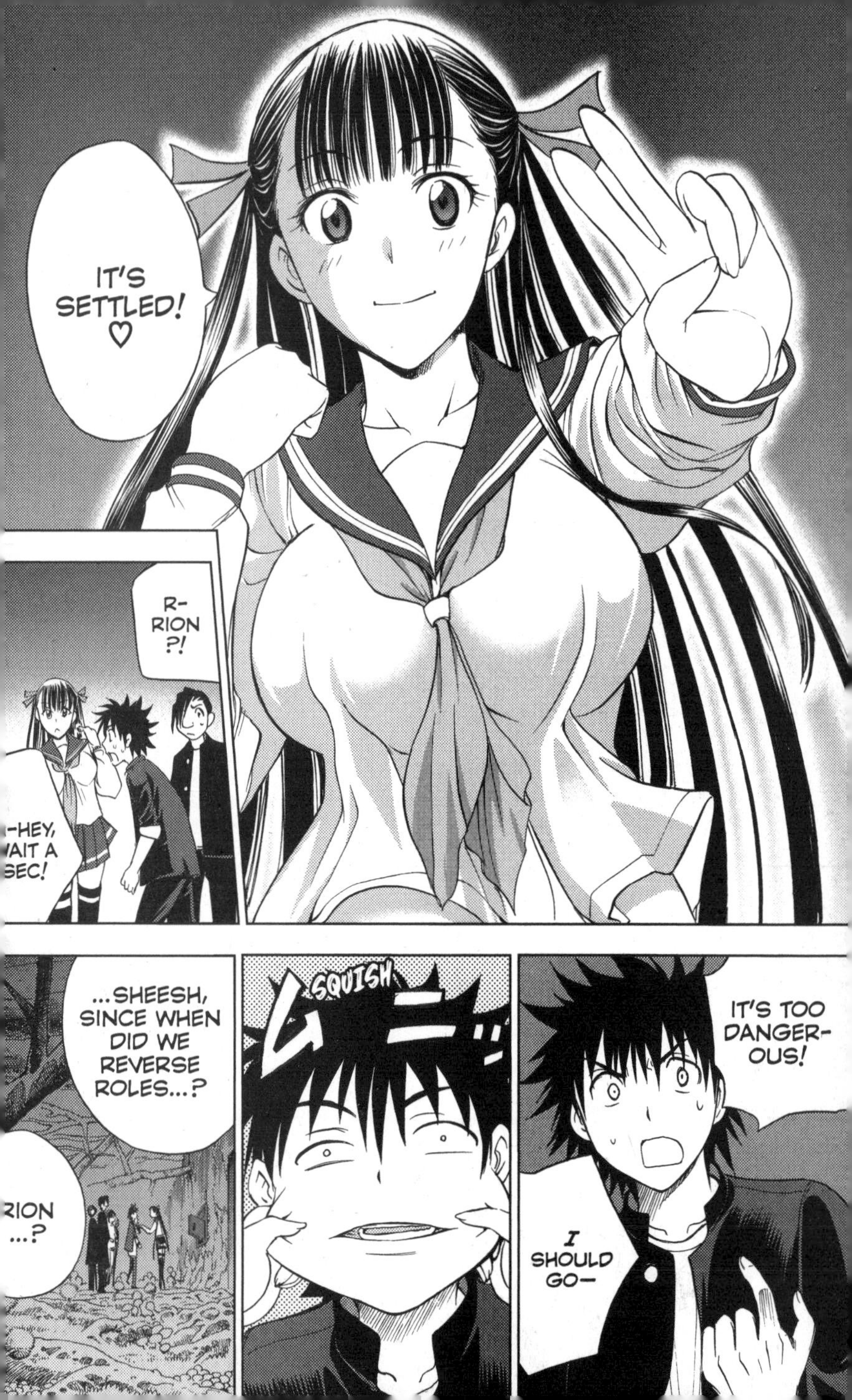
IT'S SETTLED! ♡
R-RION?!
-HEY, WAIT A SEC!
IT'S TOO DANGER-OUS!
I SHOULD GO—
SQUISH
...SHEESH, SINCE WHEN DID WE REVERSE ROLES...?
RION ...?

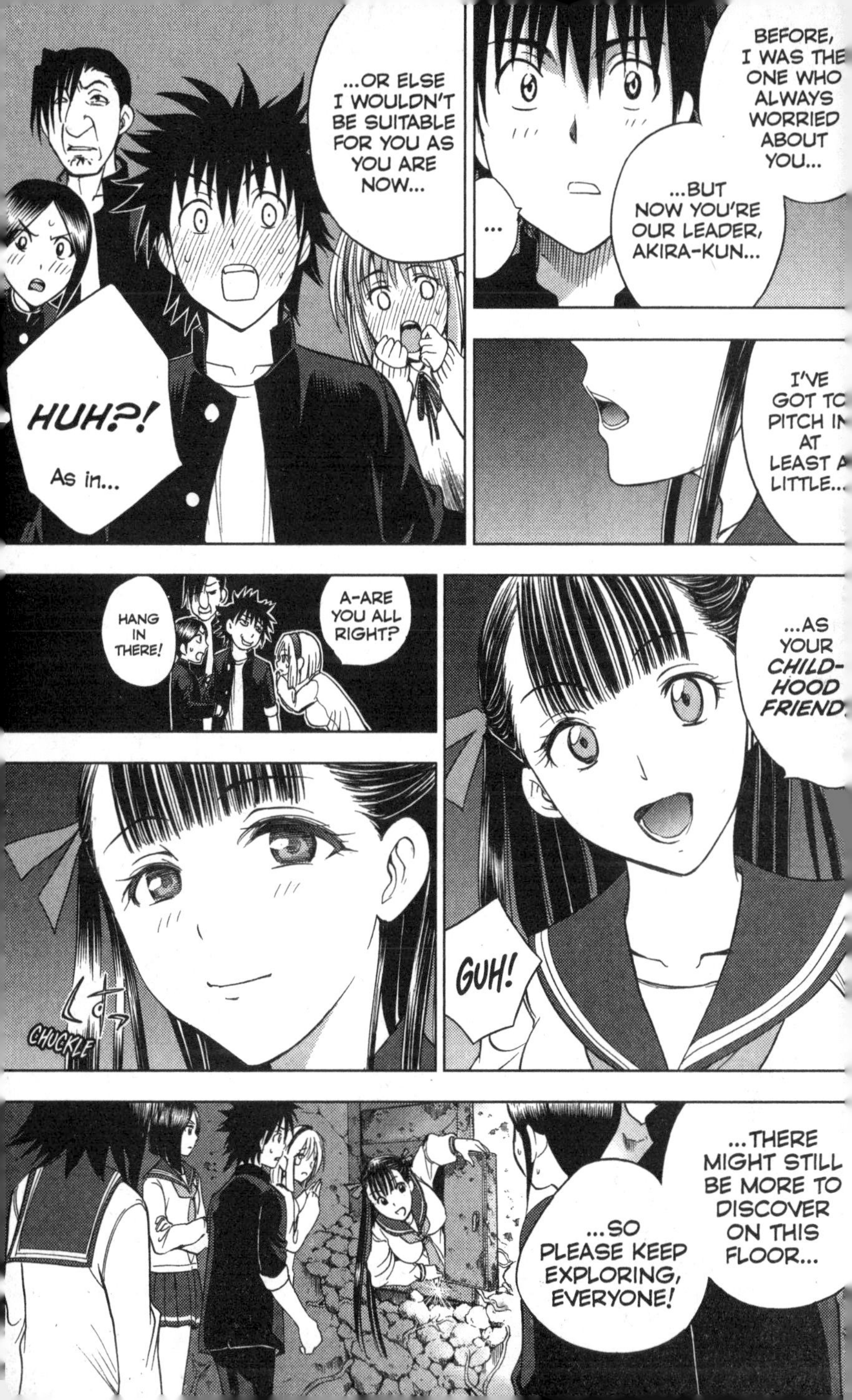
BEFORE, I WAS THE ONE WHO ALWAYS WORRIED ABOUT YOU...
...BUT NOW YOU'RE OUR LEADER, AKIRA-KUN...
...
I'VE GOT TO PITCH IN AT LEAST A LITTLE...
...OR ELSE I WOULDN'T BE SUITABLE FOR YOU AS YOU ARE NOW...
HUH?!
As in...
...AS YOUR CHILDHOOD FRIEND.
GUH!
A-ARE YOU ALL RIGHT?
HANG IN THERE!
CHUCKLE
...THERE MIGHT STILL BE MORE TO DISCOVER ON THIS FLOOR...
...SO PLEASE KEEP EXPLORING, EVERYONE!

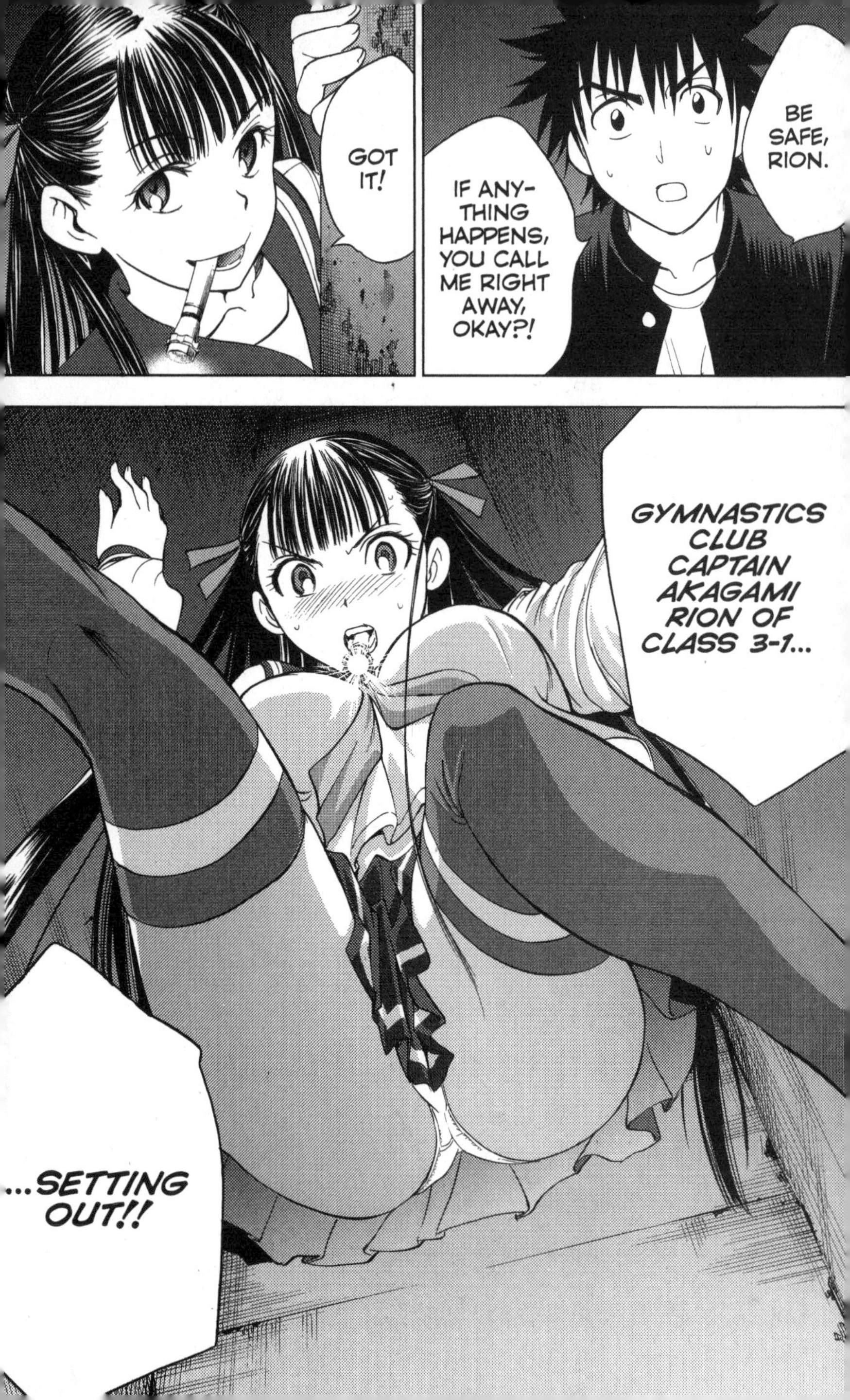
BE SAFE, RION.
IF ANY-THING HAPPENS, YOU CALL ME RIGHT AWAY, OKAY?!
GOT IT!
GYMNASTICS CLUB CAPTAIN AKAGAMI RION OF CLASS 3-1...
...SETTING OUT!!

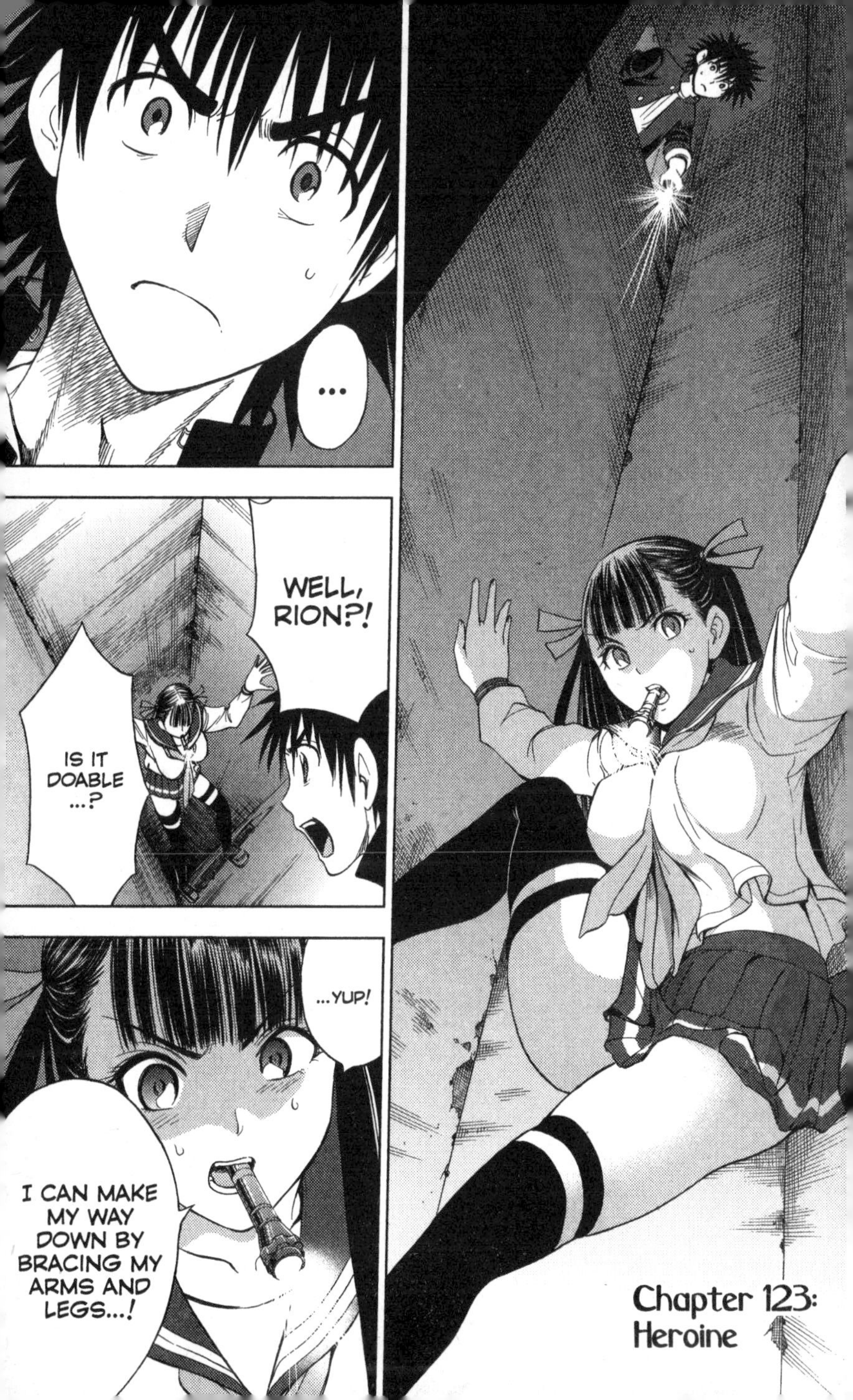
Chapter 123:
Heroine
...
WELL, RION?!
IS IT DOABLE ...?
...YUP!
I CAN MAKE MY WAY DOWN BY BRACING MY ARMS AND LEGS...!

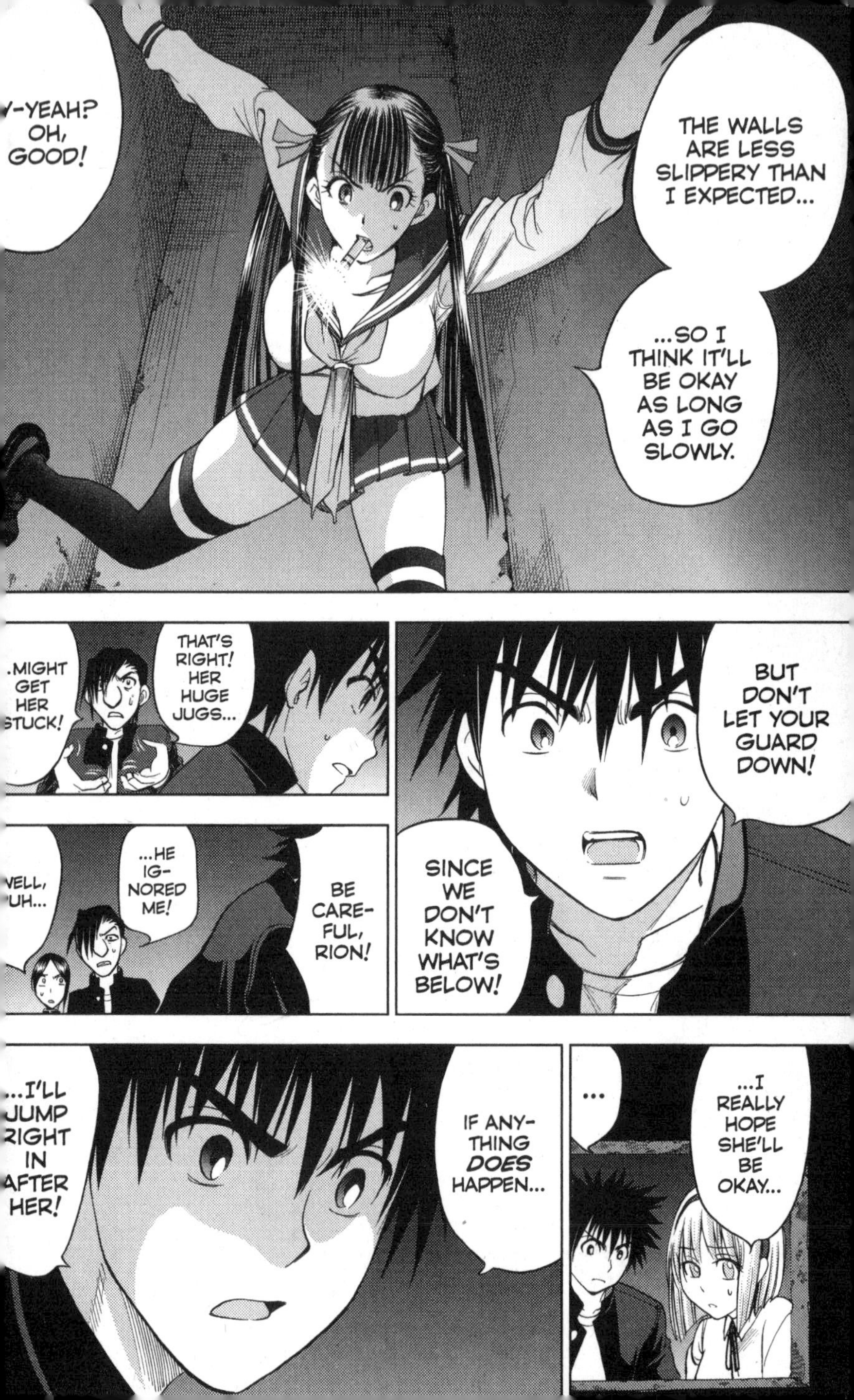
THE WALLS ARE LESS SLIPPERY THAN I EXPECTED...
...SO I THINK IT'LL BE OKAY AS LONG AS I GO SLOWLY.
-YEAH? OH, GOOD!
BUT DON'T LET YOUR GUARD DOWN!
SINCE WE DON'T KNOW WHAT'S BELOW!
THAT'S RIGHT! HER HUGE JUGS...
.MIGHT GET HER TUCK!
BE CARE-FUL, RION!
...HE IG-NORED ME!
ELL, UH...
...
...I REALLY HOPE SHE'LL BE OKAY...
IF ANY-THING *DOES* HAPPEN...
...I'LL JUMP IGHT IN FTER HER!

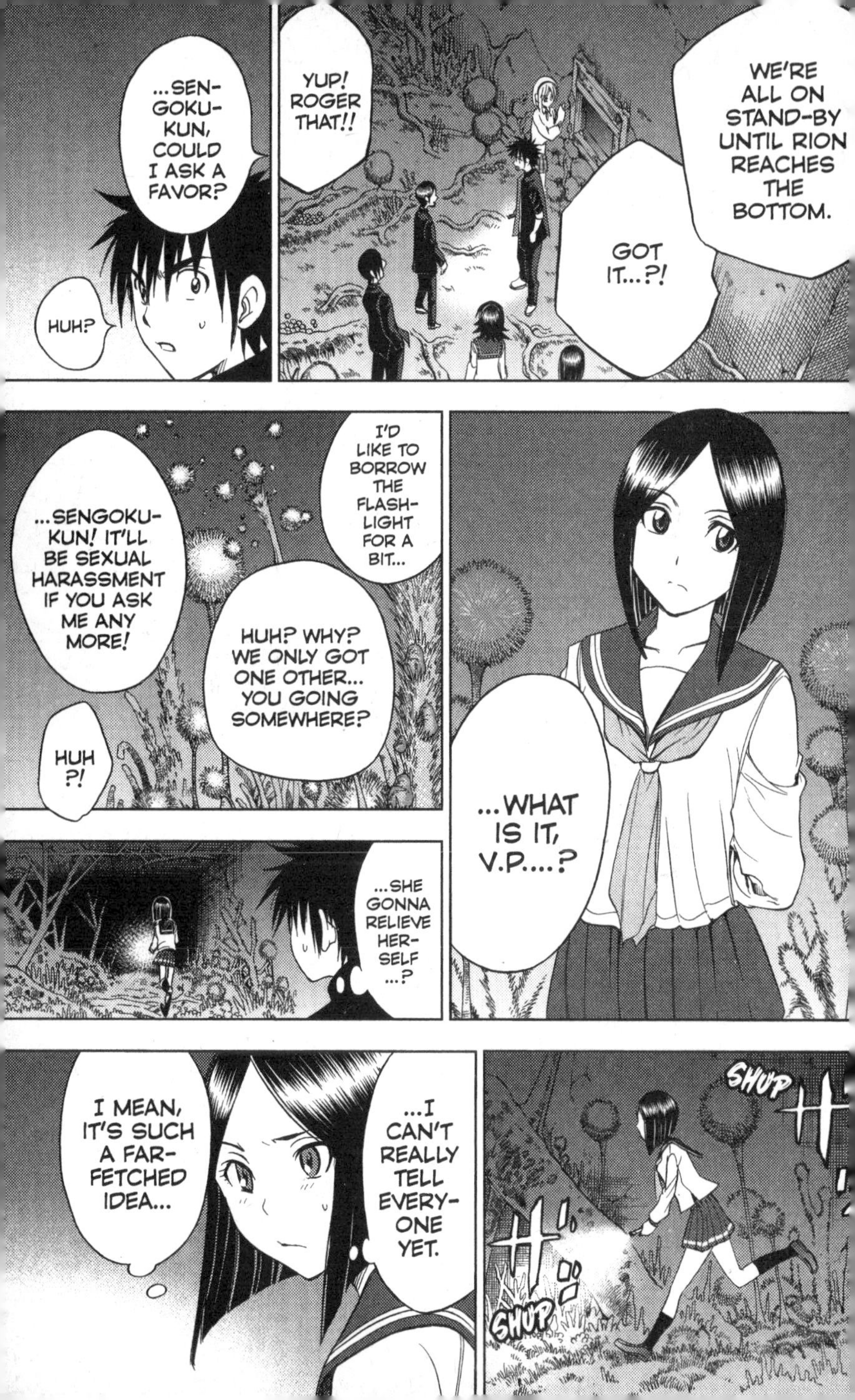
WE'RE ALL ON STAND-BY UNTIL RION REACHES THE BOTTOM.
GOT IT...?!
YUP! ROGER THAT!!
...SEN-GOKU-KUN, COULD I ASK A FAVOR?
HUH?
...WHAT IS IT, V.P....?
I'D LIKE TO BORROW THE FLASH-LIGHT FOR A BIT...
HUH? WHY? WE ONLY GOT ONE OTHER... YOU GOING SOMEWHERE?
...SENGOKU-KUN! IT'LL BE SEXUAL HARASSMENT IF YOU ASK ME ANY MORE!
HUH ?!
...SHE GONNA RELIEVE HER-SELF ...?
SHUP
SHUP
...I CAN'T REALLY TELL EVERY-ONE YET.
I MEAN, IT'S SUCH A FAR-FETCHED IDEA...

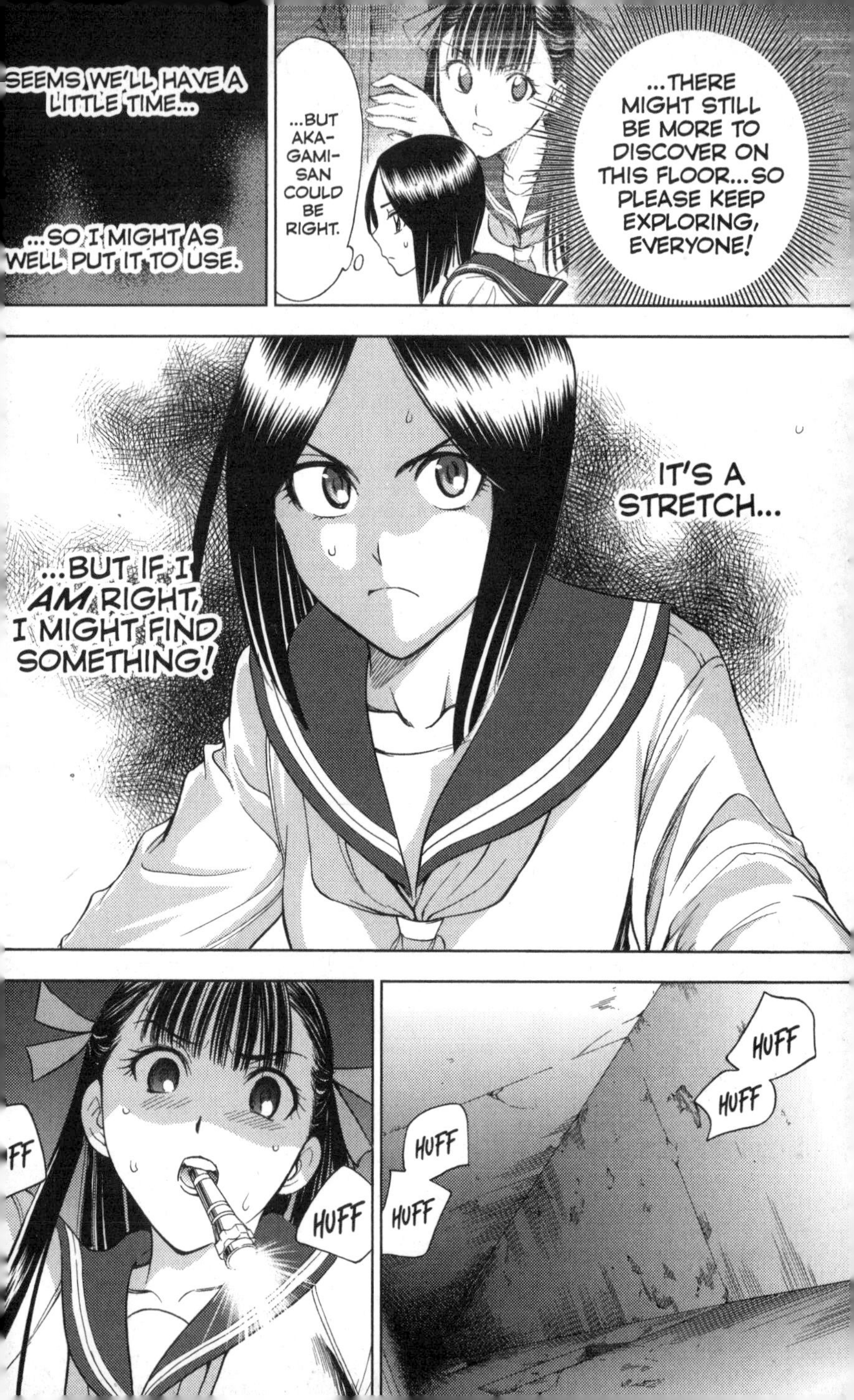
...THERE MIGHT STILL BE MORE TO DISCOVER ON THIS FLOOR...SO PLEASE KEEP EXPLORING, EVERYONE!
...BUT AKA-GAMI-SAN COULD BE RIGHT.
SEEMS WE'LL HAVE A LITTLE TIME...
...SO I MIGHT AS WELL PUT IT TO USE.
IT'S A STRETCH...
...BUT IF I AM RIGHT, I MIGHT FIND SOMETHING!
HUFF
HUFF
HUFF
HUFF
HUFF
FF

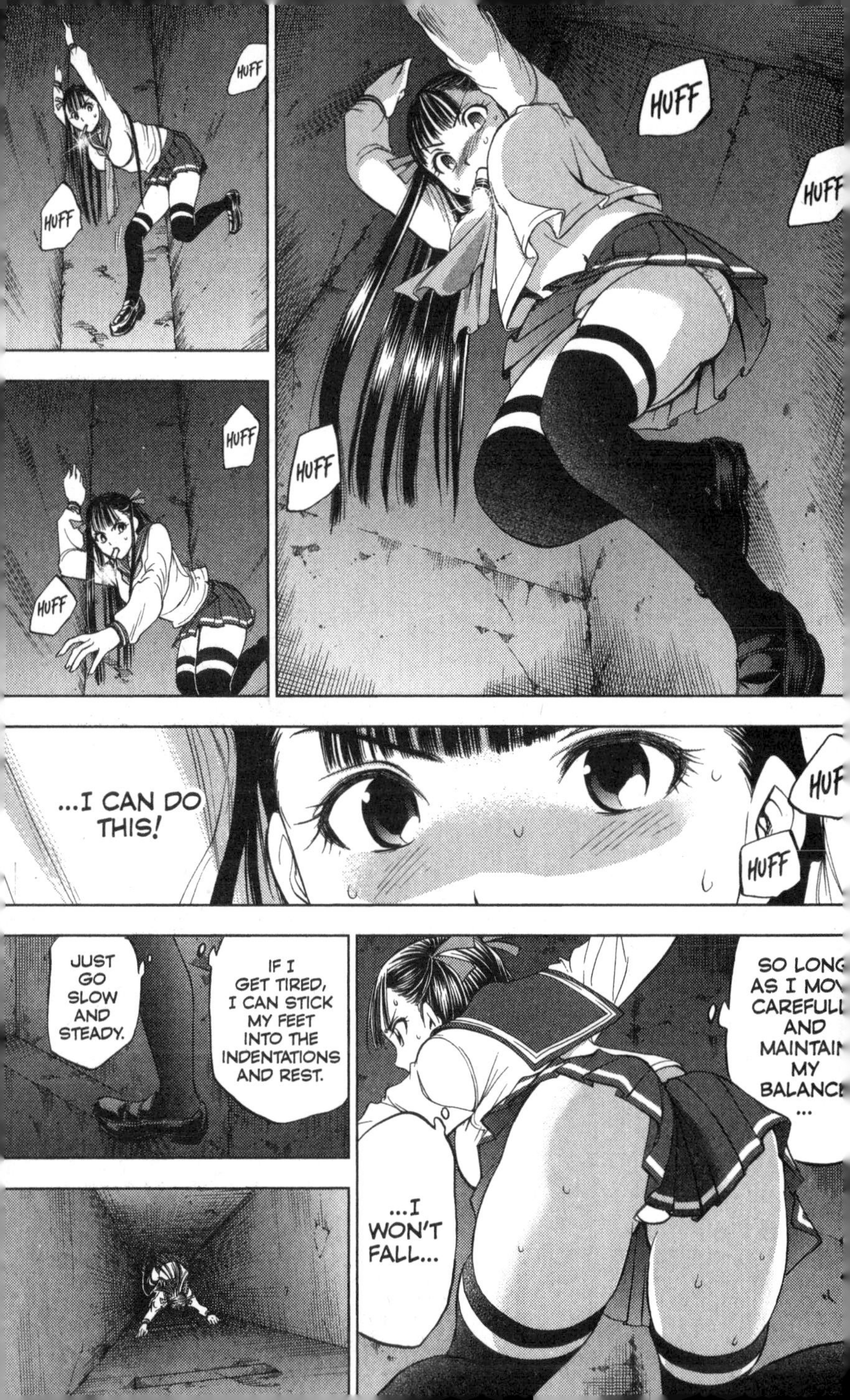
HUFF
HUFF
HUFF
HUFF
HUFF
HUFF
HUFF
HUF
HUFF
...I CAN DO THIS!
SO LONG AS I MOV CAREFULL AND MAINTAII MY BALANC ...
...I WON'T FALL...
IF I GET TIRED, I CAN STICK MY FEET INTO THE INDENTATIONS AND REST.
JUST GO SLOW AND STEADY.

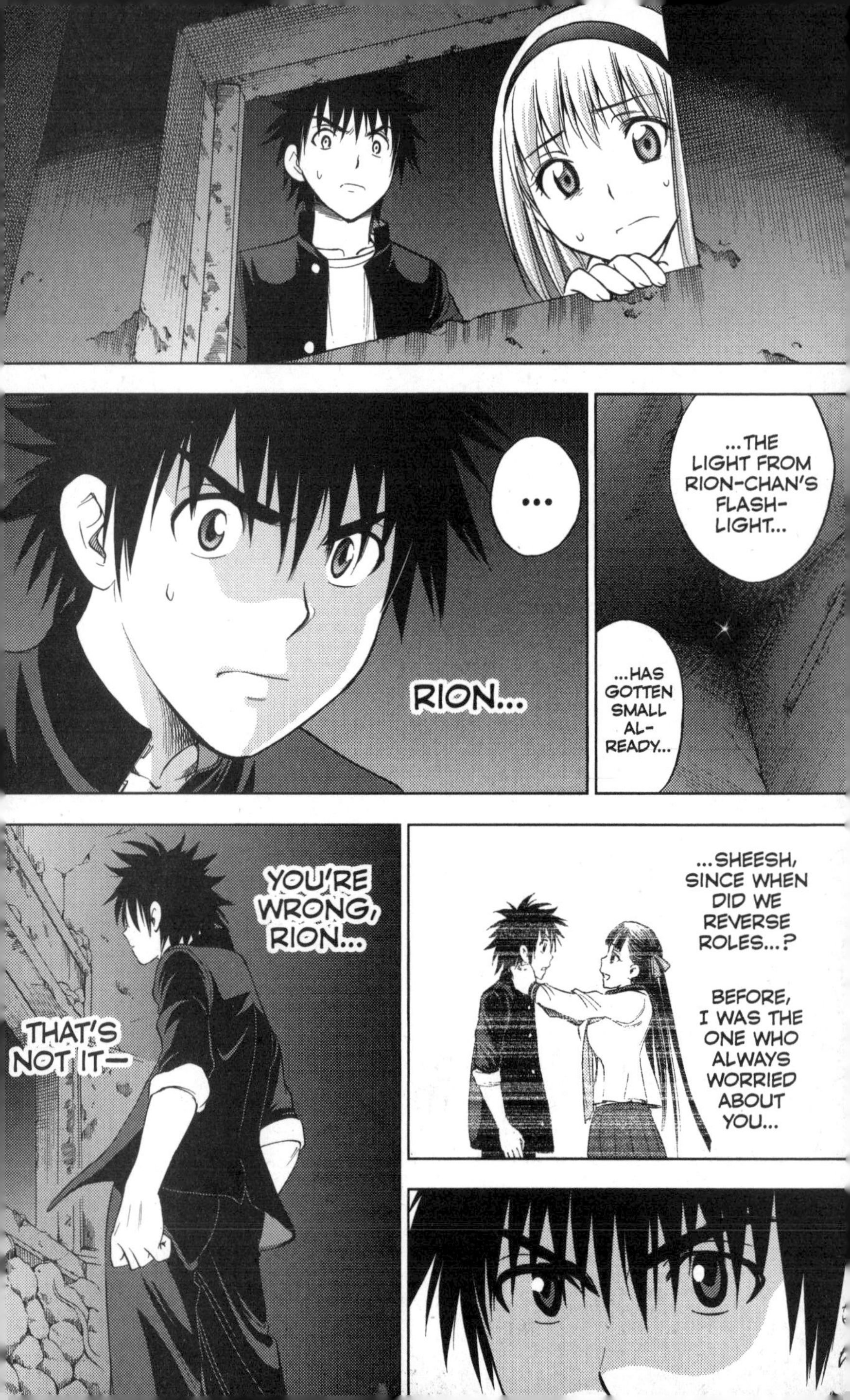
...THE LIGHT FROM RION-CHAN'S FLASH-LIGHT...
...HAS GOTTEN SMALL AL-READY...
...
RION...
...SHEESH, SINCE WHEN DID WE REVERSE ROLES...?
BEFORE, I WAS THE ONE WHO ALWAYS WORRIED ABOUT YOU...
YOU'RE WRONG, RION...
THAT'S NOT IT—

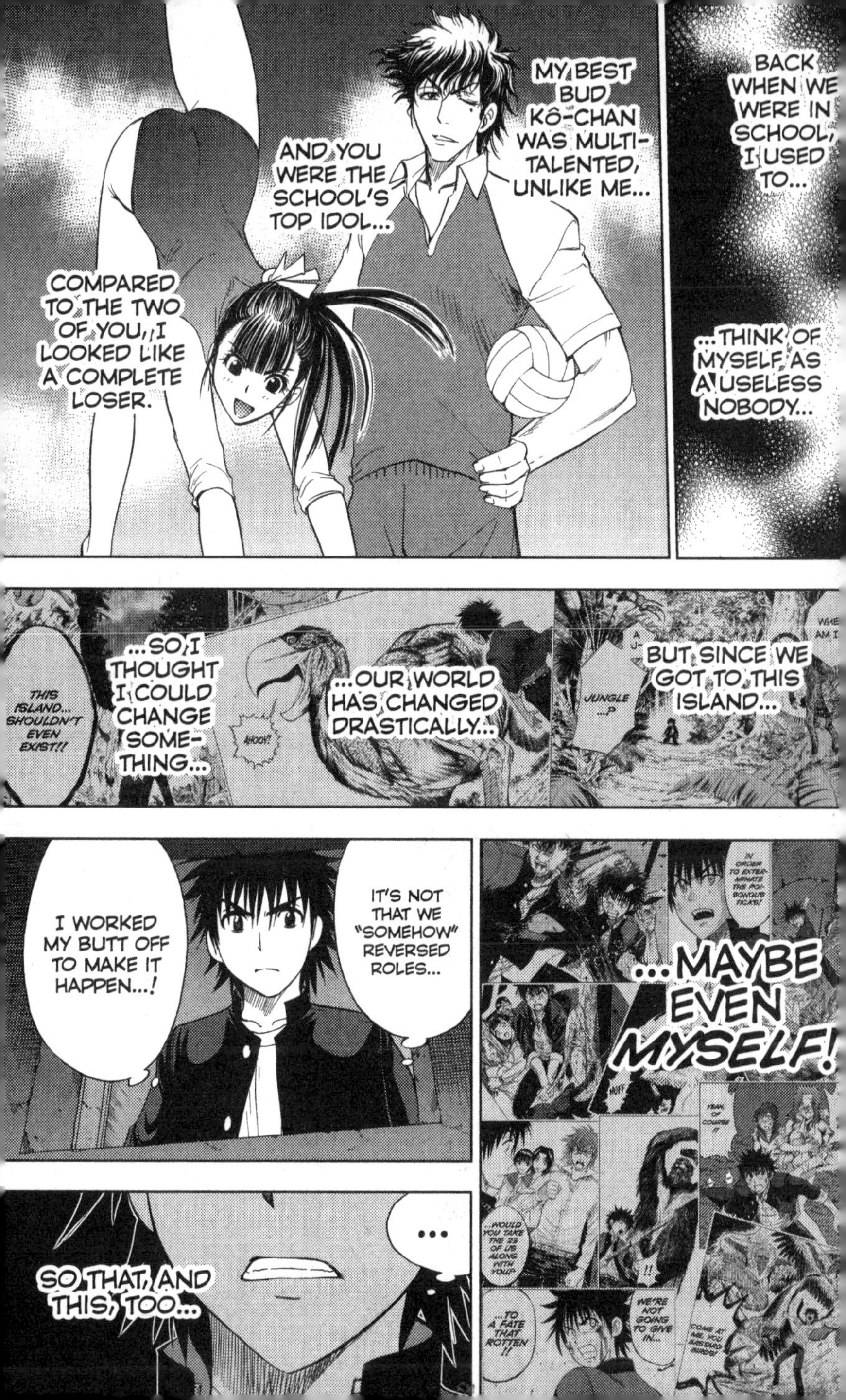
BACK WHEN WE WERE IN SCHOOL, I USED TO...
...THINK OF MYSELF AS A USELESS NOBODY...
MY BEST BUD KÔ-CHAN WAS MULTI-TALENTED, UNLIKE ME...
AND YOU WERE THE SCHOOL'S TOP IDOL...
COMPARED TO THE TWO OF YOU, I LOOKED LIKE A COMPLETE LOSER.
WHE... AM I
A J-
JUNGLE ...?
BUT SINCE WE GOT TO THIS ISLAND...
...OUR WORLD HAS CHANGED DRASTICALLY...
AHOO?!
...SO I THOUGHT I COULD CHANGE SOME-THING...
THIS ISLAND... SHOULDN'T EVEN EXIST!!
IN ORDER TO EXTER-MINATE THE POI-SONOUS TICKS!
...MAYBE EVEN MYSELF!
HUFF
YEAH, OF COURSE!!
...WOULD YOU TAKE THE 23 OF US ALONG WITH YOU?
!!
COME AT ME, YOU BASTARD BIRDS!
WE'RE NOT GOING TO GIVE IN...
...TO A FATE THAT ROTTEN!!
IT'S NOT THAT WE "SOMEHOW" REVERSED ROLES...
I WORKED MY BUTT OFF TO MAKE IT HAPPEN...!
...
SO THAT, AND THIS, TOO...

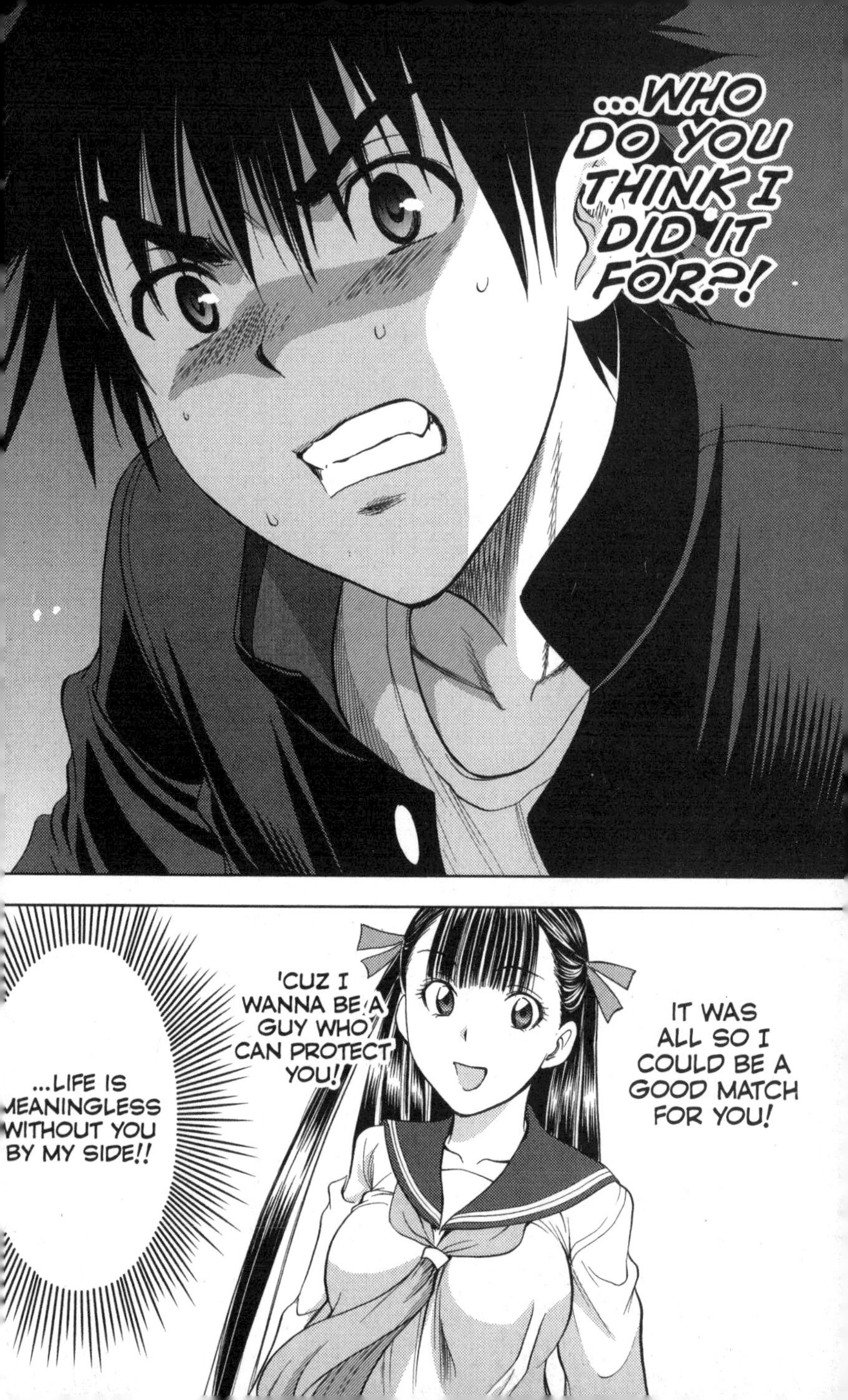
...WHO DO YOU THINK I DID IT FOR?!
IT WAS ALL SO I COULD BE A GOOD MATCH FOR YOU!
'CUZ I WANNA BE A GUY WHO CAN PROTECT YOU!
...LIFE IS MEANINGLESS WITHOUT YOU BY MY SIDE!!

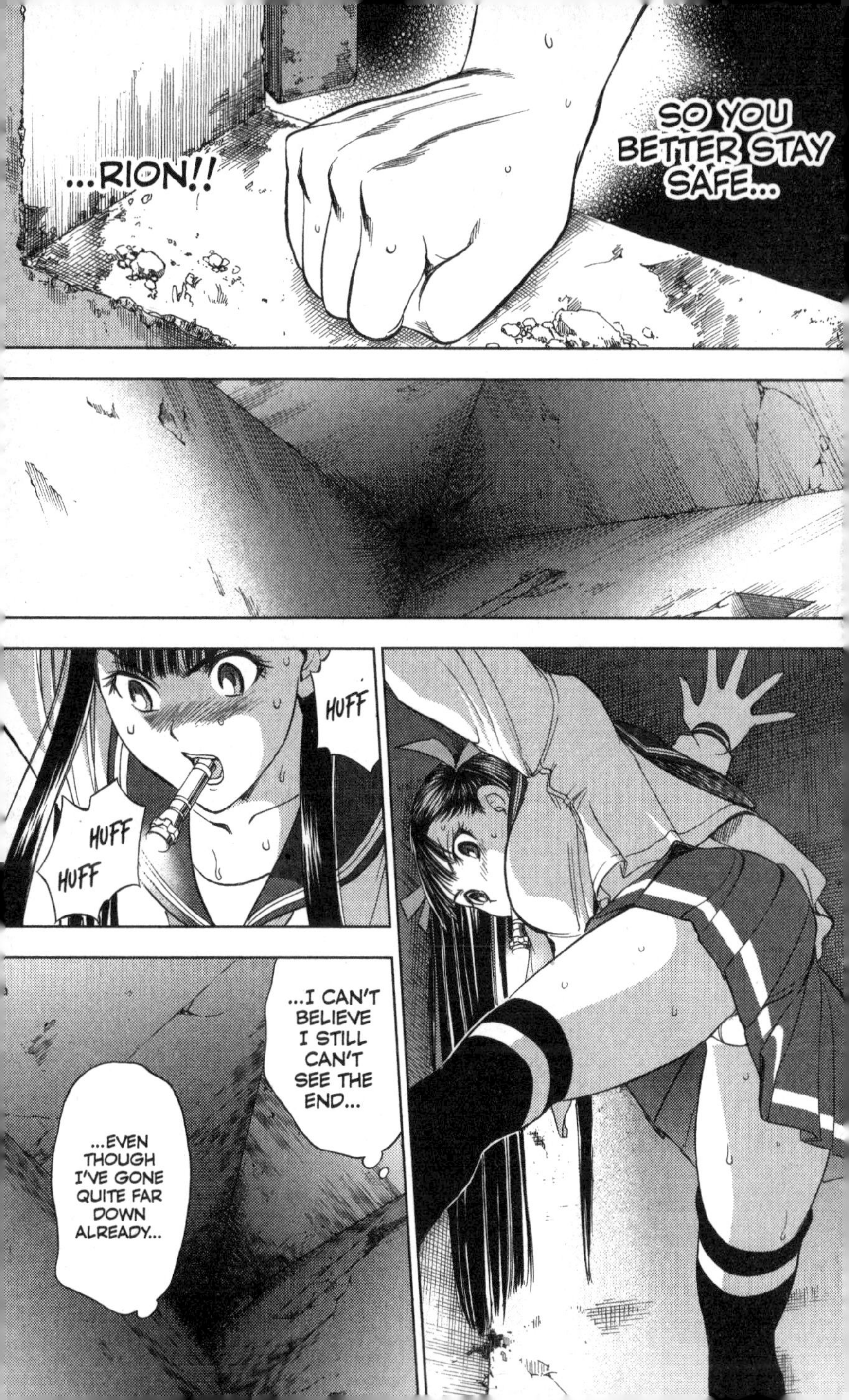
SO YOU BETTER STAY SAFE...
...RION!!
HUFF
HUFF
HUFF
...I CAN'T BELIEVE I STILL CAN'T SEE THE END...
...EVEN THOUGH I'VE GONE QUITE FAR DOWN ALREADY...

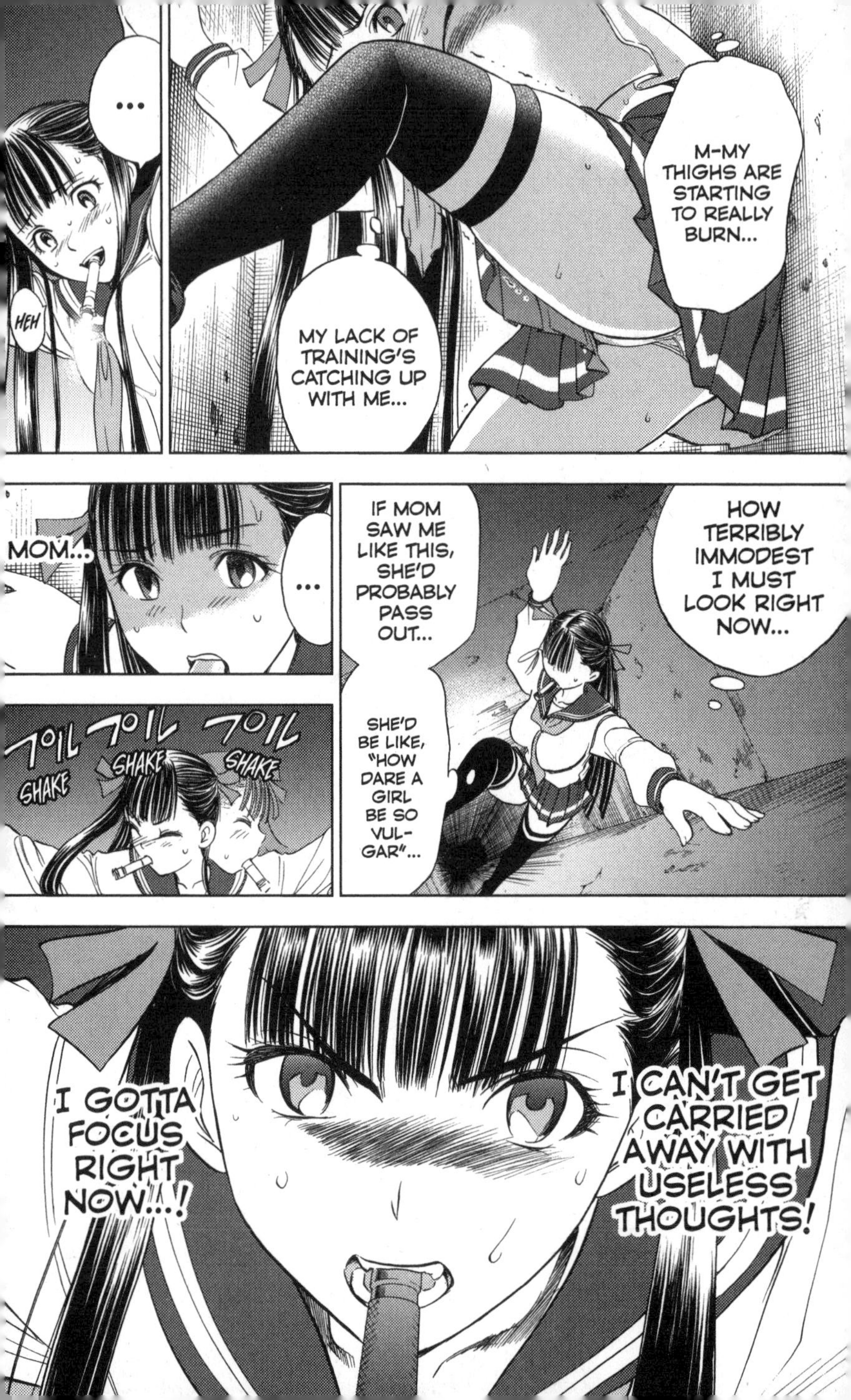
M-MY THIGHS ARE STARTING TO REALLY BURN...
MY LACK OF TRAINING'S CATCHING UP WITH ME...
...
HEH
HOW TERRIBLY IMMODEST I MUST LOOK RIGHT NOW...
IF MOM SAW ME LIKE THIS, SHE'D PROBABLY PASS OUT...
SHE'D BE LIKE, "HOW DARE A GIRL BE SO VUL-GAR"...
...
MOM...
プル プル プル
SHAKE SHAKE SHAKE
I CAN'T GET CARRIED AWAY WITH USELESS THOUGHTS!
I GOTTA FOCUS RIGHT NOW...!

THERE *HAS* TO BE SOMETHING BENEATH US!

IF WE COULD JUST FIGURE OUT WHAT...

...MAYBE WE CAN ALL GO HOME!

I CAN SEE SOMETHING!

COULD THAT POSSIBLY BE—

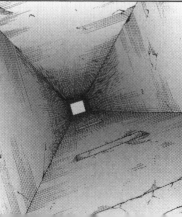

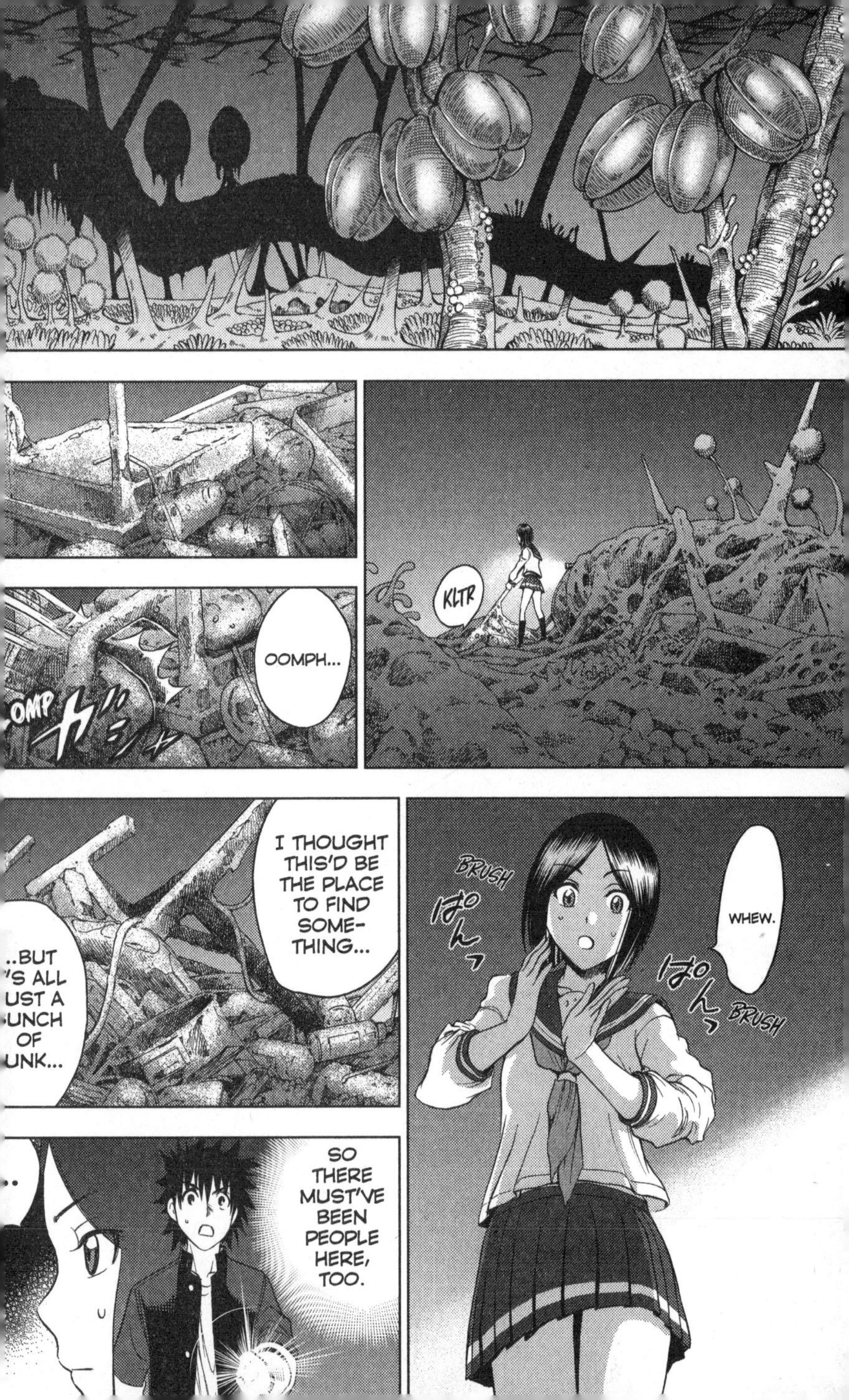
KLTR
OOMPH...
OMP
WHEW.
BRUSH
BRUSH
I THOUGHT THIS'D BE THE PLACE TO FIND SOME-THING...
..BUT 'S ALL UST A UNCH OF UNK...
SO THERE MUST'VE BEEN PEOPLE HERE, TOO.
..

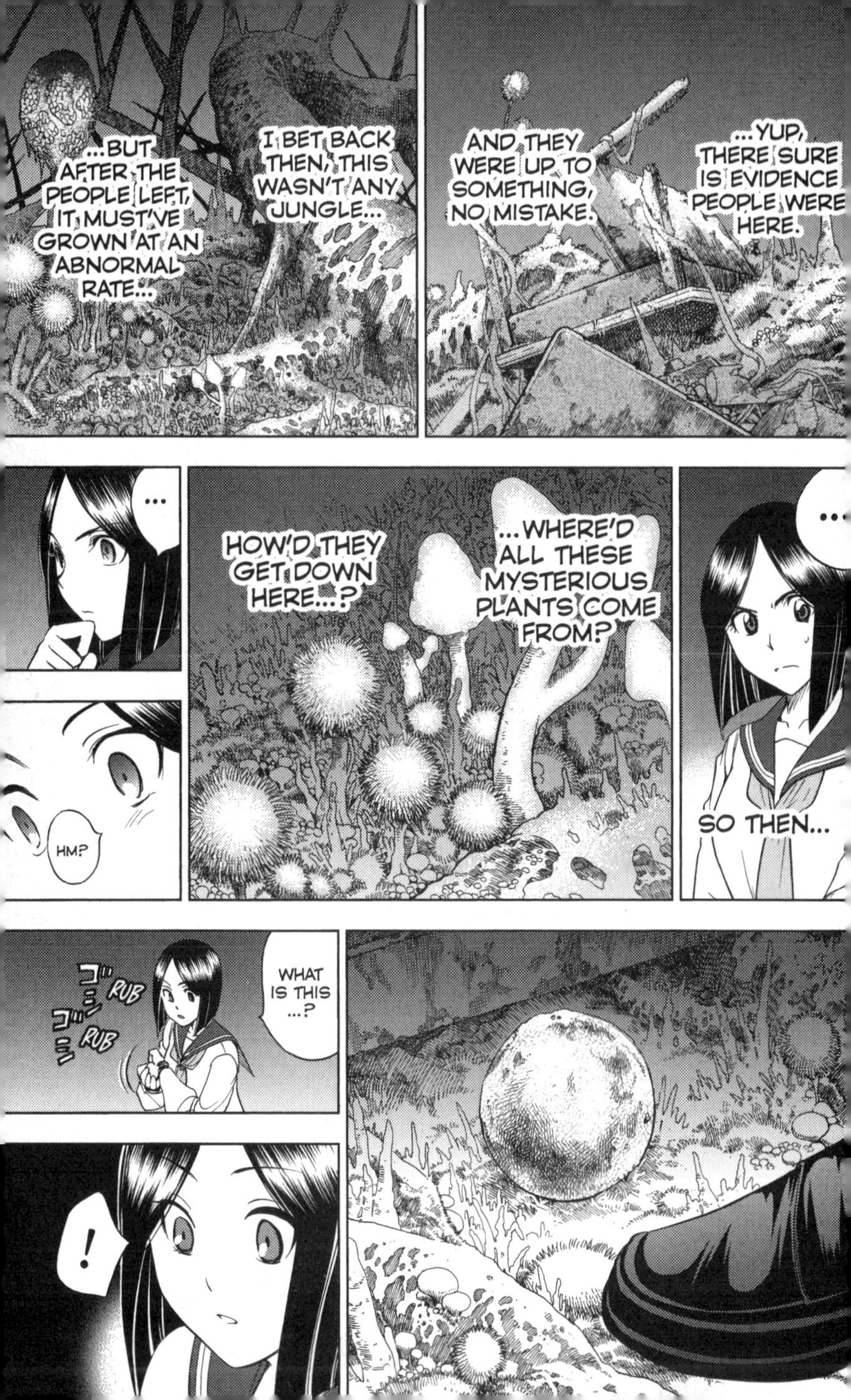
...YUP, THERE SURE IS EVIDENCE PEOPLE WERE HERE.
AND THEY WERE UP TO SOMETHING, NO MISTAKE.
I BET BACK THEN, THIS WASN'T ANY JUNGLE...
...BUT AFTER THE PEOPLE LEFT, IT MUST'VE GROWN AT AN ABNORMAL RATE...
...
SO THEN...
...WHERE'D ALL THESE MYSTERIOUS PLANTS COME FROM?
HOW'D THEY GET DOWN HERE...?
...
HM?
WHAT IS THIS ...?
ゴシ RUB
ゴシ RUB
!

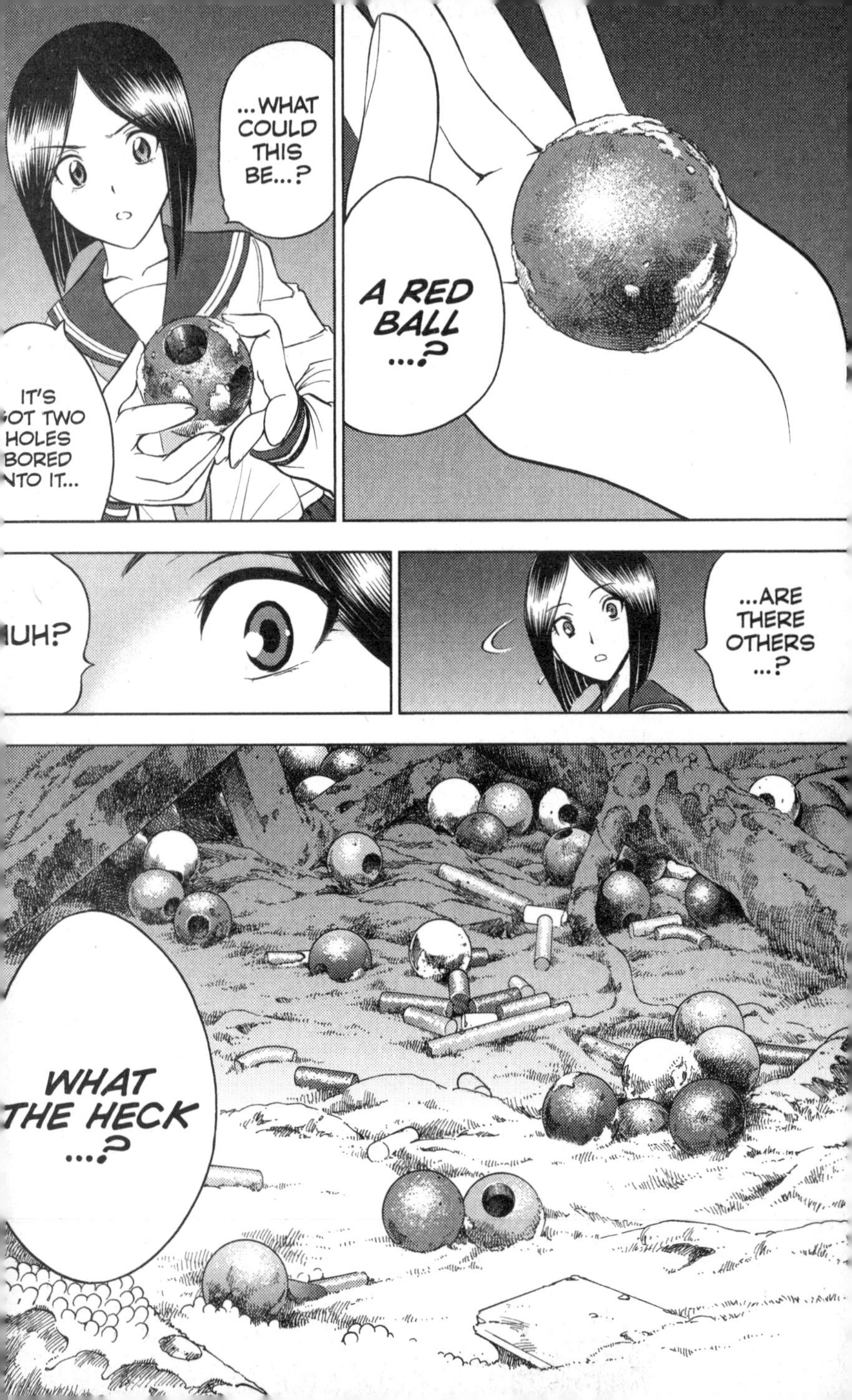
A RED BALL ...?
...WHAT COULD THIS BE...?
IT'S OT TWO HOLES BORED NTO IT...
...ARE THERE OTHERS ...?
UH?
WHAT THE HECK ...?

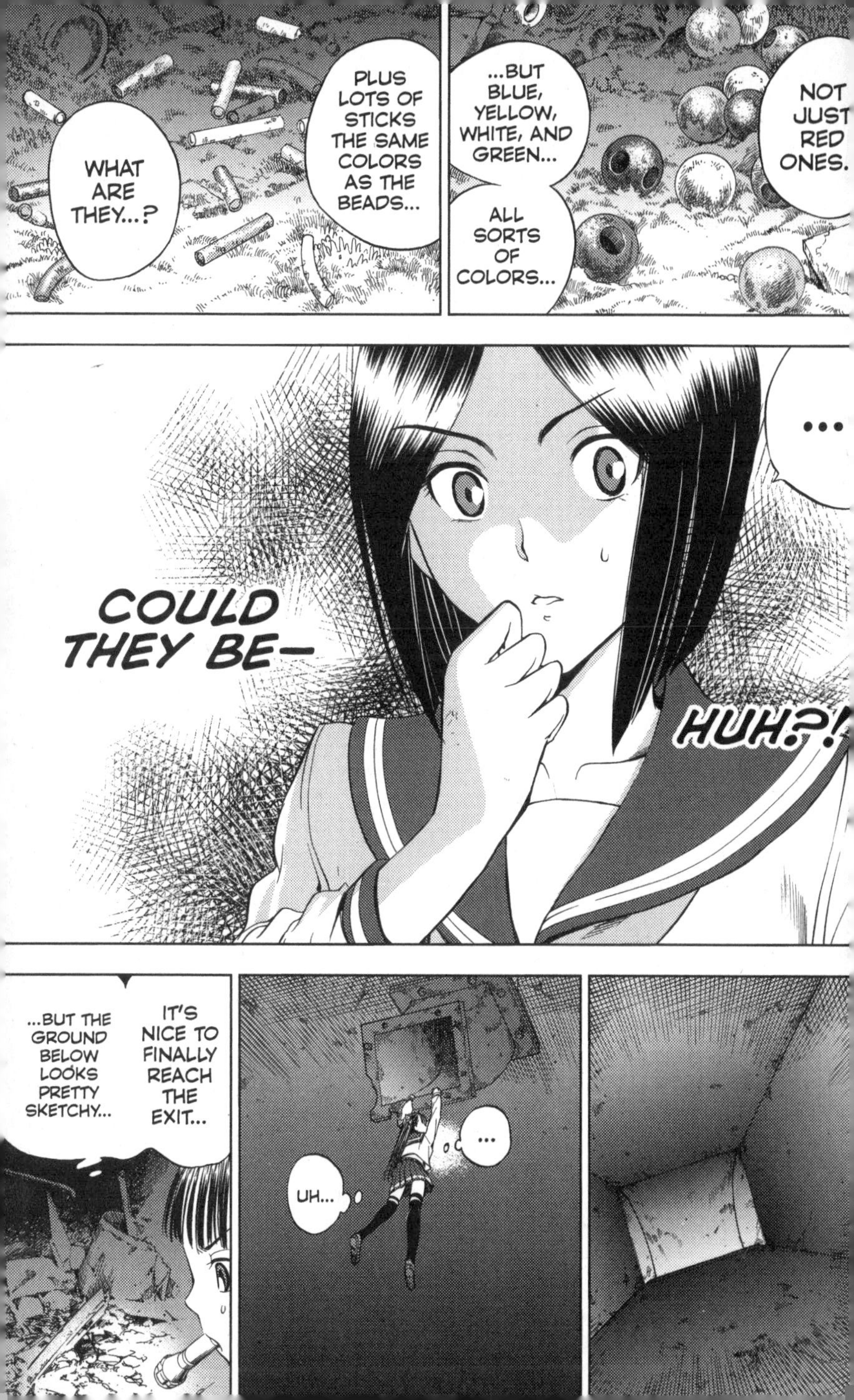
NOT JUST RED ONES.
...BUT BLUE, YELLOW, WHITE, AND GREEN...
ALL SORTS OF COLORS...
PLUS LOTS OF STICKS THE SAME COLORS AS THE BEADS...
WHAT ARE THEY...?
...
COULD THEY BE—
HUH?!
...
UH...
IT'S NICE TO FINALLY REACH THE EXIT...
...BUT THE GROUND BELOW LOOKS PRETTY SKETCHY...

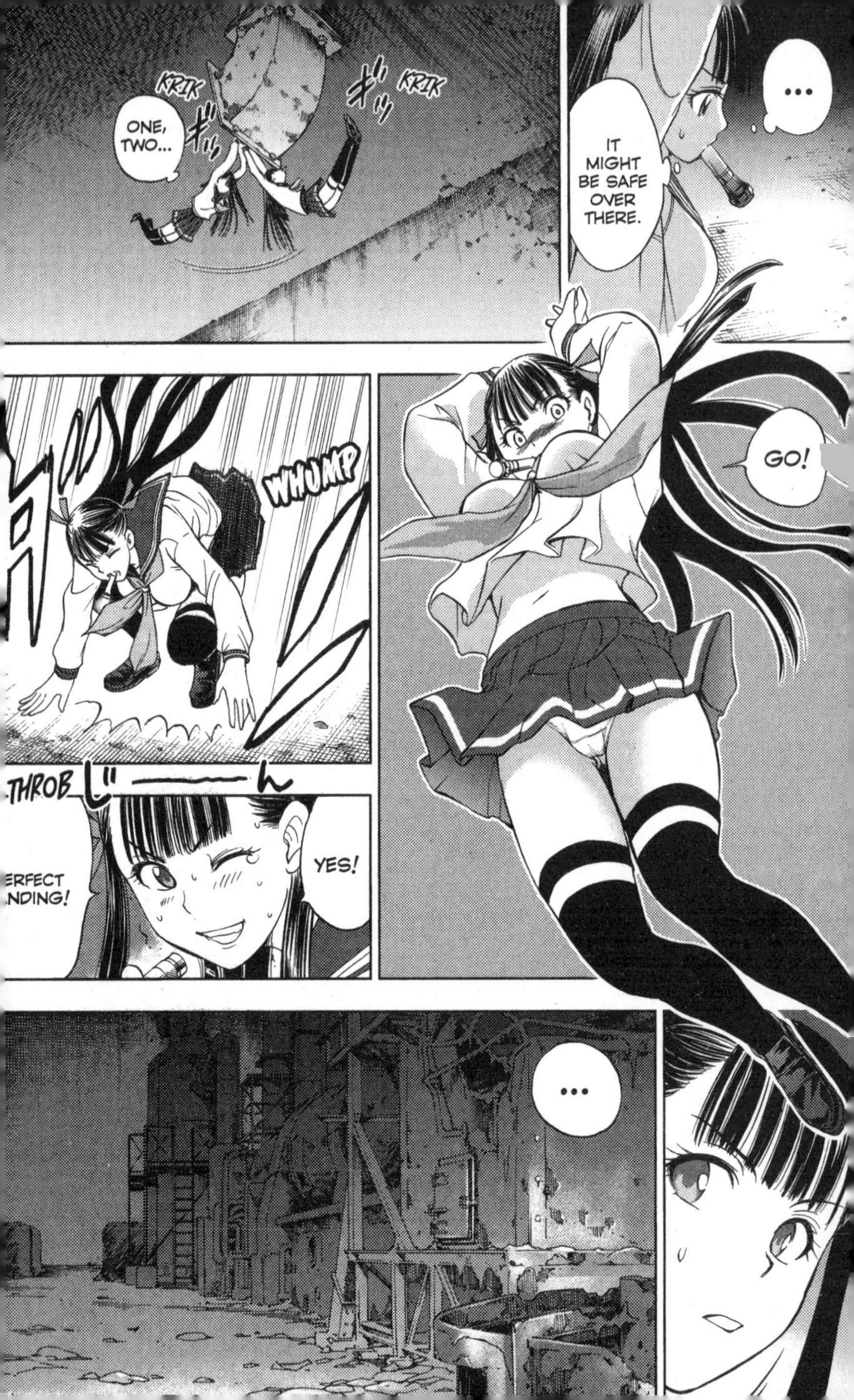
...
IT MIGHT BE SAFE OVER THERE.
KRIK
ギリ
KRIK
ギリ
ONE, TWO...
GO!
WHUMP
THROB
じーーーん
YES!
ERFECT
NDING!
...

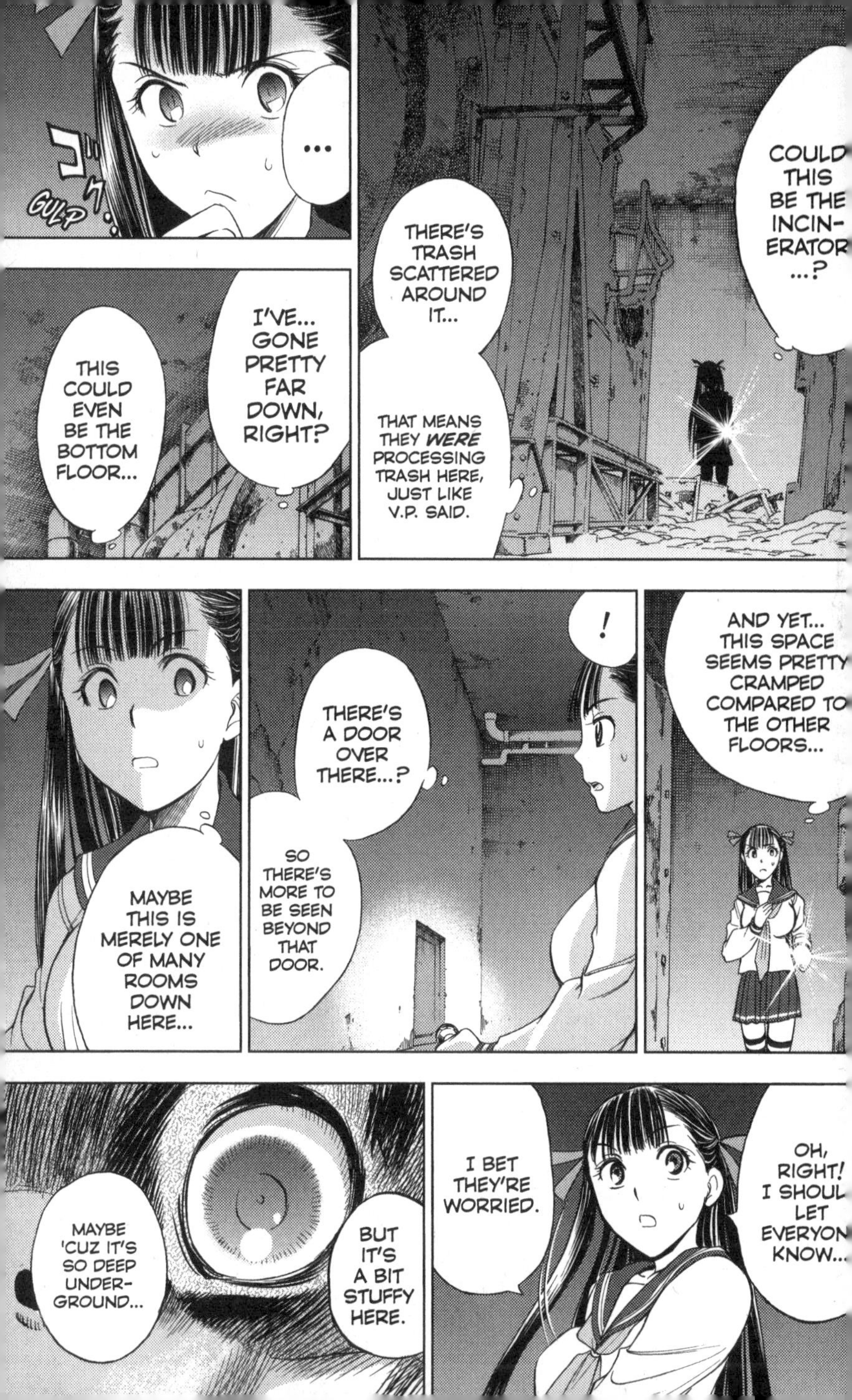
COULD THIS BE THE INCIN-ERATOR ...?
THERE'S TRASH SCATTERED AROUND IT...
THAT MEANS THEY *WERE* PROCESSING TRASH HERE, JUST LIKE V.P. SAID.
...
GULP
I'VE... GONE PRETTY FAR DOWN, RIGHT?
THIS COULD EVEN BE THE BOTTOM FLOOR...
AND YET... THIS SPACE SEEMS PRETTY CRAMPED COMPARED TO THE OTHER FLOORS...
!
THERE'S A DOOR OVER THERE...?
SO THERE'S MORE TO BE SEEN BEYOND THAT DOOR.
MAYBE THIS IS MERELY ONE OF MANY ROOMS DOWN HERE...
OH, RIGHT! I SHOUL LET EVERYON KNOW...
I BET THEY'RE WORRIED.
BUT IT'S A BIT STUFFY HERE.
MAYBE 'CUZ IT'S SO DEEP UNDER-GROUND...

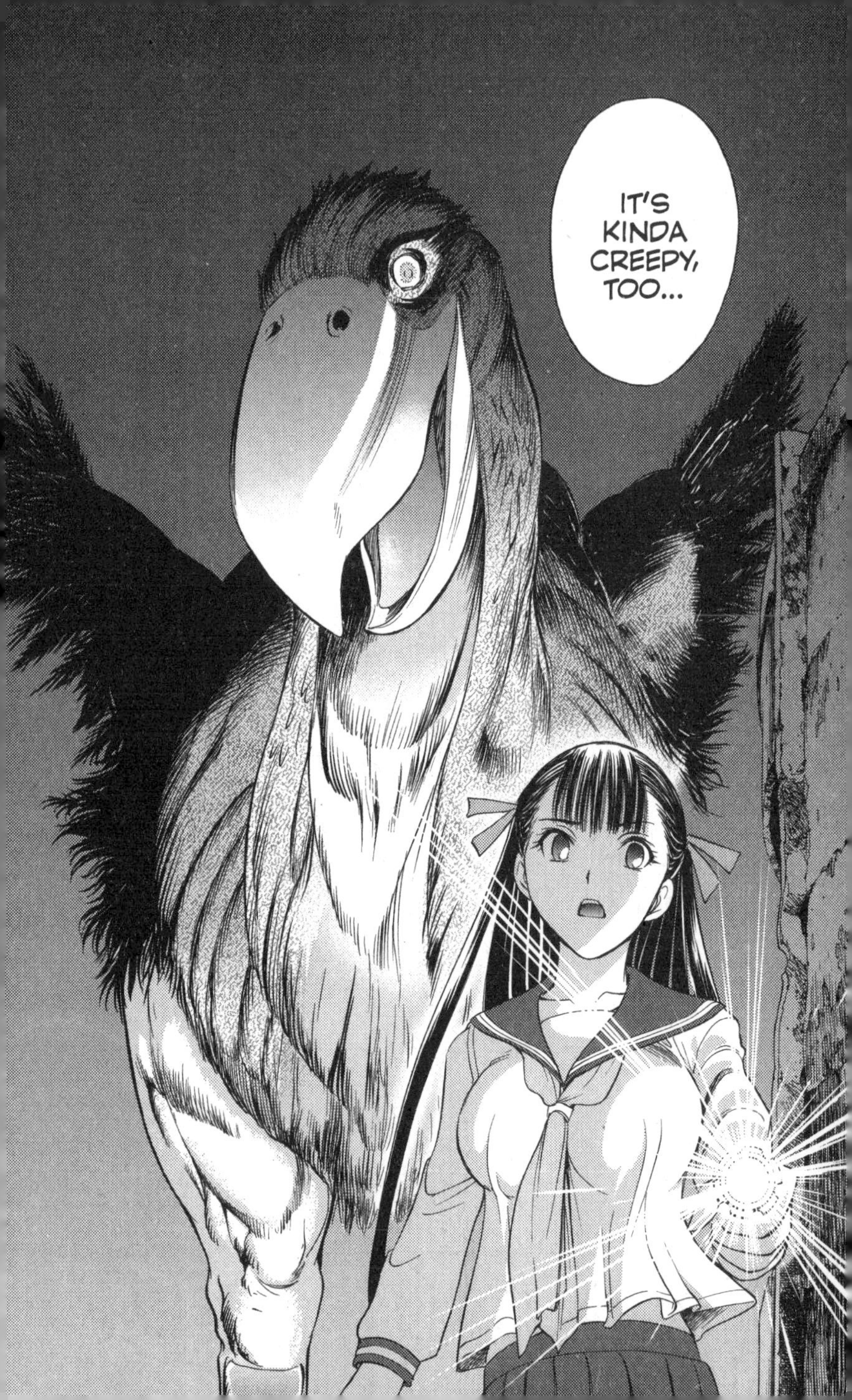
IT'S KINDA CREEPY, TOO...

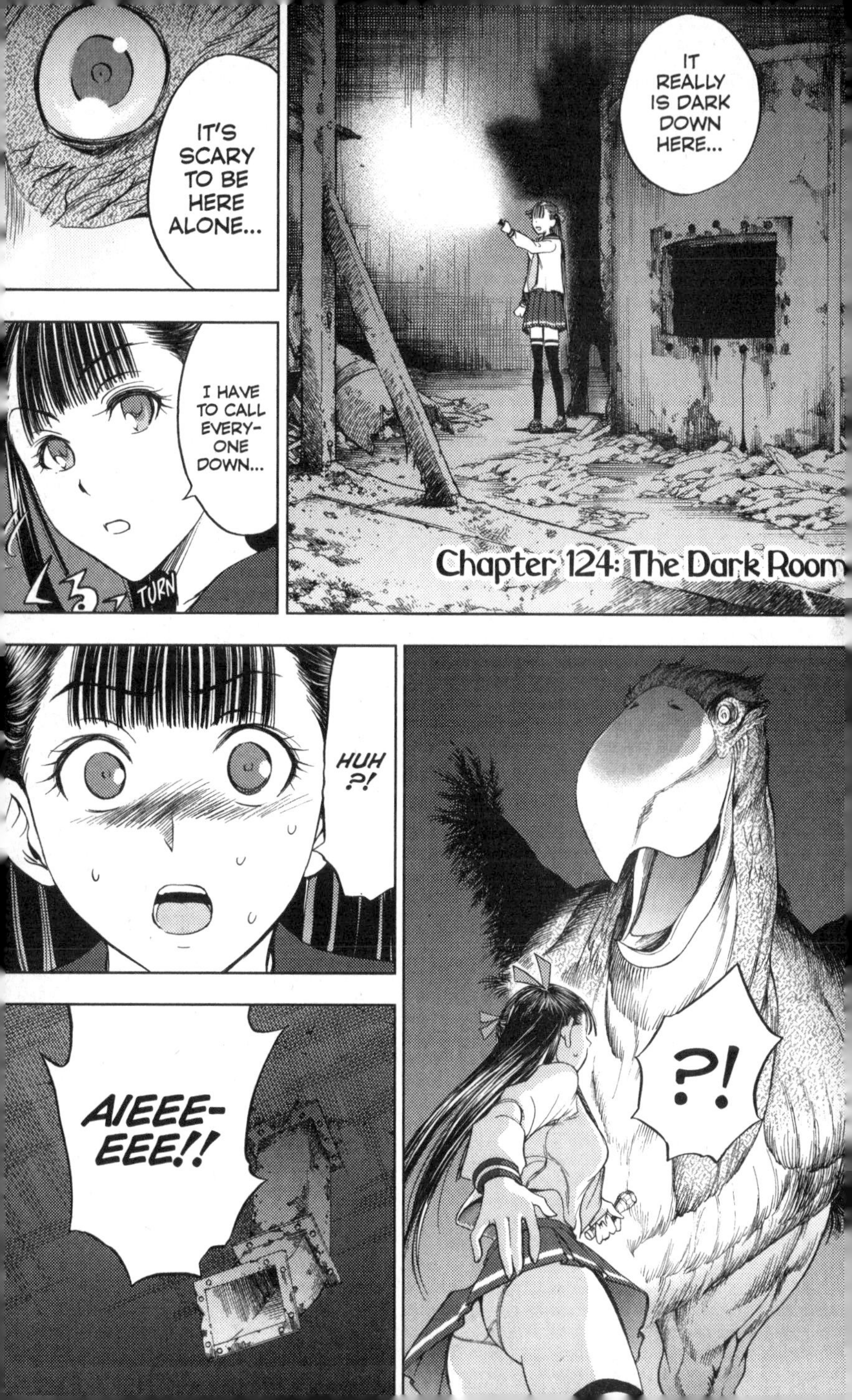
IT REALLY IS DARK DOWN HERE...
Chapter 124: The Dark Room
IT'S SCARY TO BE HERE ALONE...
I HAVE TO CALL EVERY-ONE DOWN...
TURN
?!
HUH ?!
AIEEE-EEE!!

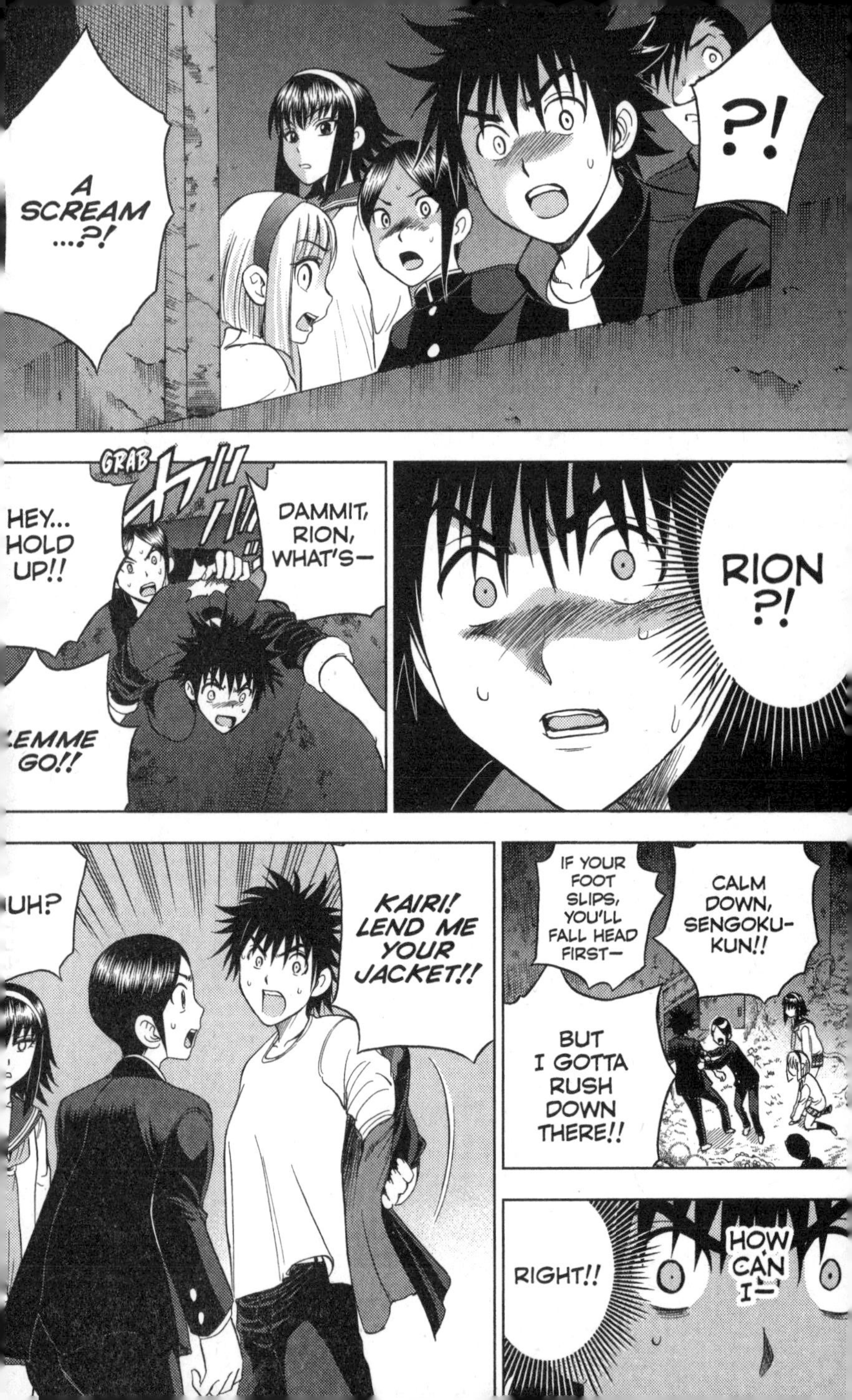
?!
A SCREAM ...?!
RION ?!
DAMMIT, RION, WHAT'S—
GRAB
HEY... HOLD UP!!
EMME GO!!
CALM DOWN, SENGOKU-KUN!!
IF YOUR FOOT SLIPS, YOU'LL FALL HEAD FIRST—
BUT I GOTTA RUSH DOWN THERE!!
HOW CAN I—
RIGHT!!
KAIRI! LEND ME YOUR JACKET!!
UH?

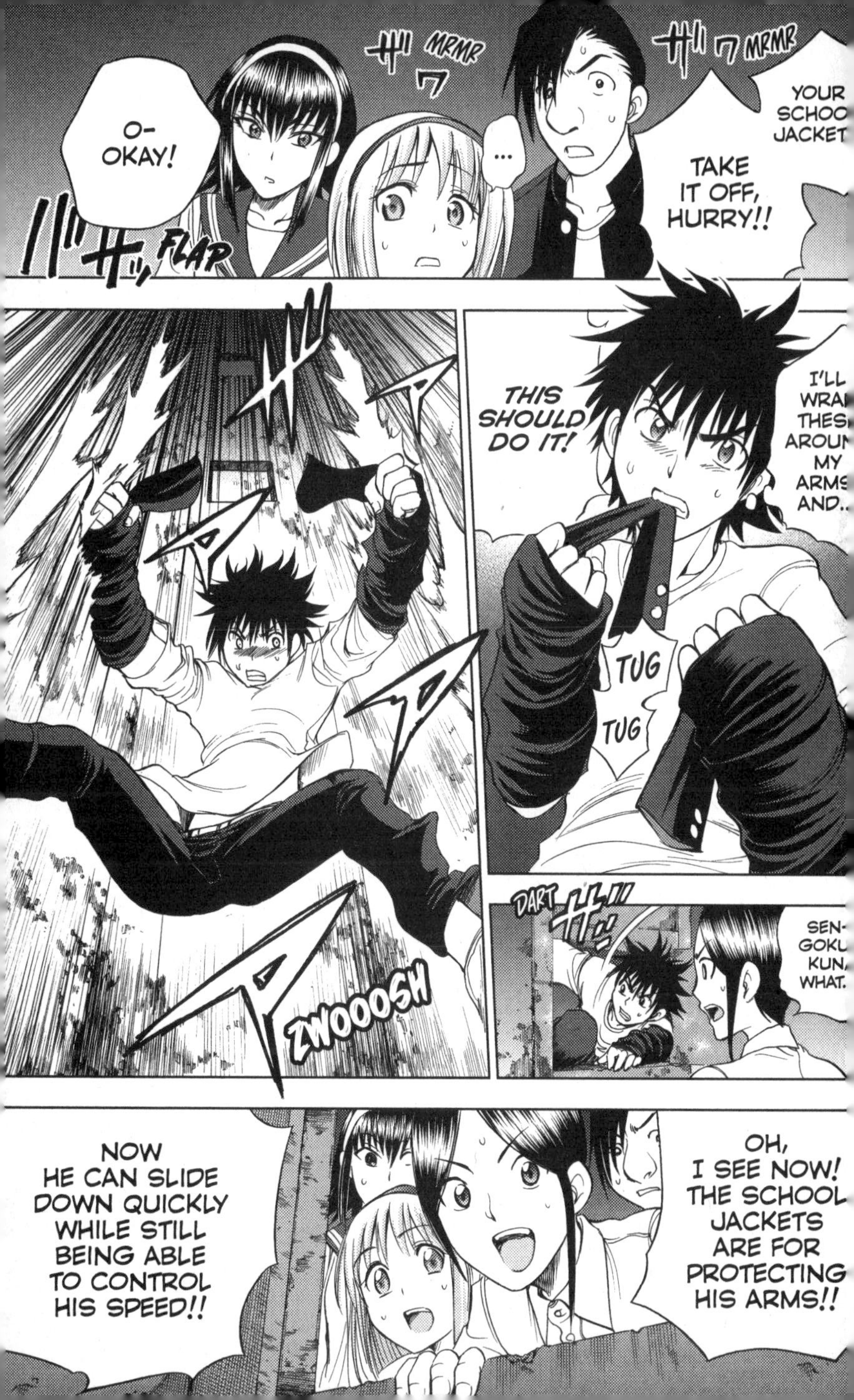
YOUR SCHOO JACKET
TAKE IT OFF, HURRY!!
MRMR
...
MRMR
O-OKAY!
FLAP
I'LL WRA THES AROUN MY ARMS AND..
THIS SHOULD DO IT!
TUG
TUG
SEN-GOKU KUN, WHAT.
DART
ZWOOOSH
OH, I SEE NOW! THE SCHOOL JACKETS ARE FOR PROTECTING HIS ARMS!!
NOW HE CAN SLIDE DOWN QUICKLY WHILE STILL BEING ABLE TO CONTROL HIS SPEED!!

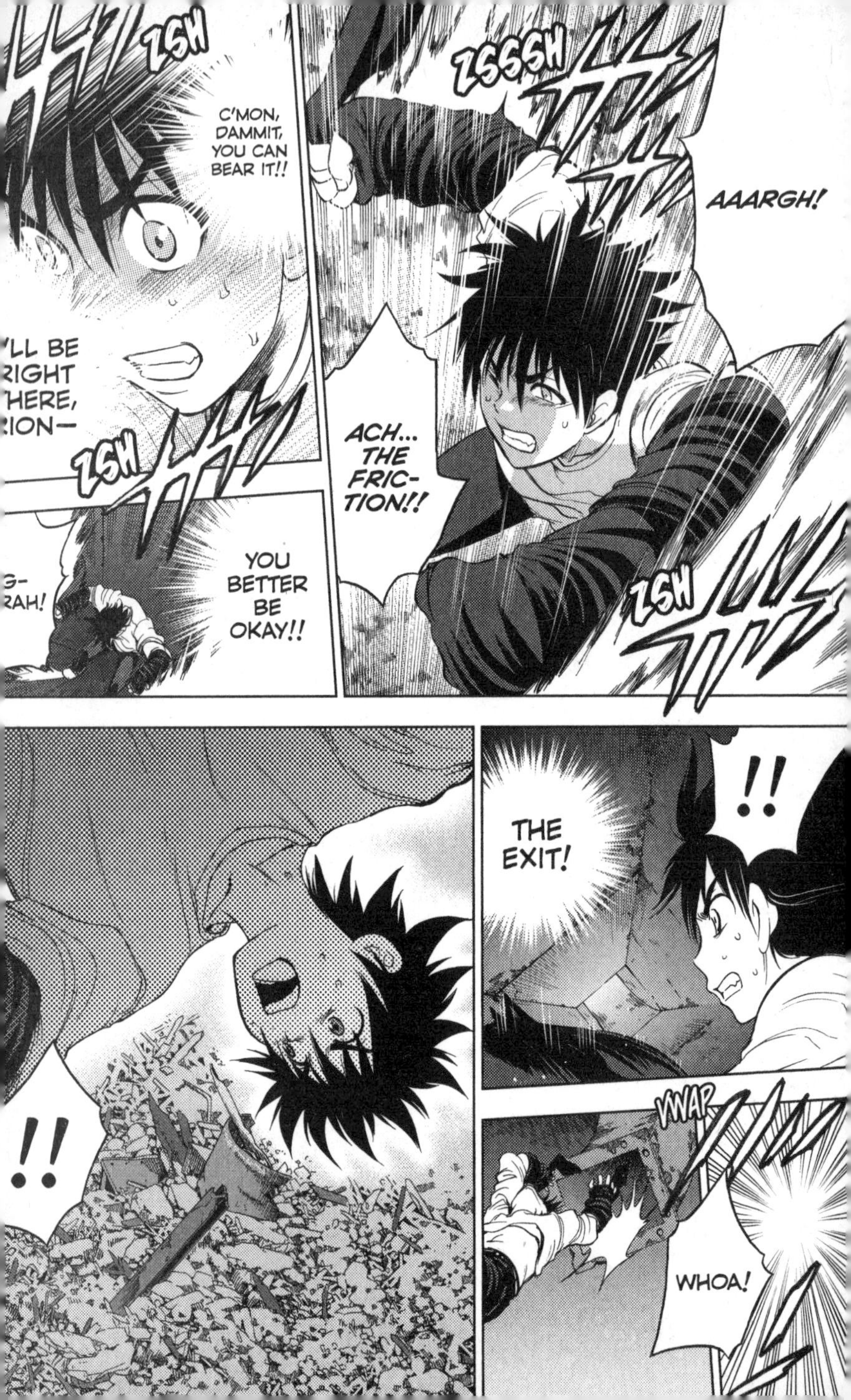

ZSSSH
AAARGH!
ACH... THE FRIC-TION!!
ZSH
ZSH
C'MON, DAMMIT, YOU CAN BEAR IT!!
'LL BE RIGHT THERE, RION—
ZSH
G-RAH!
YOU BETTER BE OKAY!!
!!
THE EXIT!
VWAP
WHOA!
!!

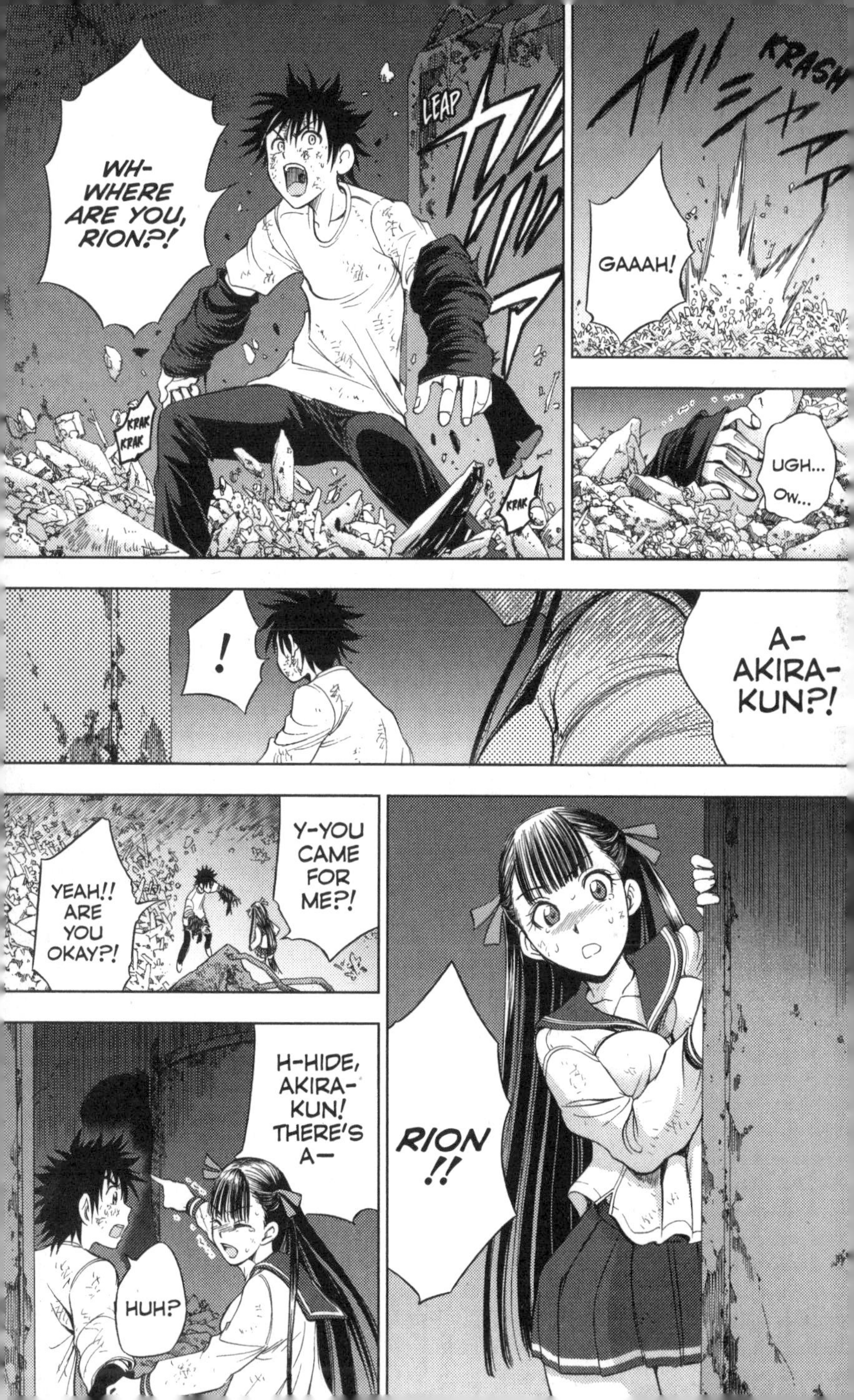
KRASH
GAAAH!
UGH... OW...
LEAP
WH- WHERE ARE YOU, RION?!
KRAK KRAK
KRAK
A- AKIRA-KUN?!
!
RION!!
Y-YOU CAME FOR ME?!
YEAH!! ARE YOU OKAY?!
H-HIDE, AKIRA-KUN! THERE'S A—
HUH?

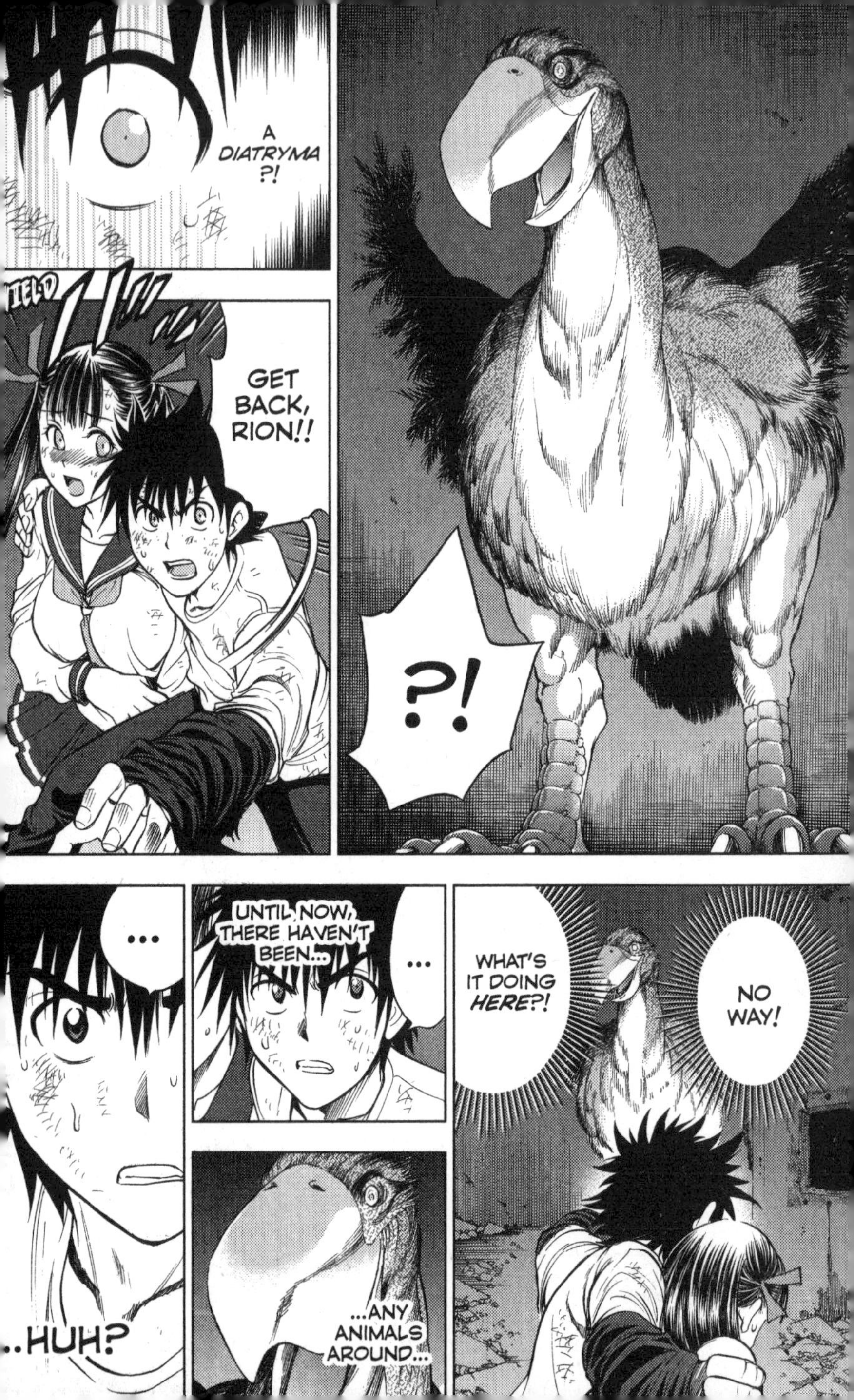
?!
A DIATRYMA ?!
GET BACK, RION!!
NO WAY!
WHAT'S IT DOING HERE?!
UNTIL NOW, THERE HAVEN'T BEEN...
...
...ANY ANIMALS AROUND...
...
..HUH?

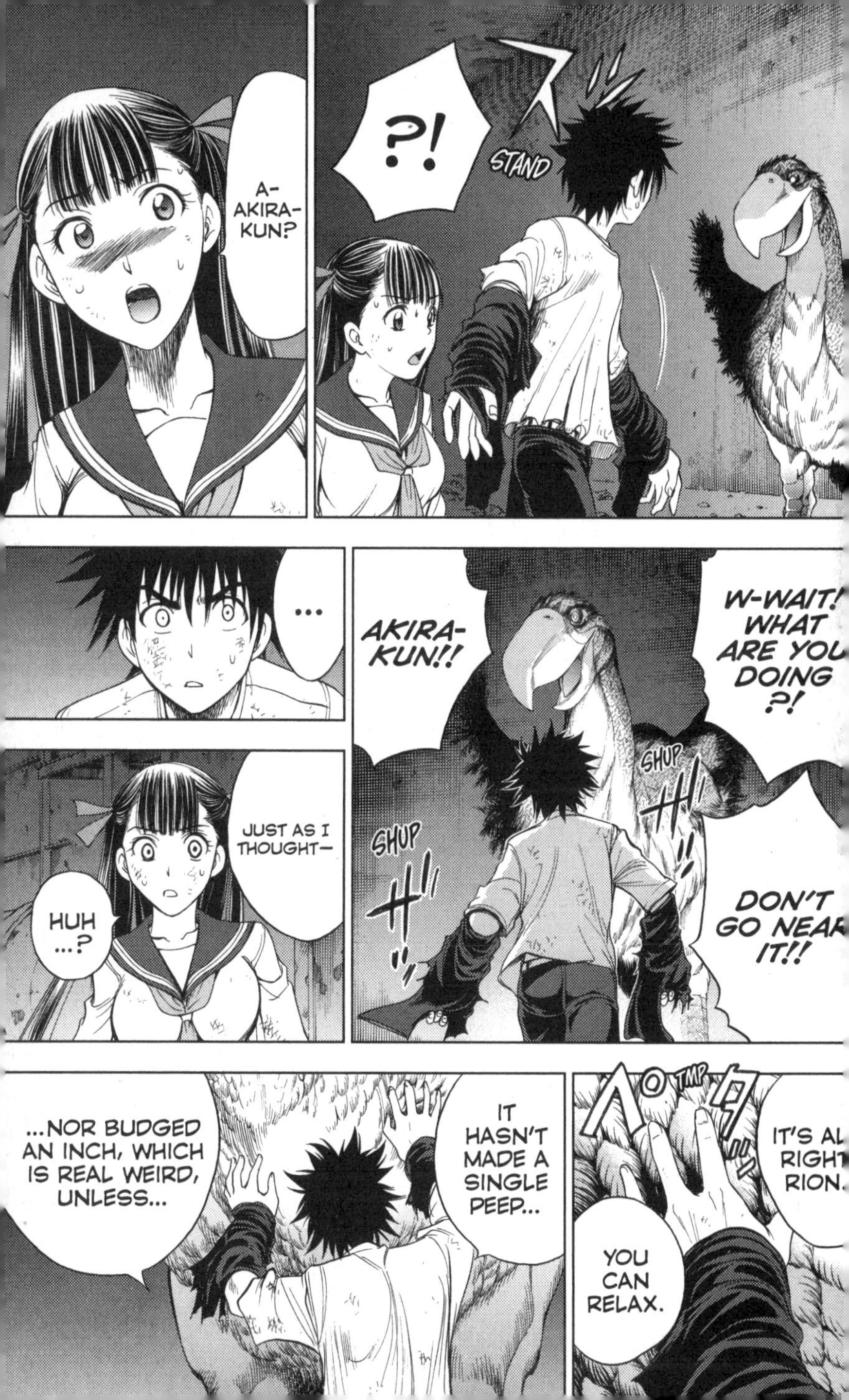
?!
STAND
A- AKIRA-KUN?
W-WAIT! WHAT ARE YOU DOING ?!
AKIRA-KUN!!
SHUP
SHUP
DON'T GO NEAR IT!!
...
JUST AS I THOUGHT—
HUH ...?
TMP
IT'S AL RIGHT RION.
YOU CAN RELAX.
IT HASN'T MADE A SINGLE PEEP...
...NOR BUDGED AN INCH, WHICH IS REAL WEIRD, UNLESS...

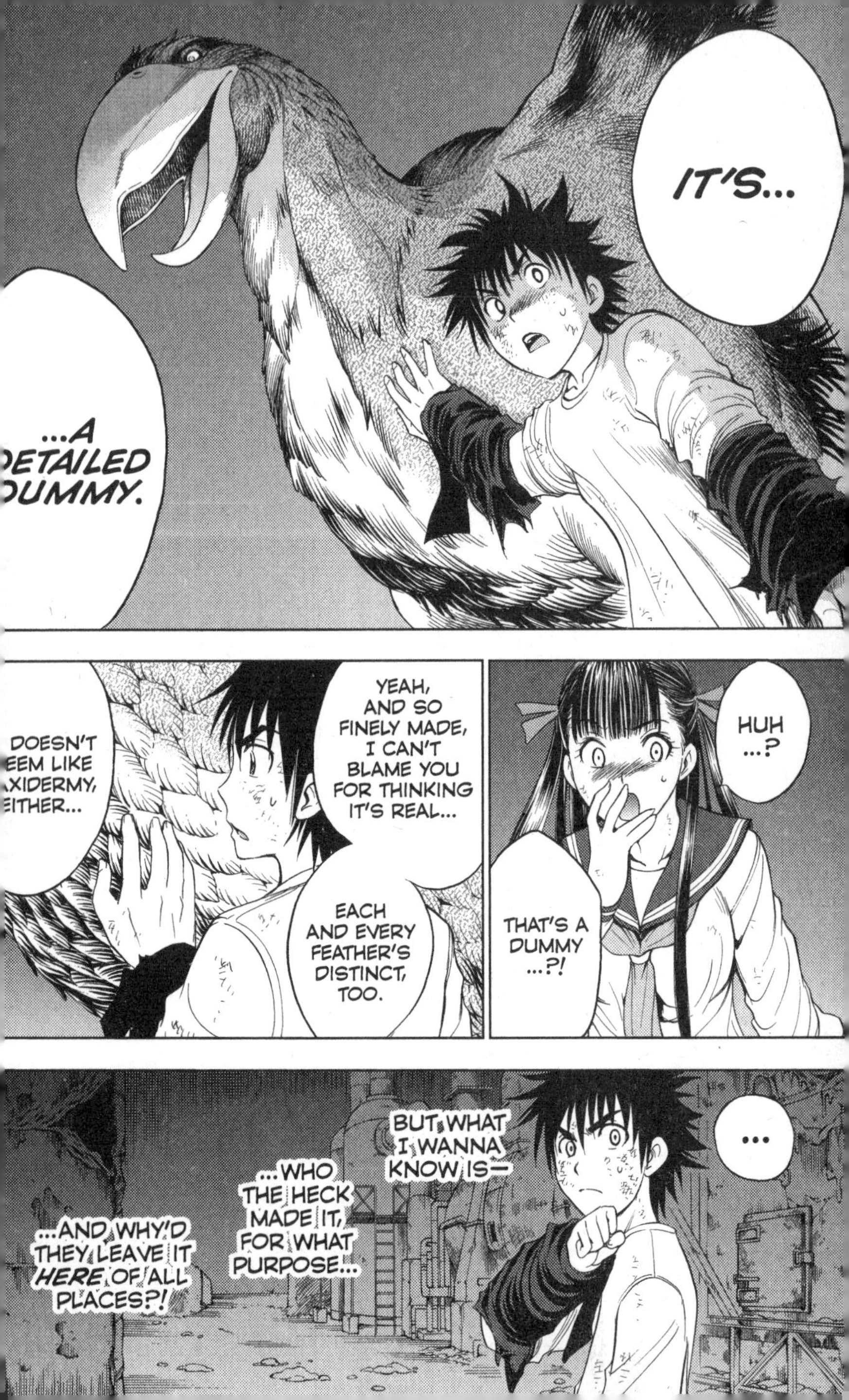
IT'S...
...A ETAILED UMMY.
HUH ...?
THAT'S A DUMMY ...?!
YEAH, AND SO FINELY MADE, I CAN'T BLAME YOU FOR THINKING IT'S REAL...
EACH AND EVERY FEATHER'S DISTINCT, TOO.
DOESN'T EEM LIKE AXIDERMY, EITHER...
...
BUT WHAT I WANNA KNOW IS—
...WHO THE HECK MADE IT, FOR WHAT PURPOSE...
...AND WHY'D THEY LEAVE IT *HERE* OF ALL PLACES?!

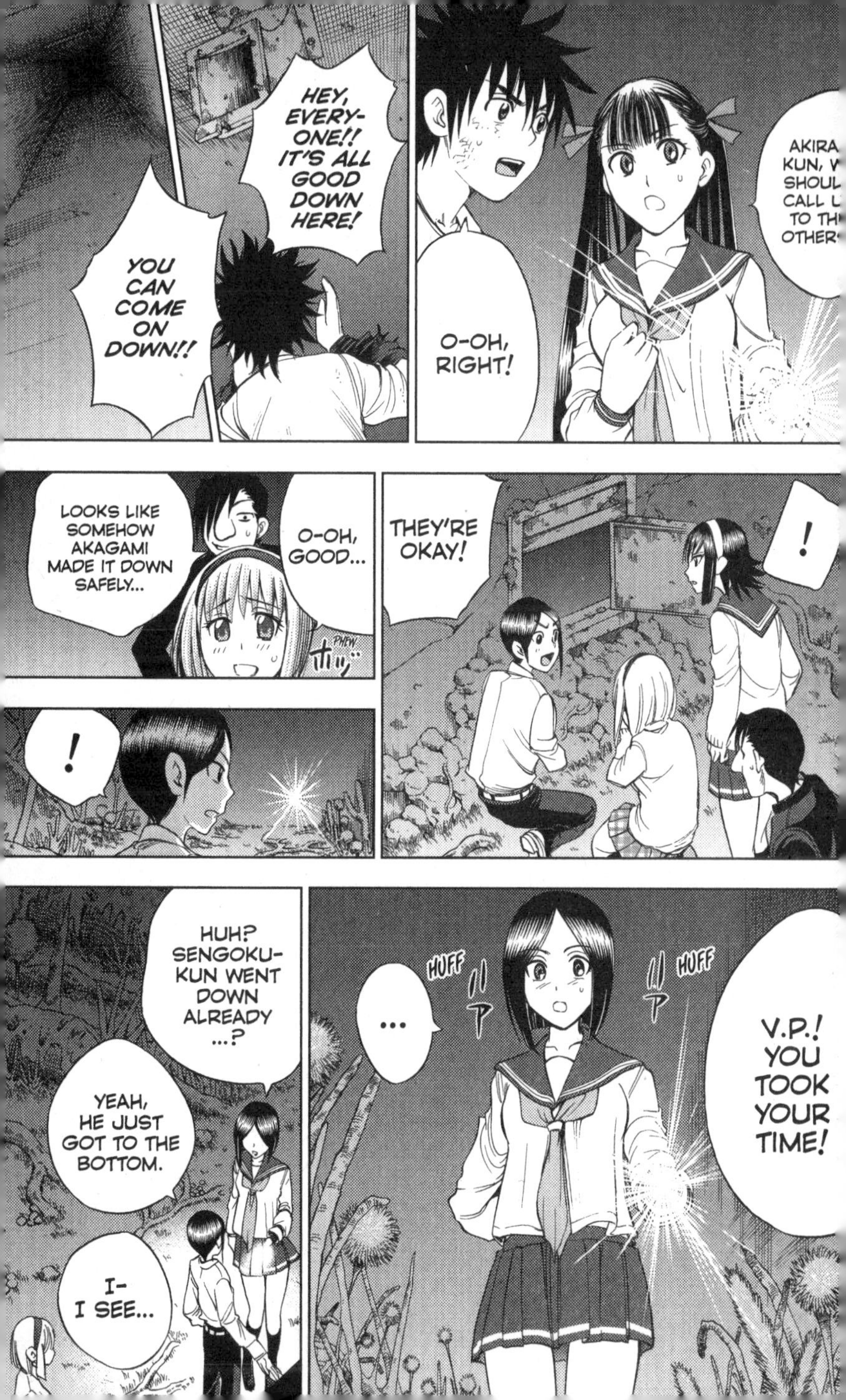
AKIRA KUN, W SHOUL CALL U TO TH OTHERS
O-OH, RIGHT!
HEY, EVERYONE!! IT'S ALL GOOD DOWN HERE!
YOU CAN COME ON DOWN!!
!
THEY'RE OKAY!
O-OH, GOOD...
LOOKS LIKE SOMEHOW AKAGAMI MADE IT DOWN SAFELY...
PHEW
!
V.P.! YOU TOOK YOUR TIME!
HUFF
HUFF
...
HUH? SENGOKU-KUN WENT DOWN ALREADY ...?
YEAH, HE JUST GOT TO THE BOTTOM.
I- I SEE...

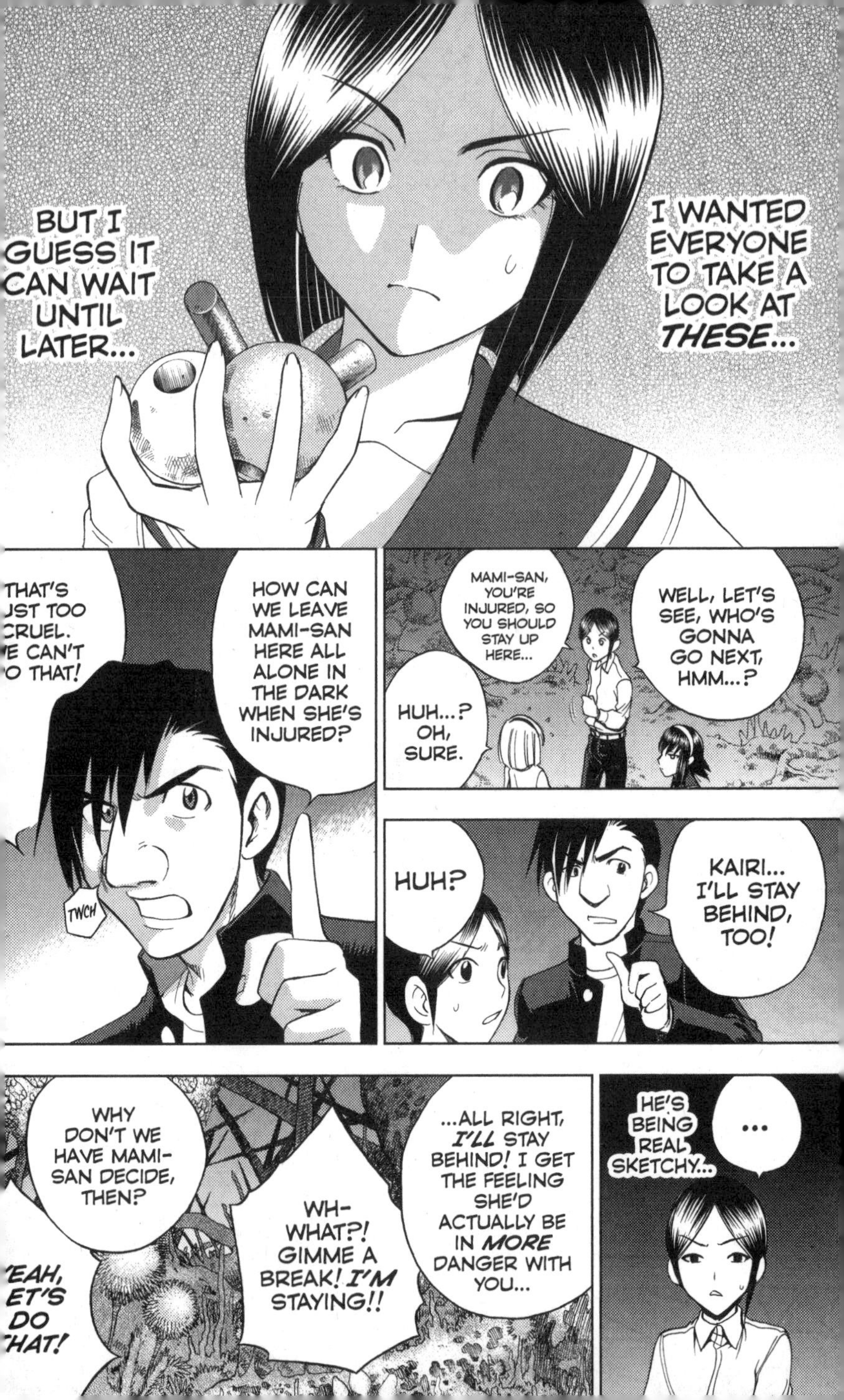
I WANTED EVERYONE TO TAKE A LOOK AT THESE...
BUT I GUESS IT CAN WAIT UNTIL LATER...
WELL, LET'S SEE, WHO'S GONNA GO NEXT, HMM...?
MAMI-SAN, YOU'RE INJURED, SO YOU SHOULD STAY UP HERE...
HUH...? OH, SURE.
KAIRI... I'LL STAY BEHIND, TOO!
HUH?
HOW CAN WE LEAVE MAMI-SAN HERE ALL ALONE IN THE DARK WHEN SHE'S INJURED?
THAT'S JST TOO CRUEL. E CAN'T O THAT!
TWCH
...
HE'S BEING REAL SKETCHY...
...ALL RIGHT, I'LL STAY BEHIND! I GET THE FEELING SHE'D ACTUALLY BE IN MORE DANGER WITH YOU...
WH-WHAT?! GIMME A BREAK! I'M STAYING!!
WHY DON'T WE HAVE MAMI-SAN DECIDE, THEN?
EAH, ET'S DO HAT!

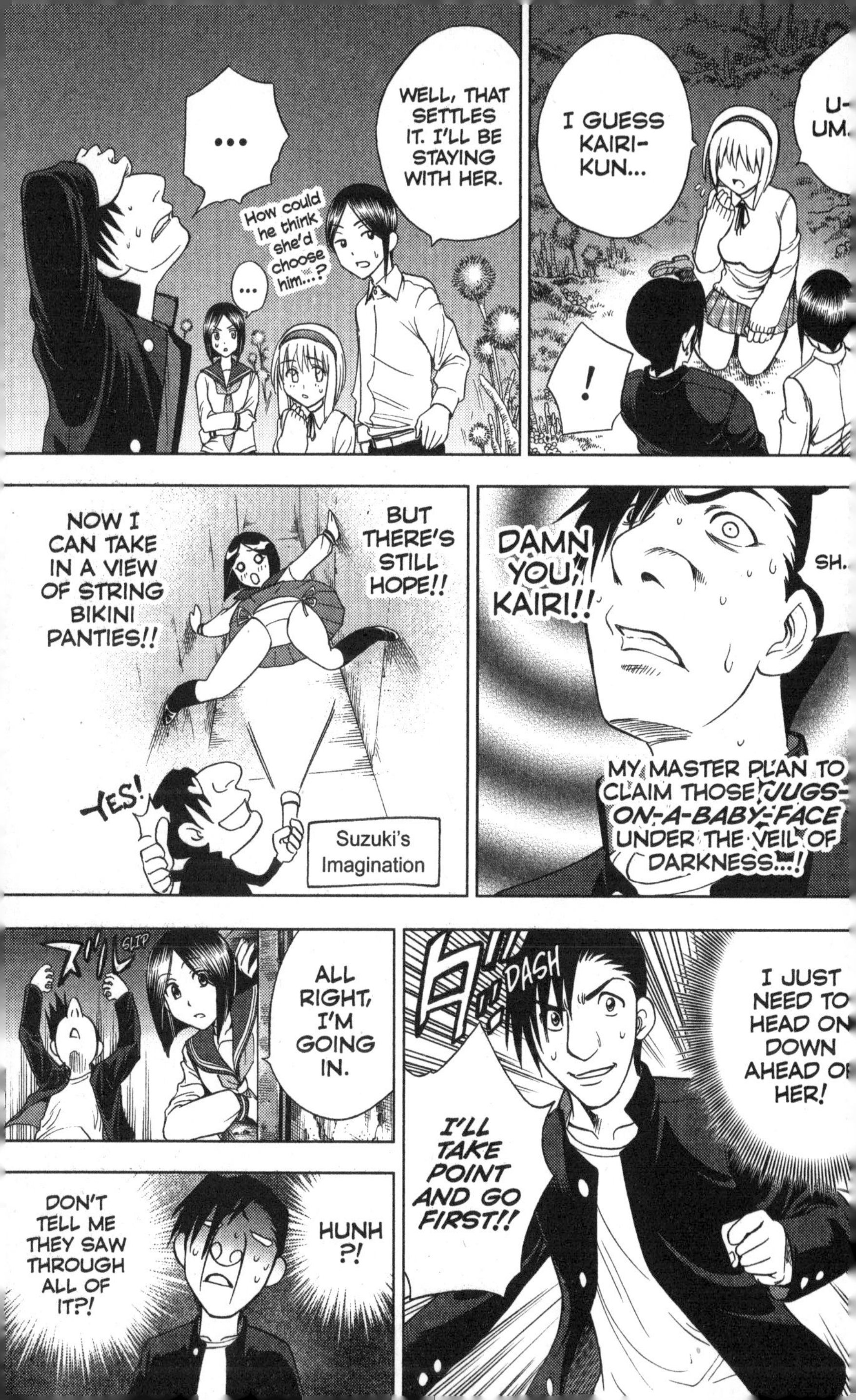
U-UM.
I GUESS KAIRI-KUN...
!
WELL, THAT SETTLES IT. I'LL BE STAYING WITH HER.
...
How could he think she'd choose him...?
...
SH.
DAMN YOU, KAIRI!!
MY MASTER PLAN TO CLAIM THOSE JUGS-ON-A-BABY-FACE UNDER THE VEIL OF DARKNESS...!
BUT THERE'S STILL HOPE!!
NOW I CAN TAKE IN A VIEW OF STRING BIKINI PANTIES!!
YES!
Suzuki's Imagination
I JUST NEED TO HEAD ON DOWN AHEAD O HER!
DASH
I'LL TAKE POINT AND GO FIRST!!
ALL RIGHT, I'M GOING IN.
SLIP
HUNH?!
DON'T TELL ME THEY SAW THROUGH ALL OF IT?!

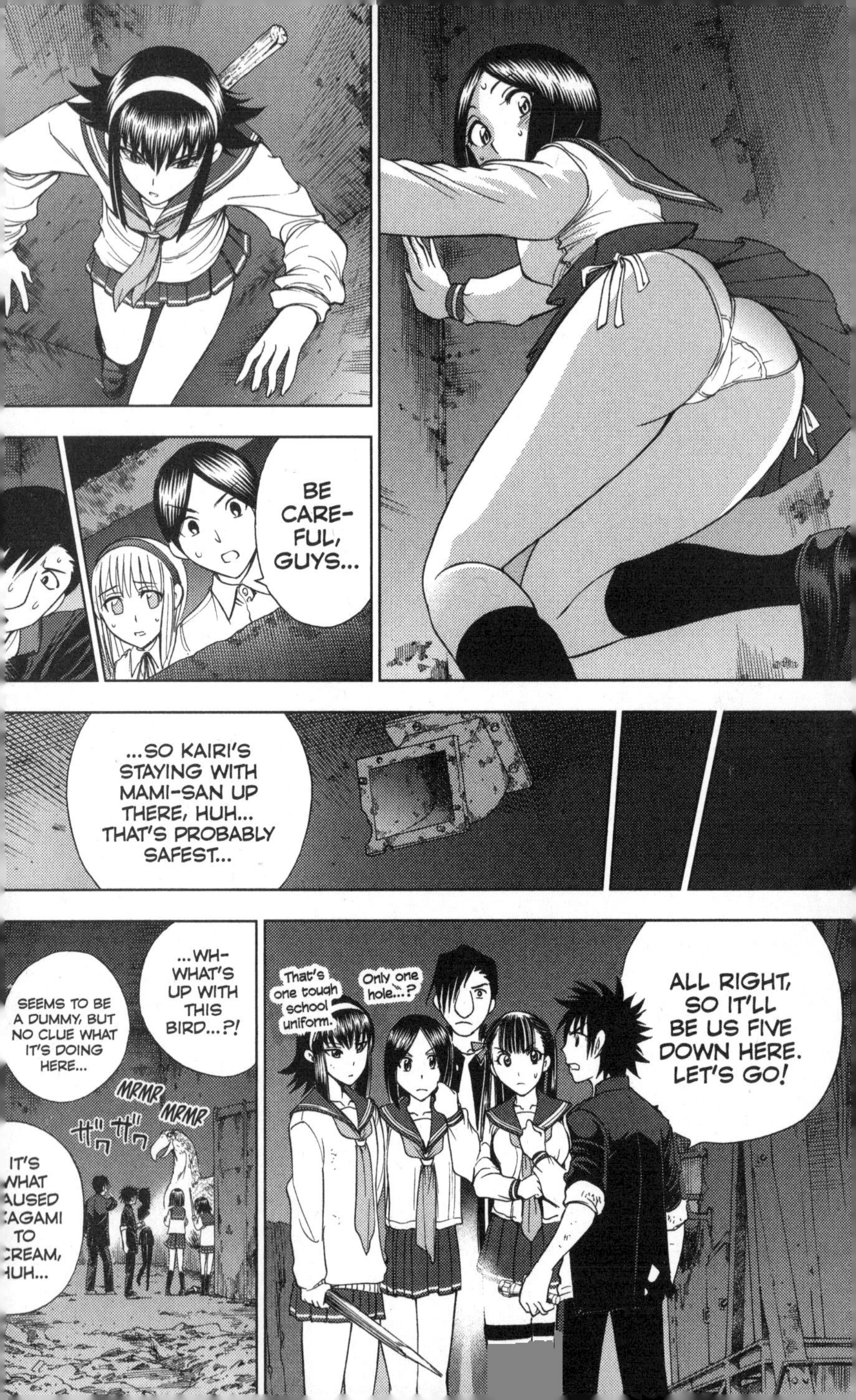
BE CARE-FUL, GUYS...
...SO KAIRI'S STAYING WITH MAMI-SAN UP THERE, HUH... THAT'S PROBABLY SAFEST...
ALL RIGHT, SO IT'LL BE US FIVE DOWN HERE. LET'S GO!
Only one hole...?
That's one tough school uniform.
...WH- WHAT'S UP WITH THIS BIRD...?!
SEEMS TO BE A DUMMY, BUT NO CLUE WHAT IT'S DOING HERE...
MRMR MRMR
ザワ ザワ
IT'S WHAT AUSED AGAMI TO CREAM, HUH...

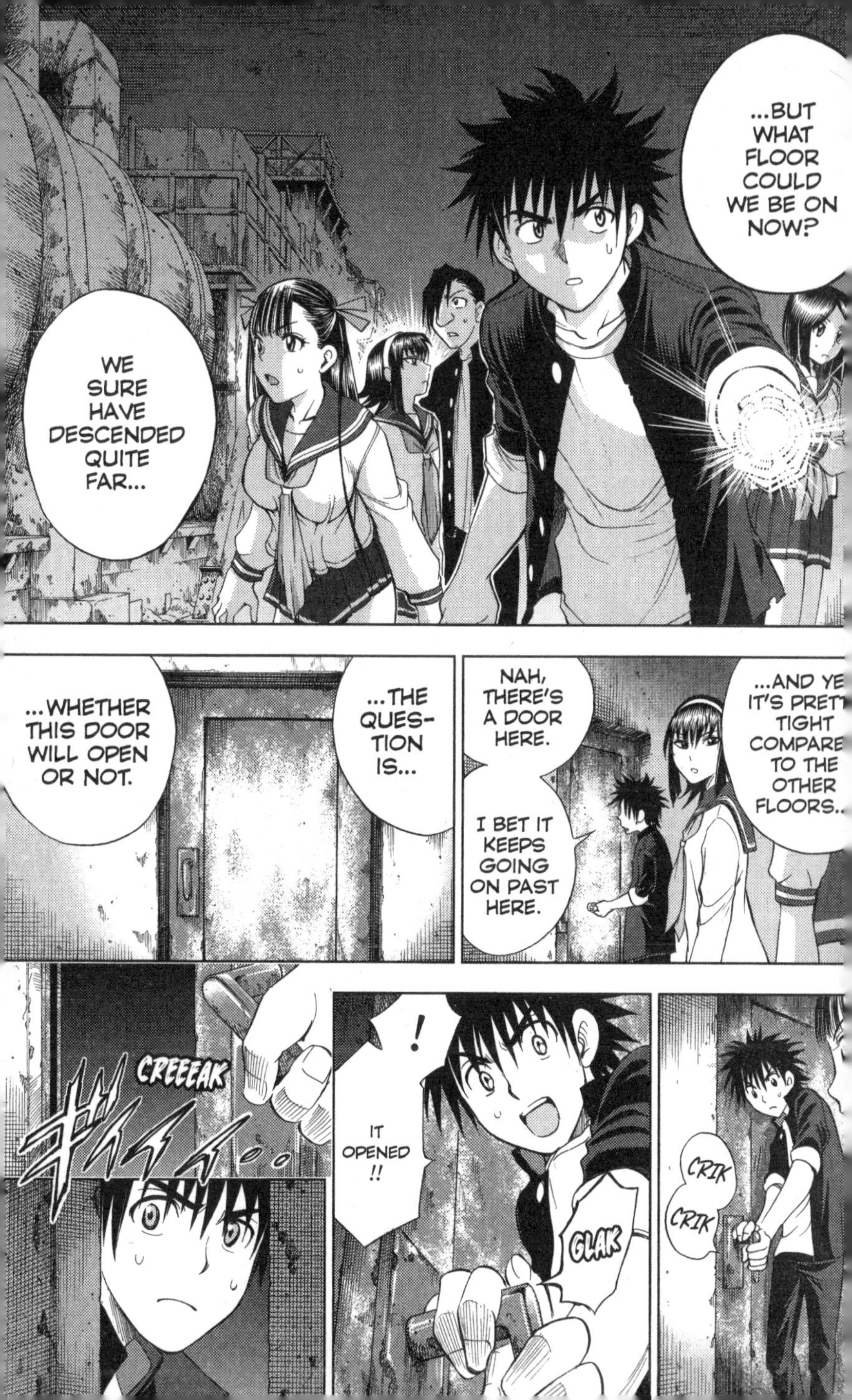

...BUT WHAT FLOOR COULD WE BE ON NOW?
WE SURE HAVE DESCENDED QUITE FAR...
...AND YE IT'S PRETT TIGHT COMPARE TO THE OTHER FLOORS..
NAH, THERE'S A DOOR HERE.
I BET IT KEEPS GOING ON PAST HERE.
...THE QUES-TION IS...
...WHETHER THIS DOOR WILL OPEN OR NOT.
CRIK
CRIK
!
GLAK
IT OPENED !!
CREEEAK

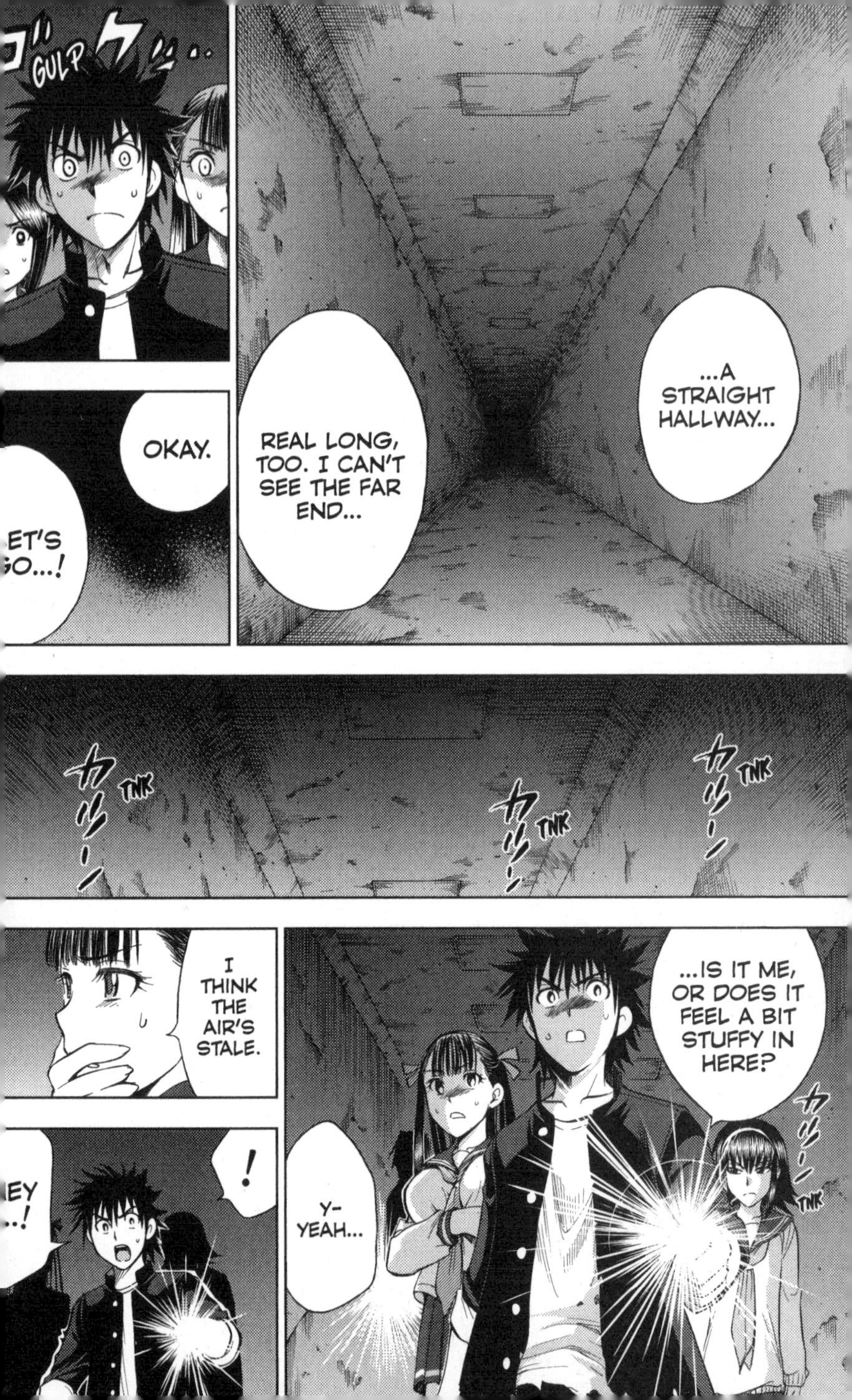
...A STRAIGHT HALLWAY...
REAL LONG, TOO. I CAN'T SEE THE FAR END...
GULP
OKAY.
ET'S GO...!
TNK
TNK
TNK
...IS IT ME, OR DOES IT FEEL A BIT STUFFY IN HERE?
Y-YEAH...
TNK
I THINK THE AIR'S STALE.
!
EY ...!

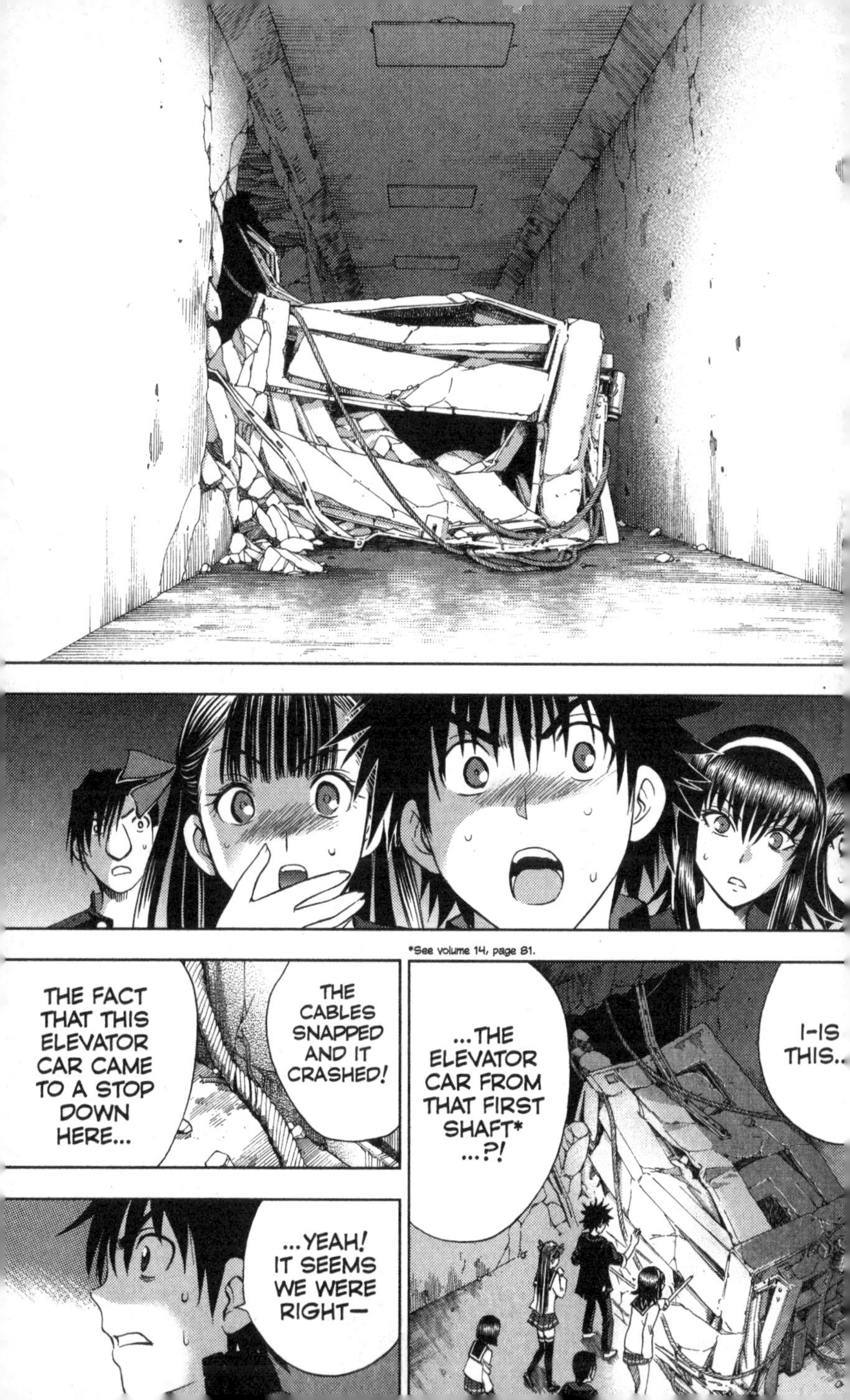
I-IS THIS..
...THE ELEVATOR CAR FROM THAT FIRST SHAFT* ...?!
THE CABLES SNAPPED AND IT CRASHED!
THE FACT THAT THIS ELEVATOR CAR CAME TO A STOP DOWN HERE...
...YEAH! IT SEEMS WE WERE RIGHT—

*See volume 14, page 81.

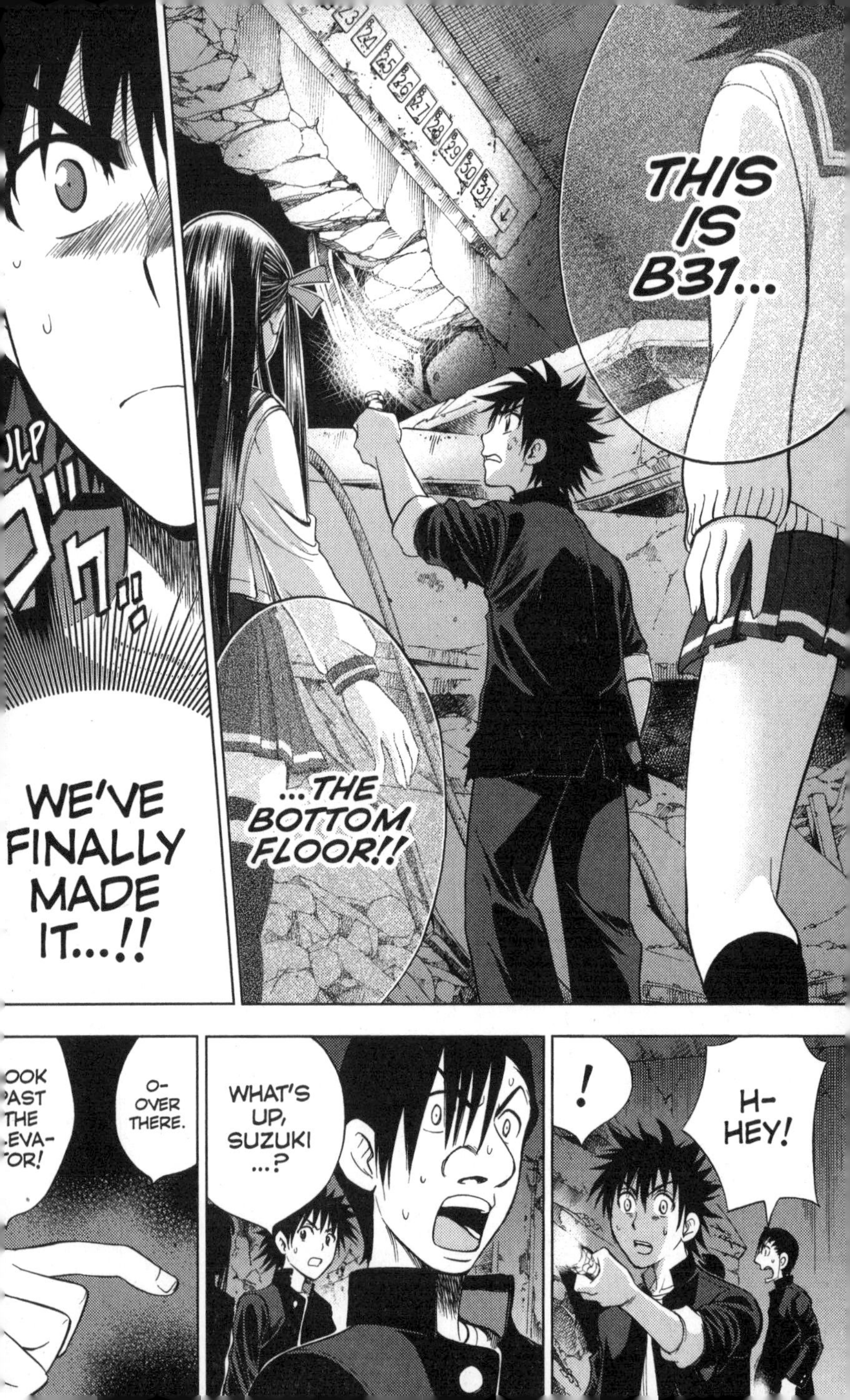
THIS IS B31...
...THE BOTTOM FLOOR!!
ULP
WE'VE FINALLY MADE IT...!!
!
H-HEY!
WHAT'S UP, SUZUKI ...?
O-OVER THERE.
OOK PAST THE EVA-TOR!

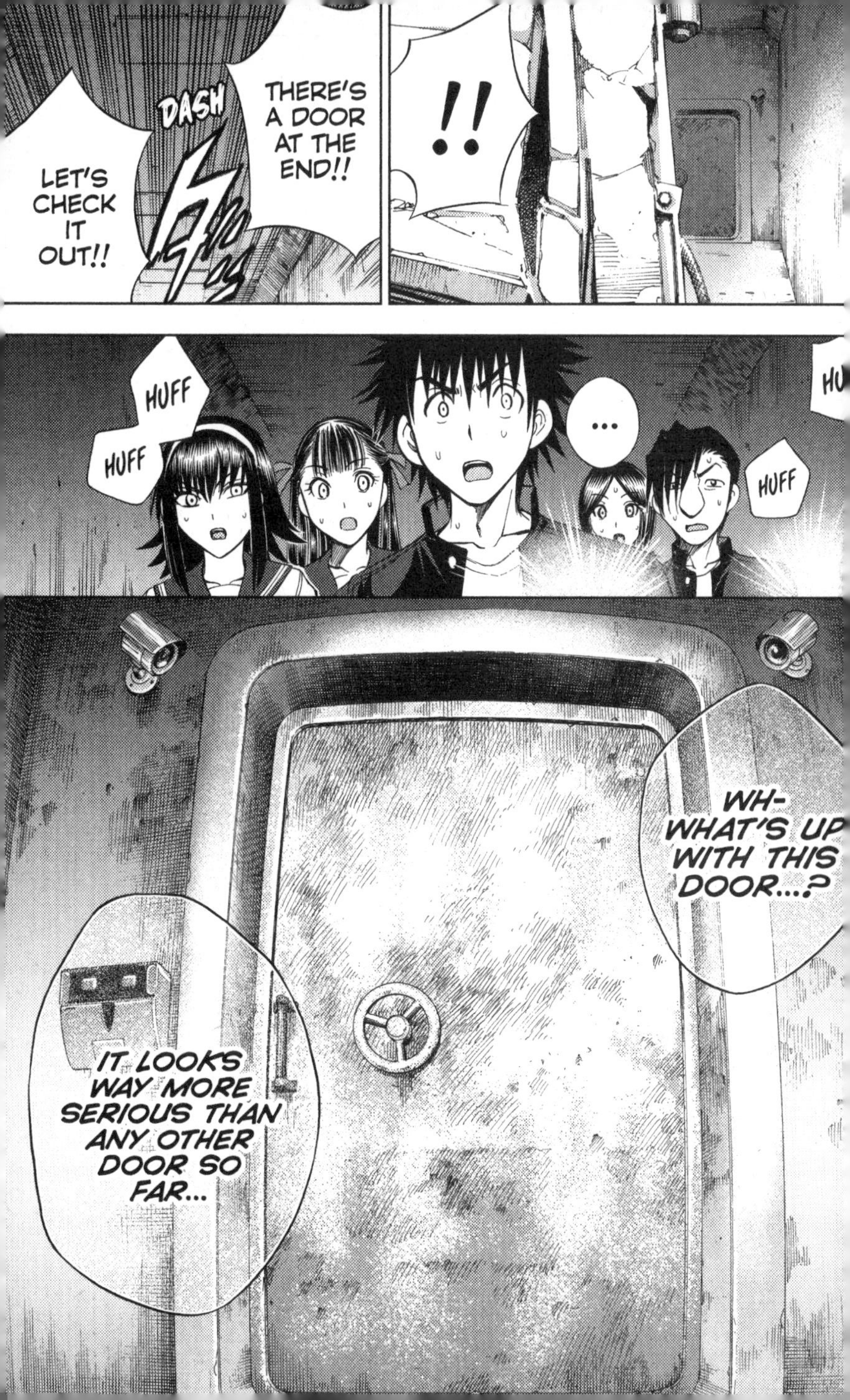
!!
THERE'S A DOOR AT THE END!!
DASH
LET'S CHECK IT OUT!!
HU
HUFF
...
HUFF
HUFF
WH- WHAT'S UP WITH THIS DOOR...?
IT LOOKS WAY MORE SERIOUS THAN ANY OTHER DOOR SO FAR...

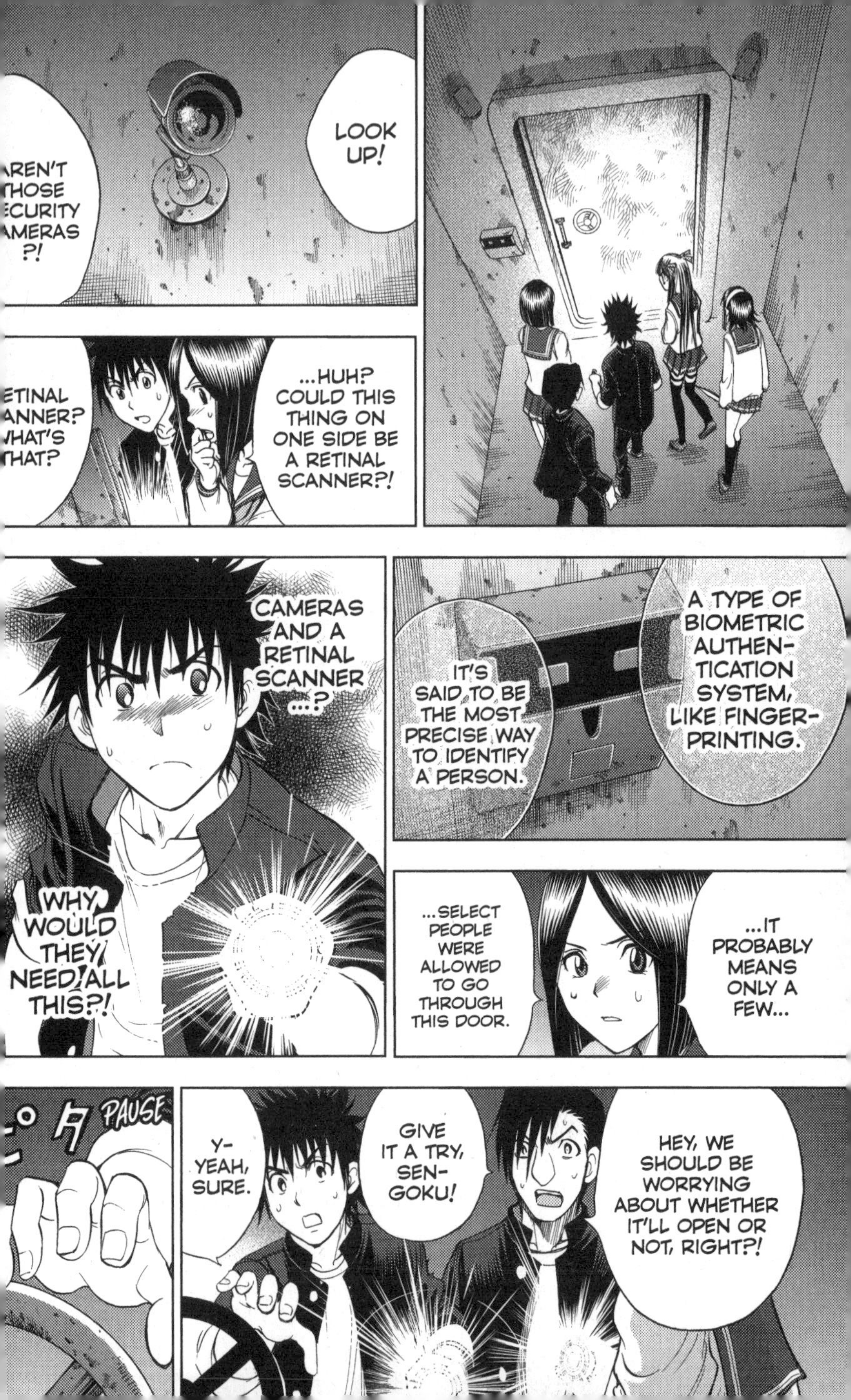
LOOK UP!
AREN'T HOSE ECURITY AMERAS ?!
...HUH? COULD THIS THING ON ONE SIDE BE A RETINAL SCANNER?!
ETINAL ANNER? VHAT'S HAT?
A TYPE OF BIOMETRIC AUTHEN-TICATION SYSTEM, LIKE FINGER-PRINTING.
IT'S SAID TO BE THE MOST PRECISE WAY TO IDENTIFY A PERSON.
...IT PROBABLY MEANS ONLY A FEW...
...SELECT PEOPLE WERE ALLOWED TO GO THROUGH THIS DOOR.
CAMERAS AND A RETINAL SCANNER ...?
WHY WOULD THEY NEED ALL THIS?!
HEY, WE SHOULD BE WORRYING ABOUT WHETHER IT'LL OPEN OR NOT, RIGHT?!
GIVE IT A TRY, SEN-GOKU!
Y-YEAH, SURE.
PAUSE

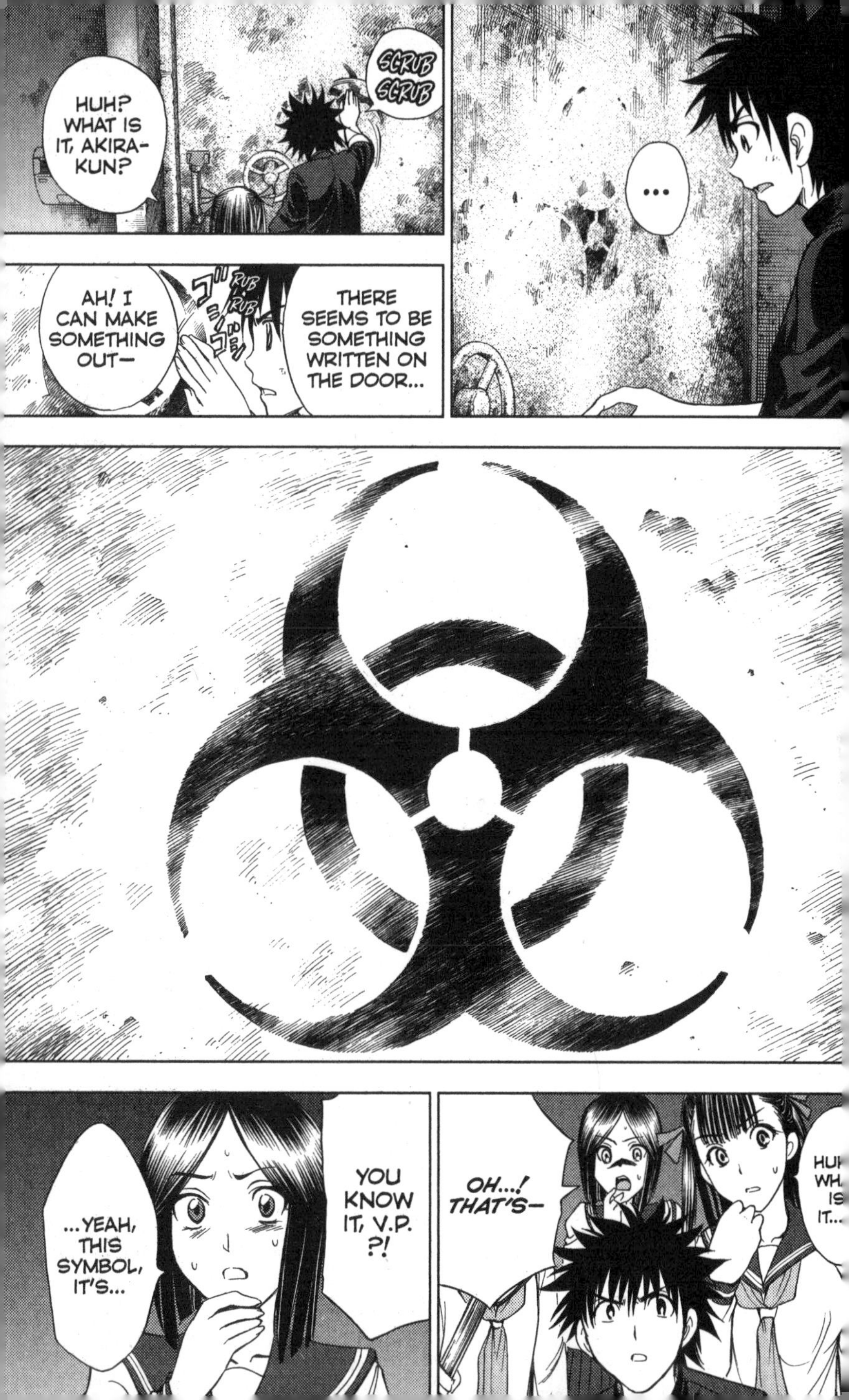
...
SGRUB SGRUB
HUH? WHAT IS IT, AKIRA-KUN?
THERE SEEMS TO BE SOMETHING WRITTEN ON THE DOOR...
RUB RUB
AH! I CAN MAKE SOMETHING OUT—
HU WHA IS IT...
OH...! THAT'S—
YOU KNOW IT, V.P. ?!
...YEAH, THIS SYMBOL, IT'S...

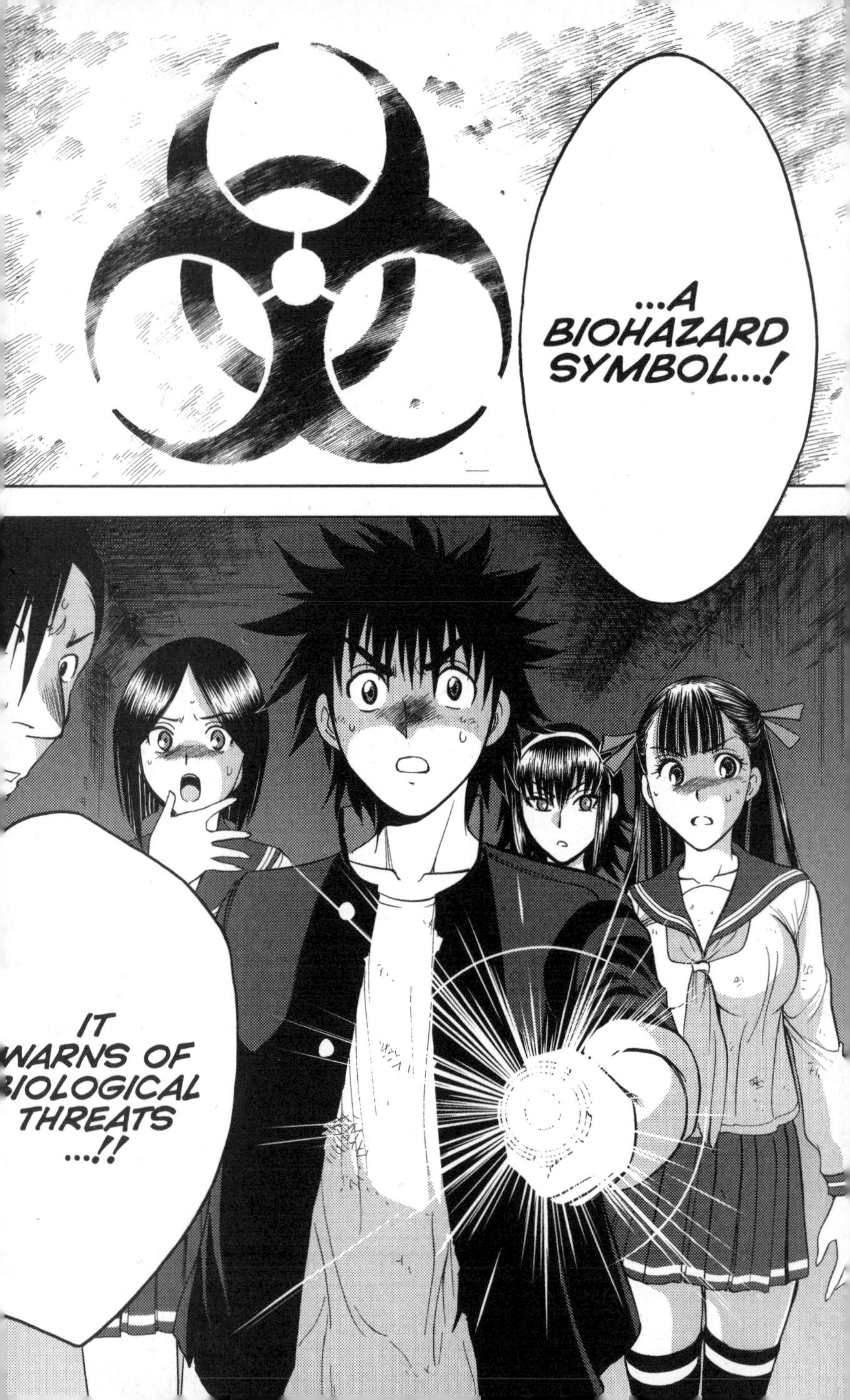
...A BIOHAZARD SYMBOL...!
IT WARNS OF BIOLOGICAL THREATS ...!!

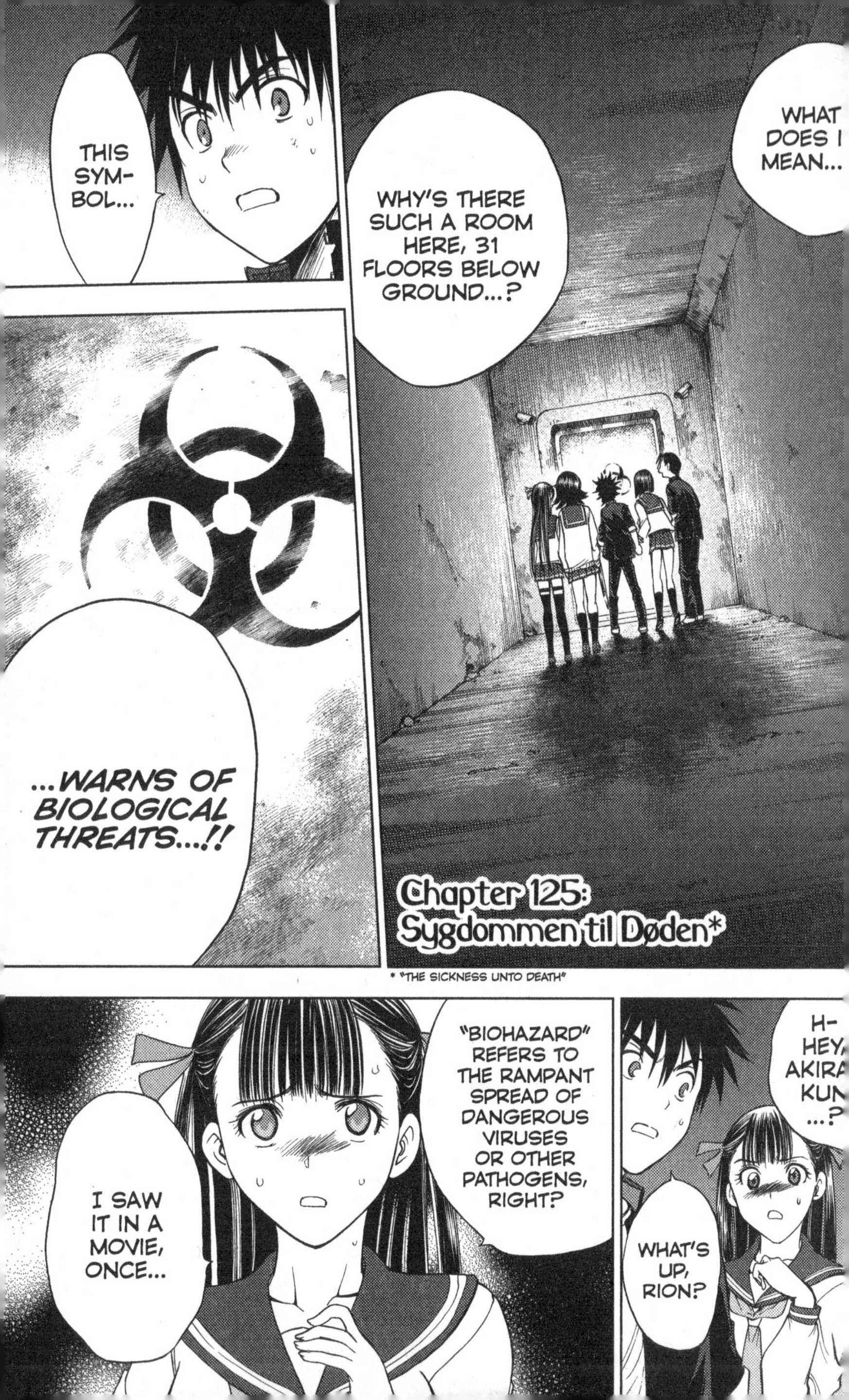
WHAT DOES I MEAN...
WHY'S THERE SUCH A ROOM HERE, 31 FLOORS BELOW GROUND...?
Chapter 125: Sygdommen til Døden*
* "THE SICKNESS UNTO DEATH"
THIS SYMBOL...
...WARNS OF BIOLOGICAL THREATS...!!
H-HEY, AKIRA KUN...?
WHAT'S UP, RION?
"BIOHAZARD" REFERS TO THE RAMPANT SPREAD OF DANGEROUS VIRUSES OR OTHER PATHOGENS, RIGHT?
I SAW IT IN A MOVIE, ONCE...

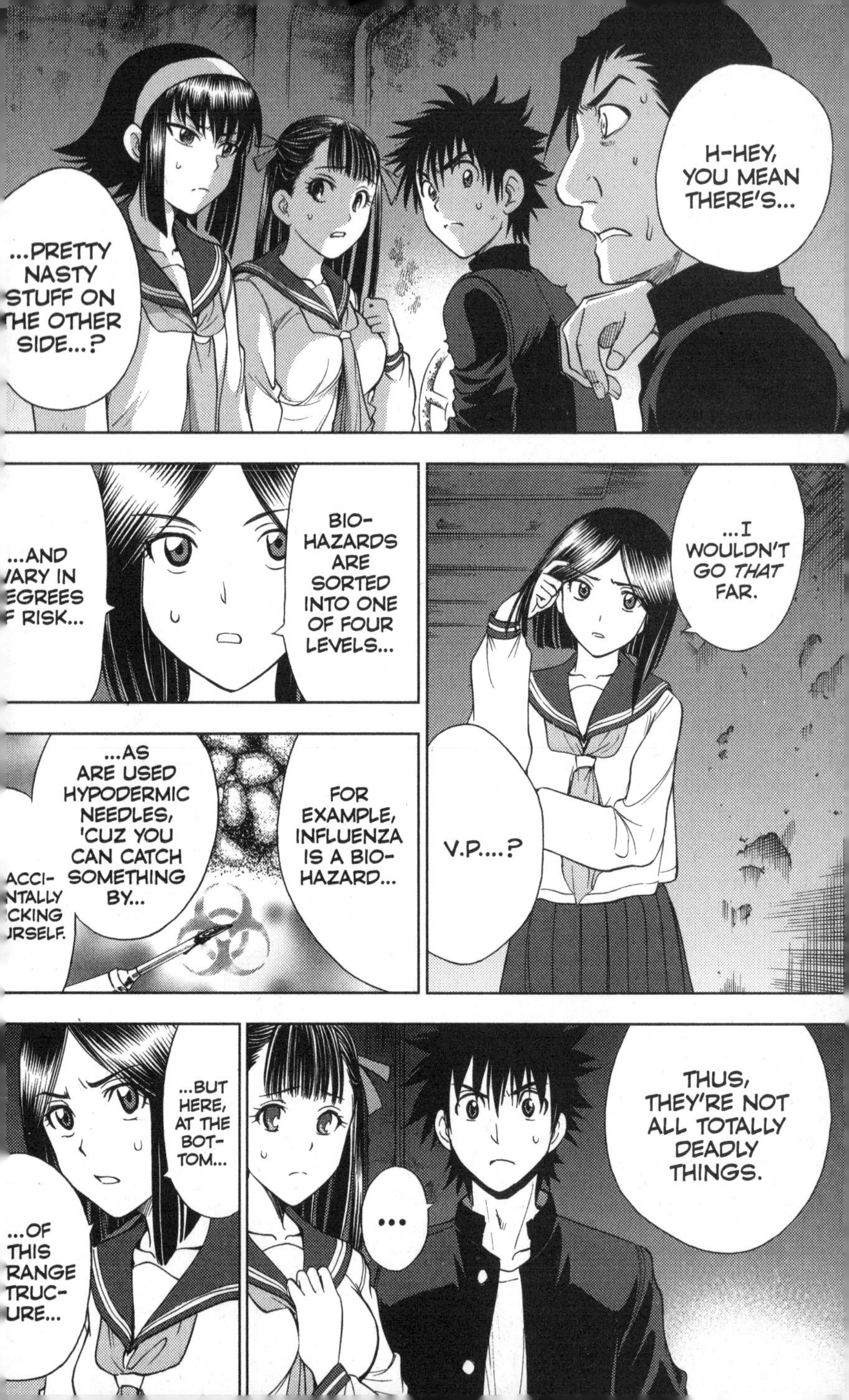
H-HEY, YOU MEAN THERE'S...
...PRETTY NASTY STUFF ON HE OTHER SIDE...?
...I WOULDN'T GO *THAT* FAR.
V.P....?
BIO-HAZARDS ARE SORTED INTO ONE OF FOUR LEVELS...
...AND ARY IN EGREES F RISK...
FOR EXAMPLE, INFLUENZA IS A BIO-HAZARD...
...AS ARE USED HYPODERMIC NEEDLES, 'CUZ YOU CAN CATCH SOMETHING BY...
ACCI- NTALLY CKING URSELF.
THUS, THEY'RE NOT ALL TOTALLY DEADLY THINGS.
...
...BUT HERE, AT THE BOT-TOM...
...OF THIS RANGE TRUC- URE...

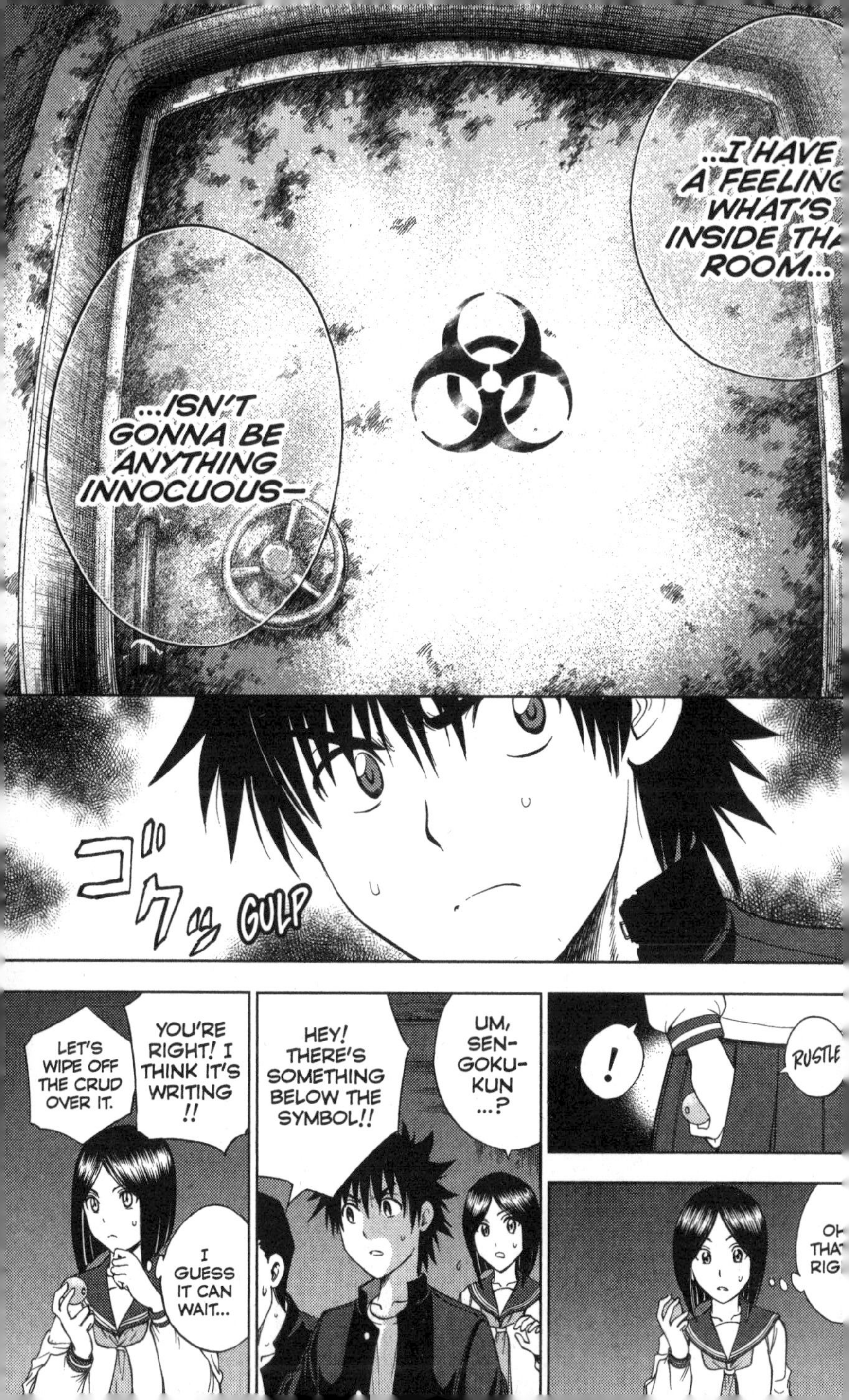

...I HAVE A FEELING WHAT'S INSIDE THA ROOM...
...ISN'T GONNA BE ANYTHING INNOCUOUS—
GULP
RUSTLE
!
OH THAT RIG
UM, SEN-GOKU-KUN ...?
HEY! THERE'S SOMETHING BELOW THE SYMBOL!!
YOU'RE RIGHT! I THINK IT'S WRITING !!
LET'S WIPE OFF THE CRUD OVER IT.
I GUESS IT CAN WAIT...

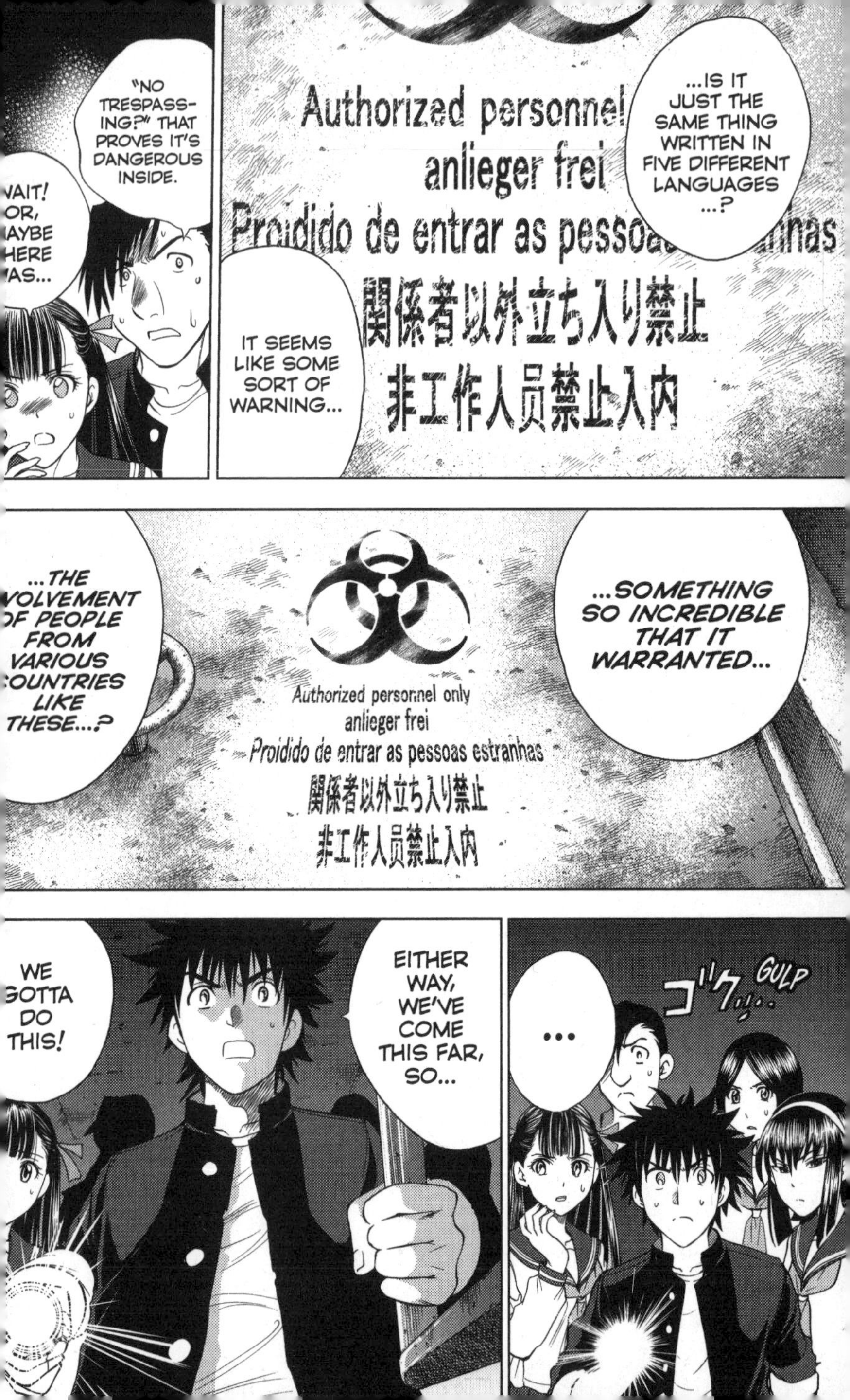
...IS IT JUST THE SAME THING WRITTEN IN FIVE DIFFERENT LANGUAGES ...?
Authorized personnel
anlieger frei
Proidido de entrar as pessoa
anhas
関係者以外立ち入り禁止
非工作人员禁止入内
IT SEEMS LIKE SOME SORT OF WARNING...
"NO TRESPASSING?" THAT PROVES IT'S DANGEROUS INSIDE.
AIT! OR, AYBE HERE AS...
...SOMETHING SO INCREDIBLE THAT IT WARRANTED...
Authorized personnel only
anlieger frei
Proidido de entrar as pessoas estranhas
関係者以外立ち入り禁止
非工作人员禁止入内
...THE OLVEMENT OF PEOPLE FROM VARIOUS OUNTRIES LIKE THESE...?
...
ゴクッ
GULP
EITHER WAY, WE'VE COME THIS FAR, SO...
WE GOTTA DO THIS!

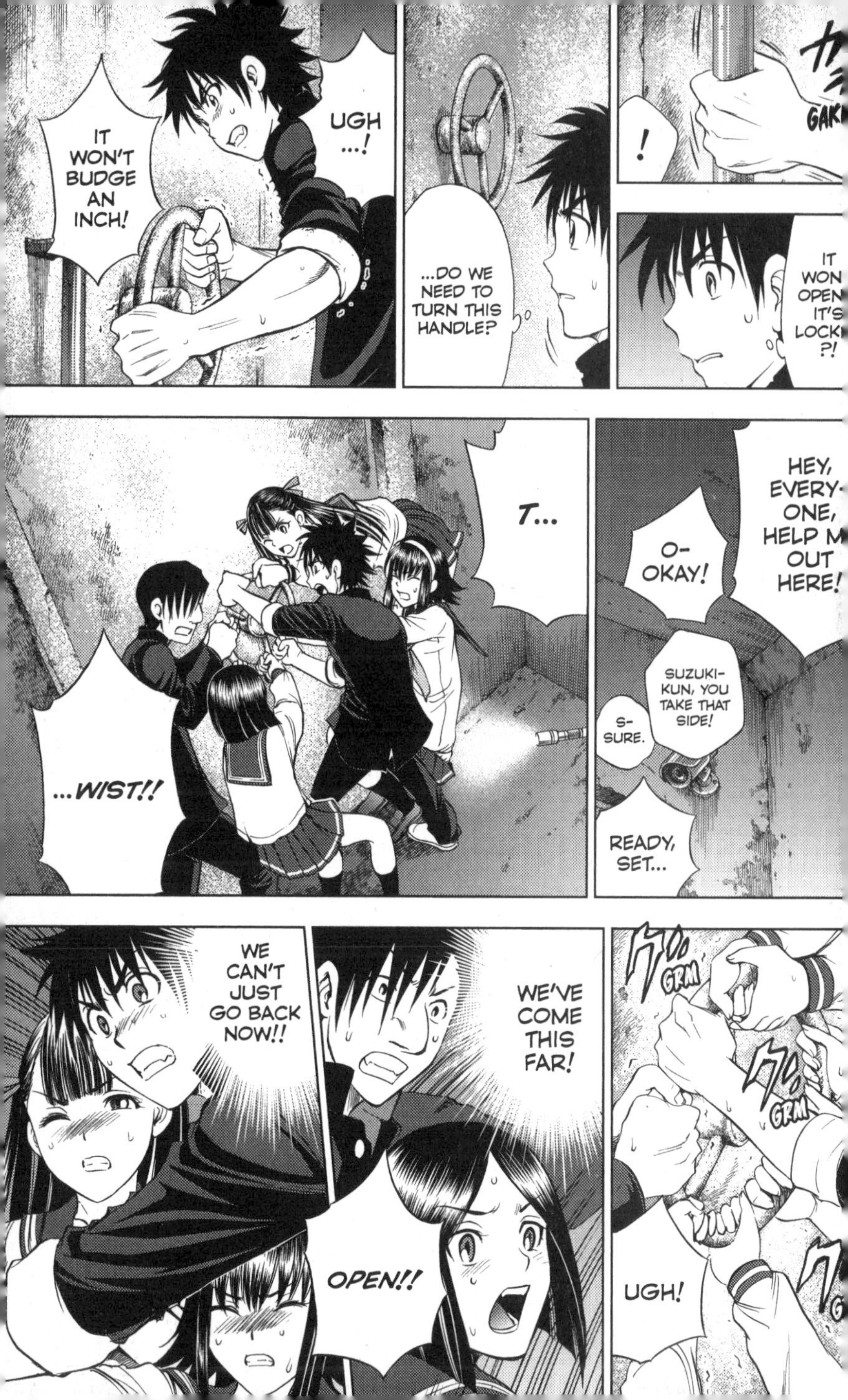
GAK
!
IT WON OPEN IT'S LOCK ?!
...DO WE NEED TO TURN THIS HANDLE?
UGH ...!
IT WON'T BUDGE AN INCH!
HEY, EVERY-ONE, HELP M OUT HERE!
O-OKAY!
SUZUKI-KUN, YOU TAKE THAT SIDE!
S-SURE.
READY, SET...
T...
...WIST!!
GRM
GRM
UGH!
WE'VE COME THIS FAR!
OPEN!!
WE CAN'T JUST GO BACK NOW!!

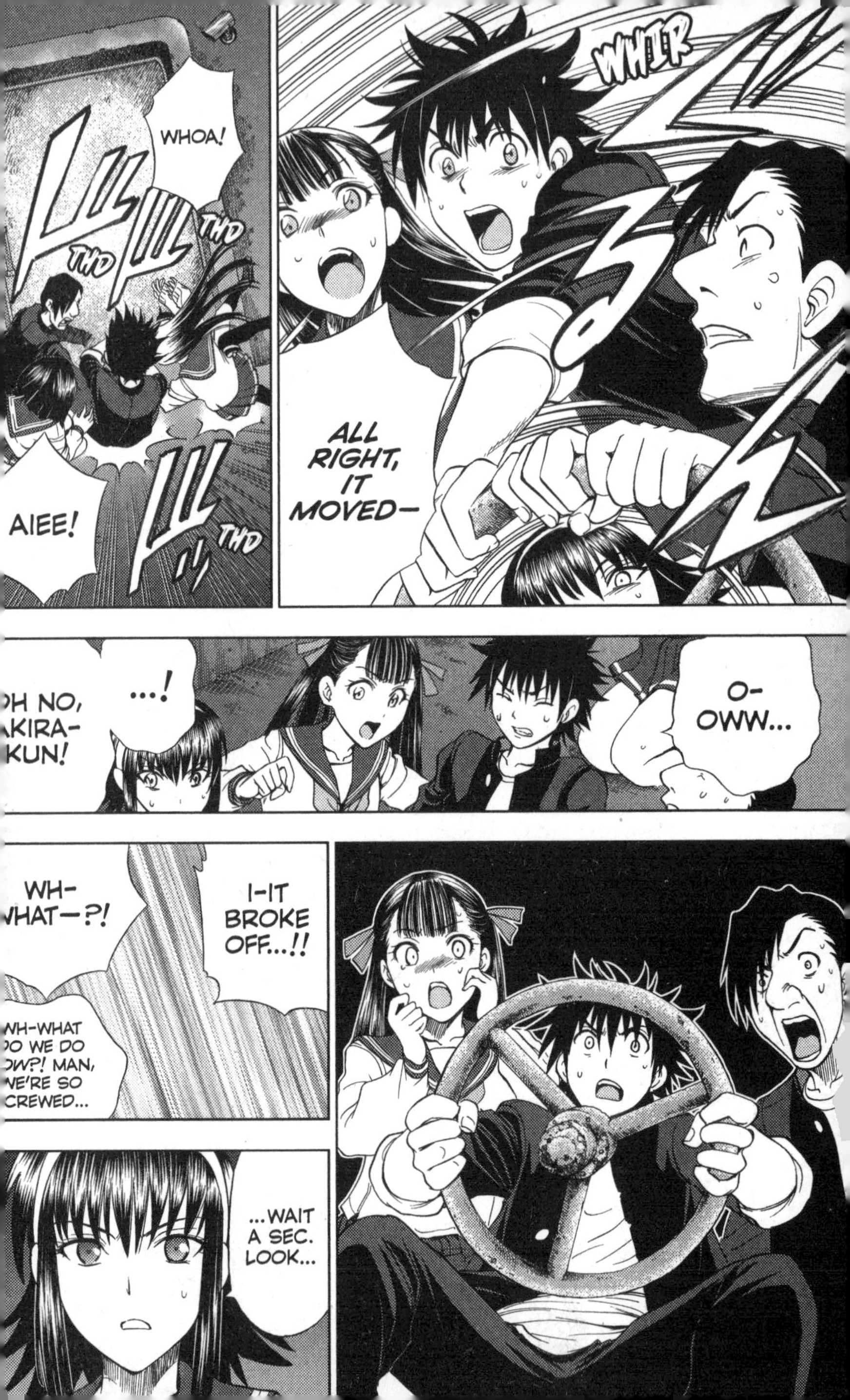
WHIR
ALL RIGHT, IT MOVED—
WHOA!
THD
THD
AIEE!
THD
O-OWW...
...!
H NO, KIRA-KUN!
I-IT BROKE OFF...!!
WH- HAT—?!
H-WHAT O WE DO OW?! MAN, E'RE SO CREWED...
...WAIT A SEC. LOOK...

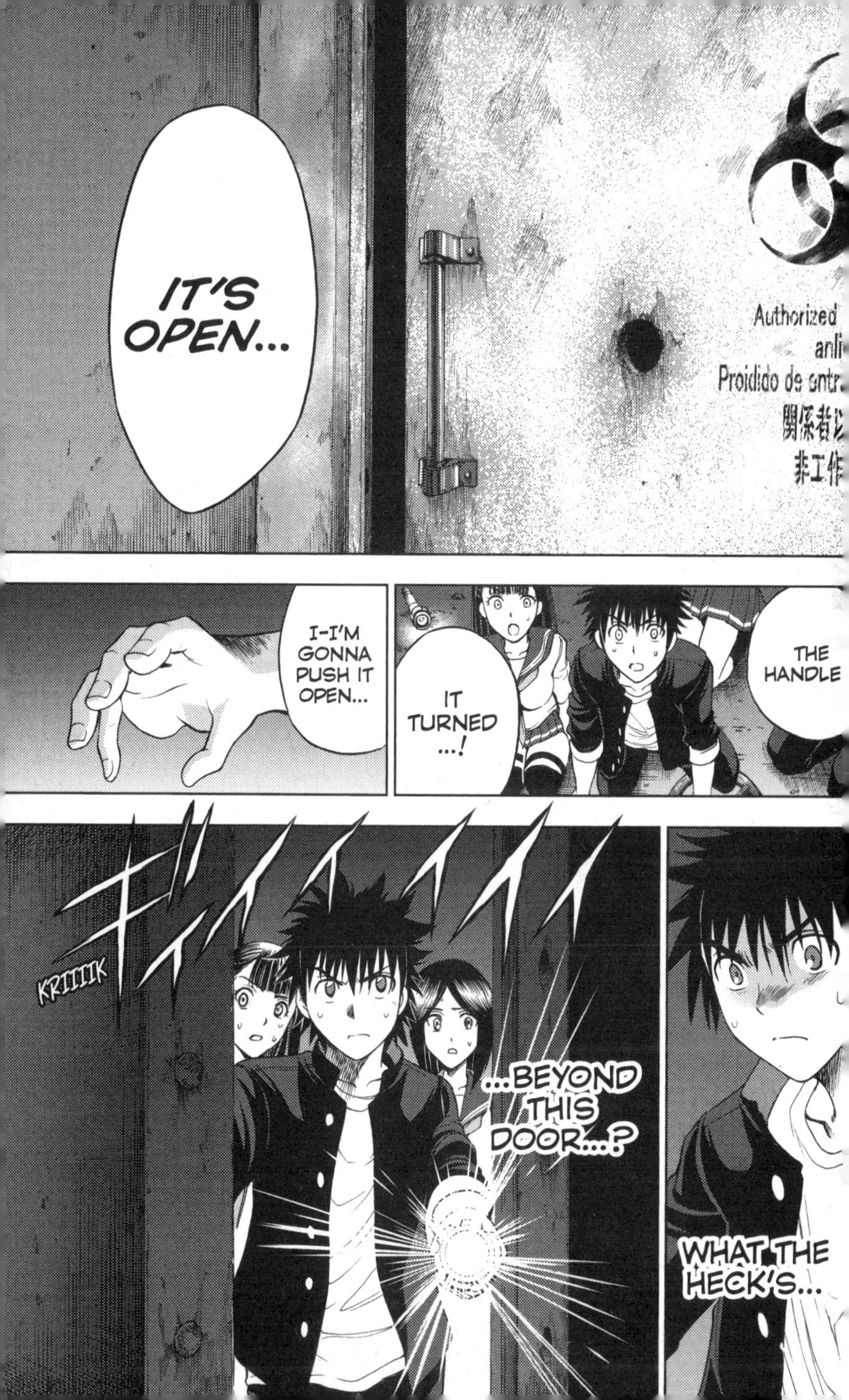
IT'S OPEN...
Authorized
THE HANDLE
IT TURNED ...!
I-I'M GONNA PUSH IT OPEN...
WHAT THE HECK'S...
KRIIIIK
...BEYOND THIS DOOR...?

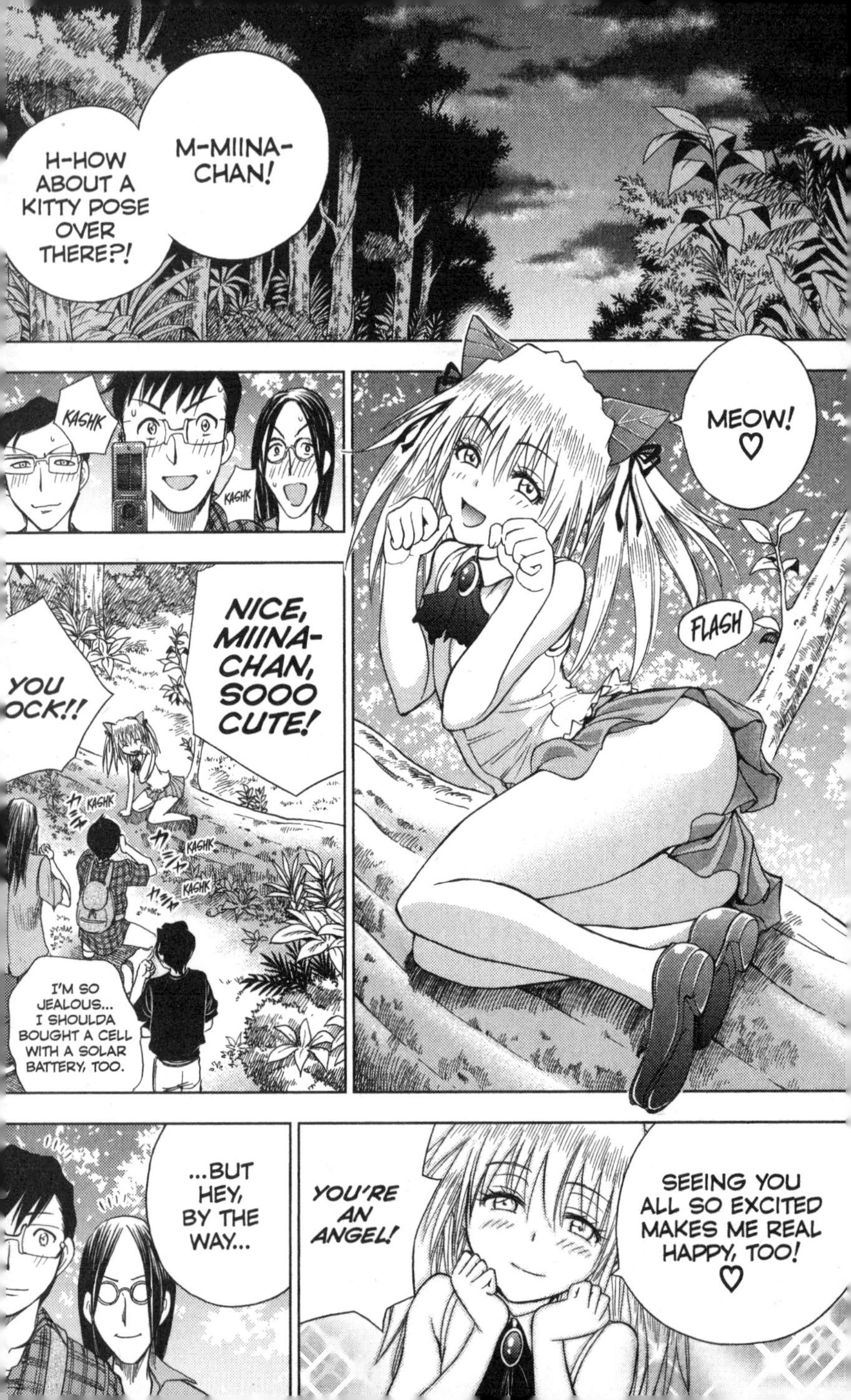
M-MIINA-CHAN!
H-HOW ABOUT A KITTY POSE OVER THERE?!
MEOW! ♡
FLASH
KASHK
KASHK
NICE, MIINA-CHAN, SOOO CUTE!
YOU OCK!!
KASHK
KASHK
KASHK
I'M SO JEALOUS... I SHOULDA BOUGHT A CELL WITH A SOLAR BATTERY, TOO.
SEEING YOU ALL SO EXCITED MAKES ME REAL HAPPY, TOO! ♡
YOU'RE AN ANGEL!
...BUT HEY, BY THE WAY...

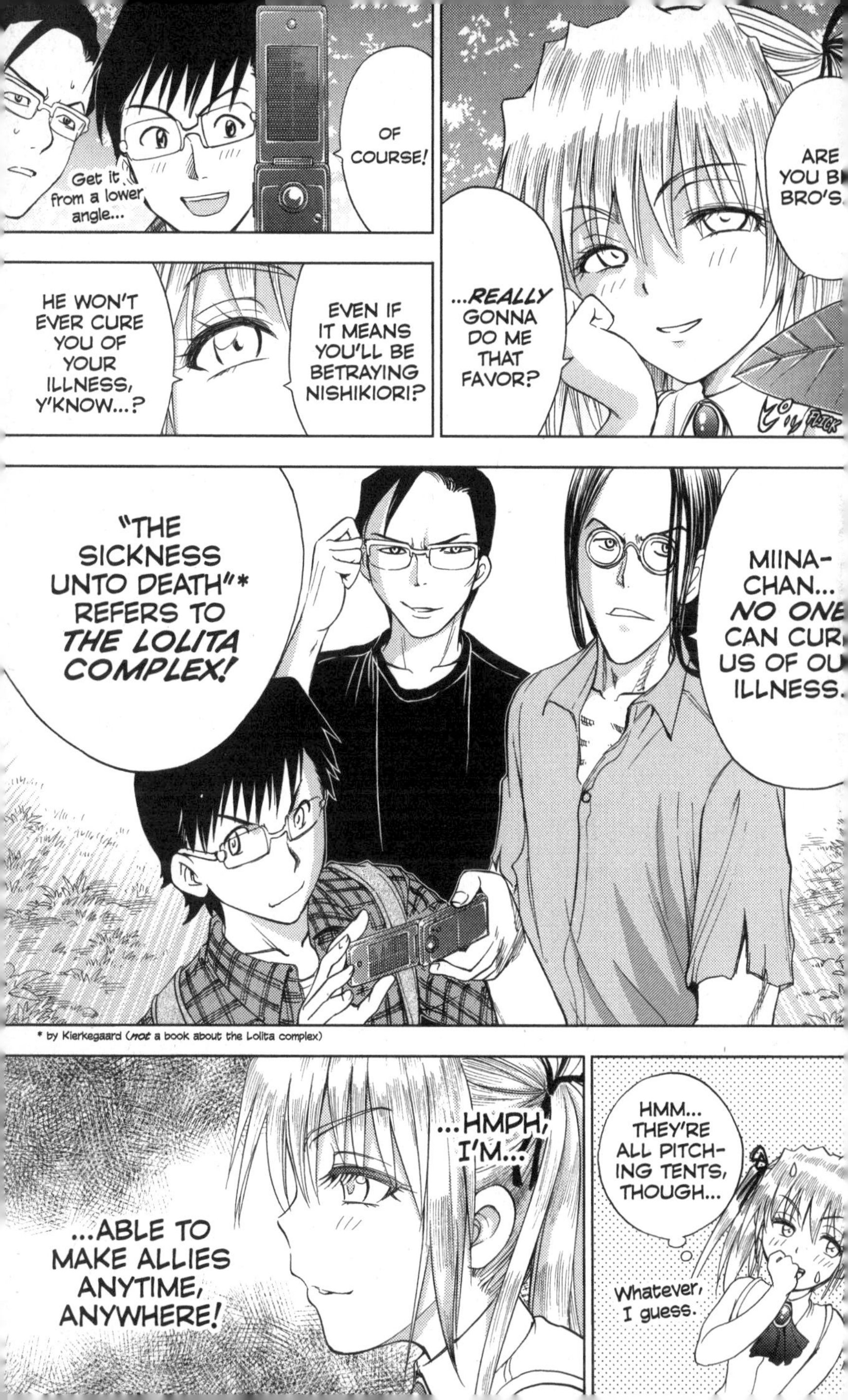
ARE YOU B BRO'S.
...REALLY GONNA DO ME THAT FAVOR?
FLICK
OF COURSE!
Get it from a lower angle...
EVEN IF IT MEANS YOU'LL BE BETRAYING NISHIKIORI?
HE WON'T EVER CURE YOU OF YOUR ILLNESS, Y'KNOW...?
MIINA-CHAN... NO ONE CAN CUR US OF OU ILLNESS.
"THE SICKNESS UNTO DEATH"* REFERS TO THE LOLITA COMPLEX!
HMM... THEY'RE ALL PITCH-ING TENTS, THOUGH...
Whatever, I guess.
...HMPH, I'M...
...ABLE TO MAKE ALLIES ANYTIME, ANYWHERE!

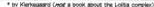

* by Kierkegaard (*not* a book about the Lolita complex)

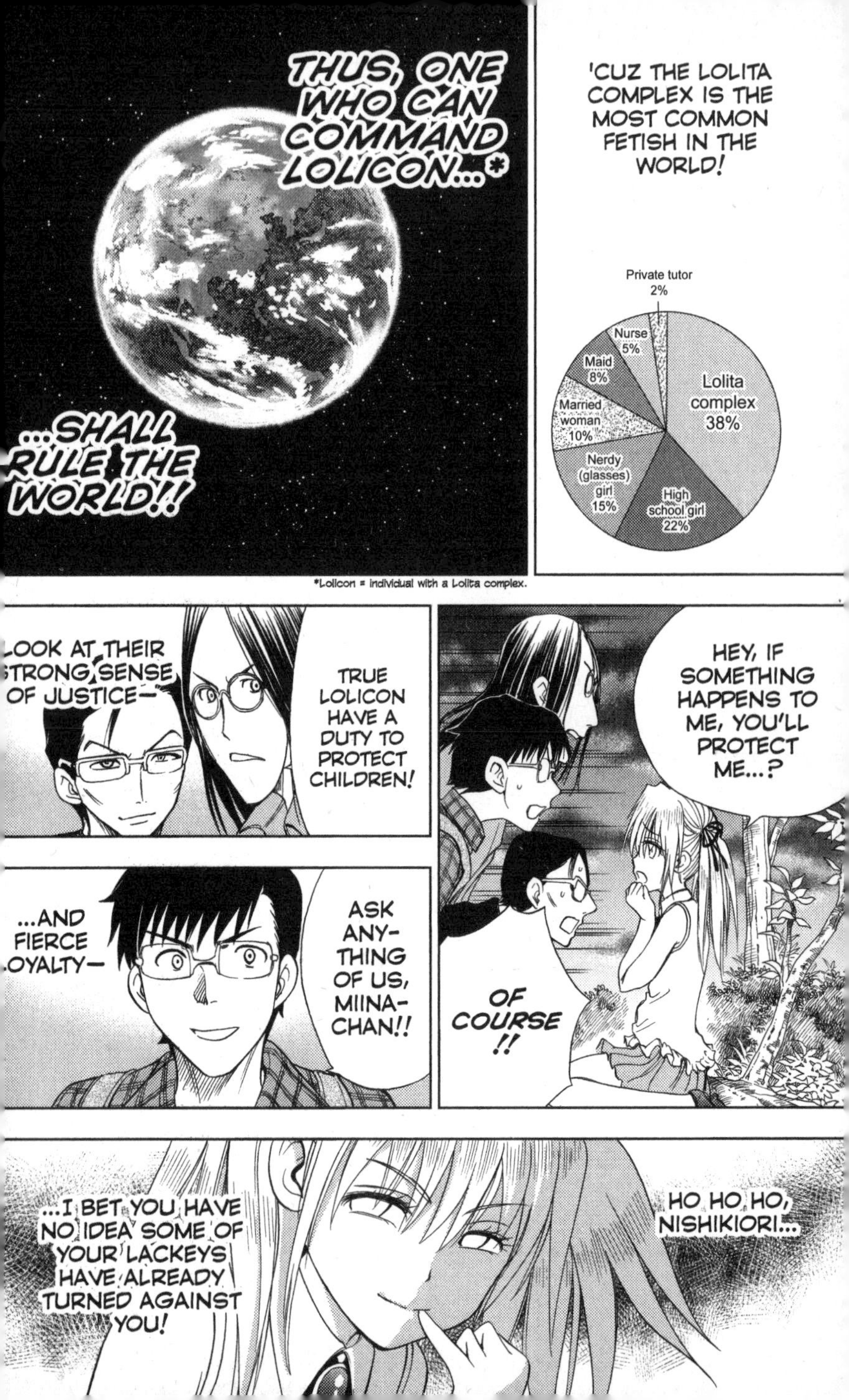
'CUZ THE LOLITA COMPLEX IS THE MOST COMMON FETISH IN THE WORLD!
Private tutor 2%
Nurse 5%
Maid 8%
Married woman 10%
Nerdy (glasses) girl 15%
High school girl 22%
Lolita complex 38%
THUS, ONE WHO CAN COMMAND LOLICON...*
...SHALL RULE THE WORLD!!
HEY, IF SOMETHING HAPPENS TO ME, YOU'LL PROTECT ME...?
OF COURSE!!
TRUE LOLICON HAVE A DUTY TO PROTECT CHILDREN!
LOOK AT THEIR STRONG SENSE OF JUSTICE—
ASK ANYTHING OF US, MIINA-CHAN!!
...AND FIERCE LOYALTY—
HO HO HO, NISHIKIORI...
...I BET YOU HAVE NO IDEA SOME OF YOUR LACKEYS HAVE ALREADY TURNED AGAINST YOU!

*Lolicon = individual with a Lolita complex.

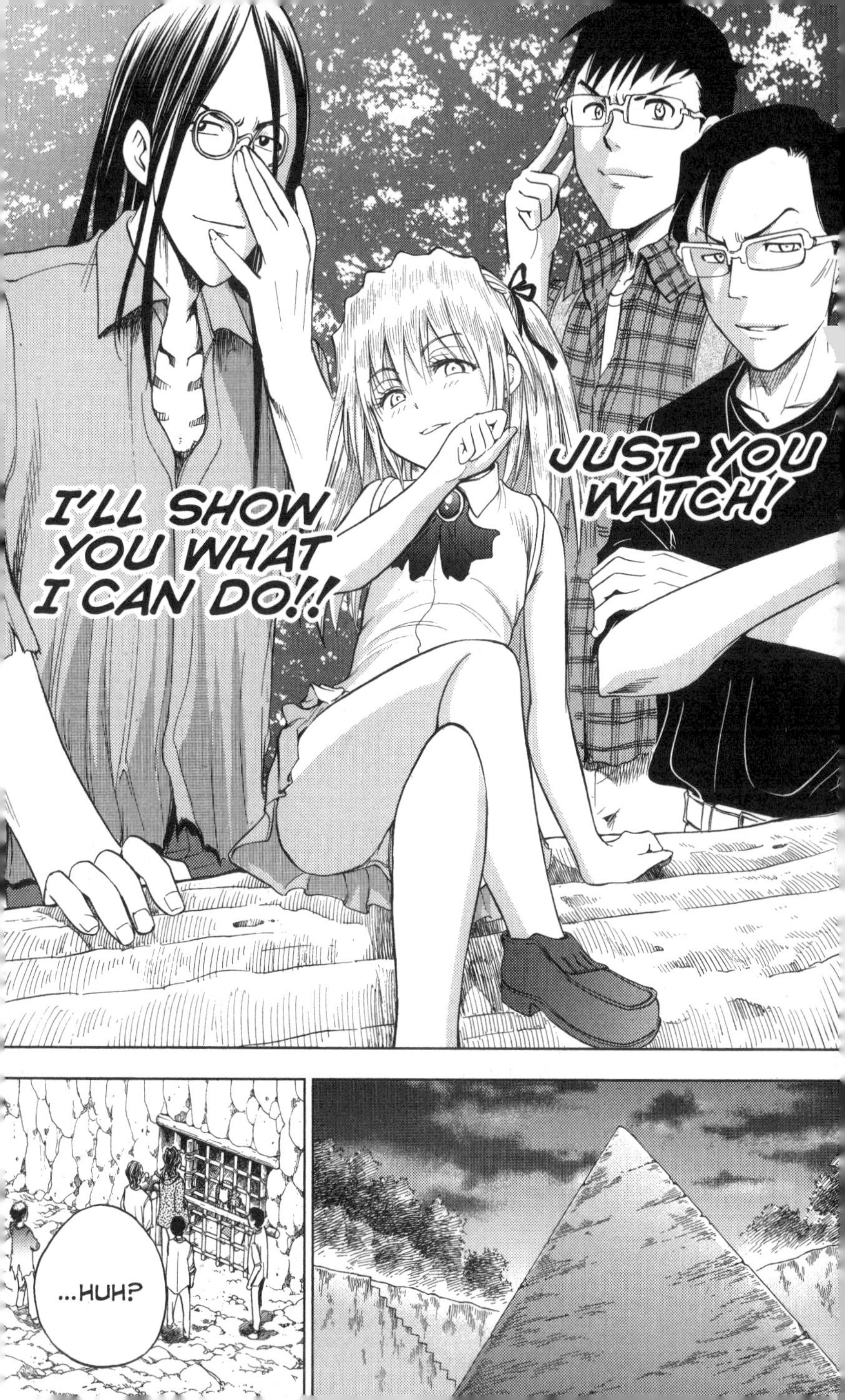
JUST YOU WATCH!
I'LL SHOW YOU WHAT I CAN DO!!
...HUH?

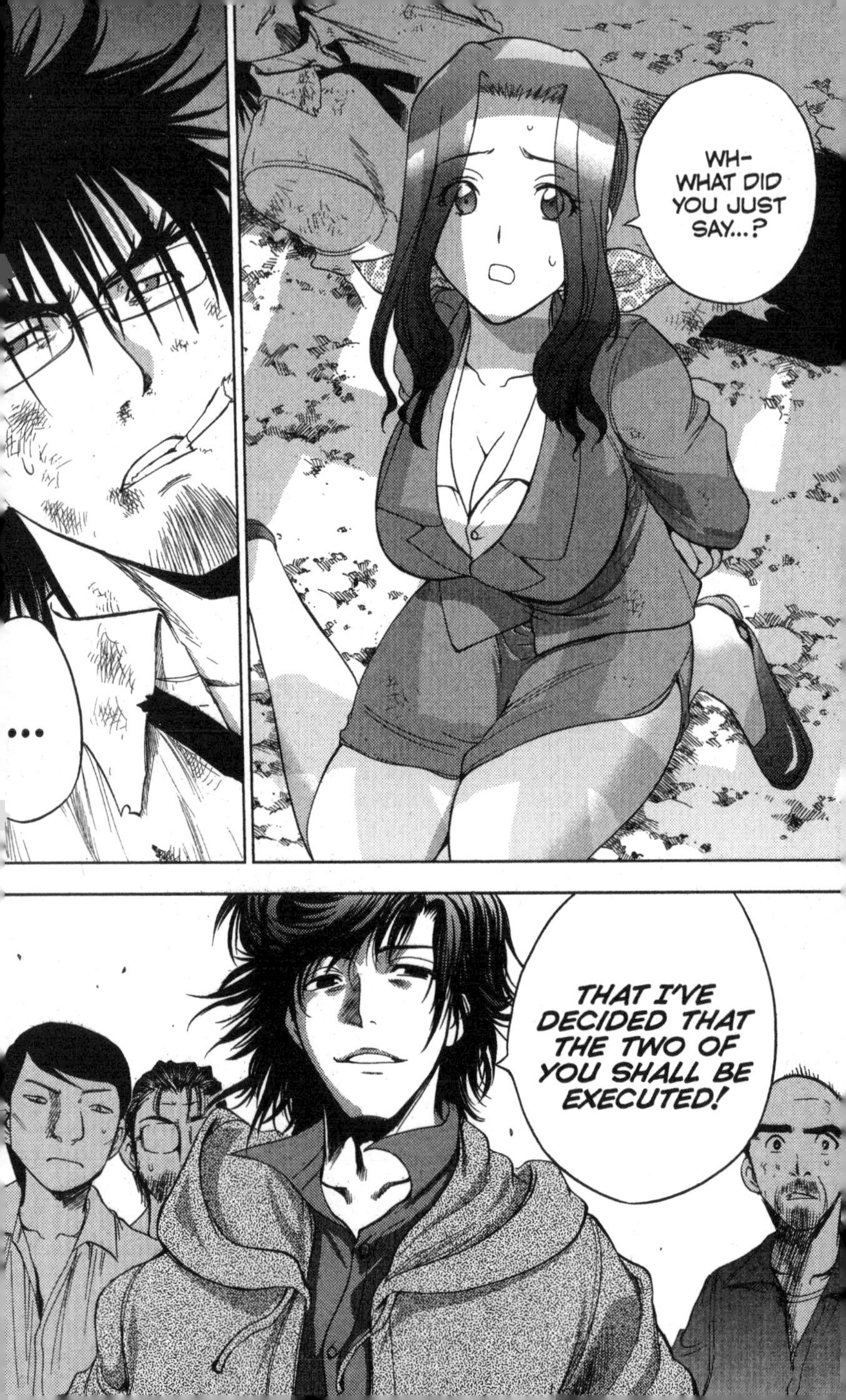
WH- WHAT DID YOU JUST SAY...?
...
THAT I'VE DECIDED THAT THE TWO OF YOU SHALL BE EXECUTED!

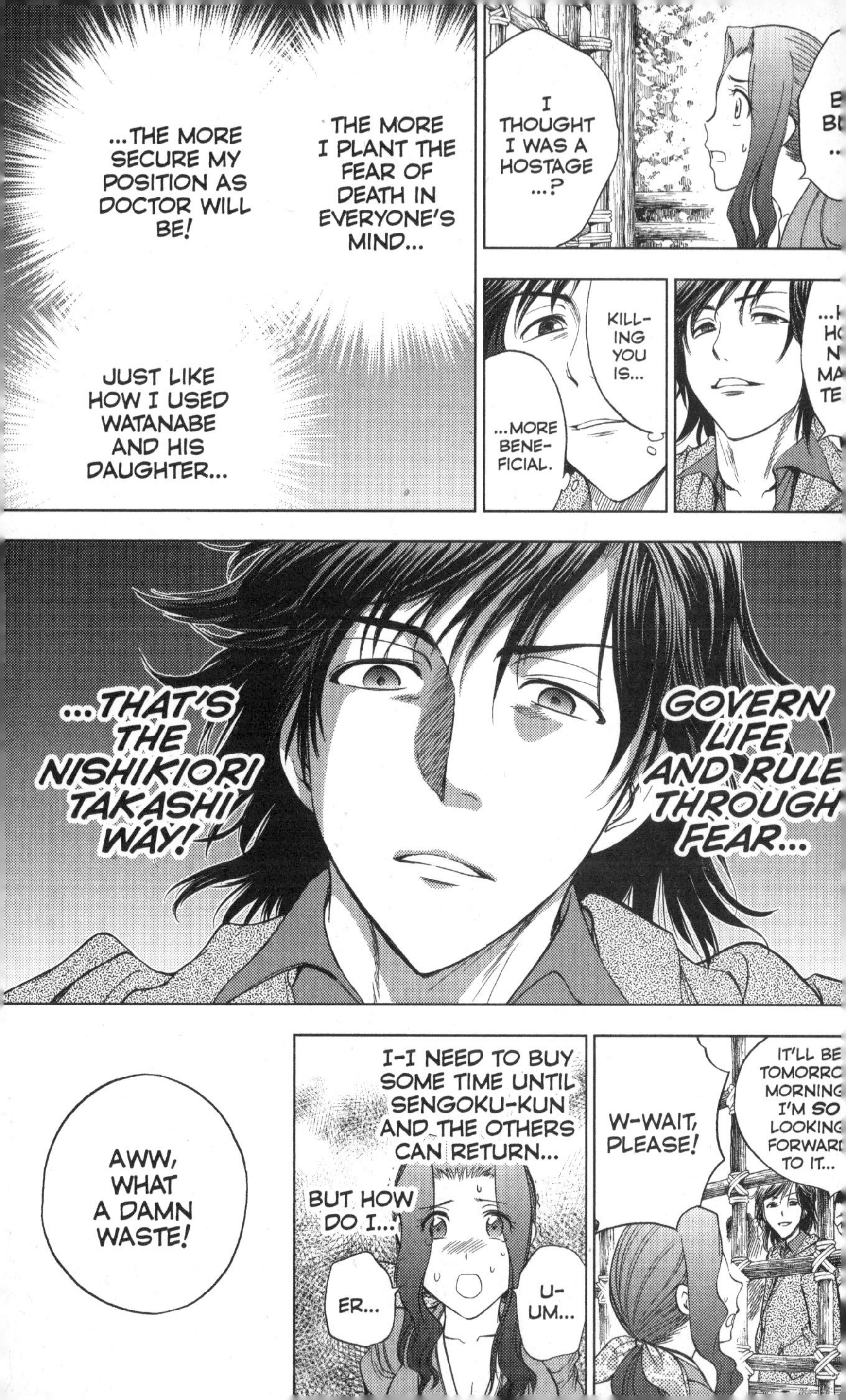
I THOUGHT I WAS A HOSTAGE ...?
KILL-ING YOU IS...
...MORE BENE-FICIAL.
THE MORE I PLANT THE FEAR OF DEATH IN EVERYONE'S MIND...
...THE MORE SECURE MY POSITION AS DOCTOR WILL BE!
JUST LIKE HOW I USED WATANABE AND HIS DAUGHTER...
GOVERN LIFE AND RULE THROUGH FEAR...
...THAT'S THE NISHIKIORI TAKASHI WAY!
IT'LL BE TOMORRO MORNING I'M SO LOOKING FORWAR TO IT...
W-WAIT, PLEASE!
I-I NEED TO BUY SOME TIME UNTIL SENGOKU-KUN AND THE OTHERS CAN RETURN...
BUT HOW DO I...
U-UM...
ER...
AWW, WHAT A DAMN WASTE!

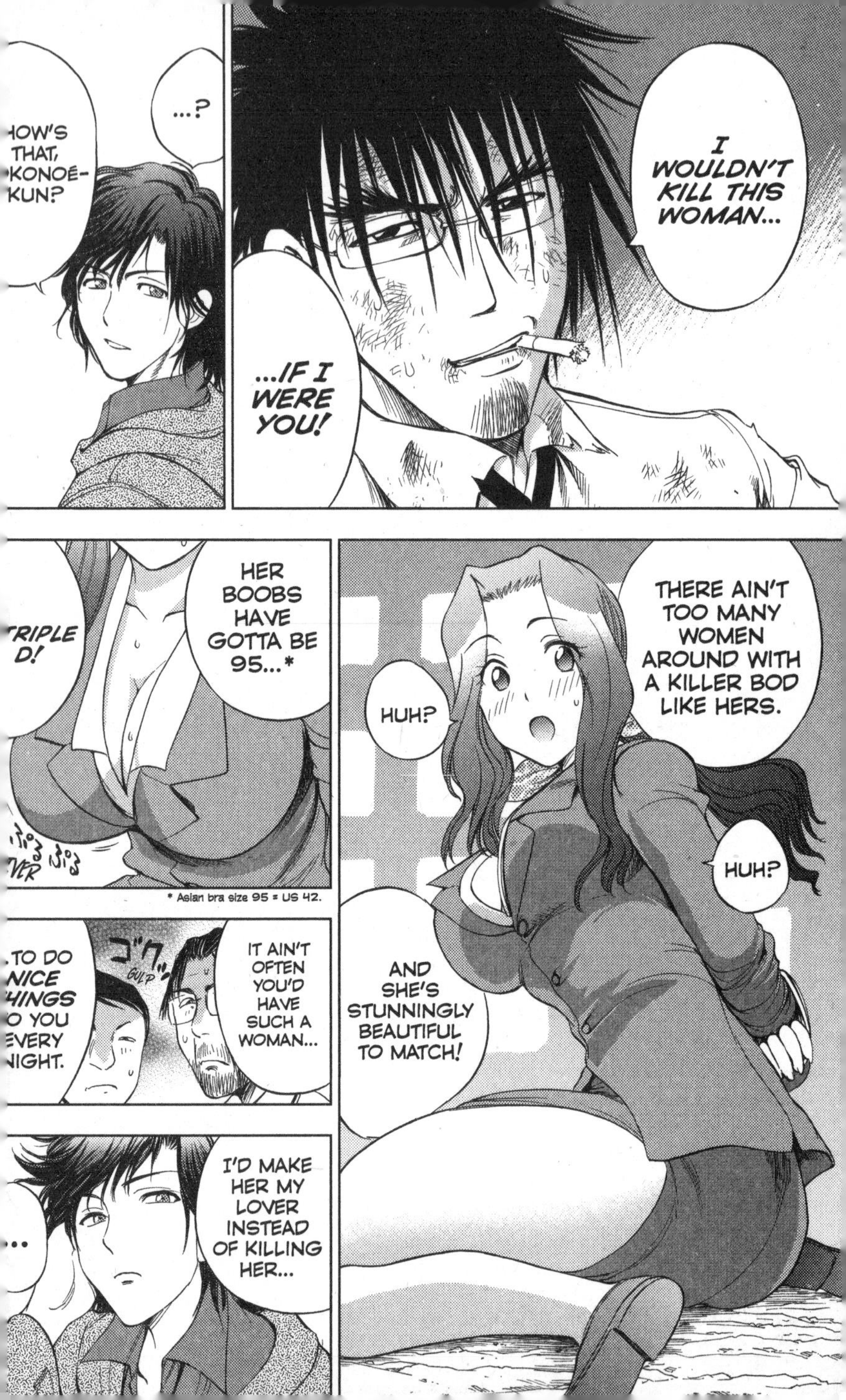
I WOULDN'T KILL THIS WOMAN...
...IF I WERE YOU!
...?
HOW'S THAT, KONOE-KUN?
THERE AIN'T TOO MANY WOMEN AROUND WITH A KILLER BOD LIKE HERS.
HUH?
HUH?
AND SHE'S STUNNINGLY BEAUTIFUL TO MATCH!
HER BOOBS HAVE GOTTA BE 95...*
TRIPLE D!
IT AIN'T OFTEN YOU'D HAVE SUCH A WOMAN...
GULP
TO DO NICE THINGS TO YOU EVERY NIGHT.
I'D MAKE HER MY LOVER INSTEAD OF KILLING HER...
...
* Asian bra size 95 = US 42.

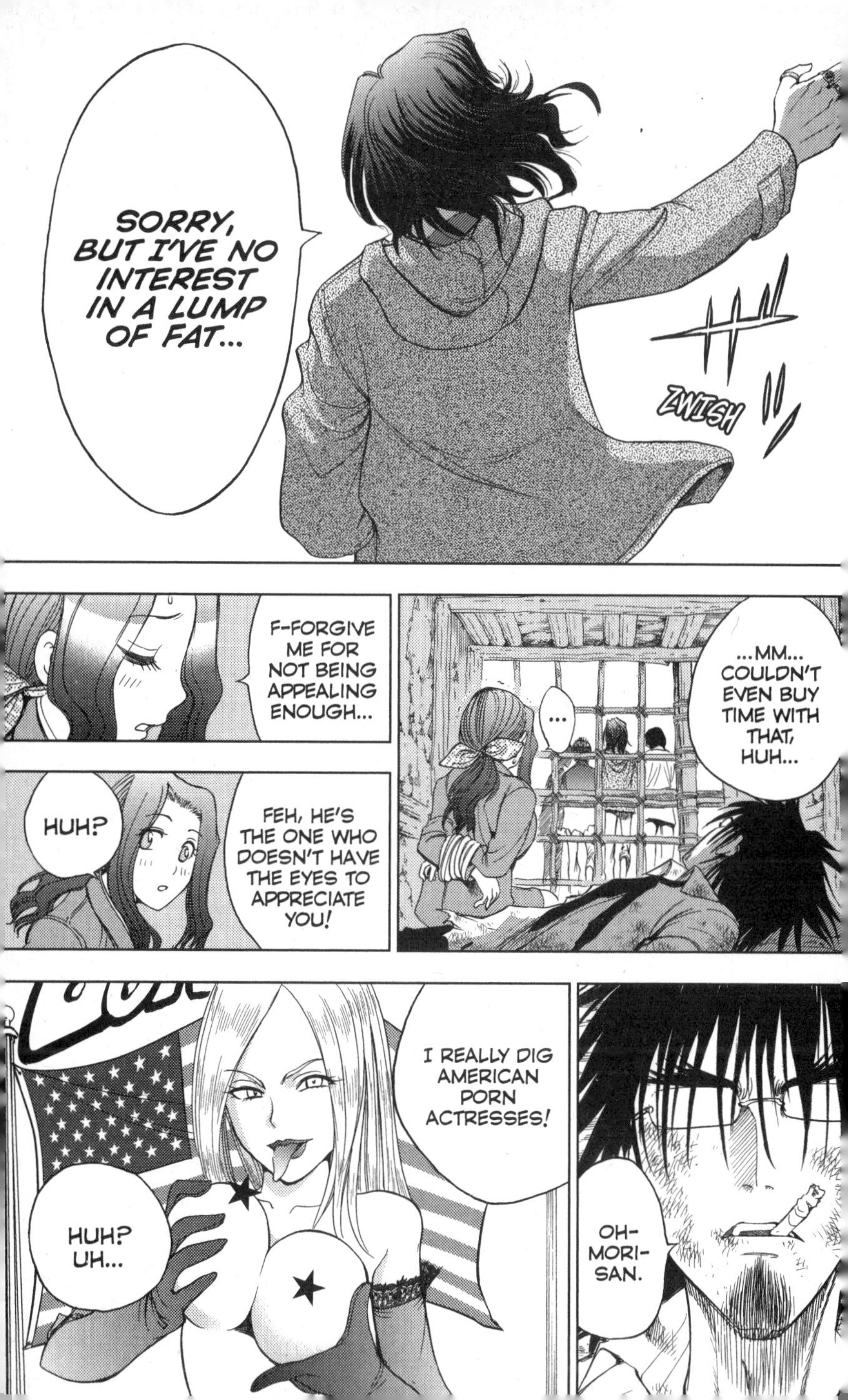
SORRY, BUT I'VE NO INTEREST IN A LUMP OF FAT...
ZWISH
...MM... COULDN'T EVEN BUY TIME WITH THAT, HUH...
...
F-FORGIVE ME FOR NOT BEING APPEALING ENOUGH...
FEH, HE'S THE ONE WHO DOESN'T HAVE THE EYES TO APPRECIATE YOU!
HUH?
OH-MORI-SAN.
I REALLY DIG AMERICAN PORN ACTRESSES!
HUH? UH...

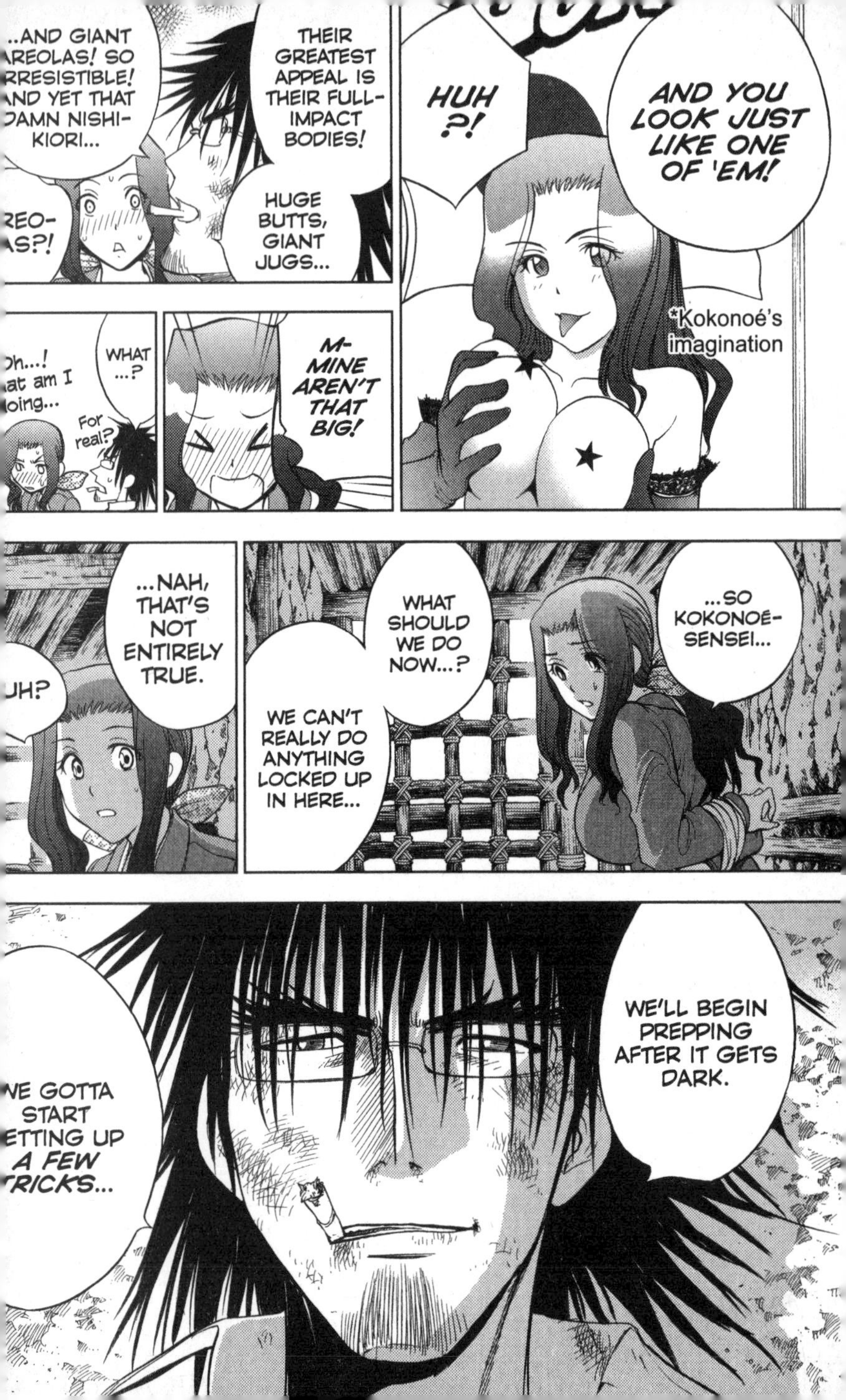
AND YOU LOOK JUST LIKE ONE OF 'EM!
HUH?!
*Kokonoé's imagination
THEIR GREATEST APPEAL IS THEIR FULL-IMPACT BODIES!
HUGE BUTTS, GIANT JUGS...
..AND GIANT AREOLAS! SO RRESISTIBLE! AND YET THAT DAMN NISHI-KIORI...
REO-AS?!
M-MINE AREN'T THAT BIG!
WHAT ...?
For real?
Oh...! at am I oing...
...SO KOKONOÉ-SENSEI...
WHAT SHOULD WE DO NOW...?
WE CAN'T REALLY DO ANYTHING LOCKED UP IN HERE...
...NAH, THAT'S NOT ENTIRELY TRUE.
UH?
WE'LL BEGIN PREPPING AFTER IT GETS DARK.
VE GOTTA START ETTING UP A FEW TRICKS...

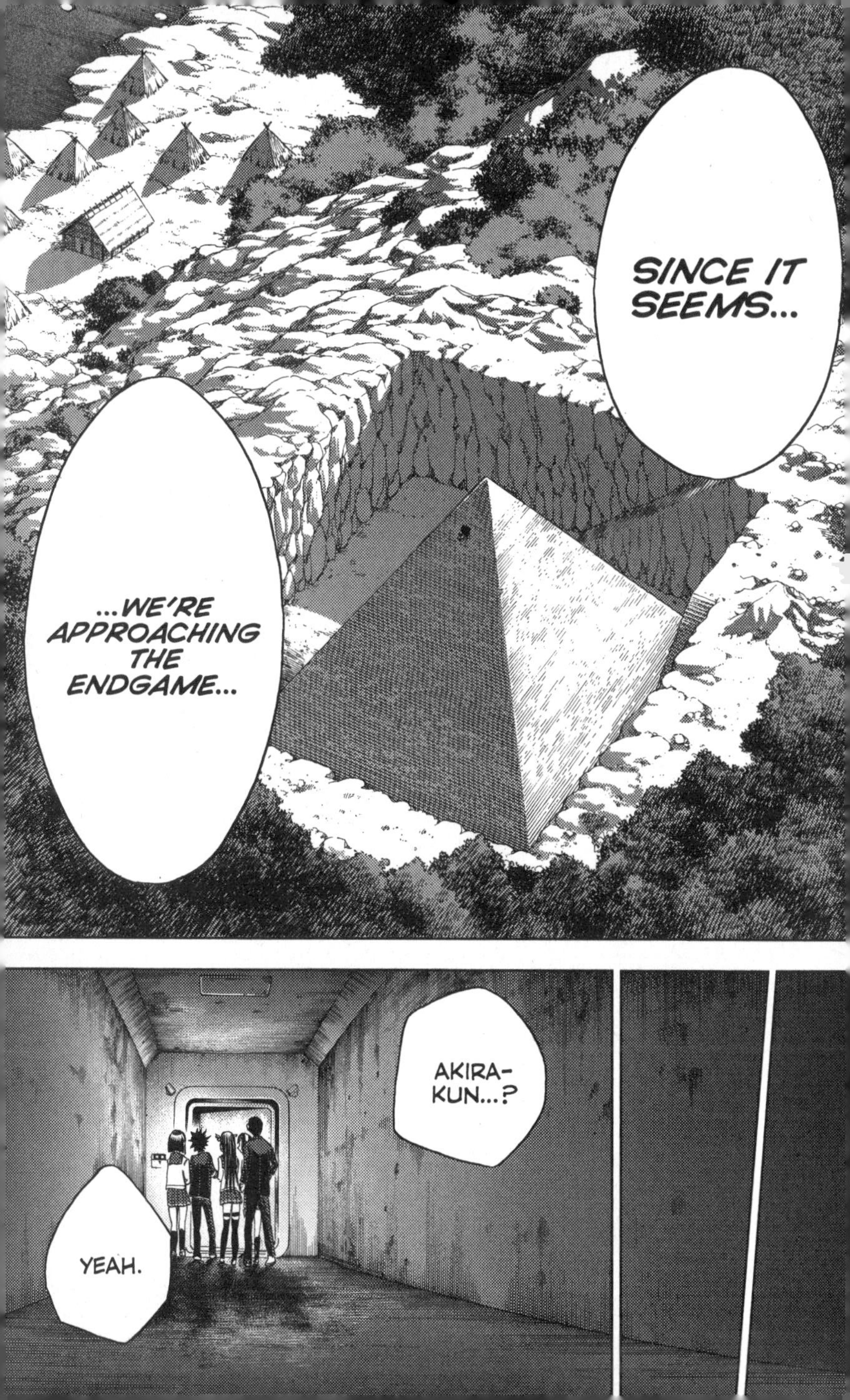
SINCE IT SEEMS...
...WE'RE APPROACHING THE ENDGAME...
AKIRA-KUN...?
YEAH.

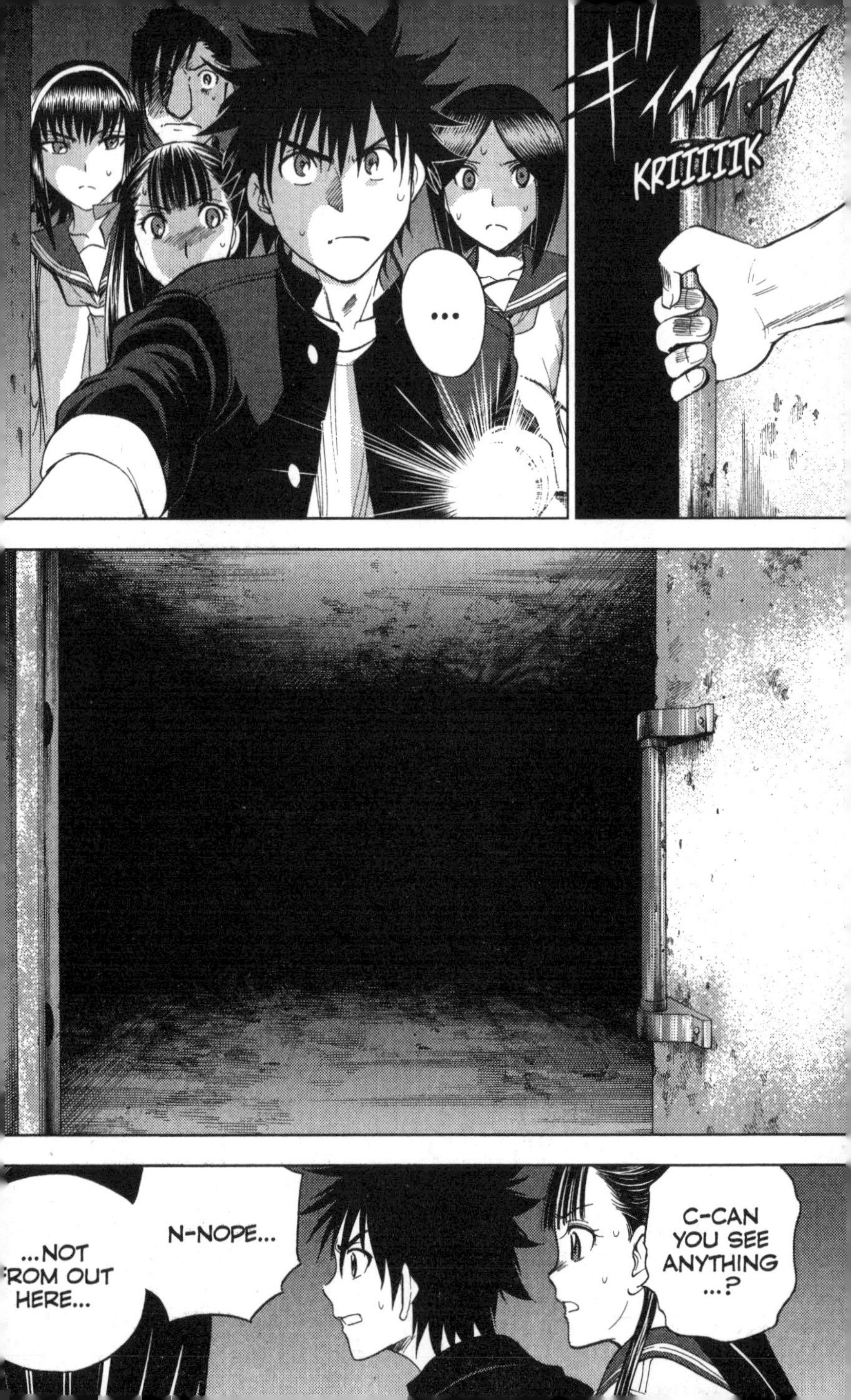
ギイイイイ
KRIIIIK
...
C-CAN YOU SEE ANYTHING ...?
N-NOPE...
...NOT FROM OUT HERE...

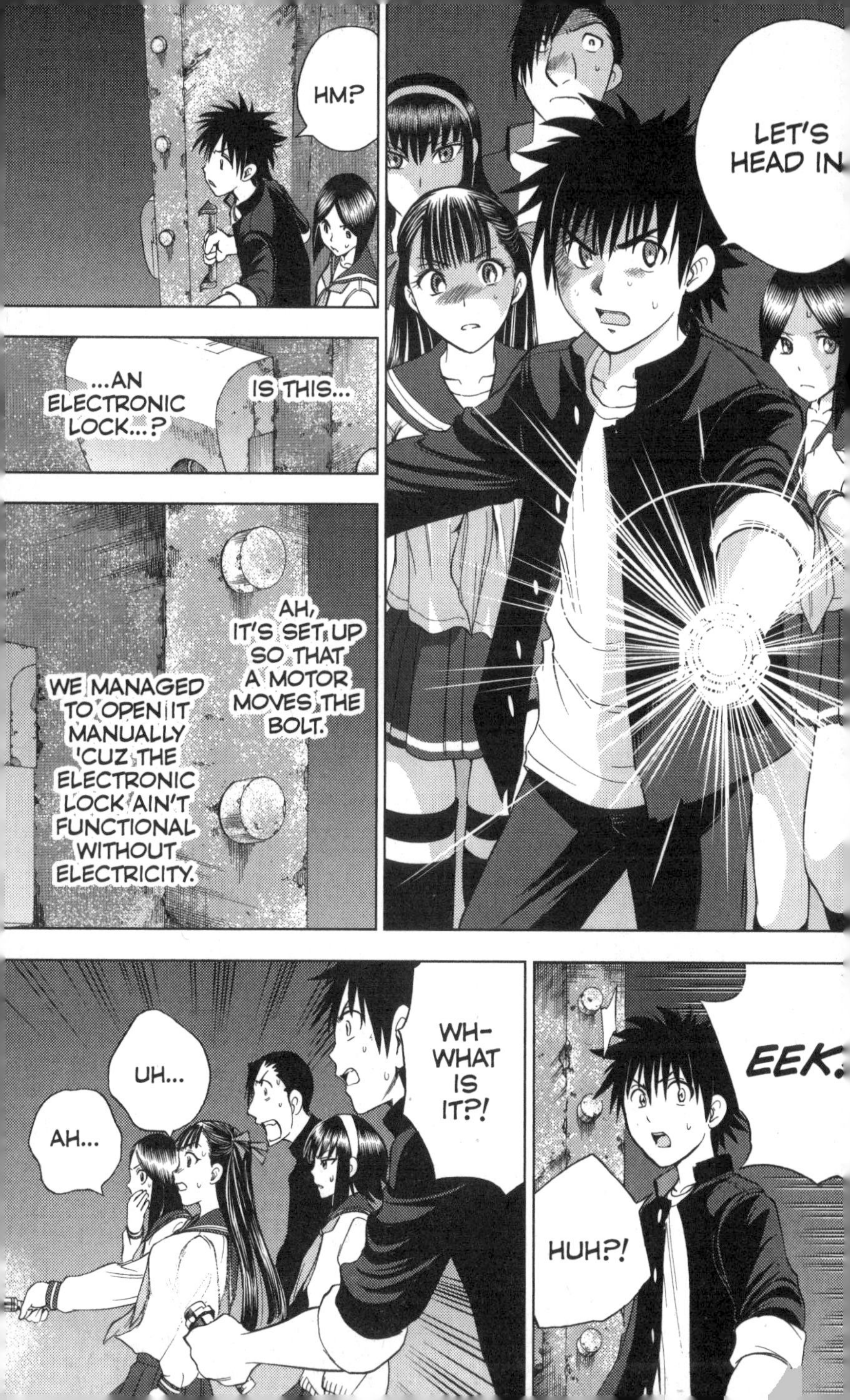
LET'S HEAD IN
HM?
IS THIS...
...AN ELECTRONIC LOCK...?
AH, IT'S SET UP SO THAT A MOTOR MOVES THE BOLT.
WE MANAGED TO OPEN IT MANUALLY 'CUZ THE ELECTRONIC LOCK AIN'T FUNCTIONAL WITHOUT ELECTRICITY.
EEK.
HUH?!
WH-WHAT IS IT?!
UH...
AH...

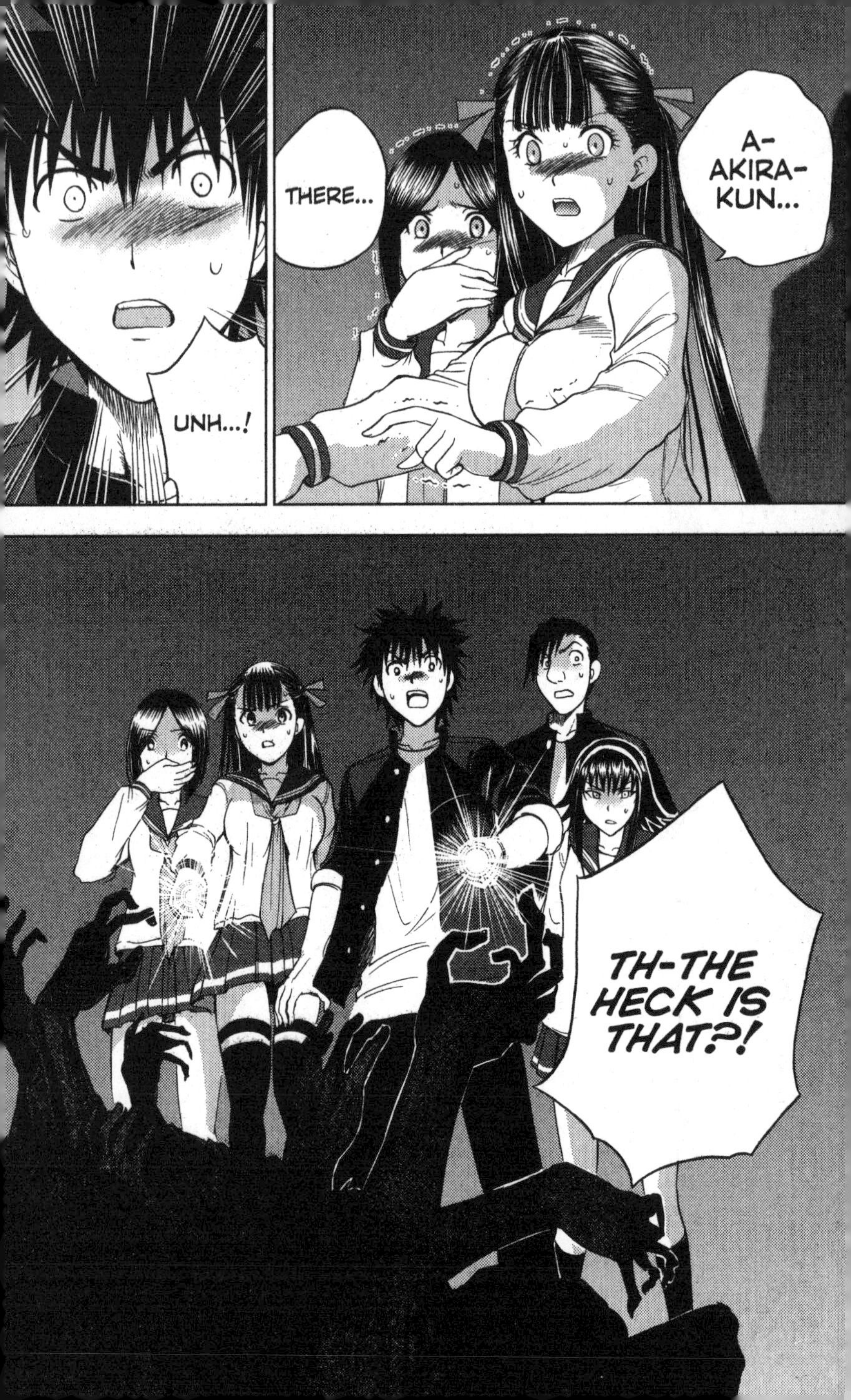
A-AKIRA-KUN...
THERE...
UNH...!
TH-THE HECK IS THAT?!

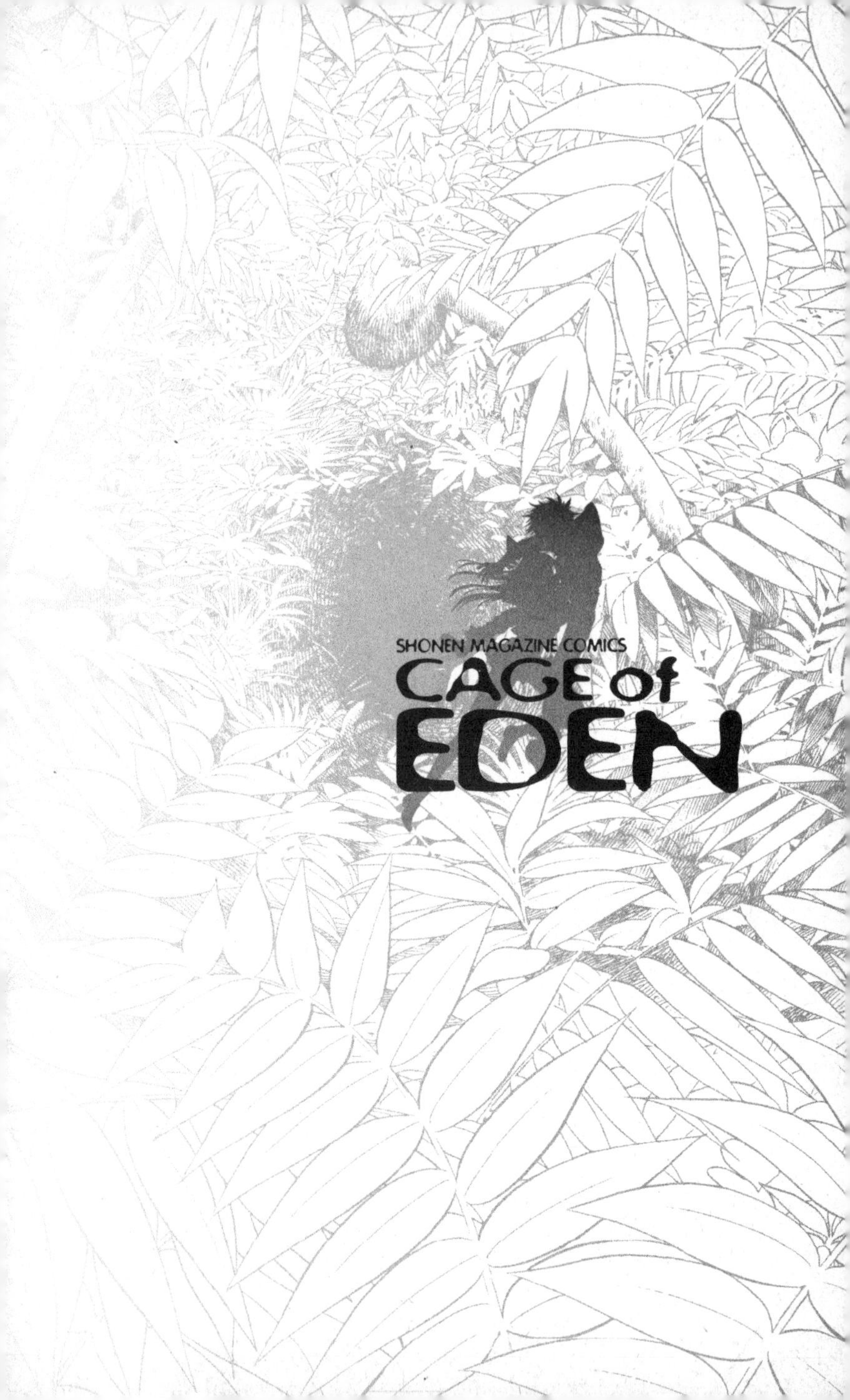
SHONEN MAGAZINE COMICS
CAGE of EDEN

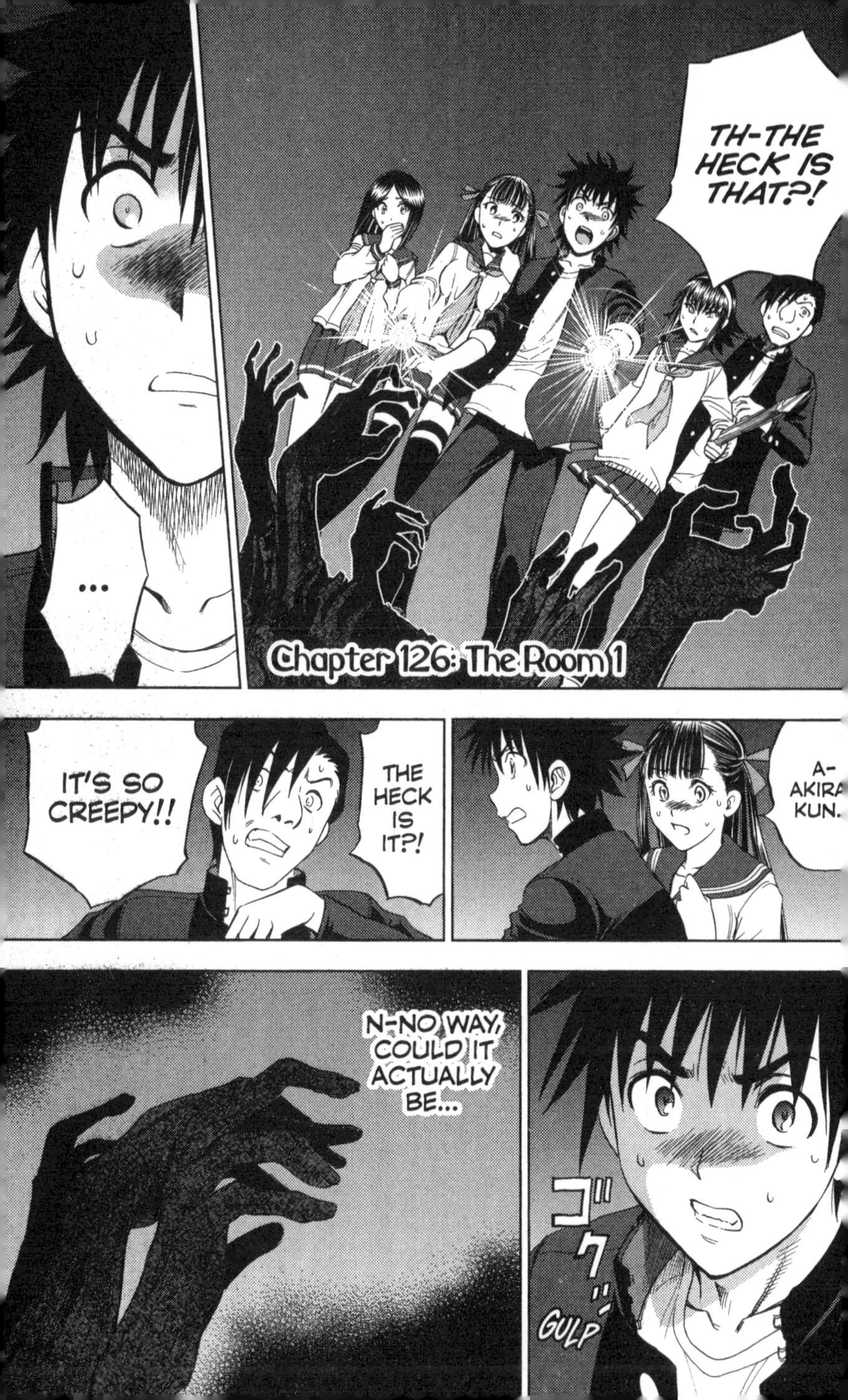
TH-THE HECK IS THAT?!
Chapter 126: The Room 1
...
A-AKIRA KUN.
THE HECK IS IT?!
IT'S SO CREEPY!!
ゴクッ
GULP
N-NO WAY, COULD IT ACTUALLY BE...

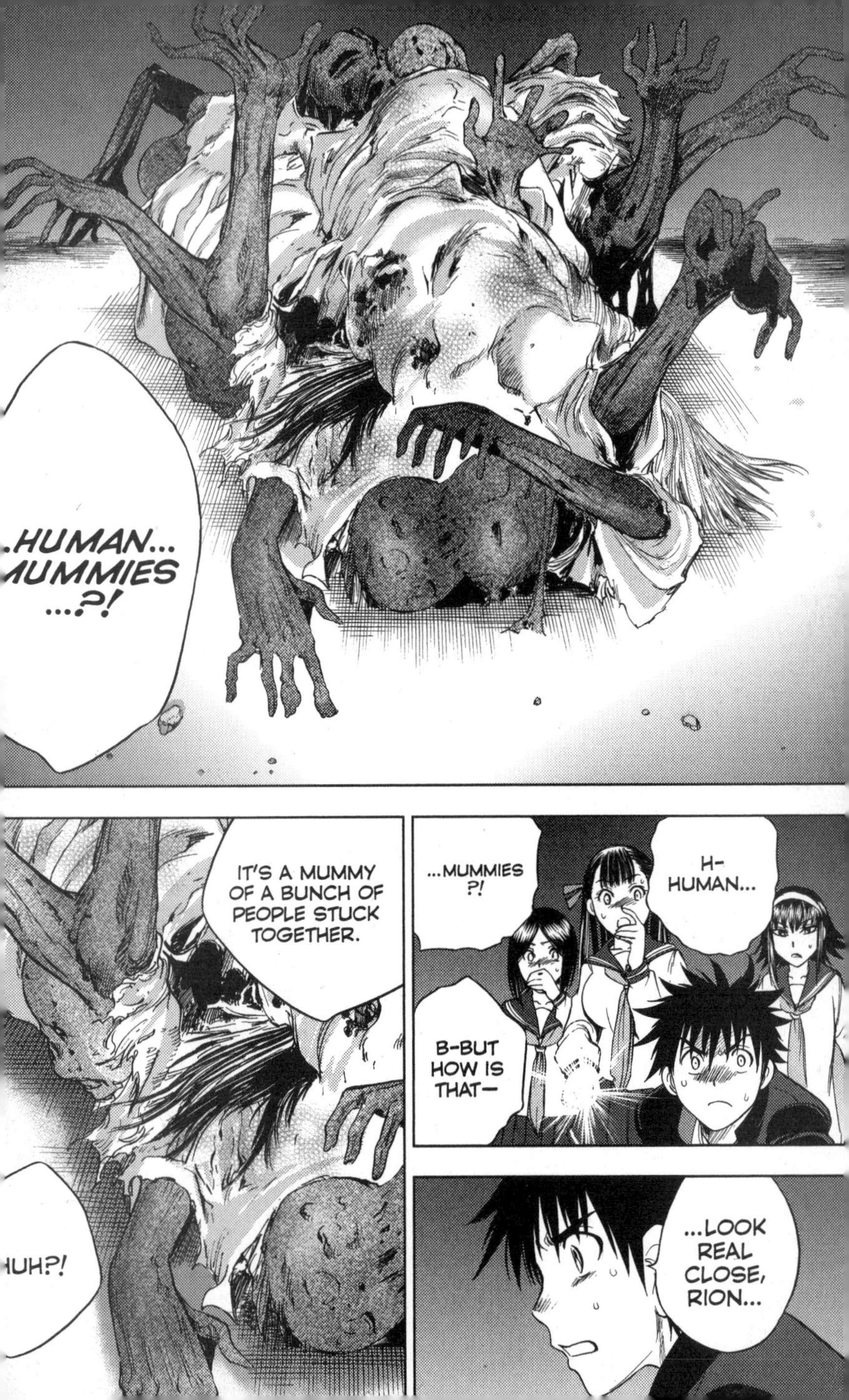

.HUMAN... MUMMIES ...?!
H- HUMAN...
...MUMMIES ?!
B-BUT HOW IS THAT—
...LOOK REAL CLOSE, RION...
IT'S A MUMMY OF A BUNCH OF PEOPLE STUCK TOGETHER.
HUH?!

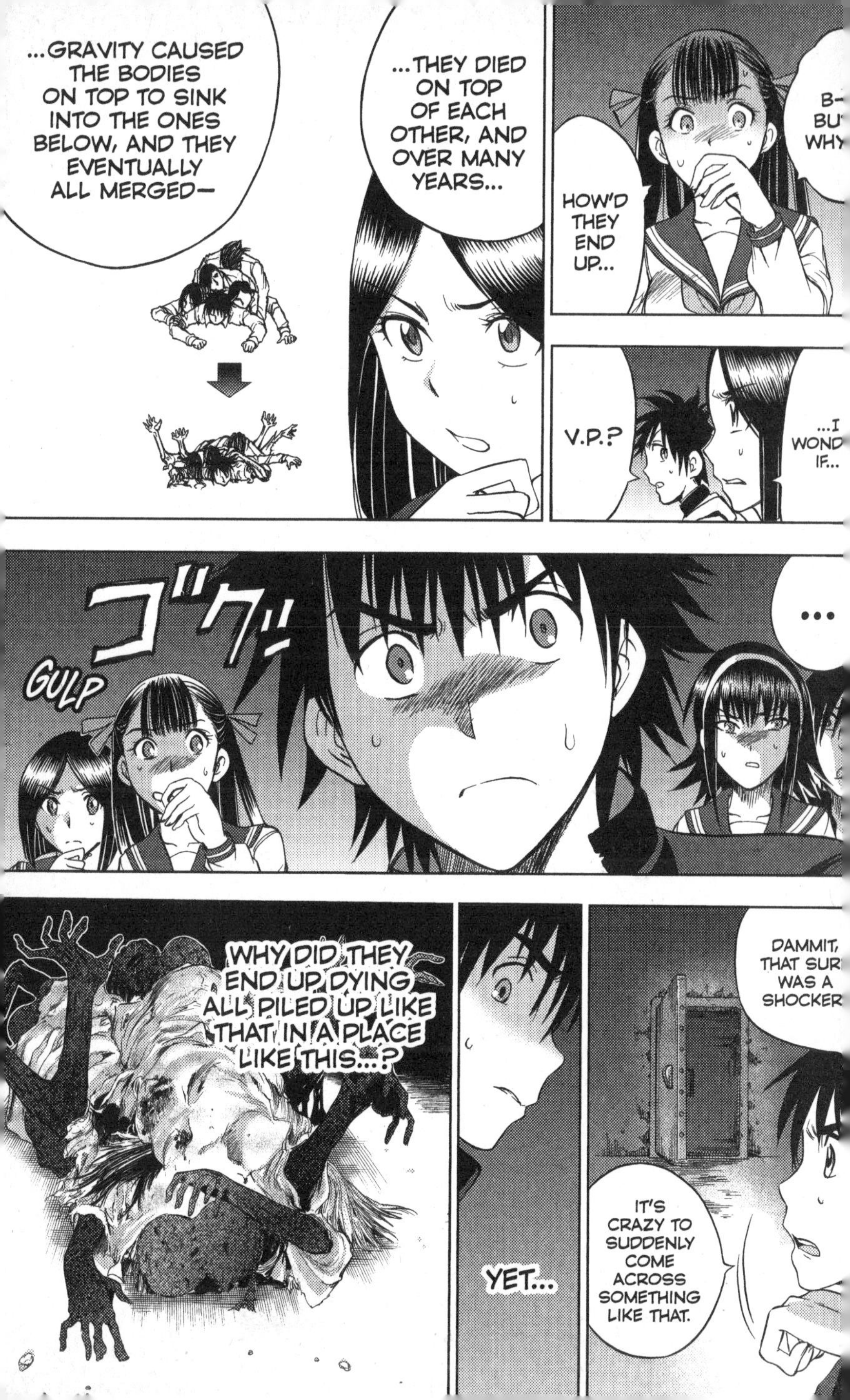
B- BU WHY
HOW'D THEY END UP...
...I WOND IF...
V.P.?
...THEY DIED ON TOP OF EACH OTHER, AND OVER MANY YEARS...
...GRAVITY CAUSED THE BODIES ON TOP TO SINK INTO THE ONES BELOW, AND THEY EVENTUALLY ALL MERGED—
...
ゴクッ
GULP
DAMMIT, THAT SUR WAS A SHOCKER
IT'S CRAZY TO SUDDENLY COME ACROSS SOMETHING LIKE THAT.
YET...
WHY DID THEY END UP DYING ALL PILED UP LIKE THAT IN A PLACE LIKE THIS...?

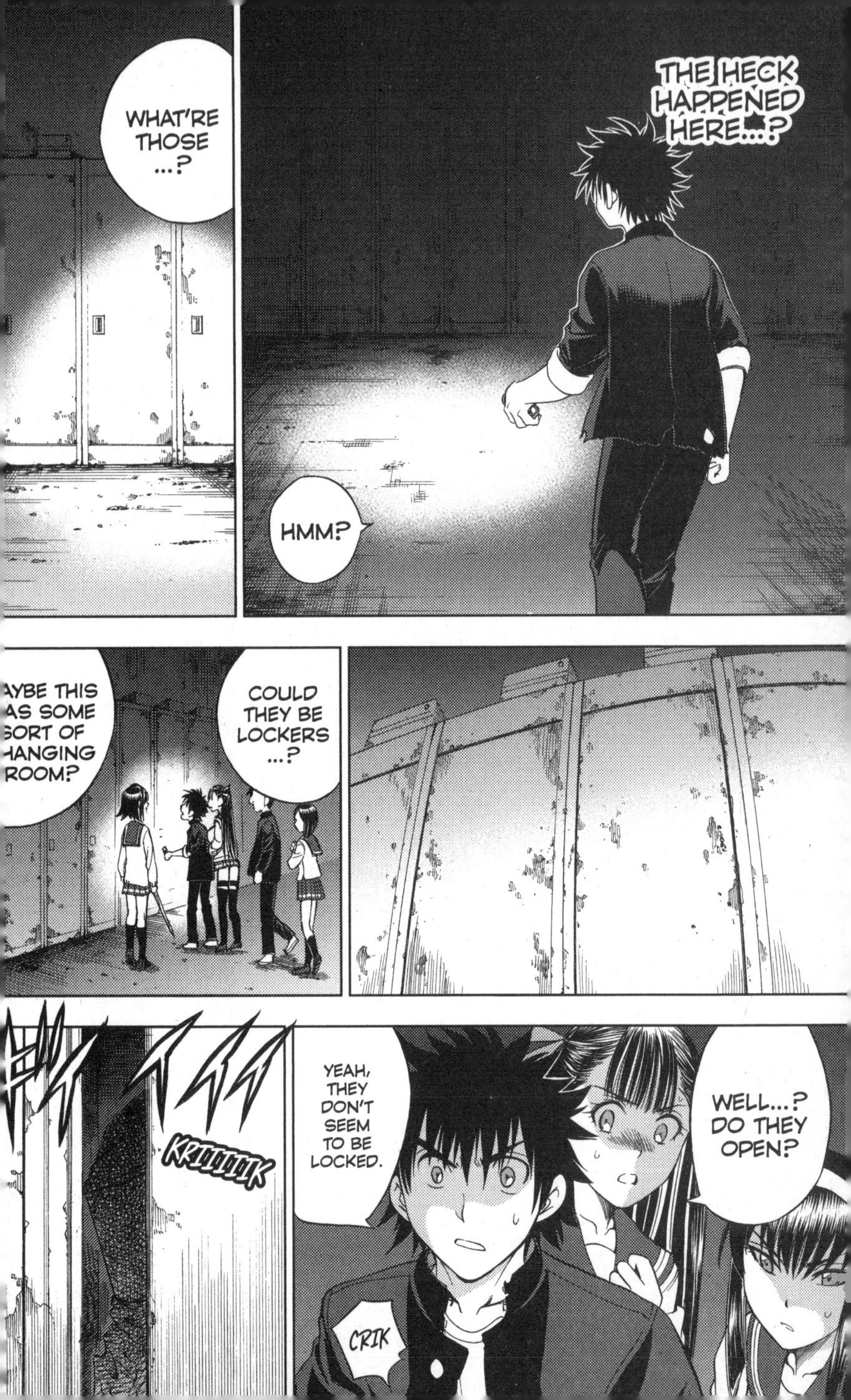
THE HECK HAPPENED HERE...?
HMM?
WHAT'RE THOSE ...?
COULD THEY BE LOCKERS ...?
AYBE THIS AS SOME SORT OF HANGING ROOM?
WELL...? DO THEY OPEN?
YEAH, THEY DON'T SEEM TO BE LOCKED.
CRIK
KRIIIIIK

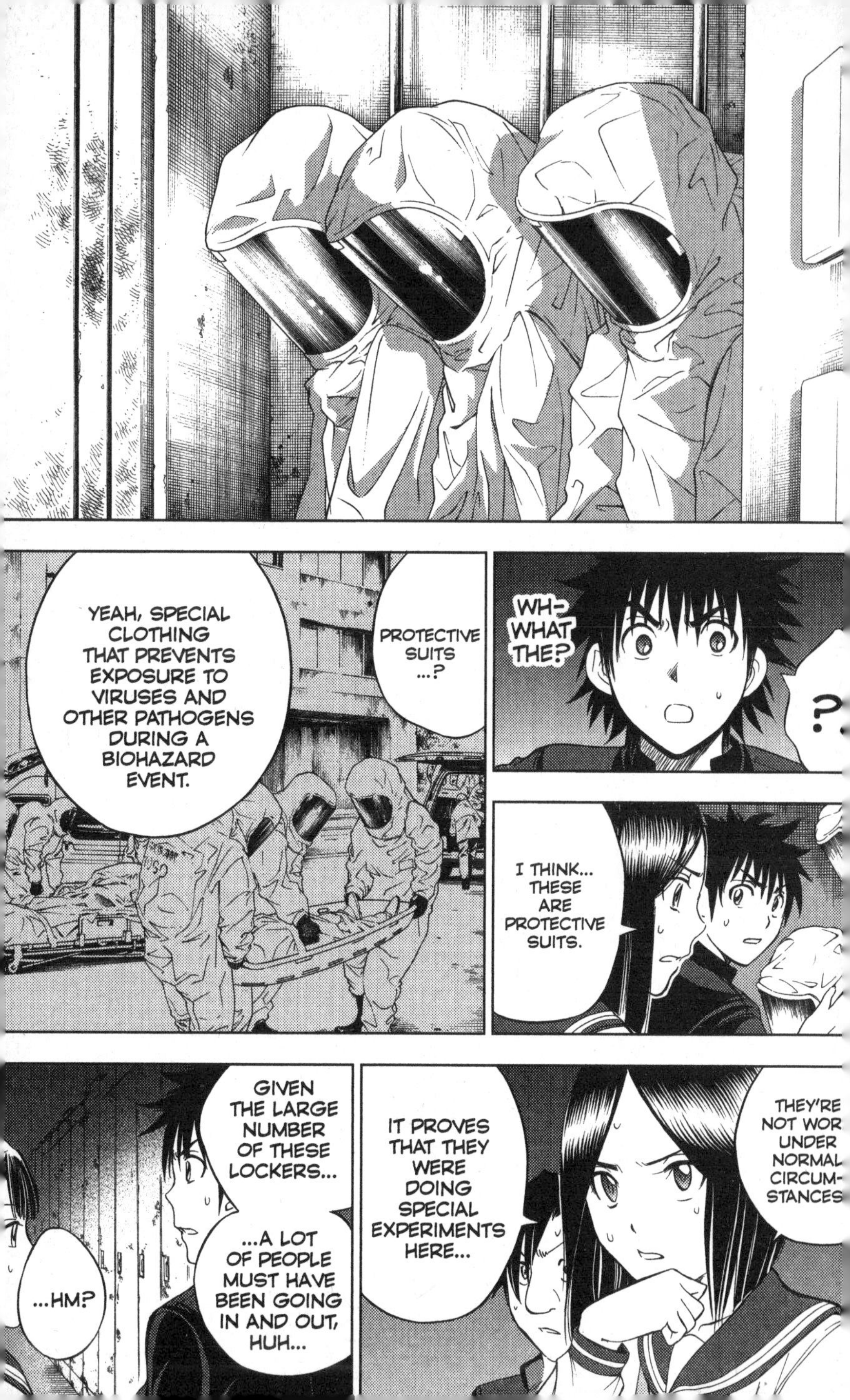
WH- WHAT THE?
?
I THINK... THESE ARE PROTECTIVE SUITS.
PROTECTIVE SUITS ...?
YEAH, SPECIAL CLOTHING THAT PREVENTS EXPOSURE TO VIRUSES AND OTHER PATHOGENS DURING A BIOHAZARD EVENT.
THEY'RE NOT WOR UNDER NORMAL CIRCUMSTANCES
IT PROVES THAT THEY WERE DOING SPECIAL EXPERIMENTS HERE...
GIVEN THE LARGE NUMBER OF THESE LOCKERS...
...A LOT OF PEOPLE MUST HAVE BEEN GOING IN AND OUT, HUH...
...HM?

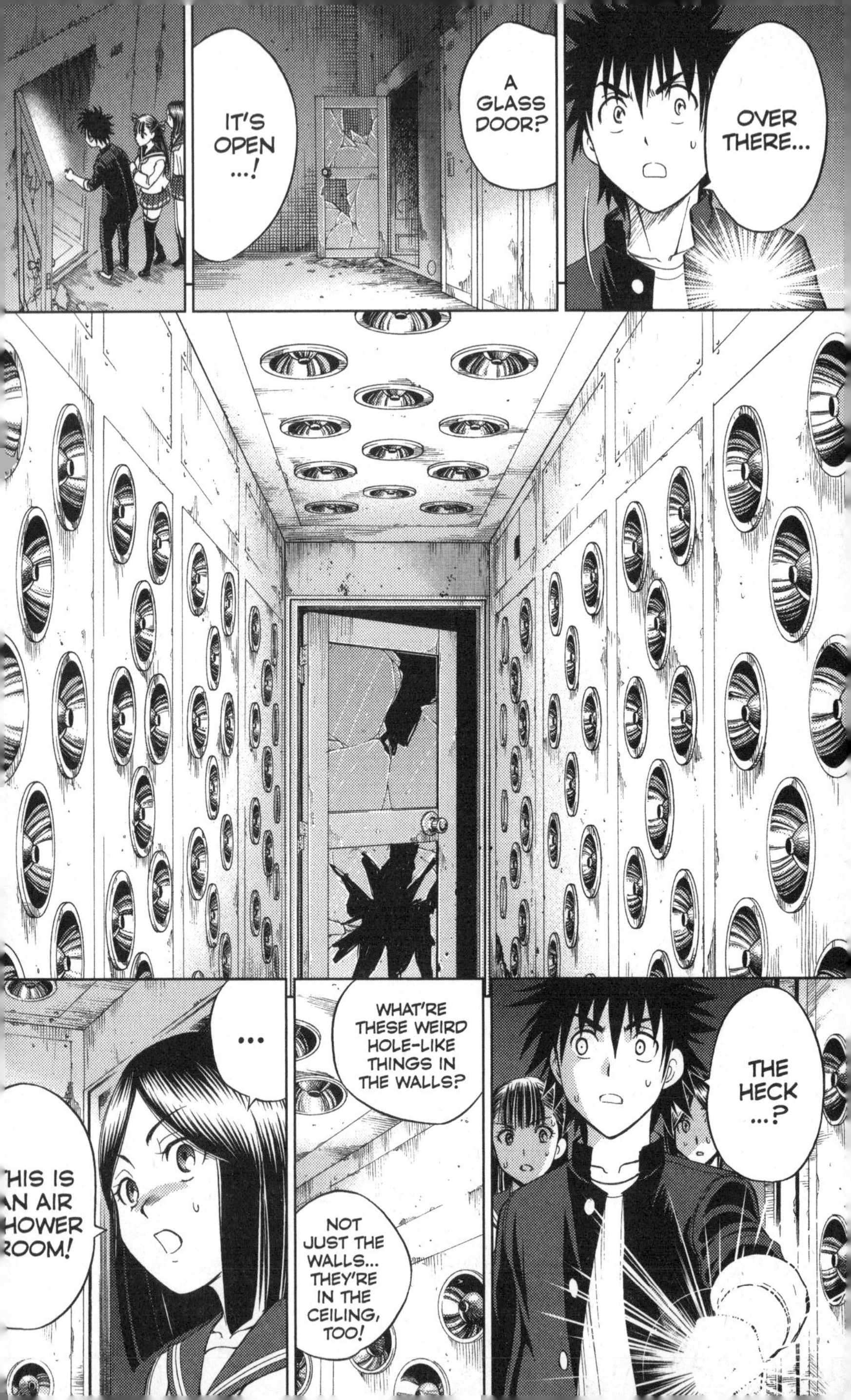

OVER THERE...
A GLASS DOOR?
IT'S OPEN ...!
THE HECK ...?
WHAT'RE THESE WEIRD HOLE-LIKE THINGS IN THE WALLS?
NOT JUST THE WALLS... THEY'RE IN THE CEILING, TOO!
...
HIS IS N AIR HOWER OOM!

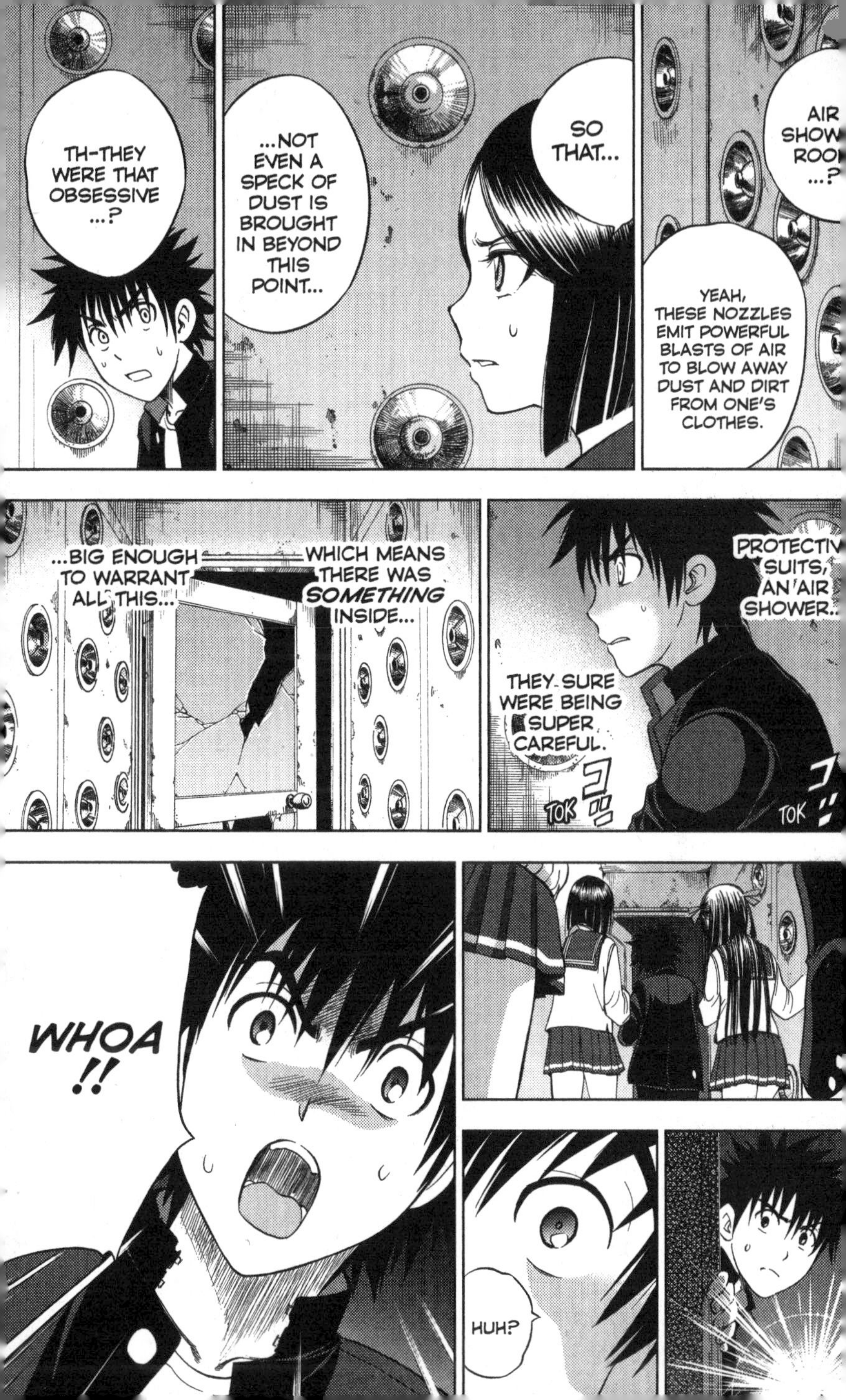
AIR SHOW ROO …?
YEAH, THESE NOZZLES EMIT POWERFUL BLASTS OF AIR TO BLOW AWAY DUST AND DIRT FROM ONE'S CLOTHES.
SO THAT…
…NOT EVEN A SPECK OF DUST IS BROUGHT IN BEYOND THIS POINT…
TH-THEY WERE THAT OBSESSIVE …?
PROTECTIV SUITS, AN AIR SHOWER…
THEY SURE WERE BEING SUPER CAREFUL.
TOK
TOK
WHICH MEANS THERE WAS *SOMETHING* INSIDE…
…BIG ENOUGH TO WARRANT ALL THIS…
HUH?
WHOA !!

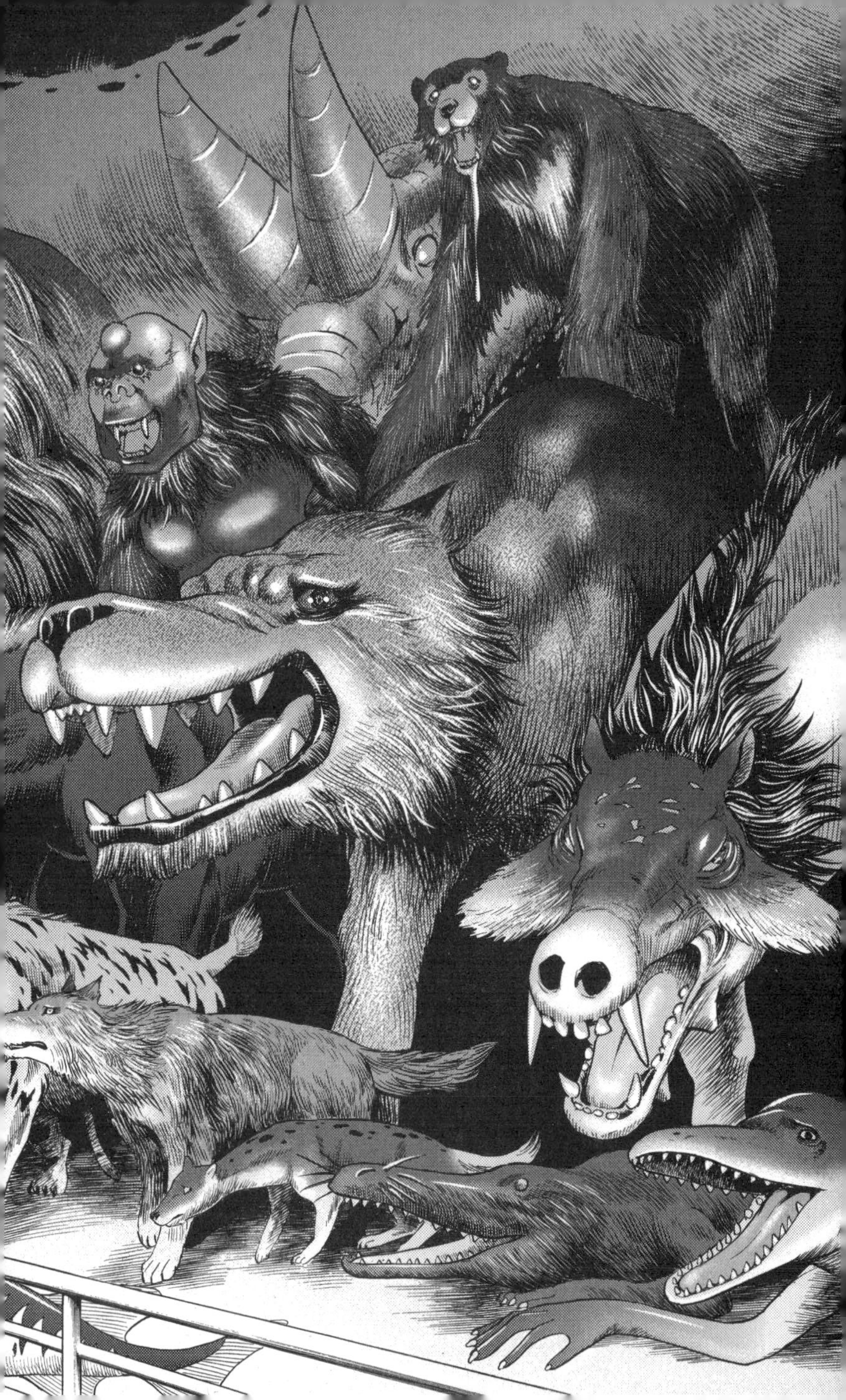

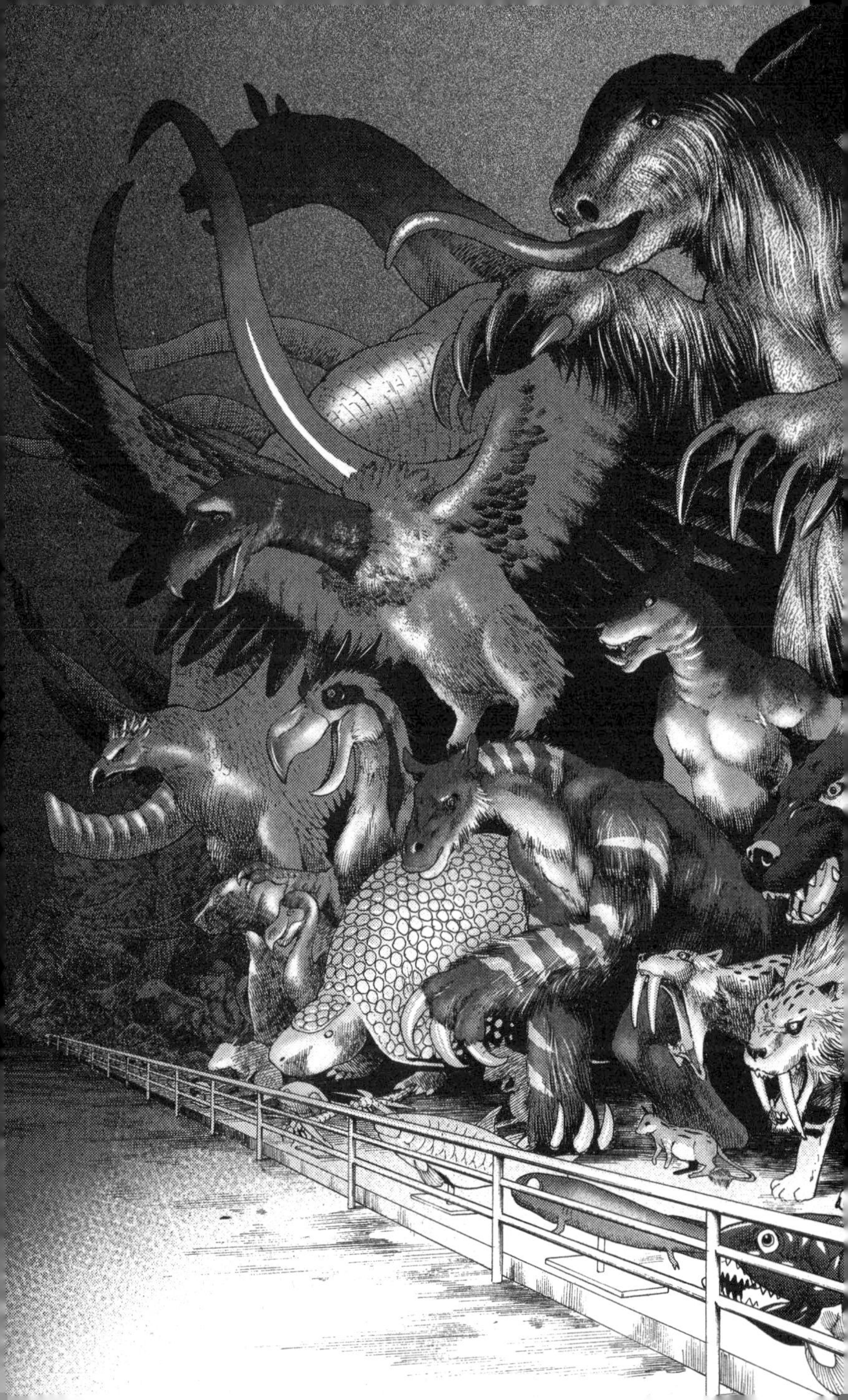

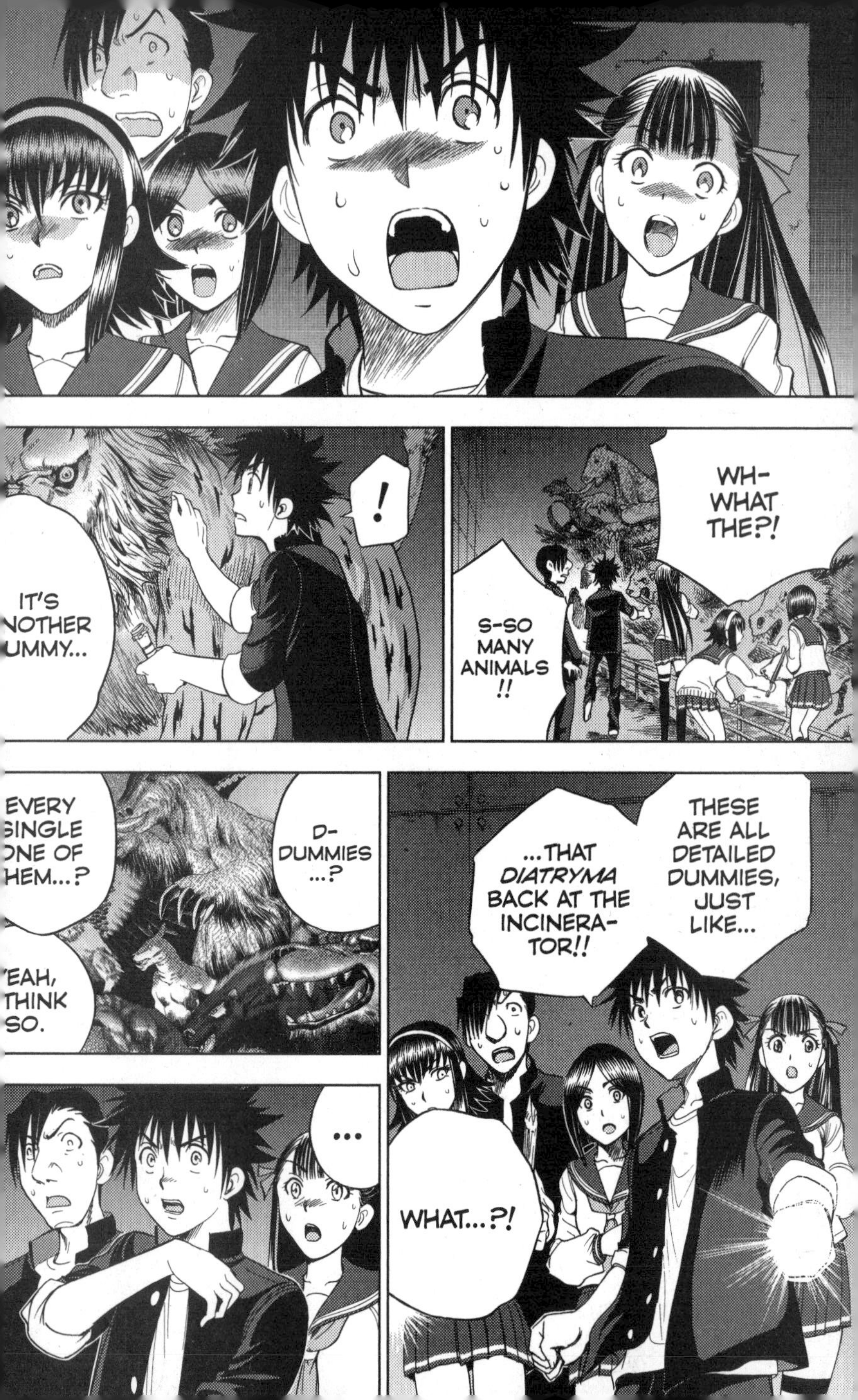

WH- WHAT THE?!
S-SO MANY ANIMALS!!
!
IT'S NOTHER UMMY...
THESE ARE ALL DETAILED DUMMIES, JUST LIKE...
...THAT *DIATRYMA* BACK AT THE INCINERA-TOR!!
WHAT...?!
D- DUMMIES ...?
EVERY SINGLE ONE OF HEM...?
EAH, THINK SO.
...

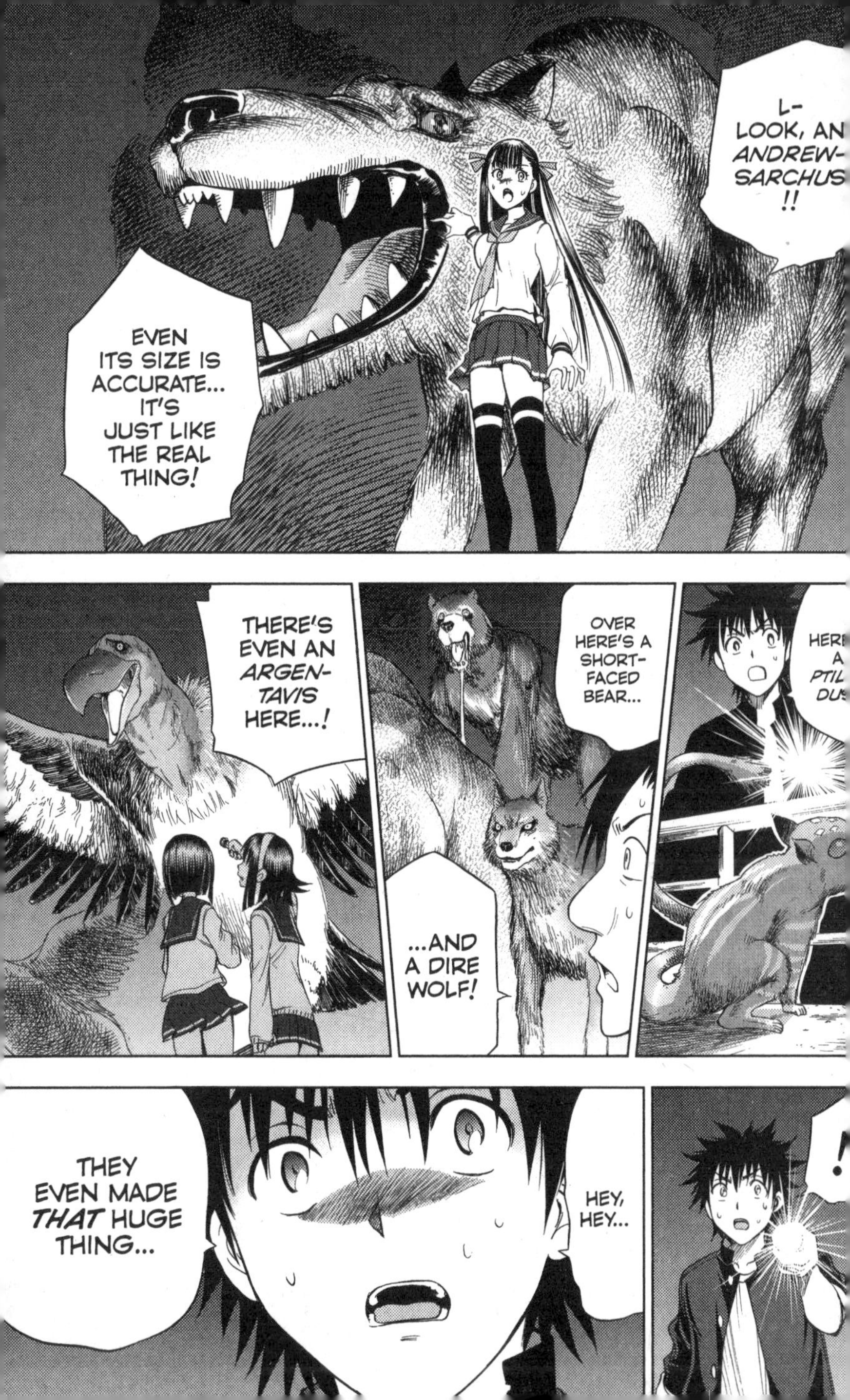
L- LOOK, AN ANDREW-SARCHUS!!
EVEN ITS SIZE IS ACCURATE... IT'S JUST LIKE THE REAL THING!
HERE A PTIL DUS
OVER HERE'S A SHORT-FACED BEAR...
...AND A DIRE WOLF!
THERE'S EVEN AN *ARGENTAVIS* HERE...!
!
HEY, HEY...
THEY EVEN MADE *THAT* HUGE THING...

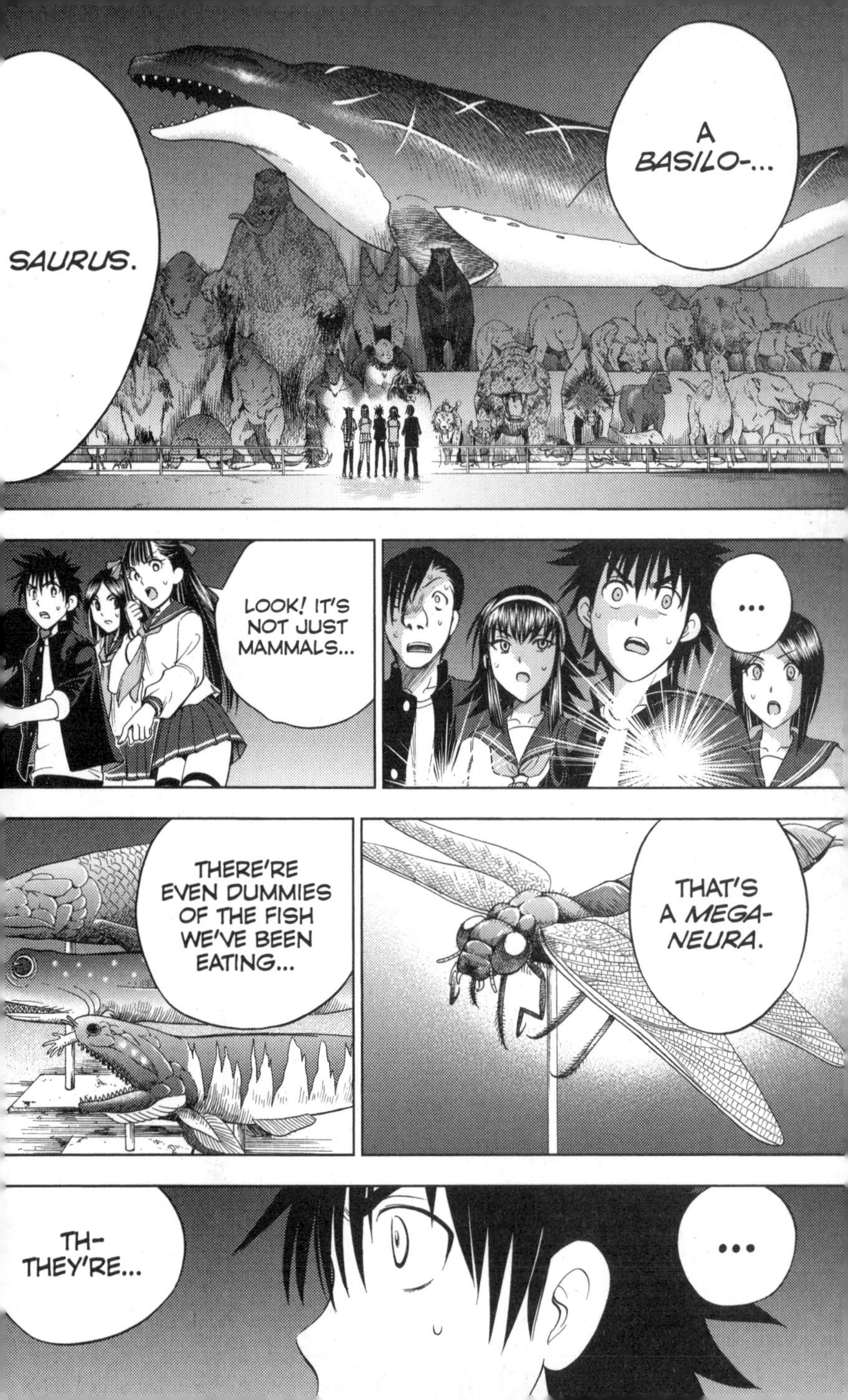
A BASILO-...
SAURUS.
...
LOOK! IT'S NOT JUST MAMMALS...
THAT'S A *MEGA-NEURA*.
THERE'RE EVEN DUMMIES OF THE FISH WE'VE BEEN EATING...
...
TH- THEY'RE...

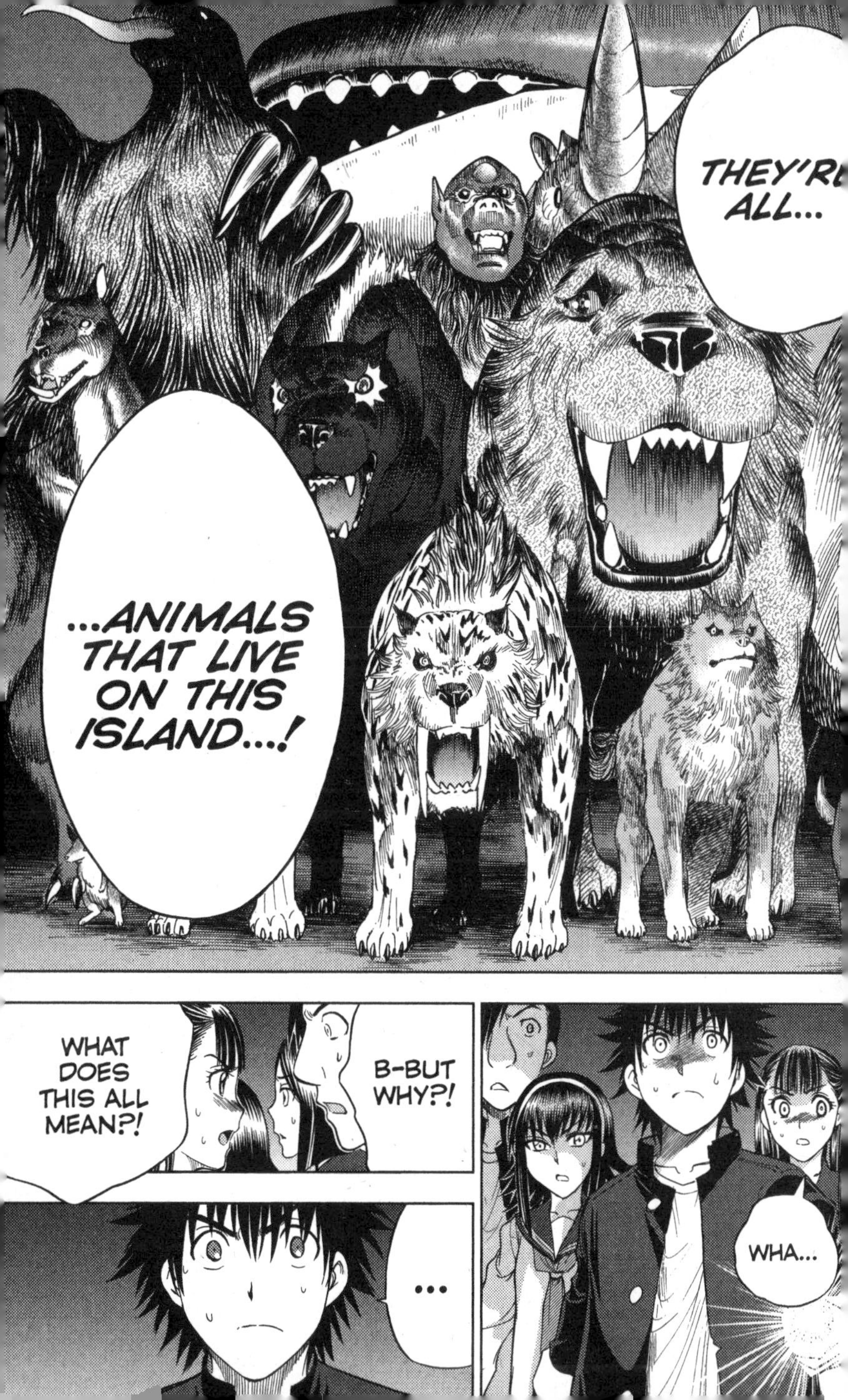
THEY'R ALL...
...ANIMALS THAT LIVE ON THIS ISLAND...!
WHA...
B-BUT WHY?!
WHAT DOES THIS ALL MEAN?!
...

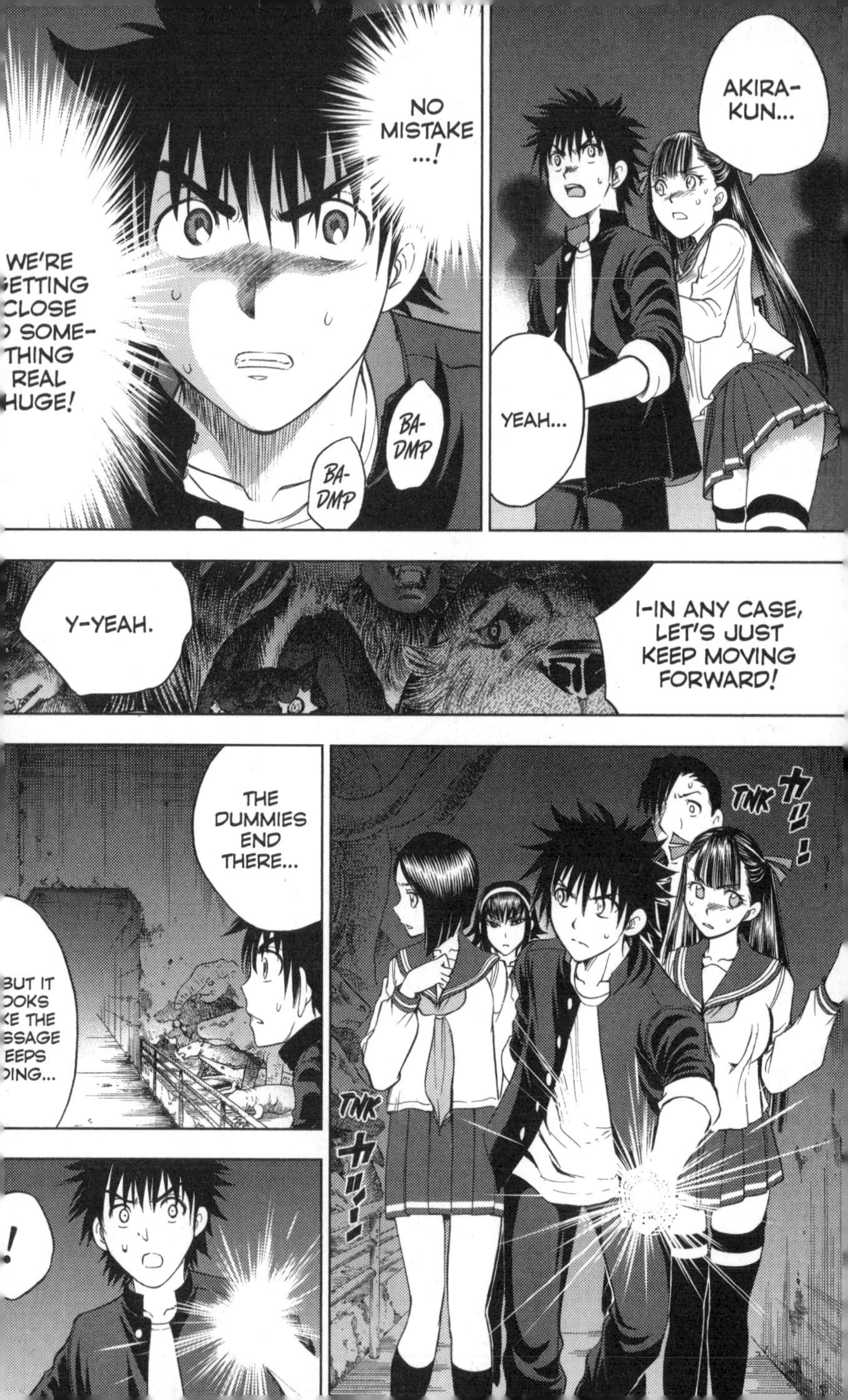
AKIRA-KUN...
YEAH...
NO MISTAKE ...!
WE'RE ETTING CLOSE O SOME-THING REAL HUGE!
BA-DMP
BA-DMP
I-IN ANY CASE, LET'S JUST KEEP MOVING FORWARD!
Y-YEAH.
TNK
TNK
THE DUMMIES END THERE...
BUT IT OOKS KE THE SSAGE EEPS OING...
!

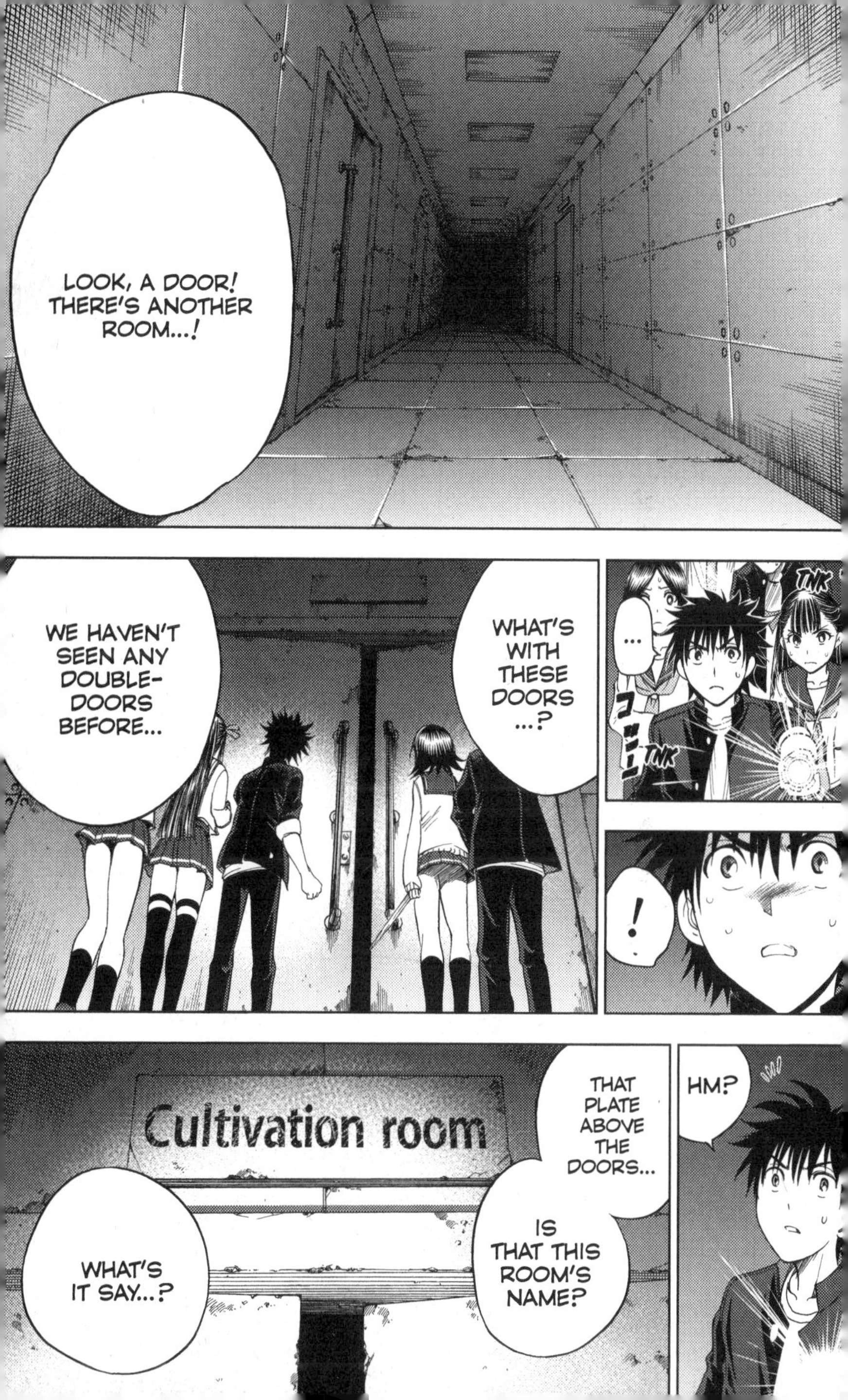
LOOK, A DOOR! THERE'S ANOTHER ROOM...!
TNK
...
TNK
!
WHAT'S WITH THESE DOORS ...?
WE HAVEN'T SEEN ANY DOUBLE-DOORS BEFORE...
HM?
THAT PLATE ABOVE THE DOORS...
Cultivation room
IS THAT THIS ROOM'S NAME?
WHAT'S IT SAY...?

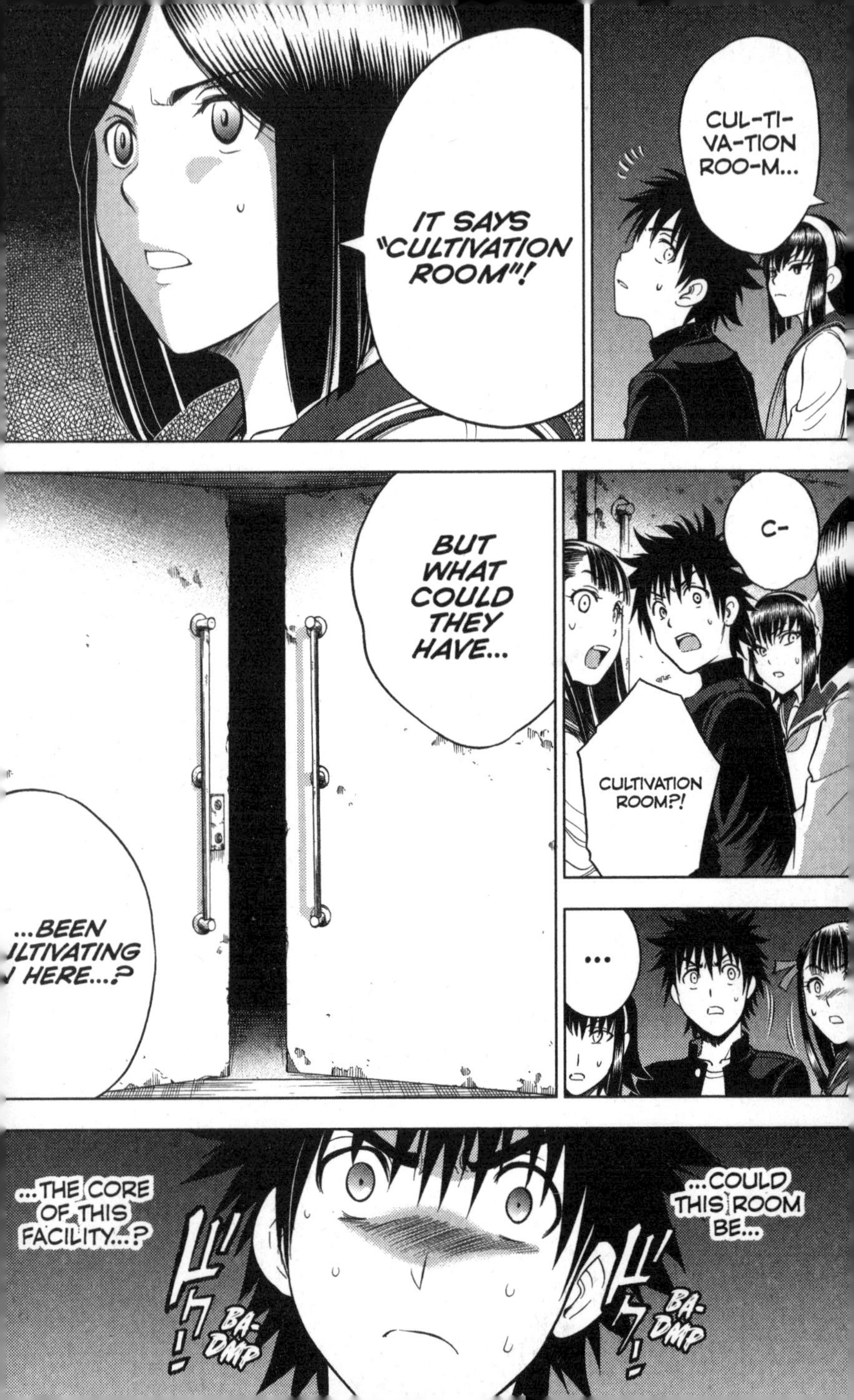
CUL-TI-VA-TION ROO-M...
IT SAYS "CULTIVATION ROOM"!
C-
CULTIVATION ROOM?!
...
BUT WHAT COULD THEY HAVE...
...BEEN LTIVATING HERE...?
...COULD THIS ROOM BE...
...THE CORE OF THIS FACILITY...?
BA-DMP
BA-DMP

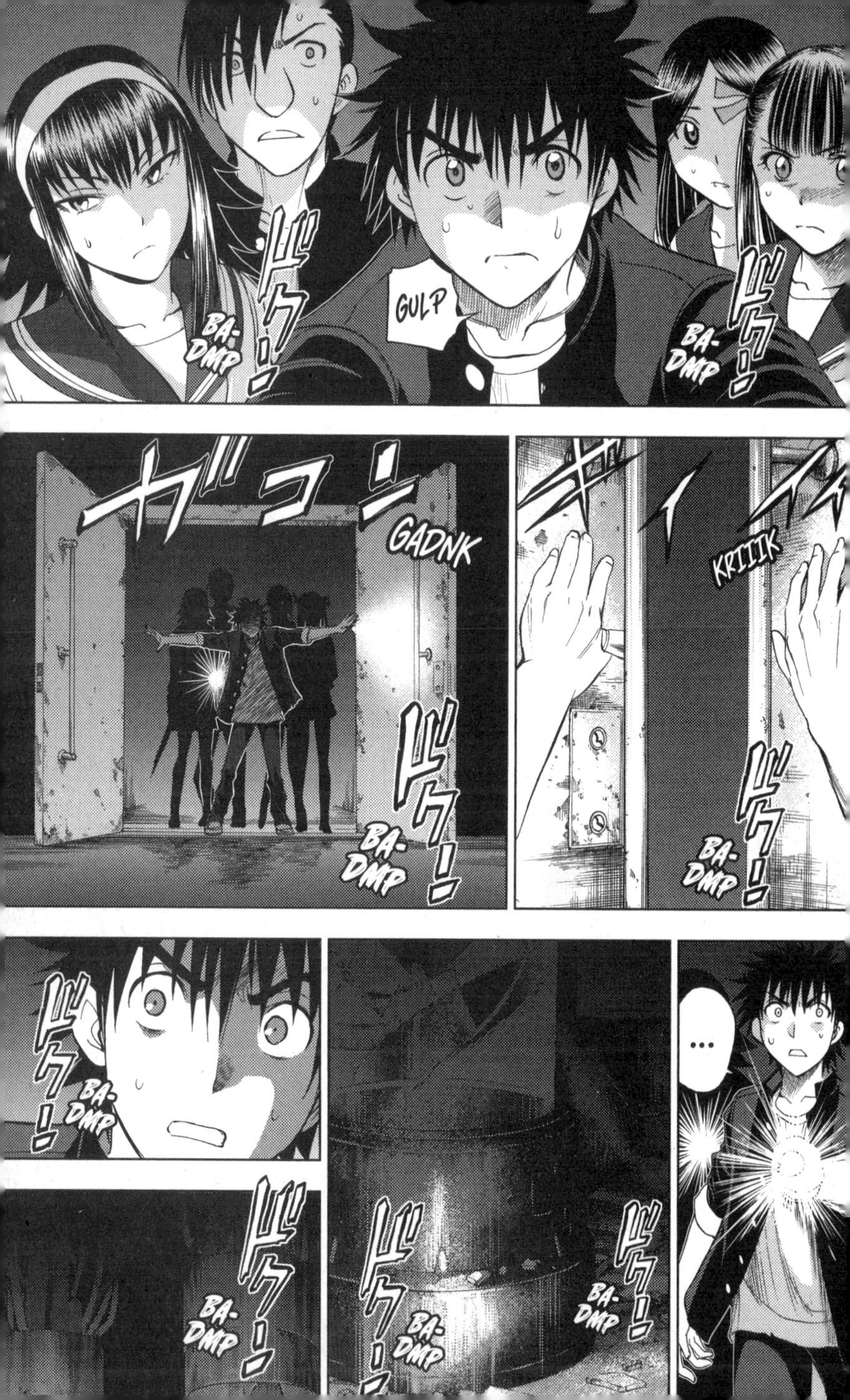
BA-DMP
GULP
BA-DMP
KRIIIK
BA-DMP
GADNK
BA-DMP
...
BA-DMP
BA-DMP
BA-DMP
BA-DMP

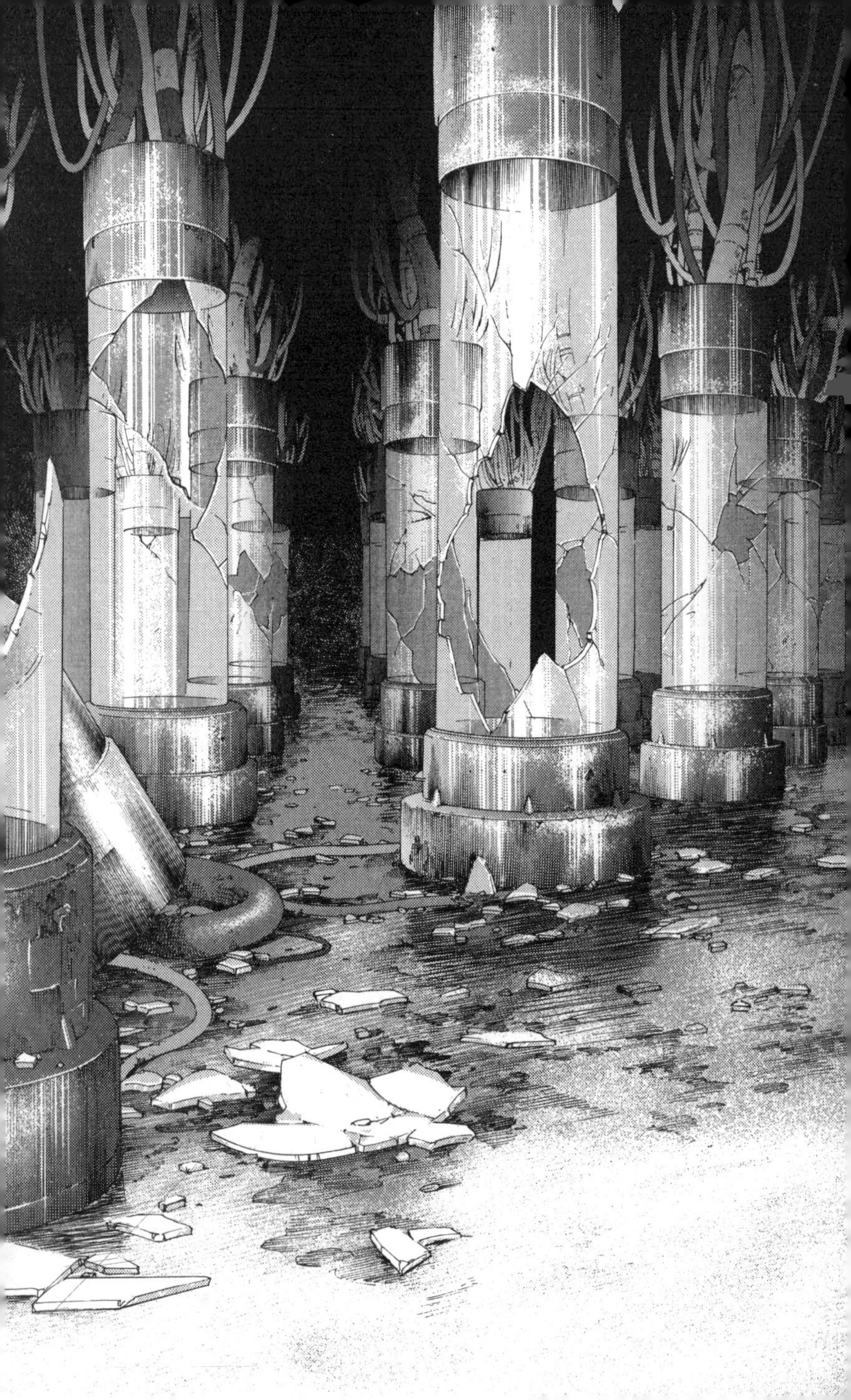

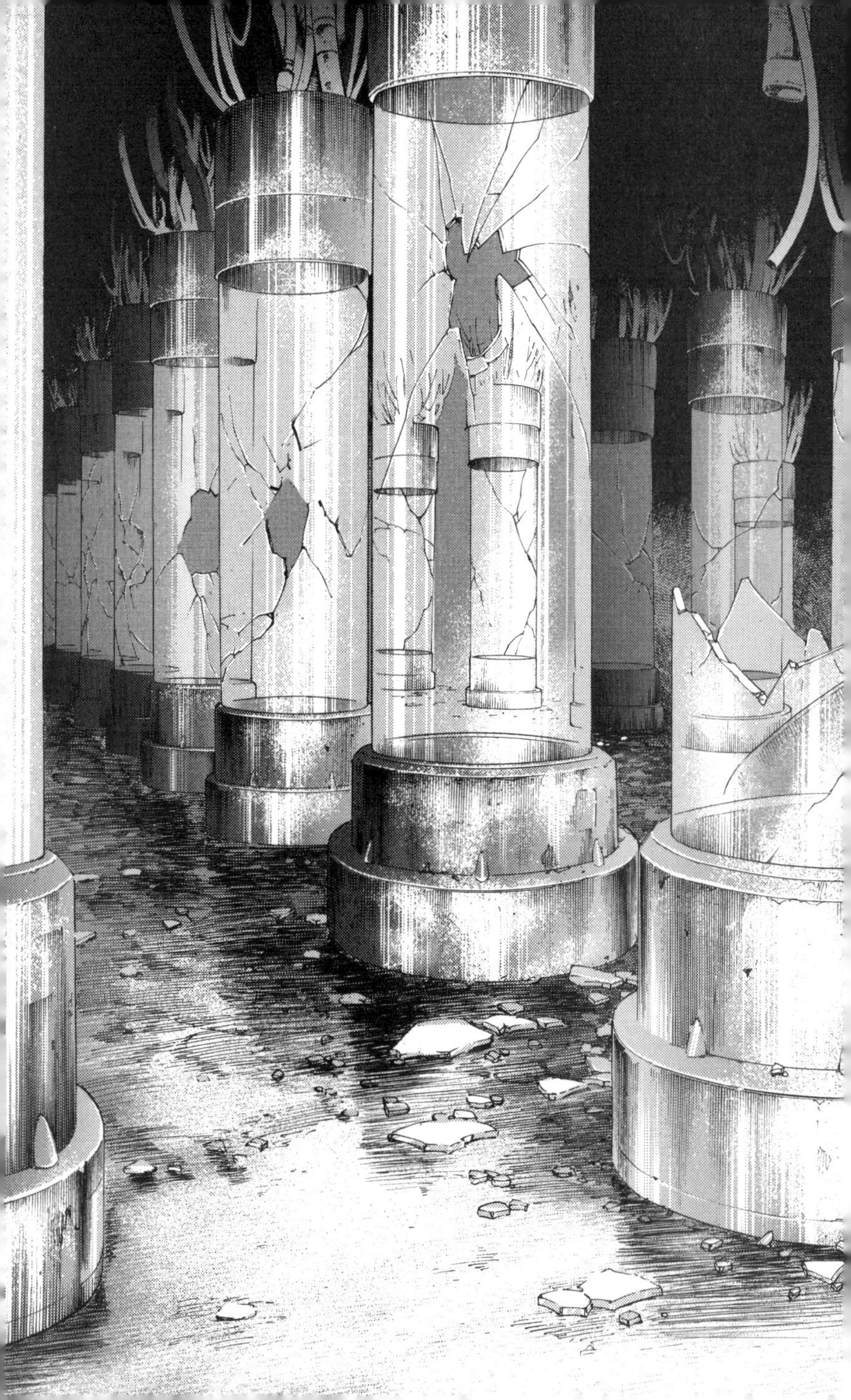

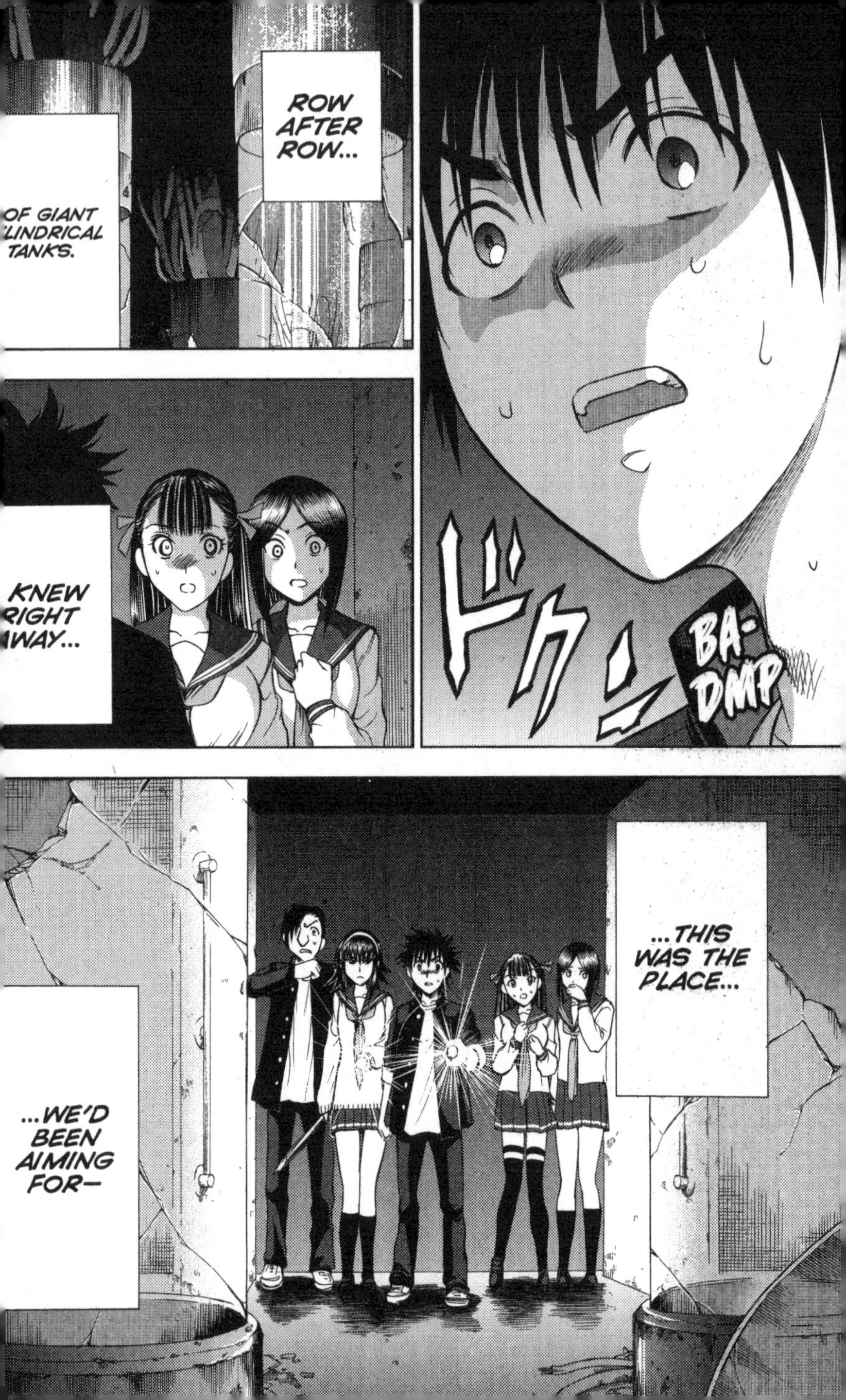
ドクン
BA-DMP
ROW AFTER ROW...
OF GIANT LINDRICAL TANKS.
KNEW RIGHT WAY...
...THIS WAS THE PLACE...
...WE'D BEEN AIMING FOR—

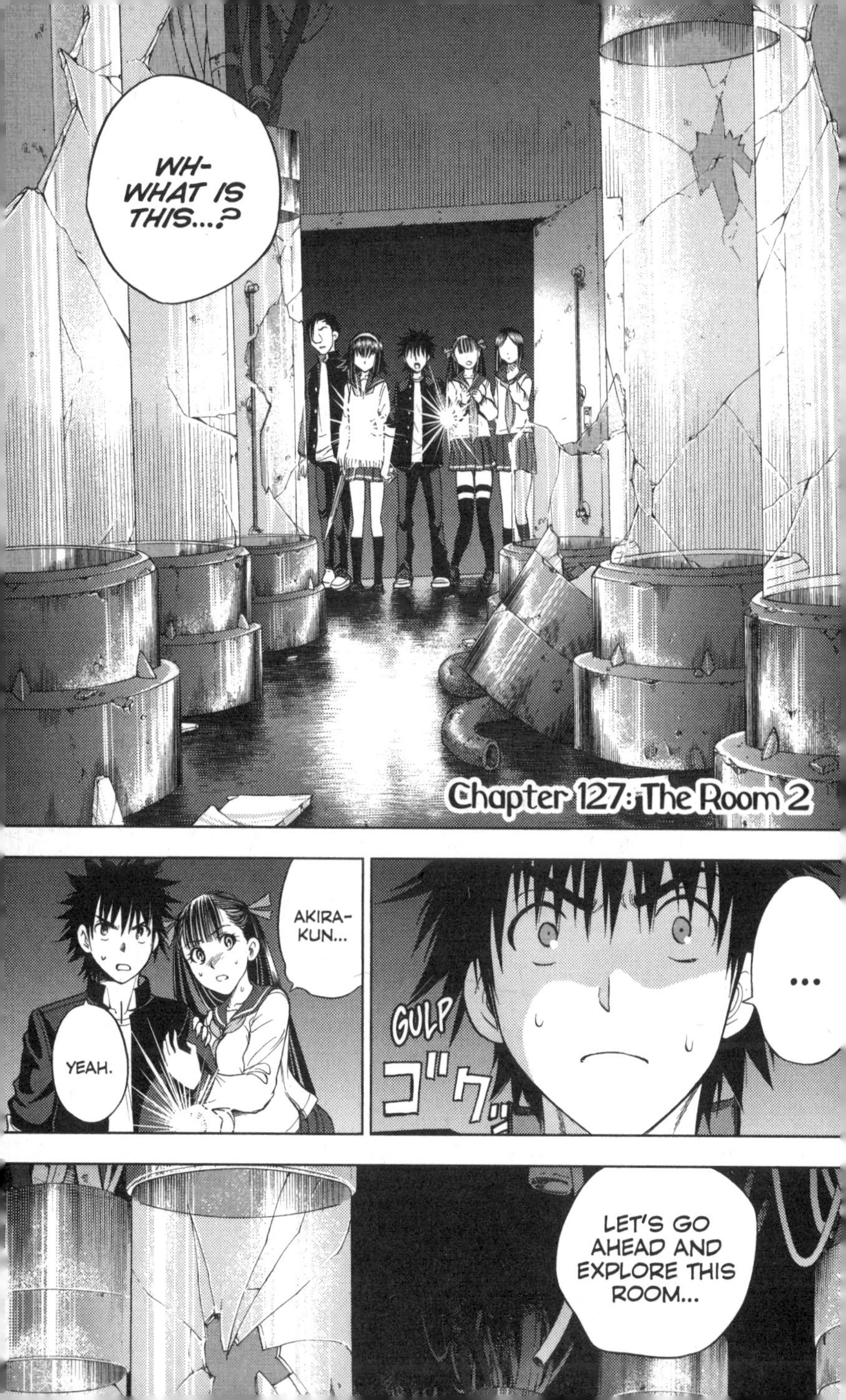
WH- WHAT IS THIS...?
Chapter 127: The Room 2
...
GULP
ゴクッ
AKIRA-KUN...
YEAH.
LET'S GO AHEAD AND EXPLORE THIS ROOM...

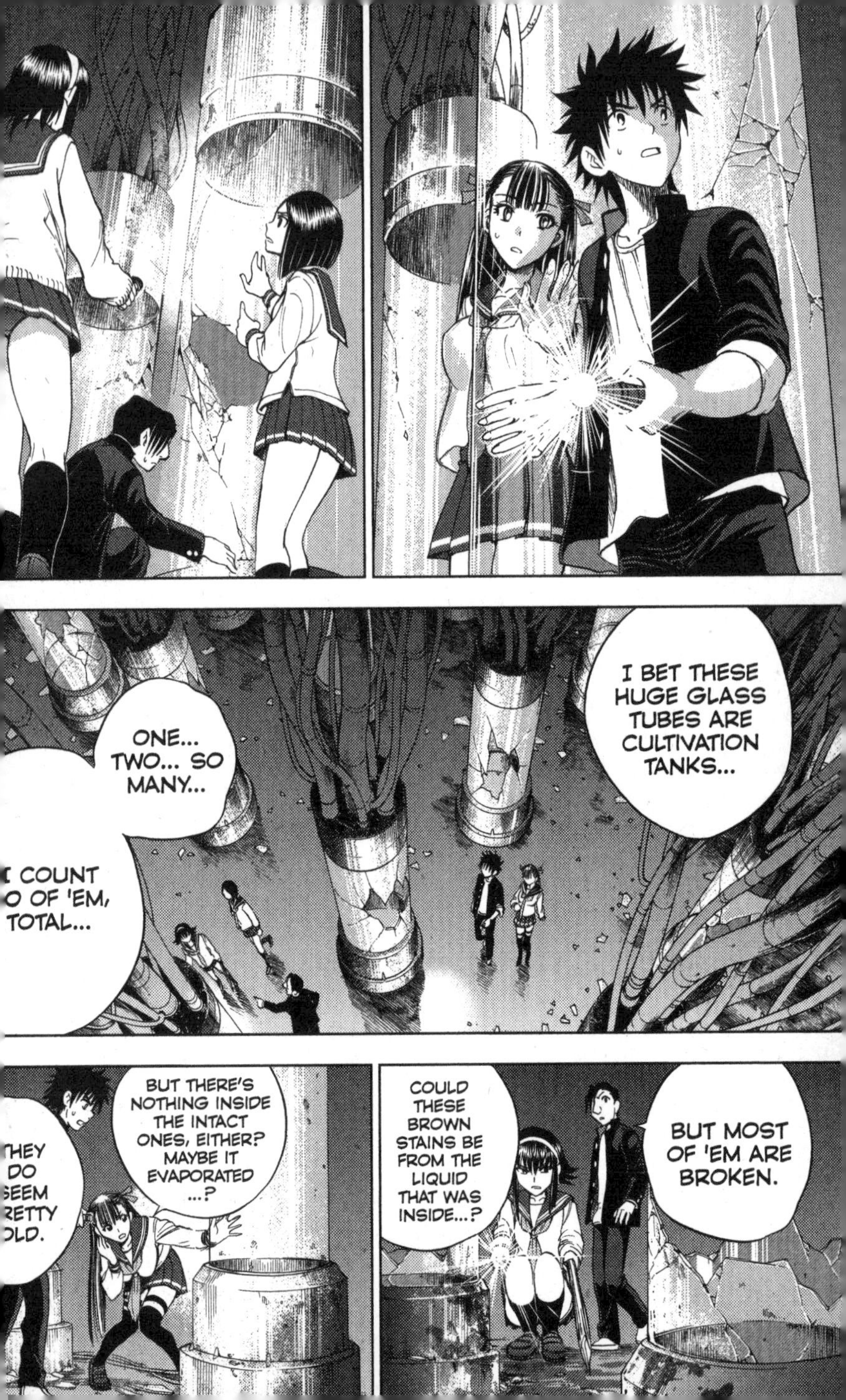
I BET THESE HUGE GLASS TUBES ARE CULTIVATION TANKS...
ONE... TWO... SO MANY...
COUNT O OF 'EM, TOTAL...
BUT MOST OF 'EM ARE BROKEN.
COULD THESE BROWN STAINS BE FROM THE LIQUID THAT WAS INSIDE...?
BUT THERE'S NOTHING INSIDE THE INTACT ONES, EITHER? MAYBE IT EVAPORATED ...?
THEY DO SEEM RETTY OLD.

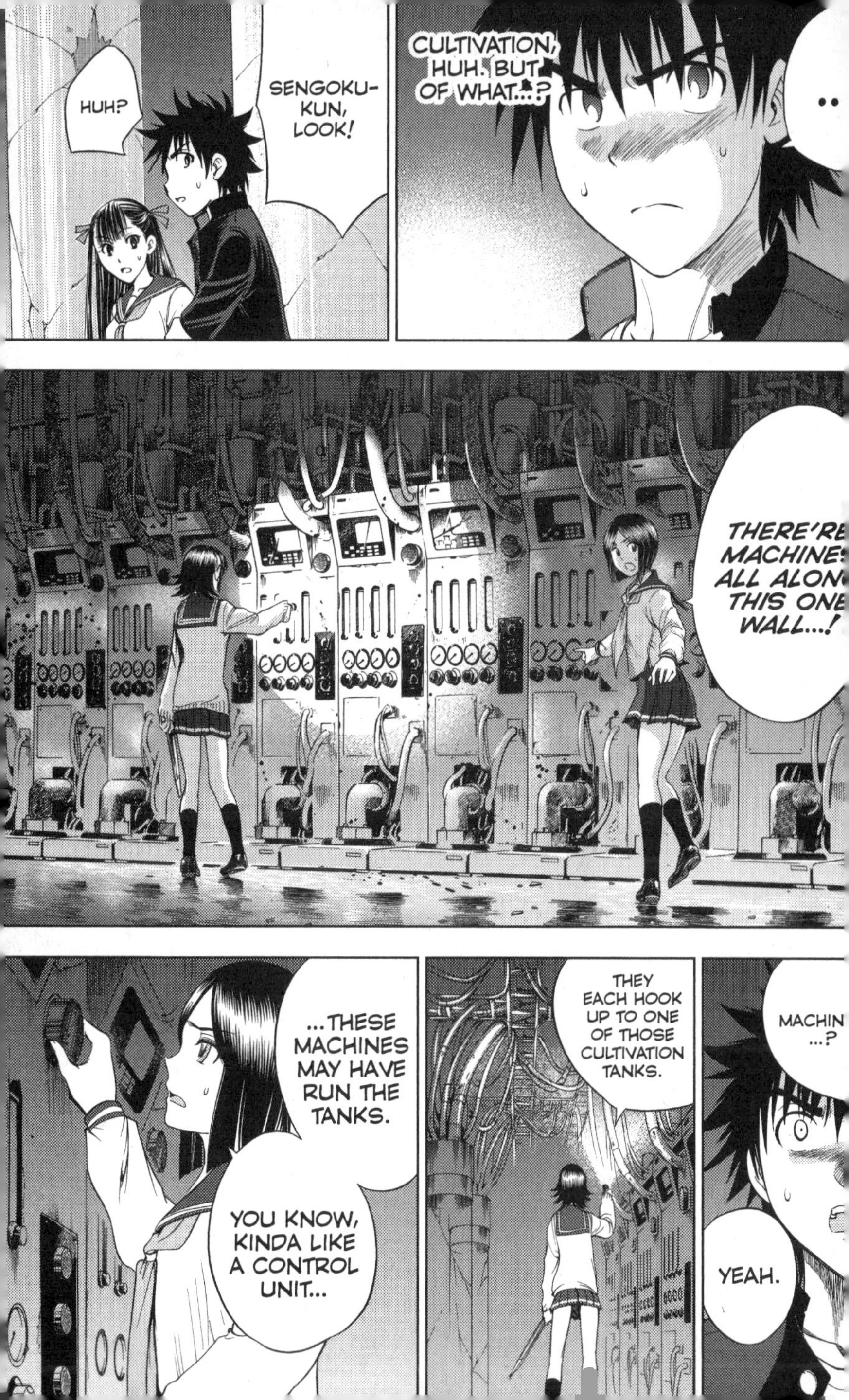
..
CULTIVATION, HUH. BUT OF WHAT...?
SENGOKU-KUN, LOOK!
HUH?
THERE'RE MACHINES ALL ALONG THIS ONE WALL...!
MACHIN ...?
YEAH.
THEY EACH HOOK UP TO ONE OF THOSE CULTIVATION TANKS.
...THESE MACHINES MAY HAVE RUN THE TANKS.
YOU KNOW, KINDA LIKE A CONTROL UNIT...

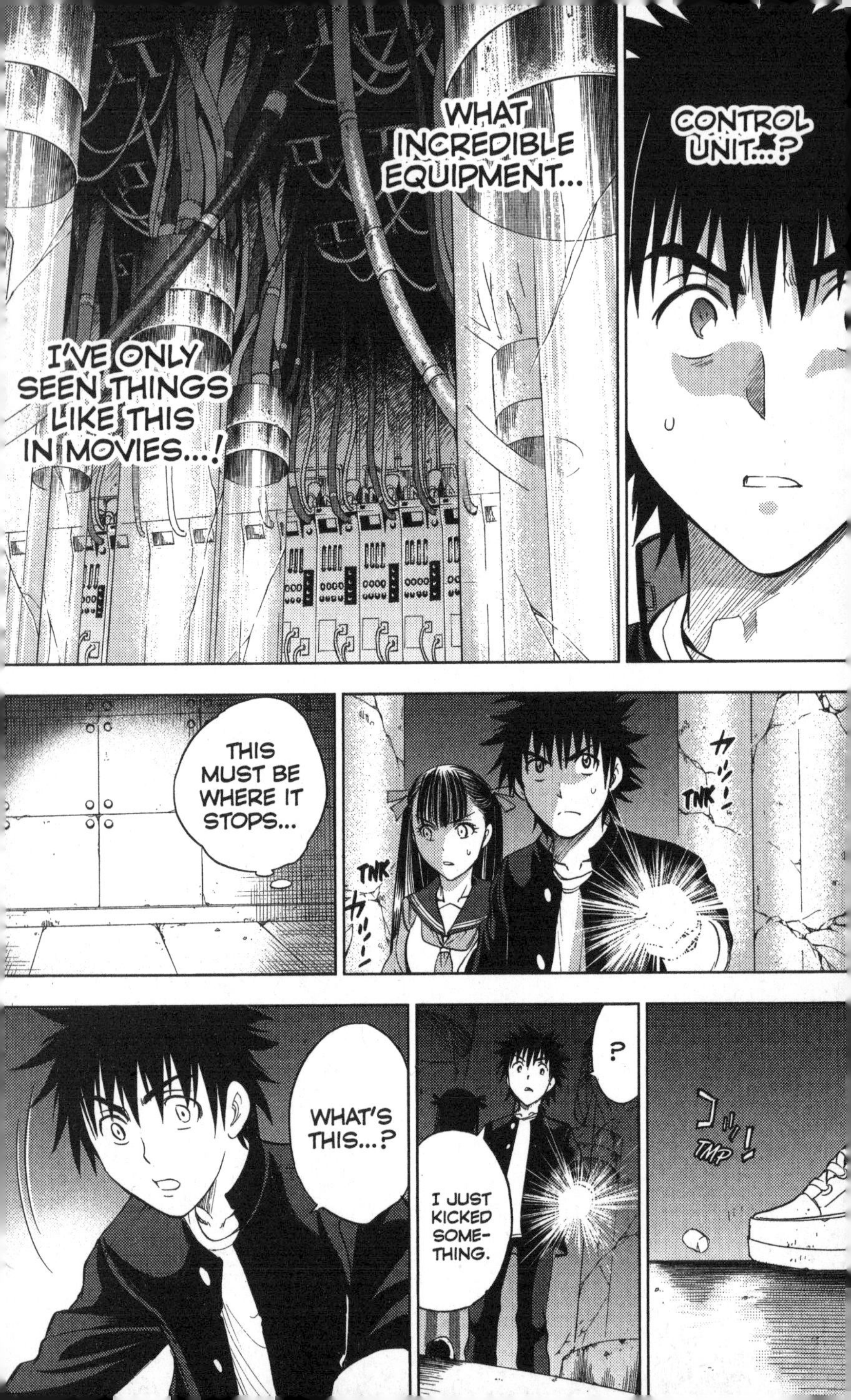
CONTROL UNIT...?
WHAT INCREDIBLE EQUIPMENT...
I'VE ONLY SEEN THINGS LIKE THIS IN MOVIES...!
TNK
TNK
THIS MUST BE WHERE IT STOPS...
TMP
?
I JUST KICKED SOME-THING.
WHAT'S THIS...?

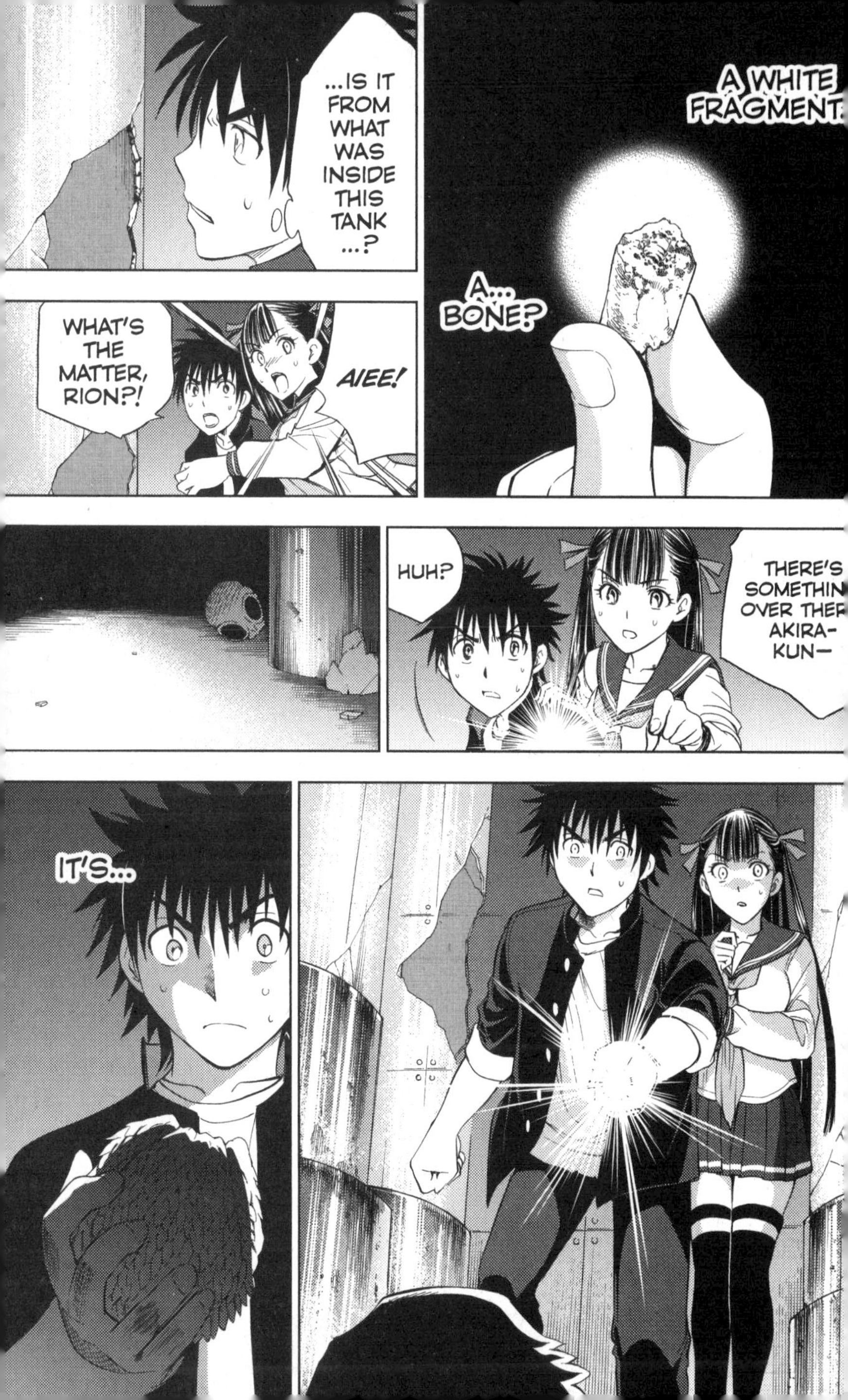

A WHITE FRAGMENT.
A... BONE?
...IS IT FROM WHAT WAS INSIDE THIS TANK...?
AIEE!
WHAT'S THE MATTER, RION?!
THERE'S SOMETHIN OVER THER AKIRA-KUN—
HUH?
IT'S...

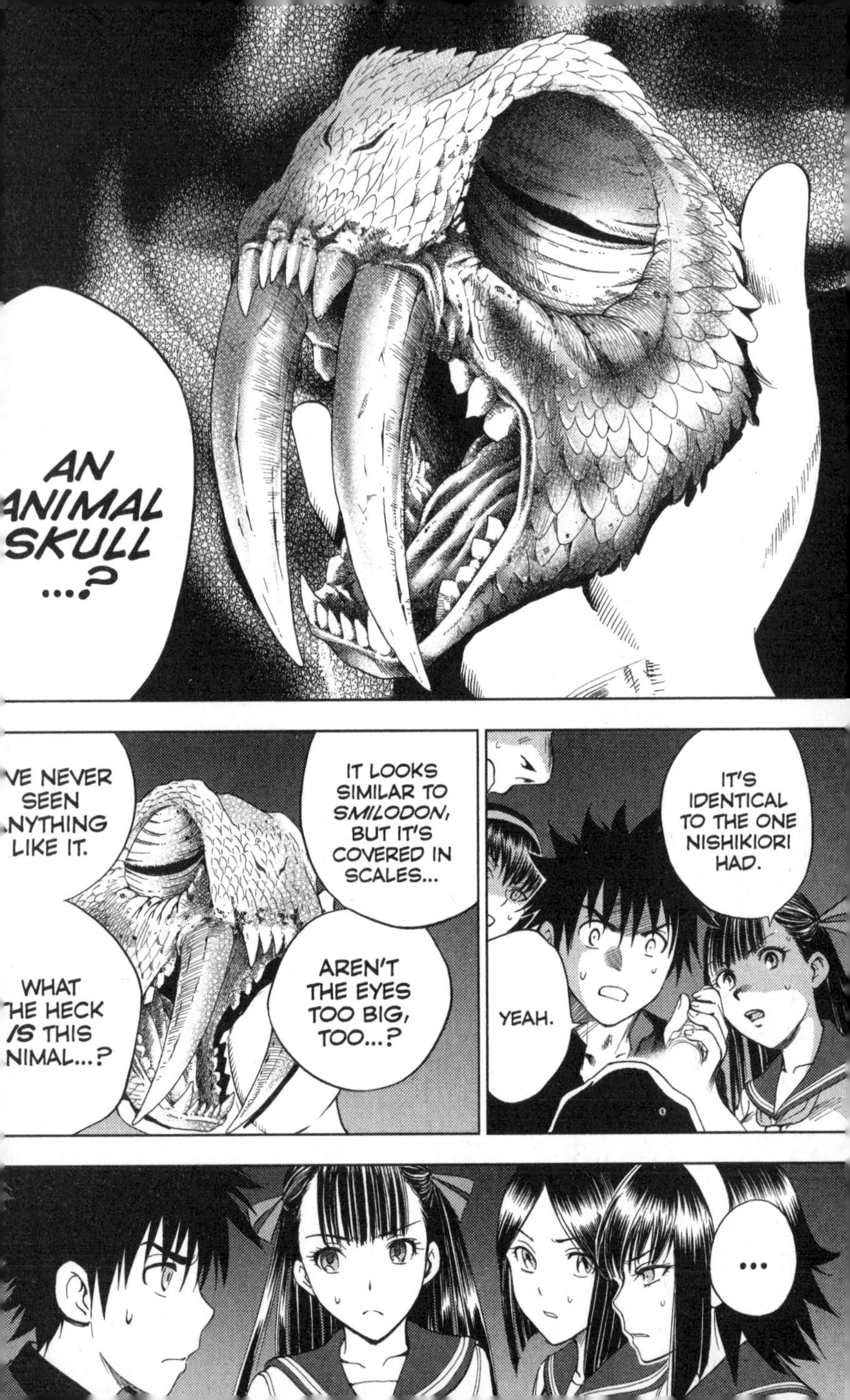
AN ANIMAL SKULL ...?
IT'S IDENTICAL TO THE ONE NISHIKIORI HAD.
YEAH.
IT LOOKS SIMILAR TO *SMILODON*, BUT IT'S COVERED IN SCALES...
VE NEVER SEEN NYTHING LIKE IT.
AREN'T THE EYES TOO BIG, TOO...?
WHAT HE HECK *IS* THIS NIMAL...?
...

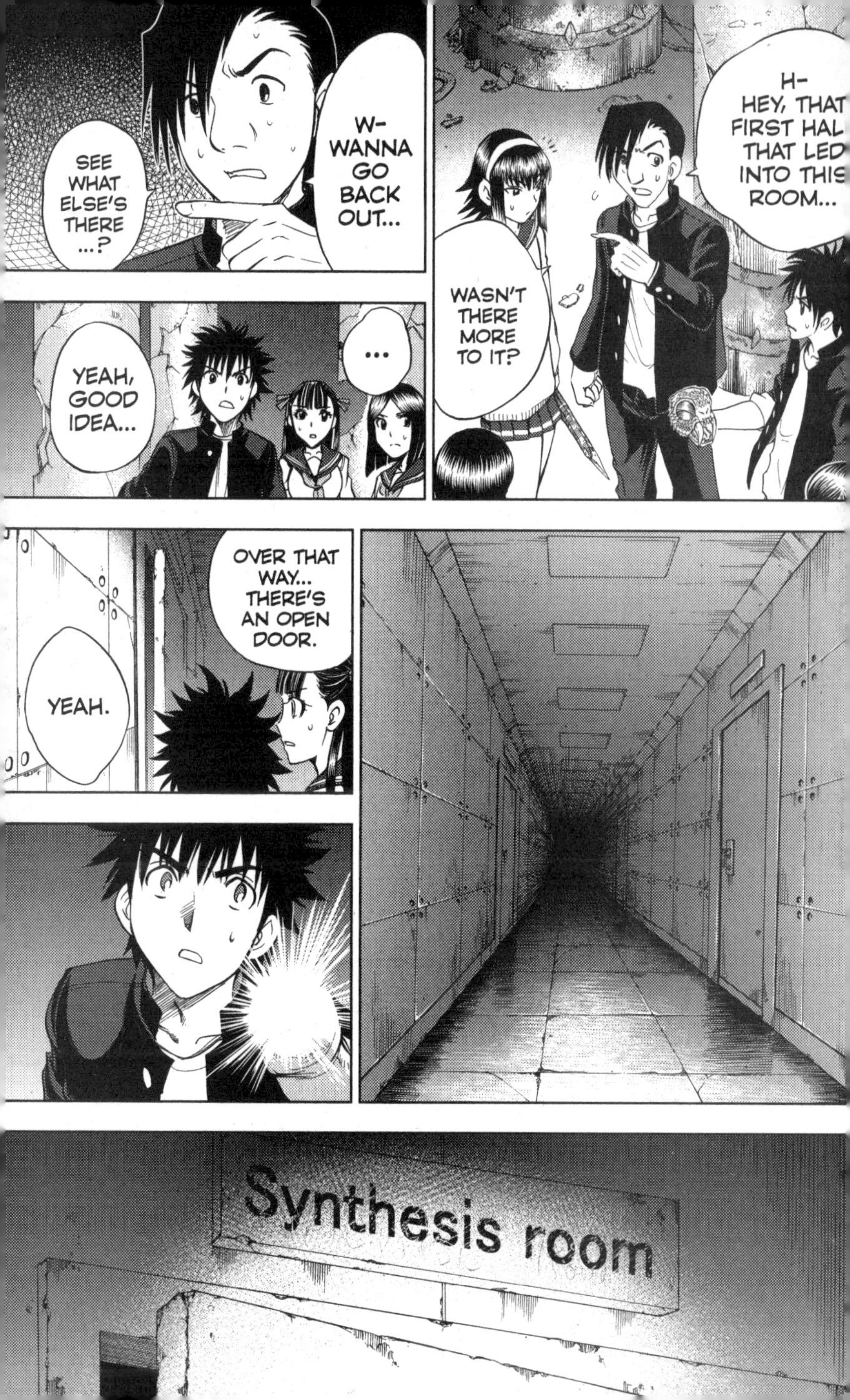
H- HEY, THAT FIRST HAL THAT LED INTO THIS ROOM...
WASN'T THERE MORE TO IT?
W- WANNA GO BACK OUT...
SEE WHAT ELSE'S THERE ...?
...
YEAH, GOOD IDEA...
OVER THAT WAY... THERE'S AN OPEN DOOR.
YEAH.
Synthesis room

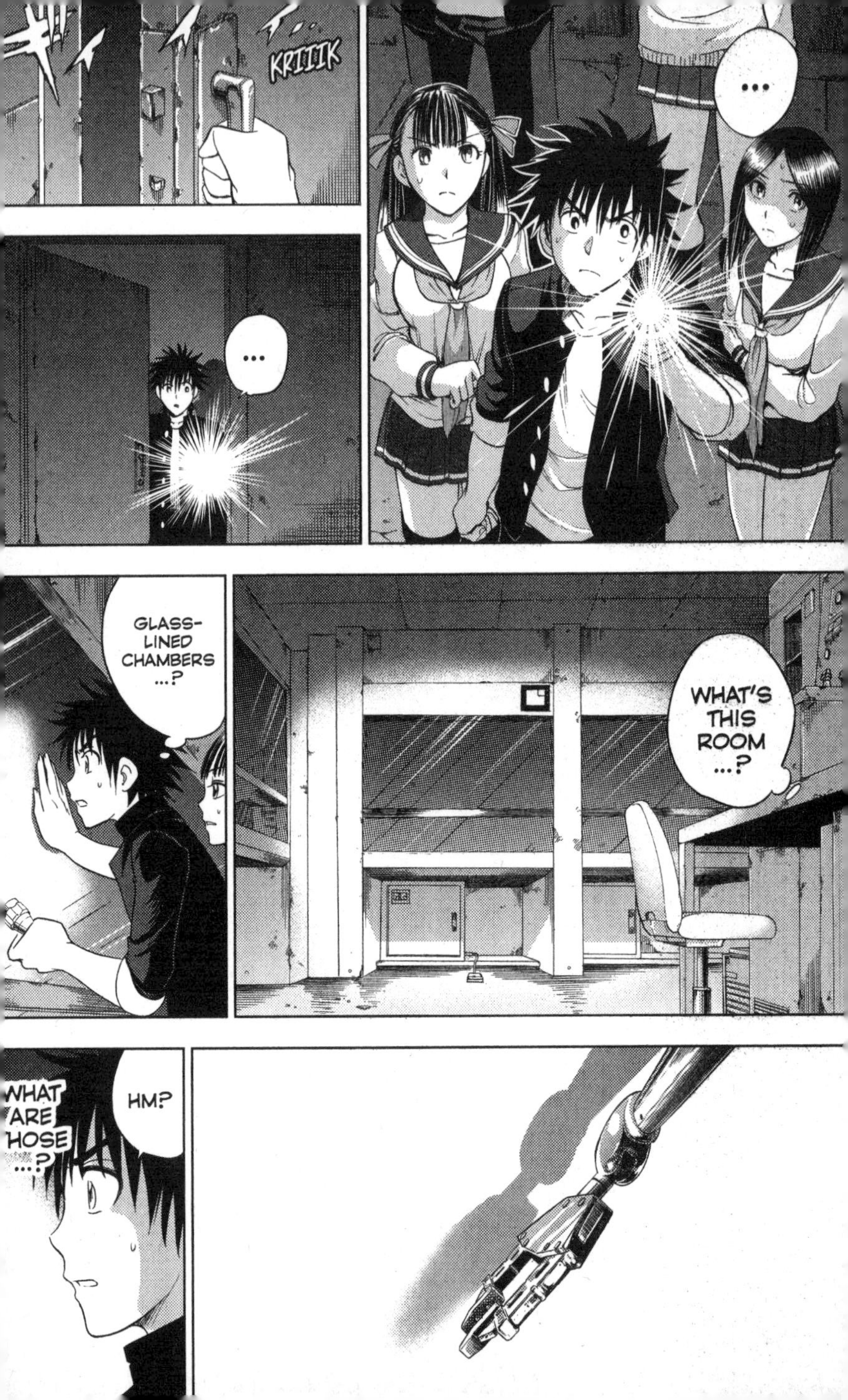
...
KRIIIK
...
WHAT'S THIS ROOM ...?
GLASS-LINED CHAMBERS ...?
HM?
WHAT ARE HOSE ...?

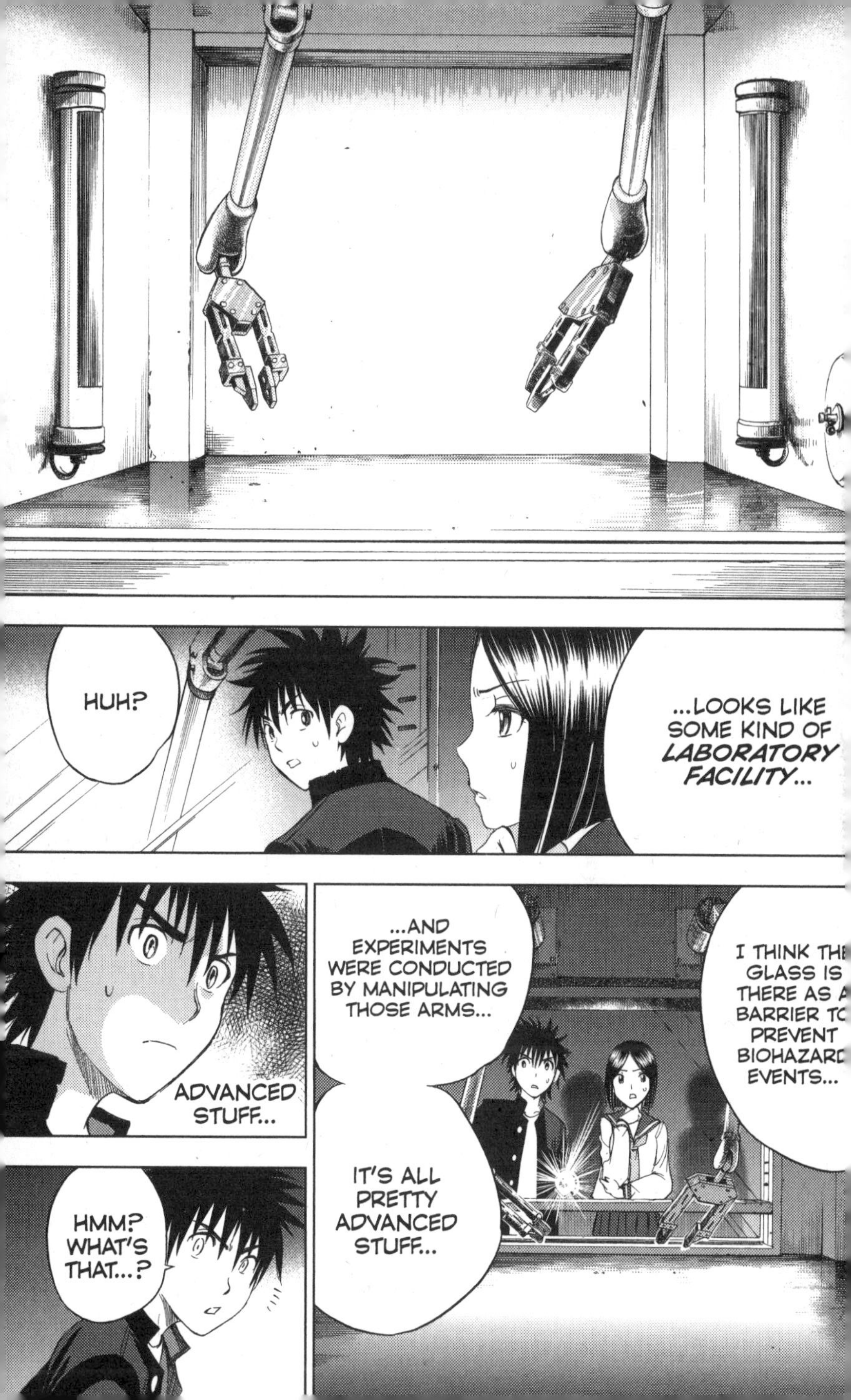
...LOOKS LIKE SOME KIND OF *LABORATORY FACILITY*...
HUH?
I THINK THE GLASS IS THERE AS A BARRIER TO PREVENT BIOHAZARD EVENTS...
...AND EXPERIMENTS WERE CONDUCTED BY MANIPULATING THOSE ARMS...
IT'S ALL PRETTY ADVANCED STUFF...
ADVANCED STUFF...
HMM? WHAT'S THAT...?

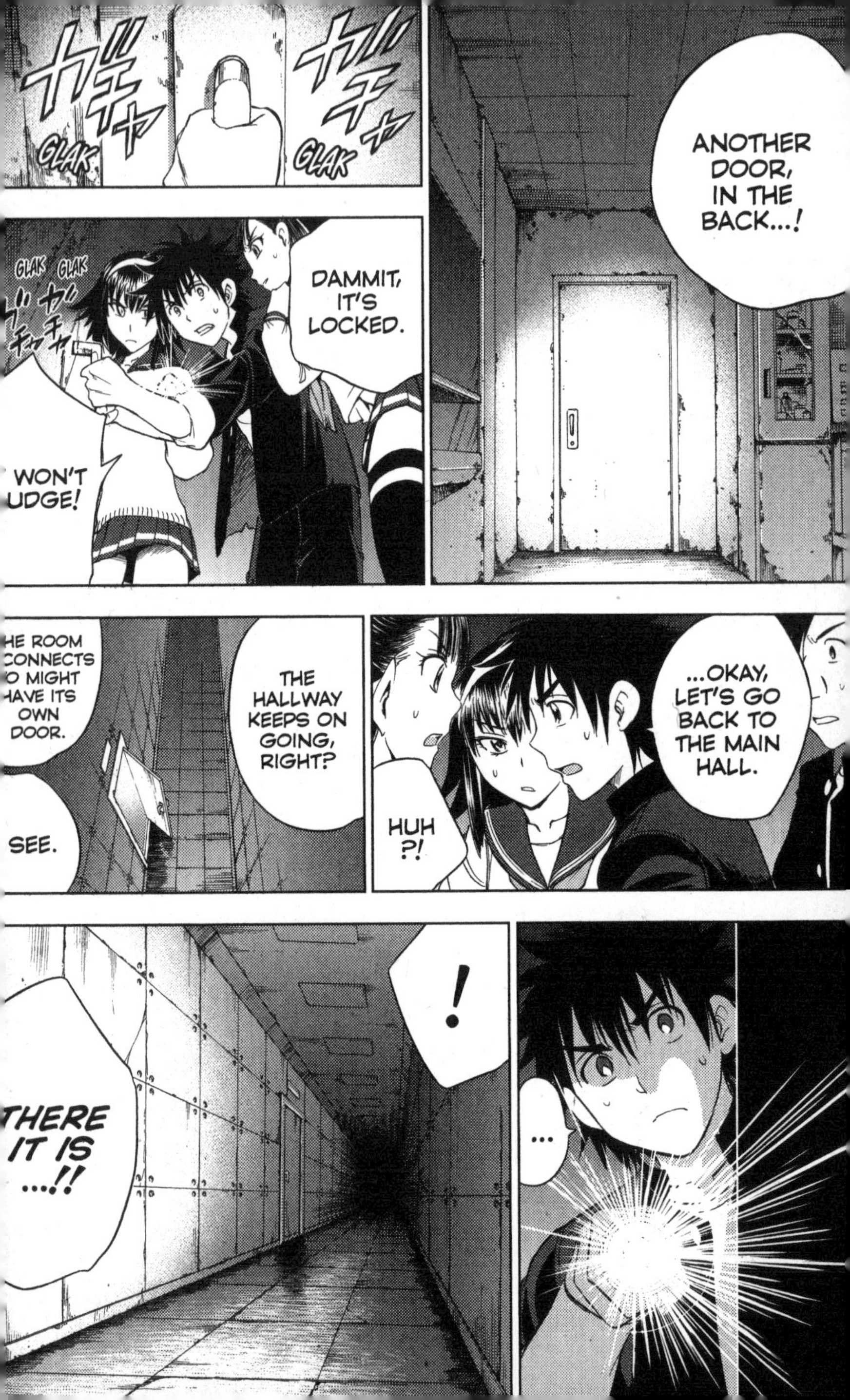

ANOTHER DOOR, IN THE BACK...!
GLAK
GLAK
GLAK GLAK
DAMMIT, IT'S LOCKED.
WON'T
UDGE!
...OKAY, LET'S GO BACK TO THE MAIN HALL.
HUH ?!
THE HALLWAY KEEPS ON GOING, RIGHT?
HE ROOM CONNECTS
O MIGHT HAVE ITS OWN DOOR.
SEE.
...
!
THERE IT IS ...!!

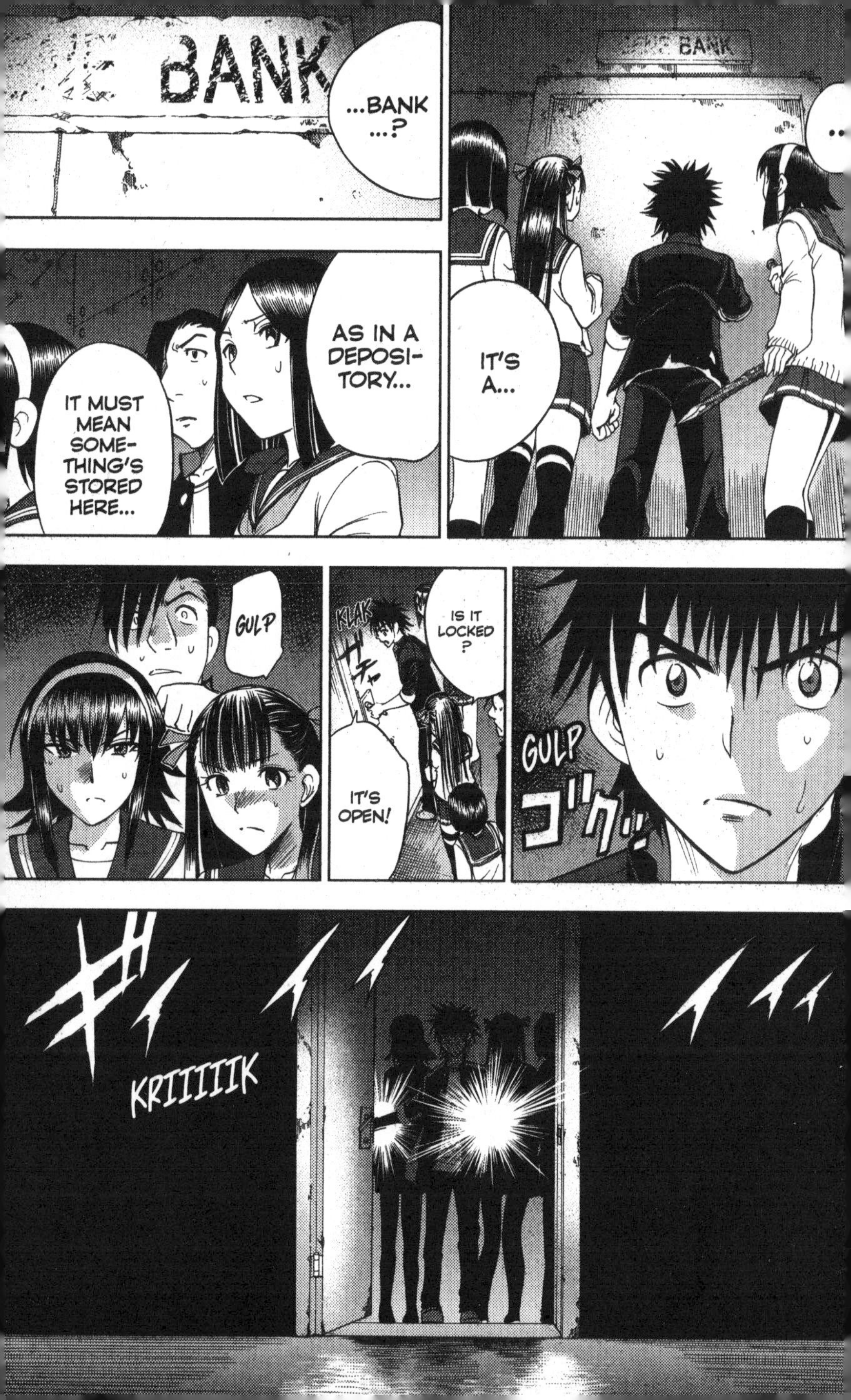

BANK
...
IT'S A...
BANK
...BANK ...?
AS IN A DEPOSITORY...
IT MUST MEAN SOMETHING'S STORED HERE...
GULP
ゴクッ
IS IT LOCKED?
KLAK
ガチャ
IT'S OPEN!
GULP
ギイイイ
KRIIIIIK

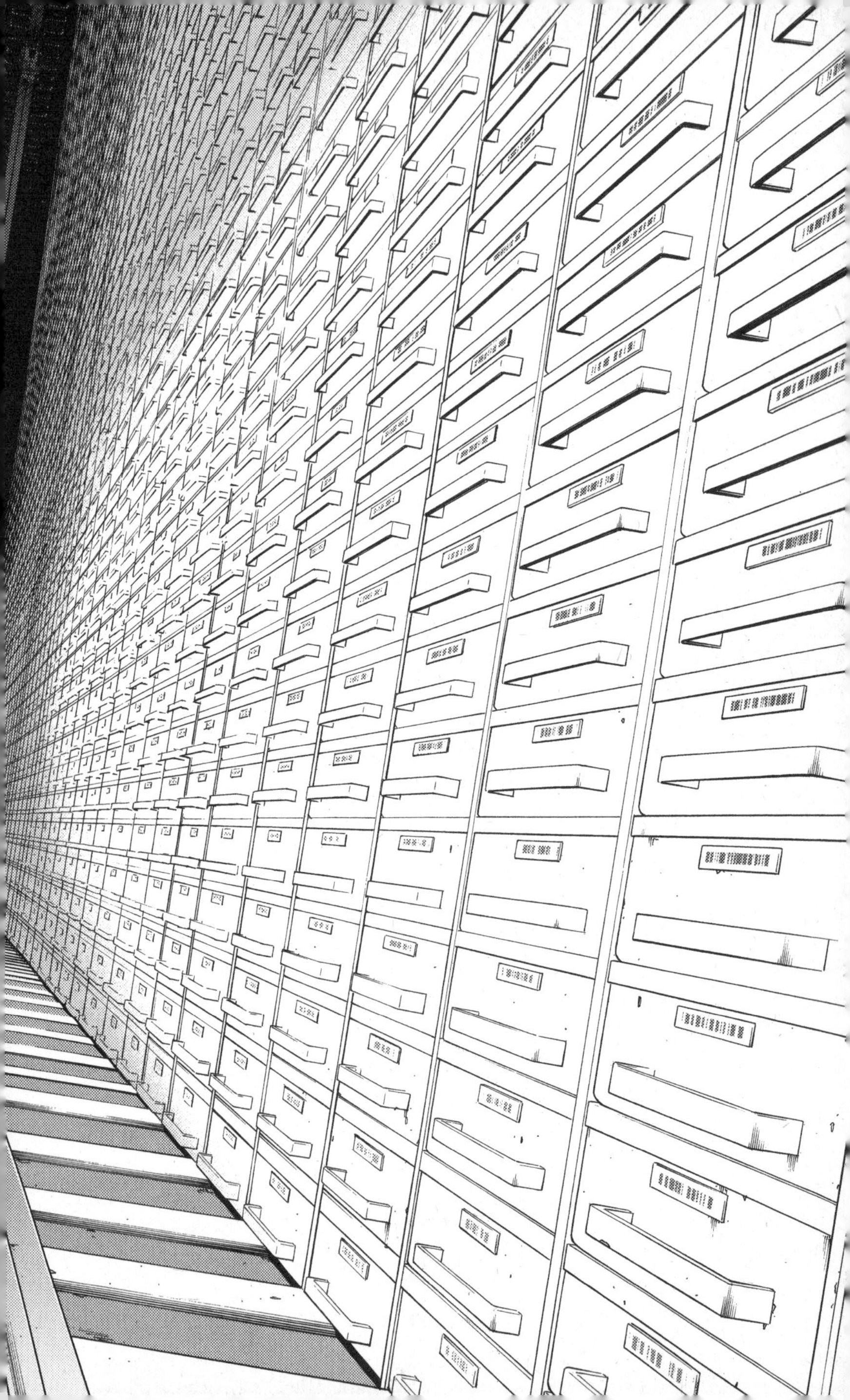

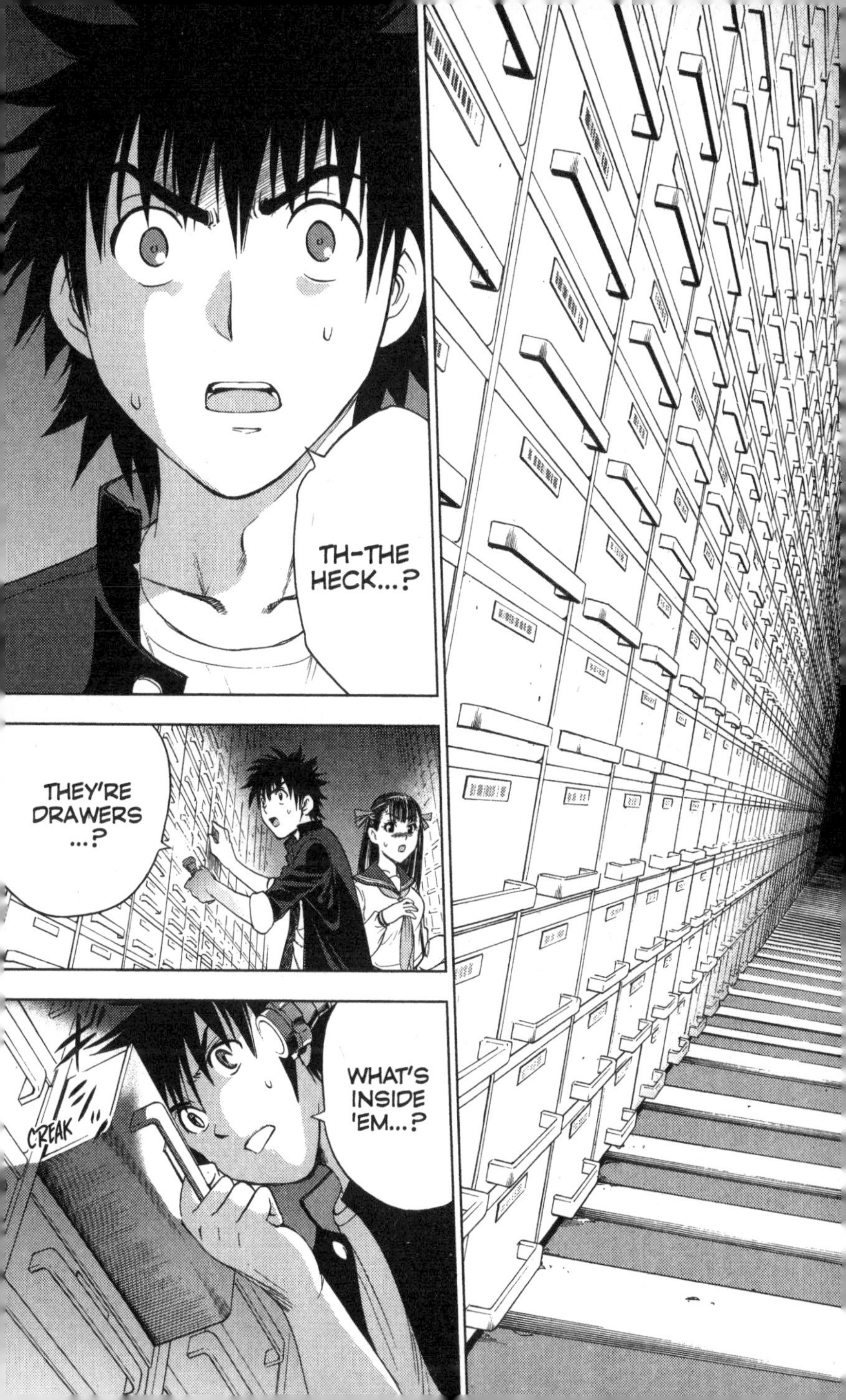
TH-THE HECK...?
THEY'RE DRAWERS ...?
WHAT'S INSIDE 'EM...?
CREAK

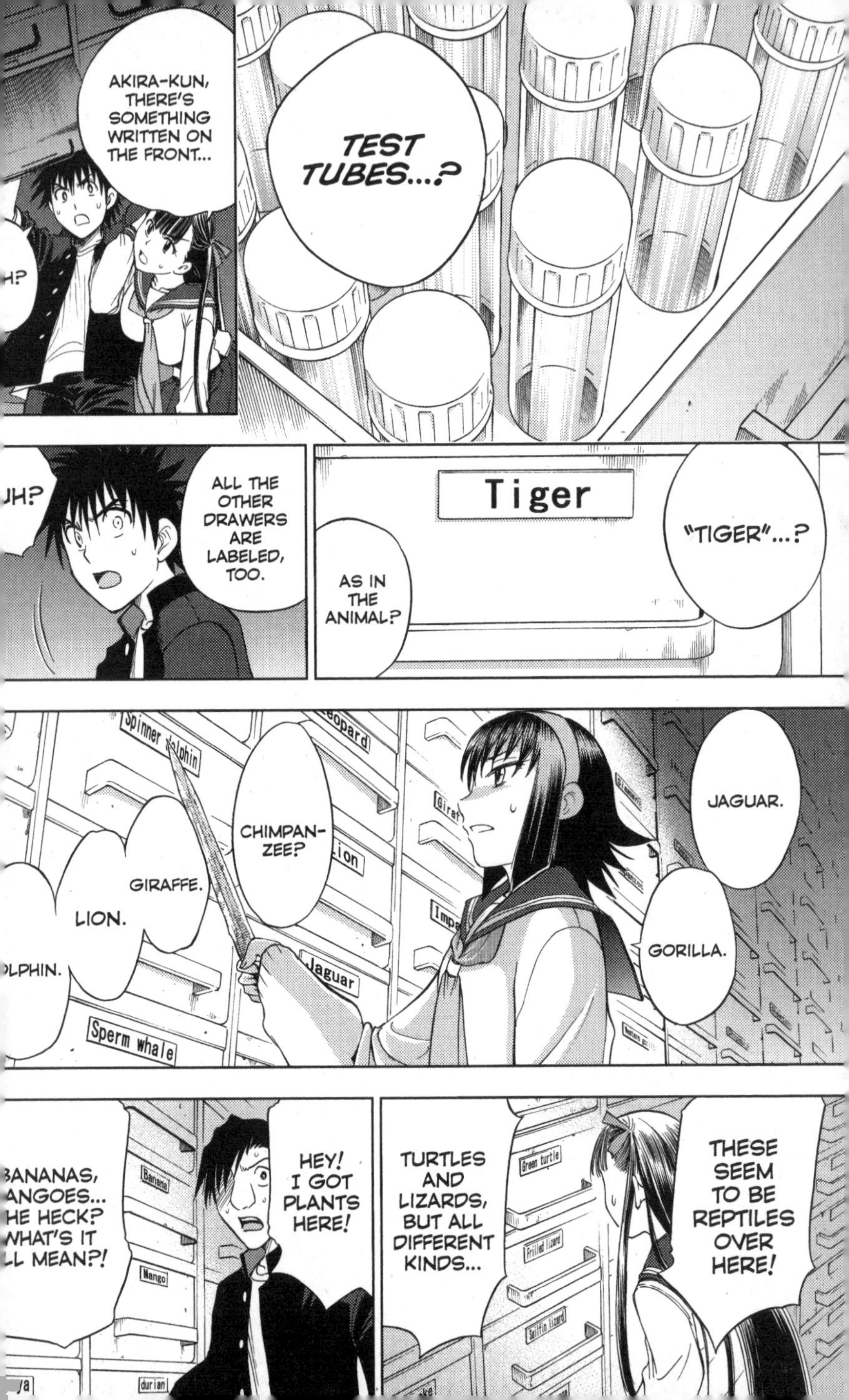
TEST TUBES...?
AKIRA-KUN, THERE'S SOMETHING WRITTEN ON THE FRONT...
H?
"TIGER"...?
Tiger
AS IN THE ANIMAL?
ALL THE OTHER DRAWERS ARE LABELED, TOO.
JH?
JAGUAR.
GORILLA.
CHIMPANZEE?
Leopard
Spinner dolphin
Jaguar
GIRAFFE.
LION.
LPHIN.
Sperm whale
THESE SEEM TO BE REPTILES OVER HERE!
TURTLES AND LIZARDS, BUT ALL DIFFERENT KINDS...
Green turtle
Frilled lizard
Sailfin lizard
HEY! I GOT PLANTS HERE!
BANANAS, ANGOES... HE HECK? WHAT'S IT LL MEAN?!
Banana
Mango
durian

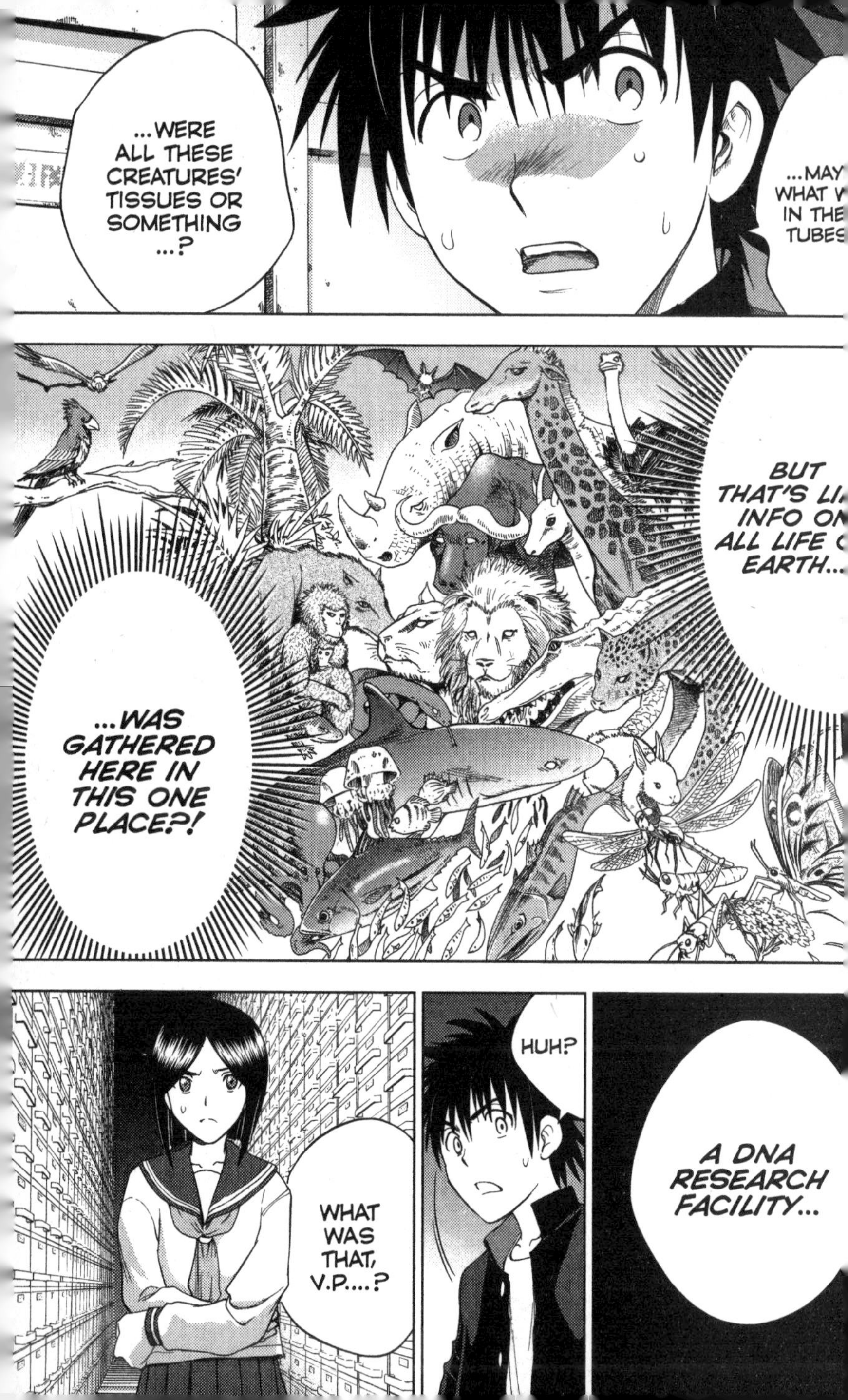
...MAY WHAT W IN THE TUBES
...WERE ALL THESE CREATURES' TISSUES OR SOMETHING ...?
BUT THAT'S LI INFO ON ALL LIFE EARTH...
...WAS GATHERED HERE IN THIS ONE PLACE?!
A DNA RESEARCH FACILITY...
HUH?
WHAT WAS THAT, V.P....?

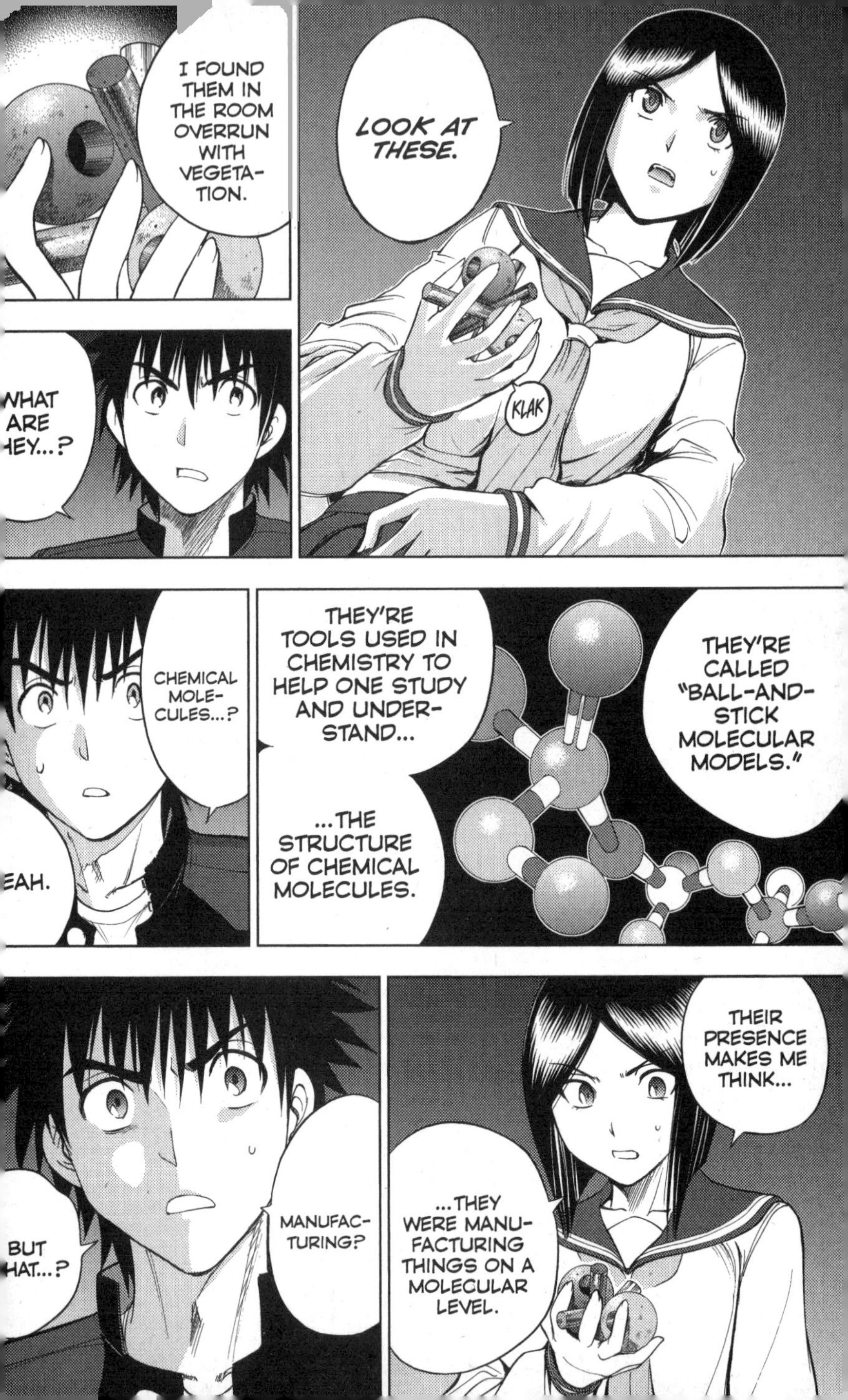
LOOK AT THESE.
KLAK
I FOUND THEM IN THE ROOM OVERRUN WITH VEGETATION.
WHAT ARE HEY...?
THEY'RE CALLED "BALL-AND-STICK MOLECULAR MODELS."
THEY'RE TOOLS USED IN CHEMISTRY TO HELP ONE STUDY AND UNDERSTAND...
...THE STRUCTURE OF CHEMICAL MOLECULES.
CHEMICAL MOLECULES...?
EAH.
THEIR PRESENCE MAKES ME THINK...
...THEY WERE MANUFACTURING THINGS ON A MOLECULAR LEVEL.
MANUFACTURING?
BUT HAT...?

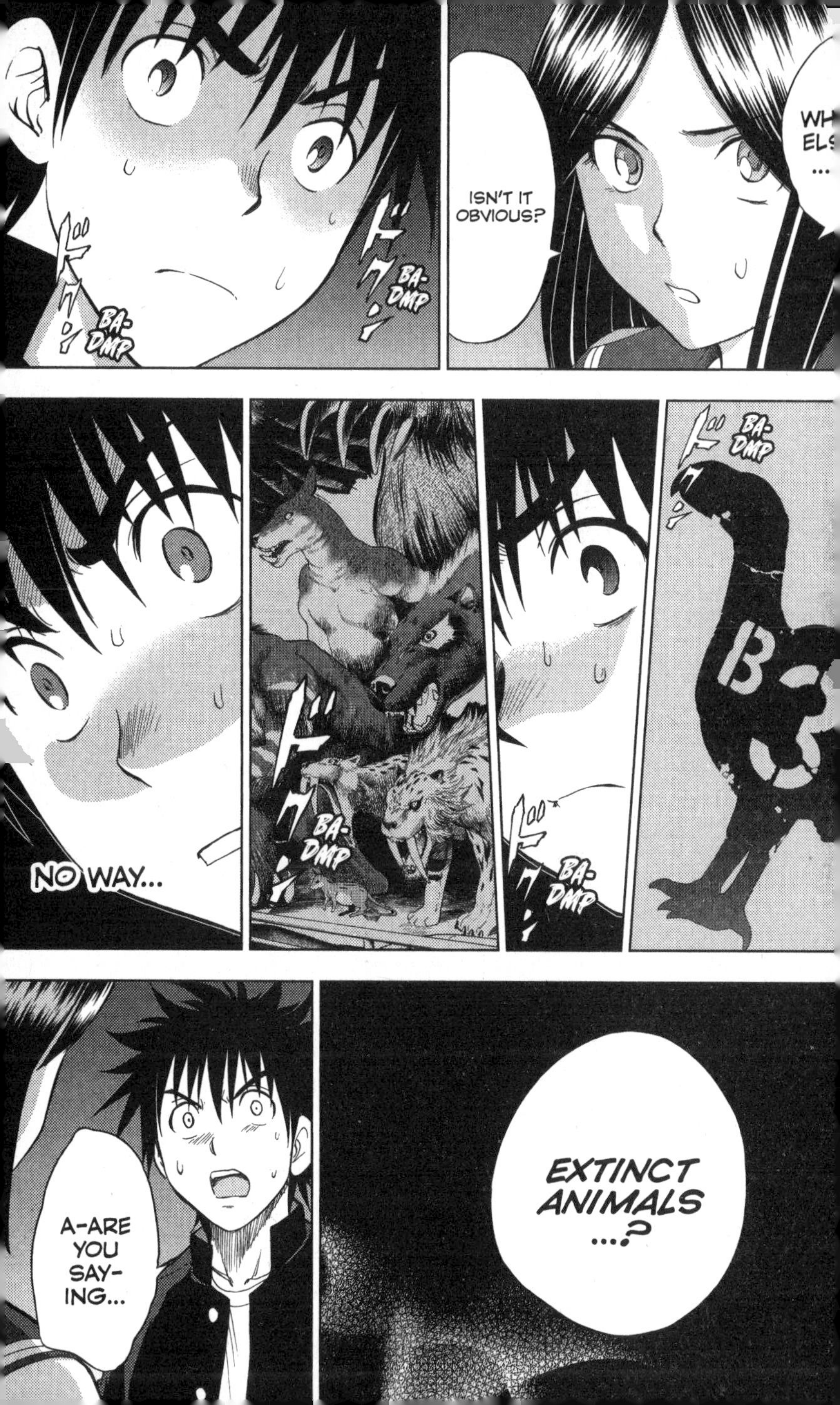
WH
ELS
...
ISN'T IT OBVIOUS?
BA-DMP
BA-DMP
BA-DMP
BA-DMP
BA-DMP
NO WAY...
EXTINCT ANIMALS ...?
A-ARE YOU SAY-ING...

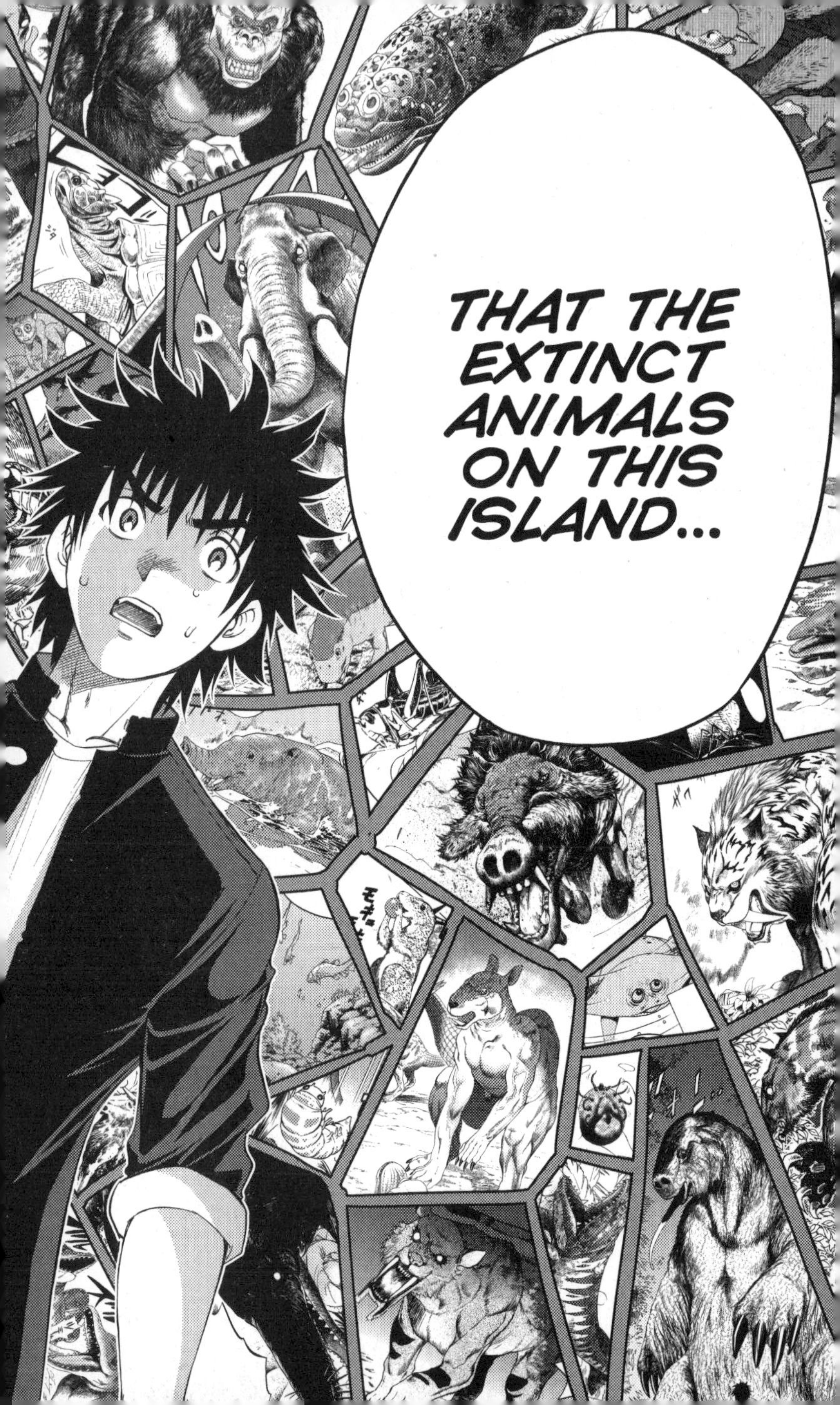
THAT THE EXTINCT ANIMALS ON THIS ISLAND...

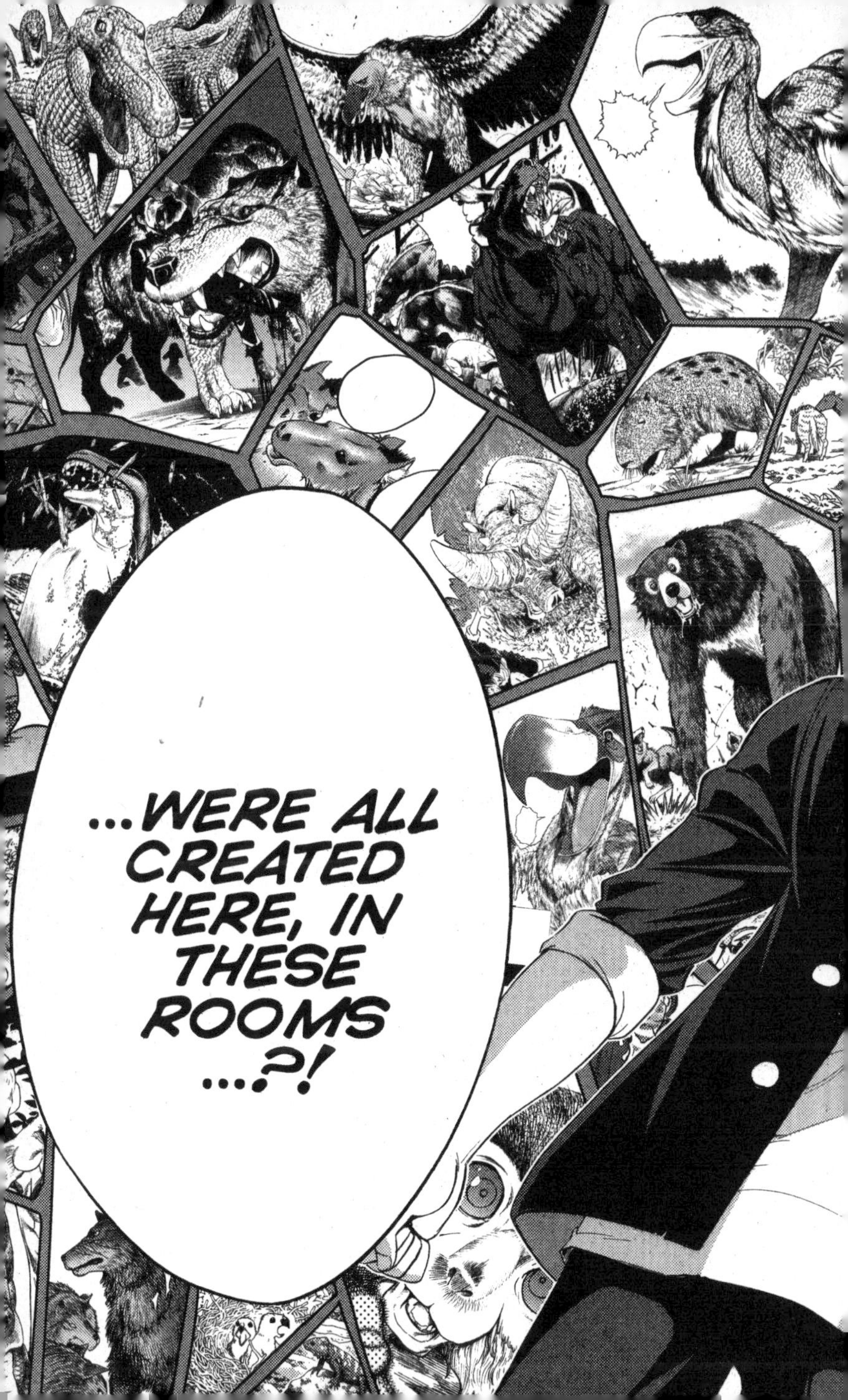
...WERE ALL CREATED HERE, IN THESE ROOMS ...?!

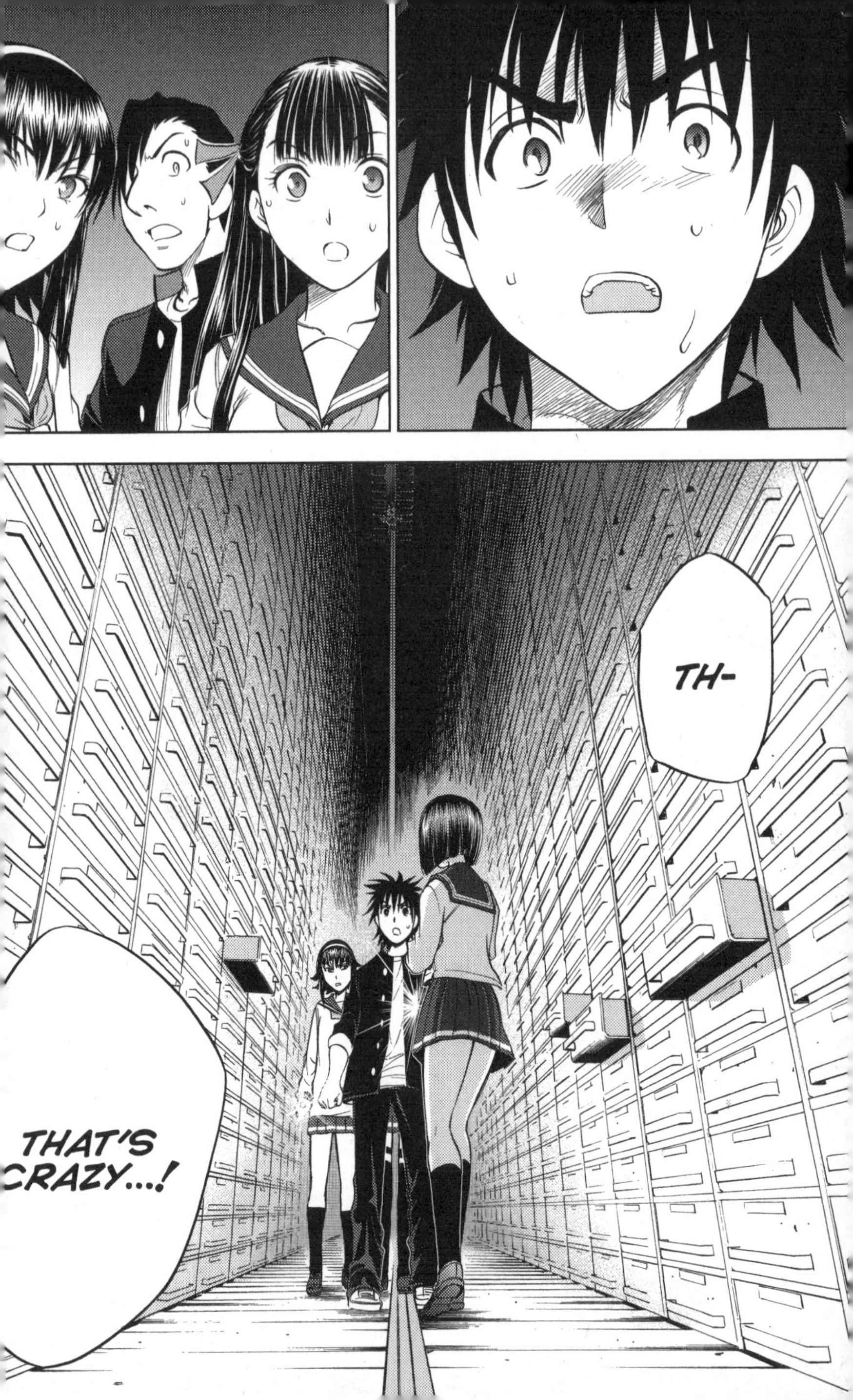
TH-
THAT'S CRAZY...!

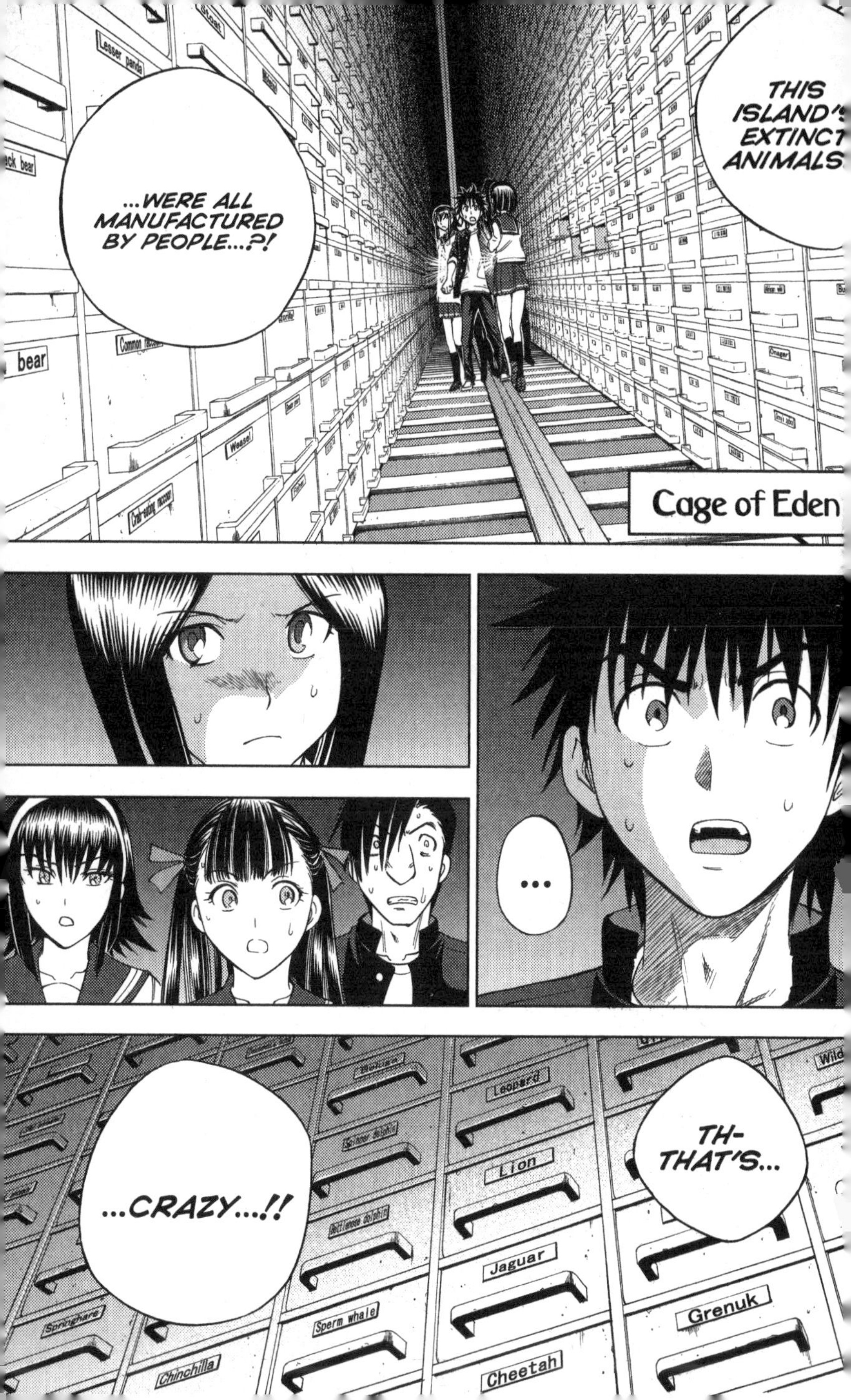
THIS ISLAND'S EXTINCT ANIMALS
...WERE ALL MANUFACTURED BY PEOPLE...?!
Lesser panda
Stoat
bear
Weasel
Crab-eating raccoon
Onager
Cage of Eden
...
TH- THAT'S...
...CRAZY...!!
Leopard
Lion
Jaguar
Grenuk
Cheetah
Sperm whale
Springhare
Chinchilla

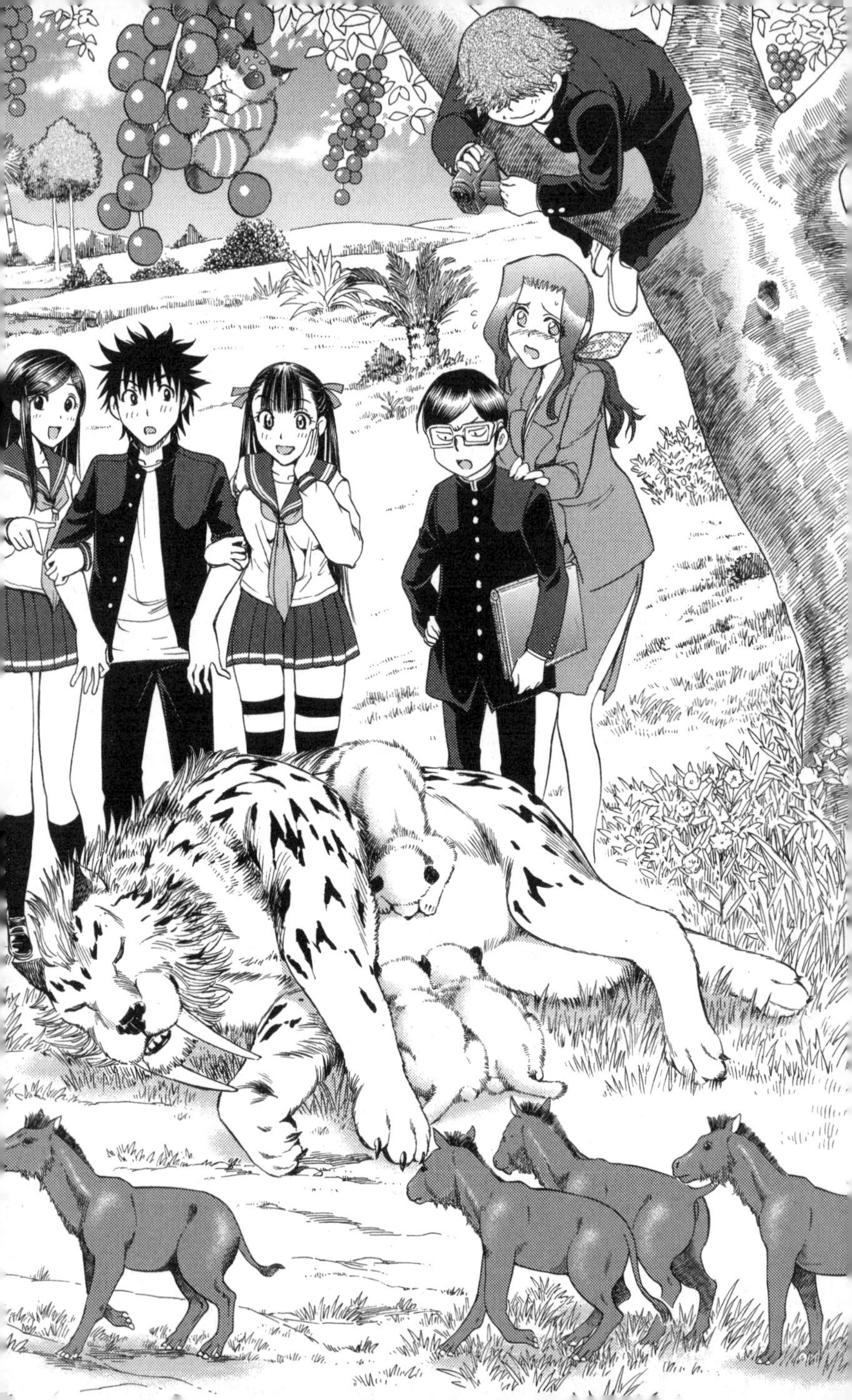

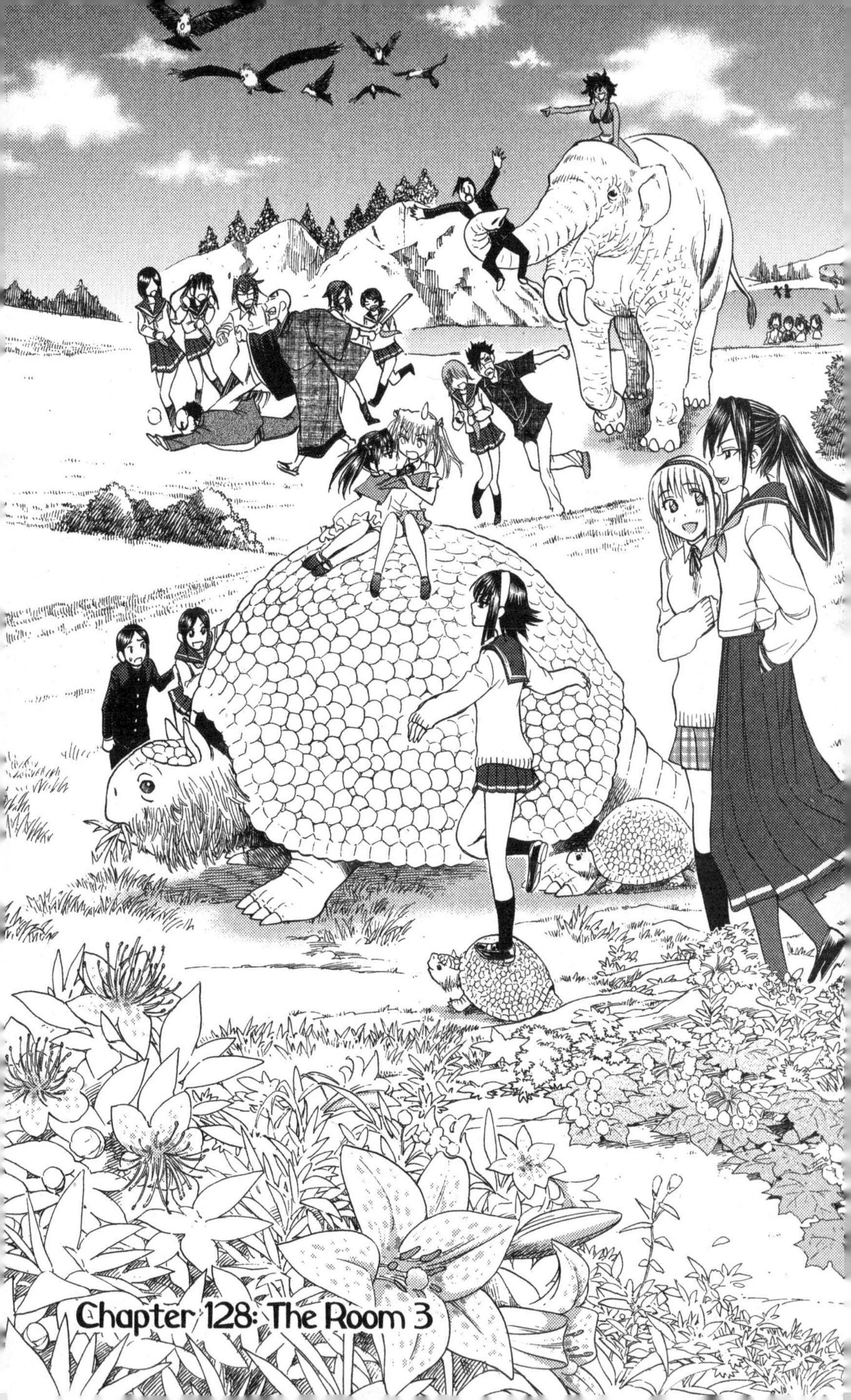
Chapter 128: The Room 3

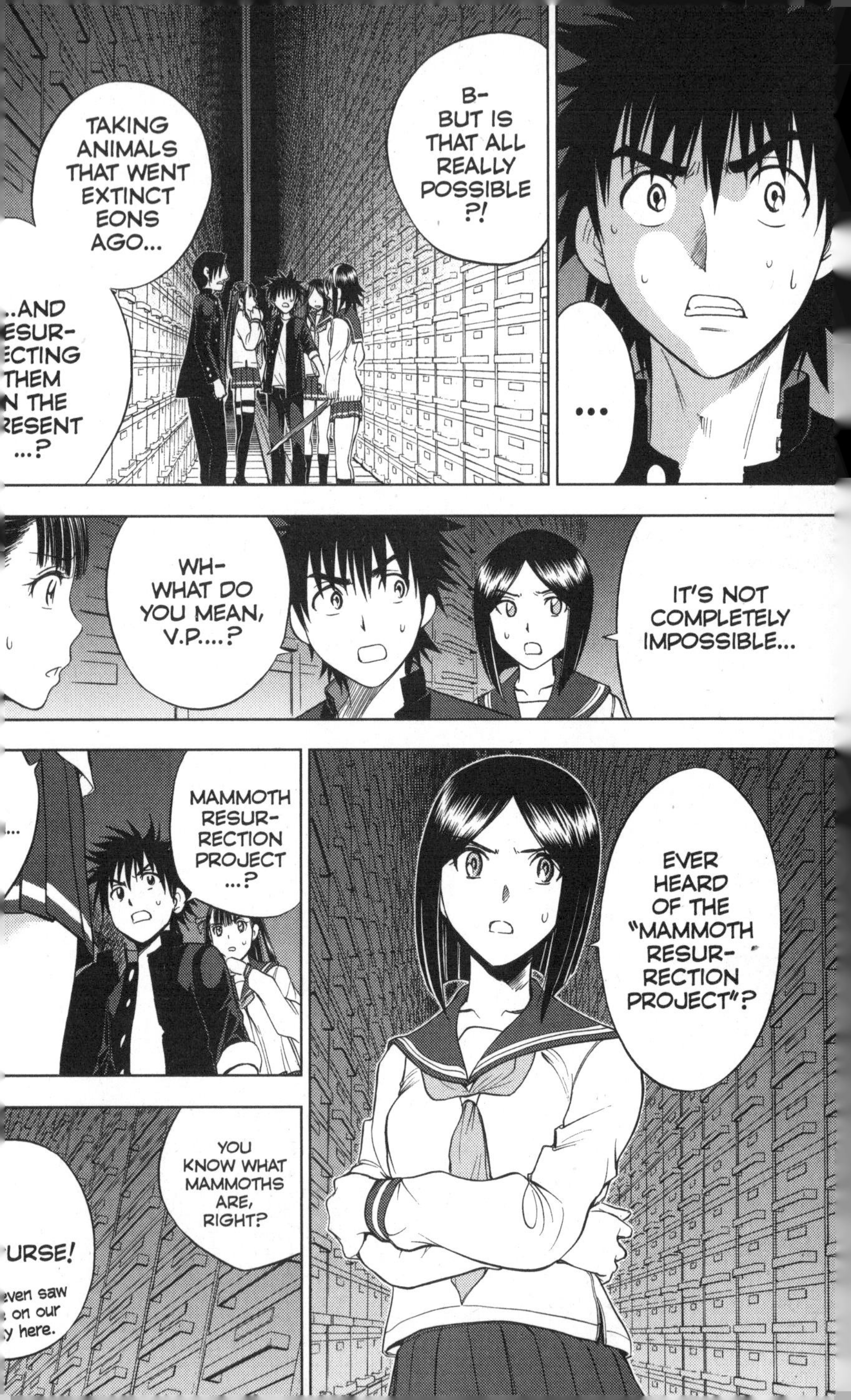
...
B- BUT IS THAT ALL REALLY POSSIBLE?!
TAKING ANIMALS THAT WENT EXTINCT EONS AGO...
..AND ESUR- ECTING THEM N THE RESENT ...?
IT'S NOT COMPLETELY IMPOSSIBLE...
WH- WHAT DO YOU MEAN, V.P....?
EVER HEARD OF THE "MAMMOTH RESURRECTION PROJECT"?
MAMMOTH RESURRECTION PROJECT ...?
YOU KNOW WHAT MAMMOTHS ARE, RIGHT?
URSE!
even saw on our y here.

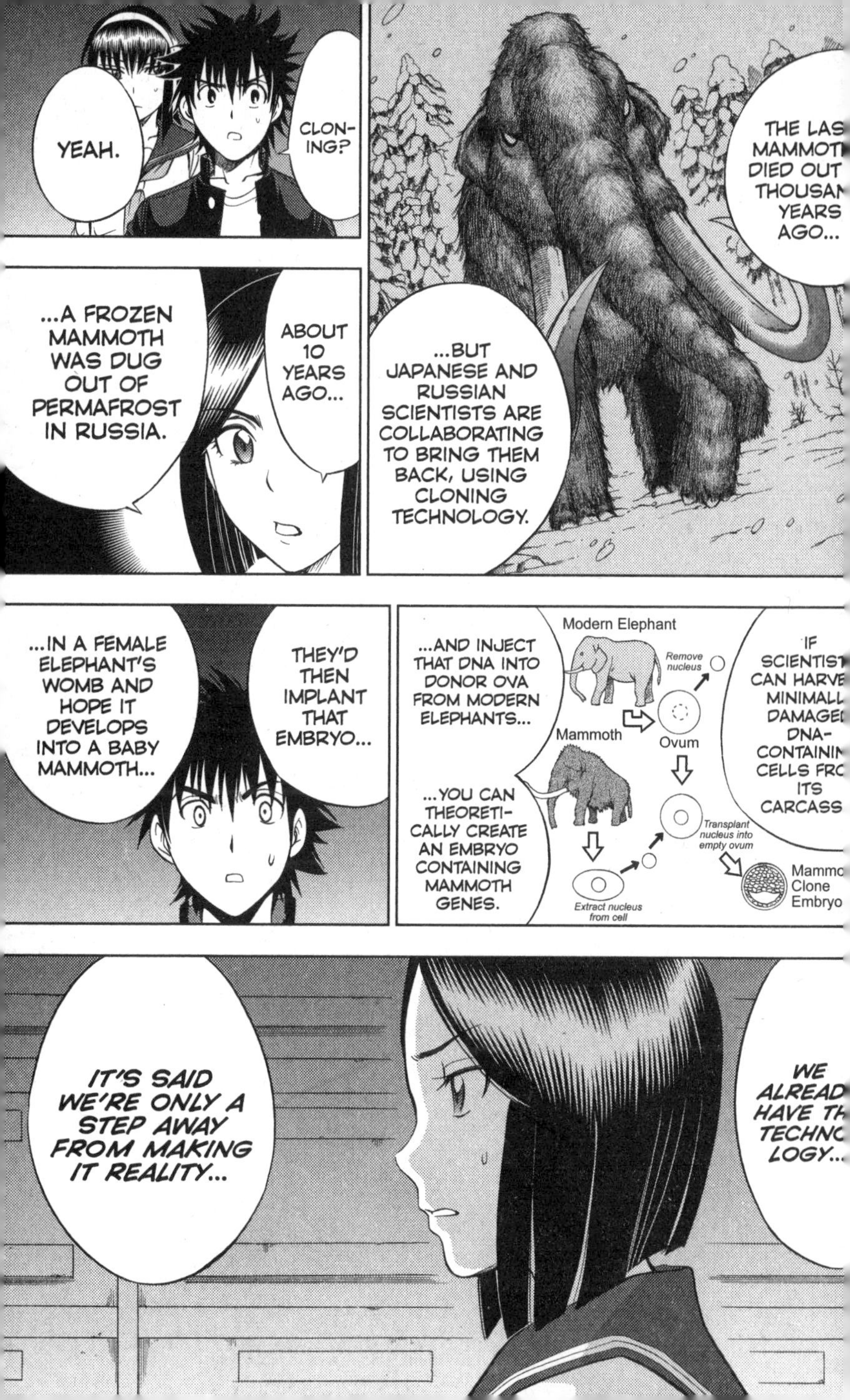
THE LAS MAMMOT DIED OUT THOUSAN YEARS AGO...
...BUT JAPANESE AND RUSSIAN SCIENTISTS ARE COLLABORATING TO BRING THEM BACK, USING CLONING TECHNOLOGY.
CLON-ING?
YEAH.
ABOUT 10 YEARS AGO...
...A FROZEN MAMMOTH WAS DUG OUT OF PERMAFROST IN RUSSIA.
IF SCIENTIST CAN HARVE MINIMALL DAMAGEI DNA-CONTAININ CELLS FRO ITS CARCASS
...AND INJECT THAT DNA INTO DONOR OVA FROM MODERN ELEPHANTS...
...YOU CAN THEORETI-CALLY CREATE AN EMBRYO CONTAINING MAMMOTH GENES.
Modern Elephant
Remove nucleus
Ovum
Mammoth
Transplant nucleus into empty ovum
Extract nucleus from cell
Mammo Clone Embryo
THEY'D THEN IMPLANT THAT EMBRYO...
...IN A FEMALE ELEPHANT'S WOMB AND HOPE IT DEVELOPS INTO A BABY MAMMOTH...
WE ALREAD HAVE TH TECHNC LOGY...
IT'S SAID WE'RE ONLY A STEP AWAY FROM MAKING IT REALITY...

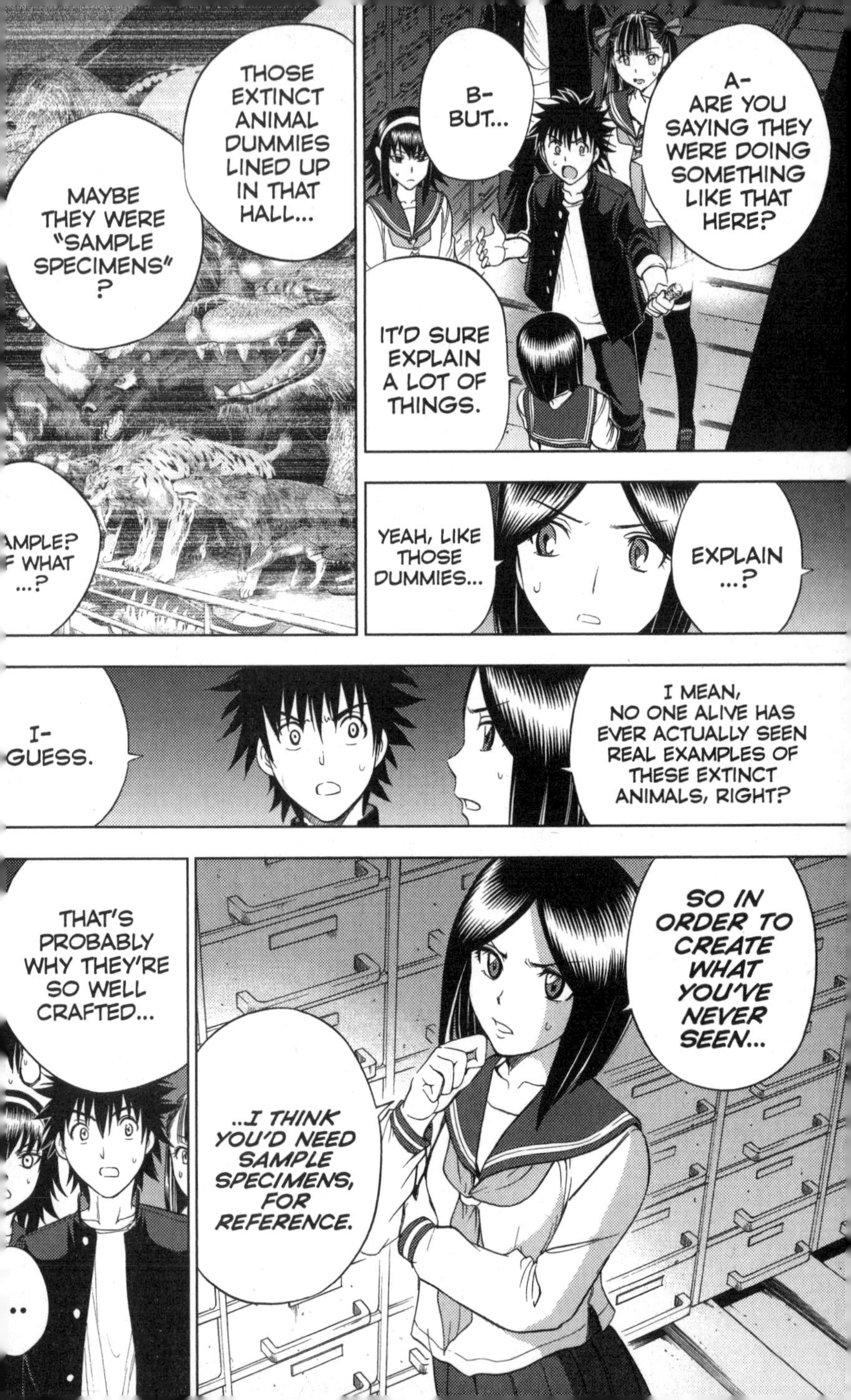
A- ARE YOU SAYING THEY WERE DOING SOMETHING LIKE THAT HERE?
B- BUT...
IT'D SURE EXPLAIN A LOT OF THINGS.
THOSE EXTINCT ANIMAL DUMMIES LINED UP IN THAT HALL...
MAYBE THEY WERE "SAMPLE SPECIMENS"?
AMPLE? F WHAT ...?
EXPLAIN ...?
YEAH, LIKE THOSE DUMMIES...
I MEAN, NO ONE ALIVE HAS EVER ACTUALLY SEEN REAL EXAMPLES OF THESE EXTINCT ANIMALS, RIGHT?
I- GUESS.
SO IN ORDER TO CREATE WHAT YOU'VE NEVER SEEN...
...I THINK YOU'D NEED SAMPLE SPECIMENS, FOR REFERENCE.
THAT'S PROBABLY WHY THEY'RE SO WELL CRAFTED...
..

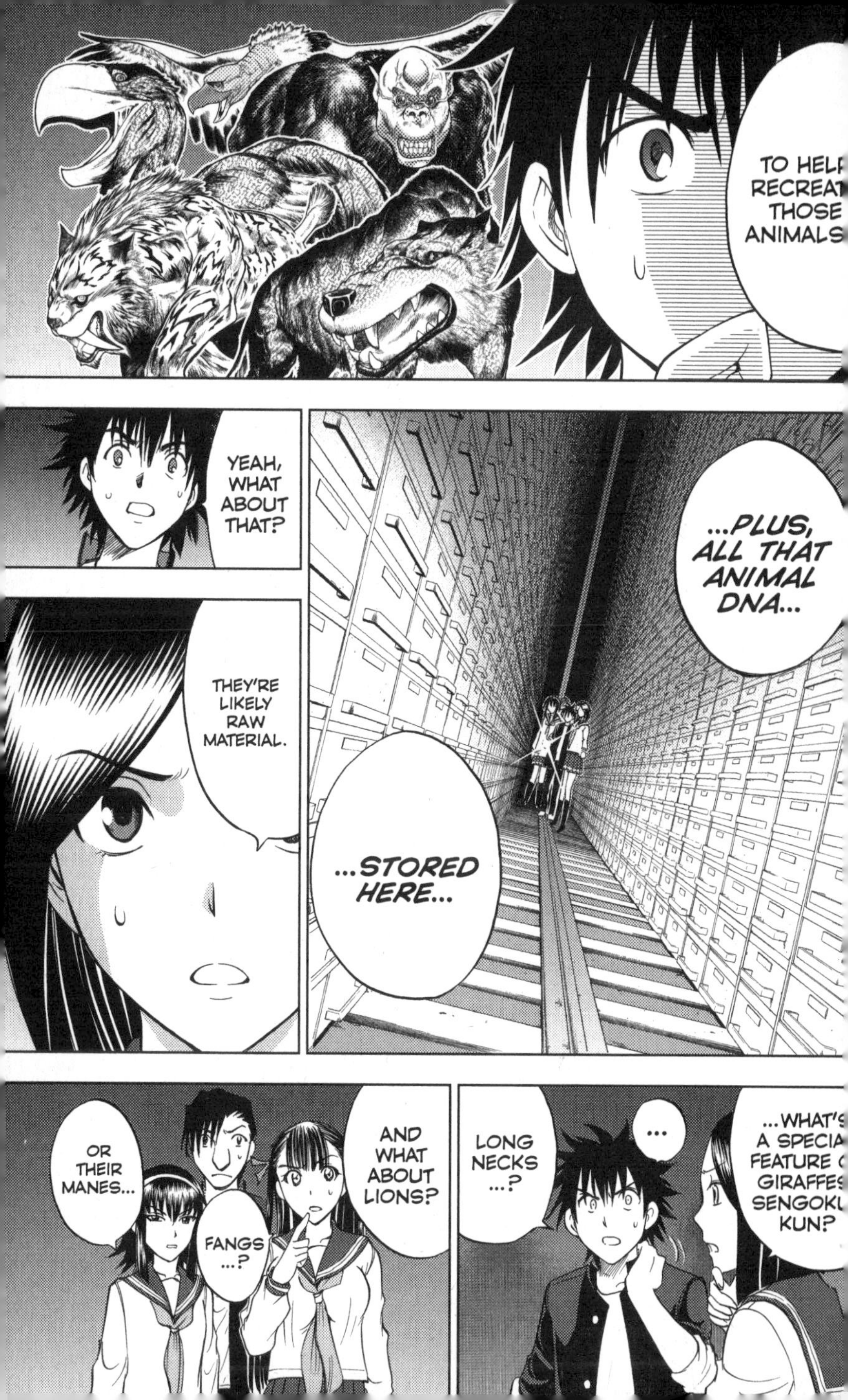
TO HELP RECREAT THOSE ANIMALS
...PLUS, ALL THAT ANIMAL DNA...
...STORED HERE...
YEAH, WHAT ABOUT THAT?
THEY'RE LIKELY RAW MATERIAL.
...WHAT'S A SPECIA FEATURE GIRAFFES SENGOKU KUN?
...
LONG NECKS ...?
AND WHAT ABOUT LIONS?
FANGS ...?
OR THEIR MANES...

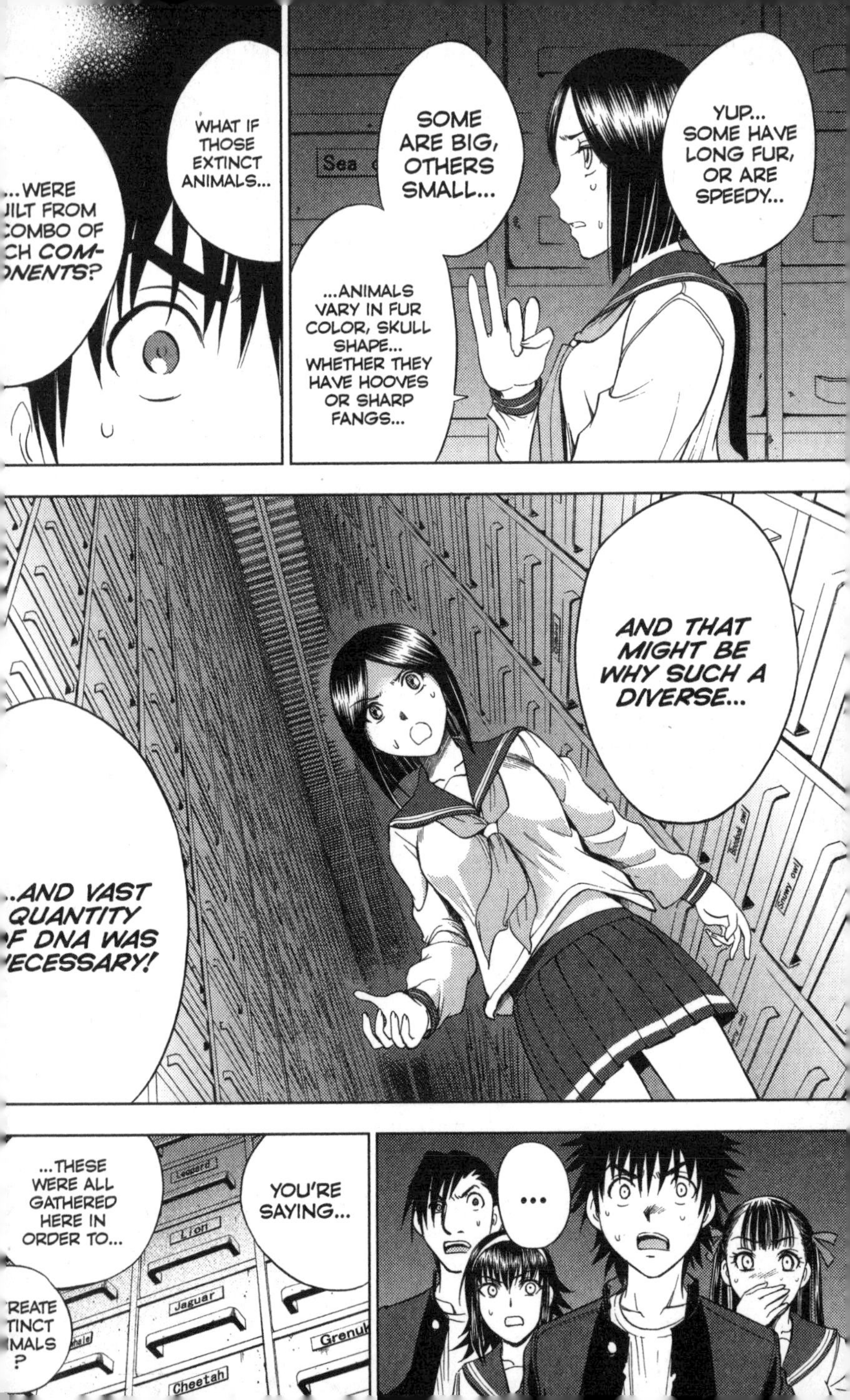
YUP... SOME HAVE LONG FUR, OR ARE SPEEDY...
SOME ARE BIG, OTHERS SMALL...
...ANIMALS VARY IN FUR COLOR, SKULL SHAPE... WHETHER THEY HAVE HOOVES OR SHARP FANGS...
WHAT IF THOSE EXTINCT ANIMALS...
...WERE UILT FROM OMBO OF CH COM- ONENTS?
AND THAT MIGHT BE WHY SUCH A DIVERSE...
..AND VAST QUANTITY F DNA WAS ECESSARY!
...
YOU'RE SAYING...
...THESE WERE ALL GATHERED HERE IN ORDER TO...
REATE TINCT MALS ?
Lion
Jaguar
Cheetah

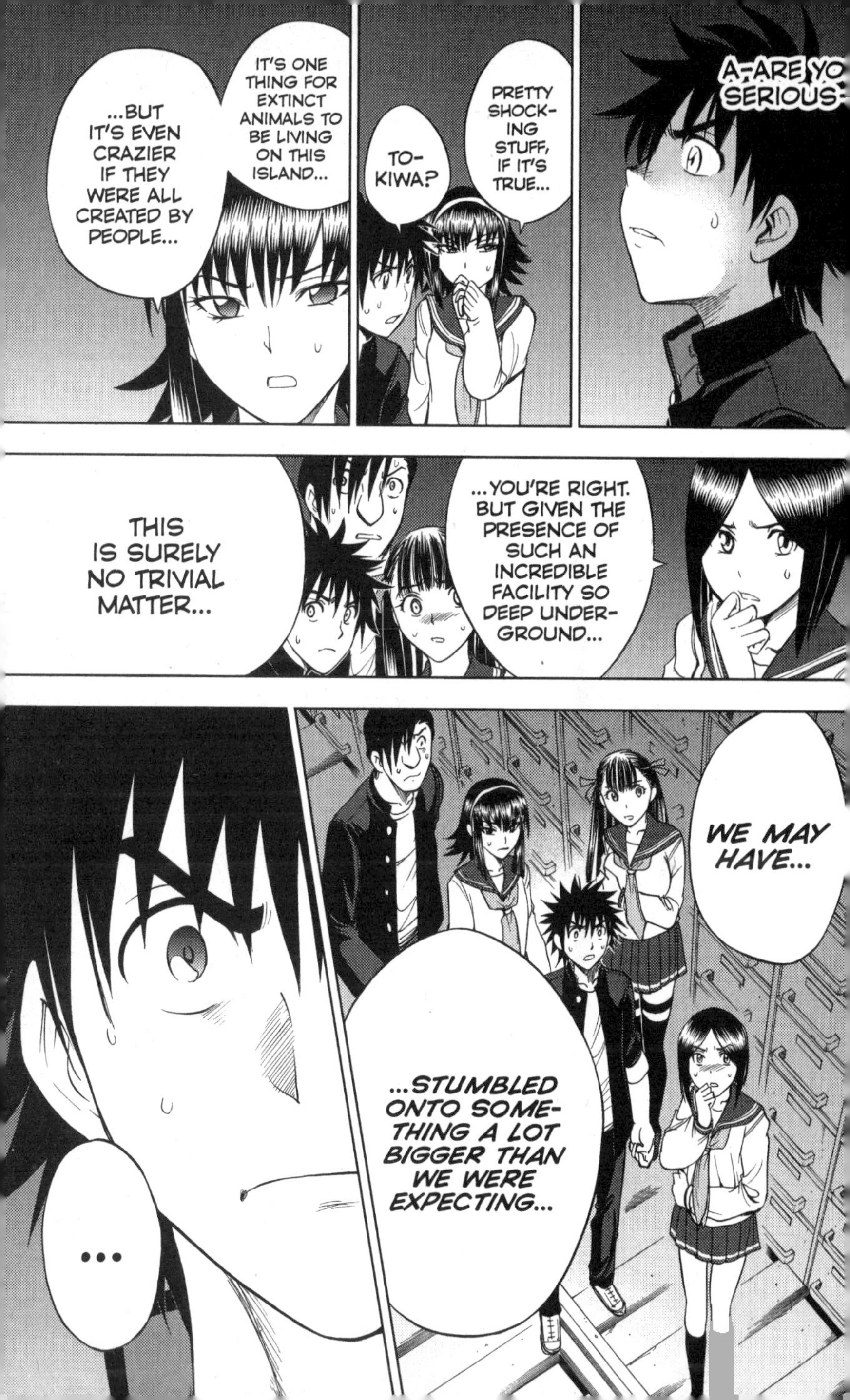
A-ARE YO SERIOUS-
PRETTY SHOCKING STUFF, IF IT'S TRUE...
TO-KIWA?
IT'S ONE THING FOR EXTINCT ANIMALS TO BE LIVING ON THIS ISLAND...
...BUT IT'S EVEN CRAZIER IF THEY WERE ALL CREATED BY PEOPLE...
...YOU'RE RIGHT. BUT GIVEN THE PRESENCE OF SUCH AN INCREDIBLE FACILITY SO DEEP UNDER-GROUND...
THIS IS SURELY NO TRIVIAL MATTER...
WE MAY HAVE...
...STUMBLED ONTO SOME-THING A LOT BIGGER THAN WE WERE EXPECTING...
...

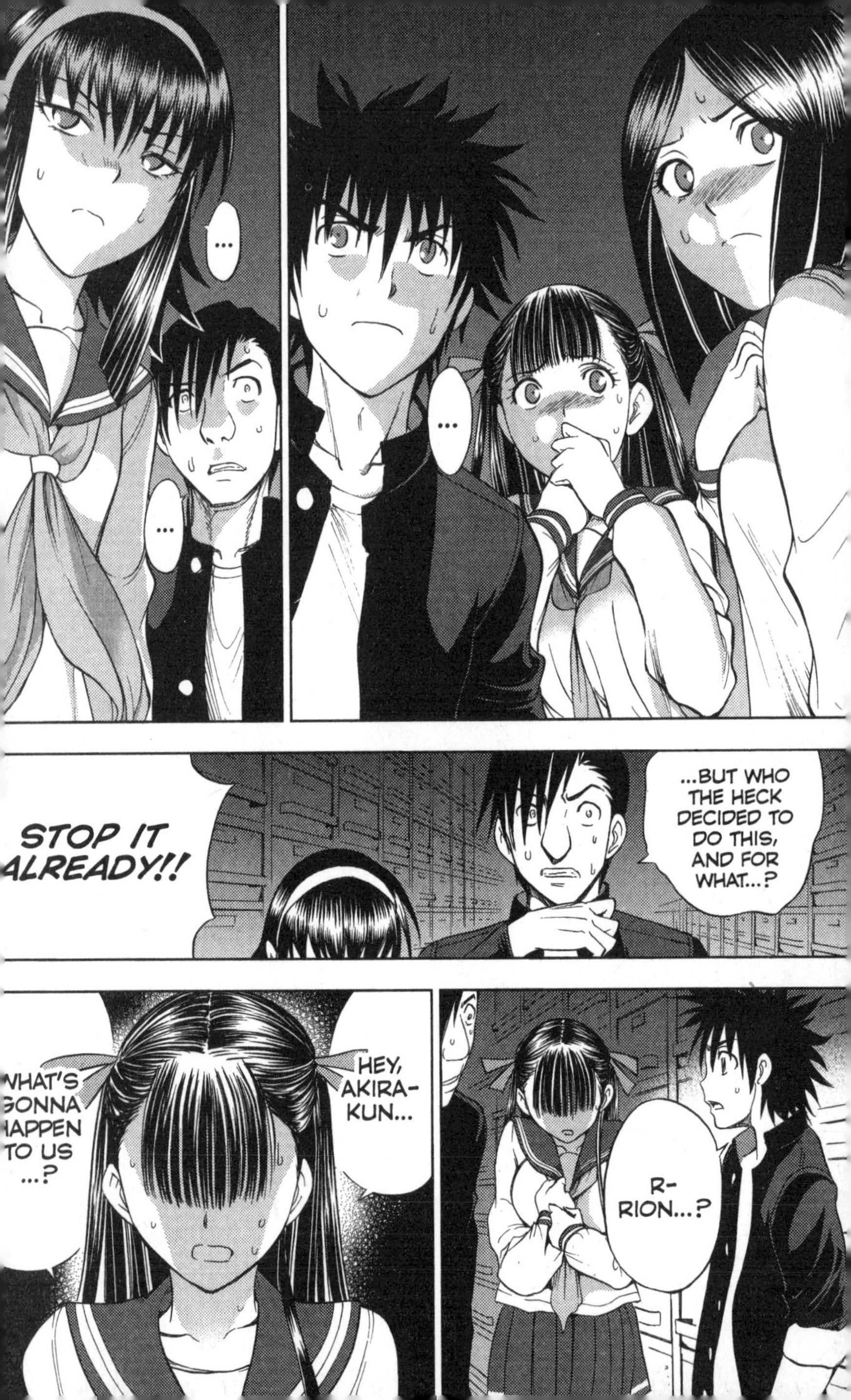
...
...
...
...BUT WHO THE HECK DECIDED TO DO THIS, AND FOR WHAT...?
STOP IT ALREADY!!
R-RION...?
HEY, AKIRA-KUN...
WHAT'S GONNA HAPPEN TO US ...?

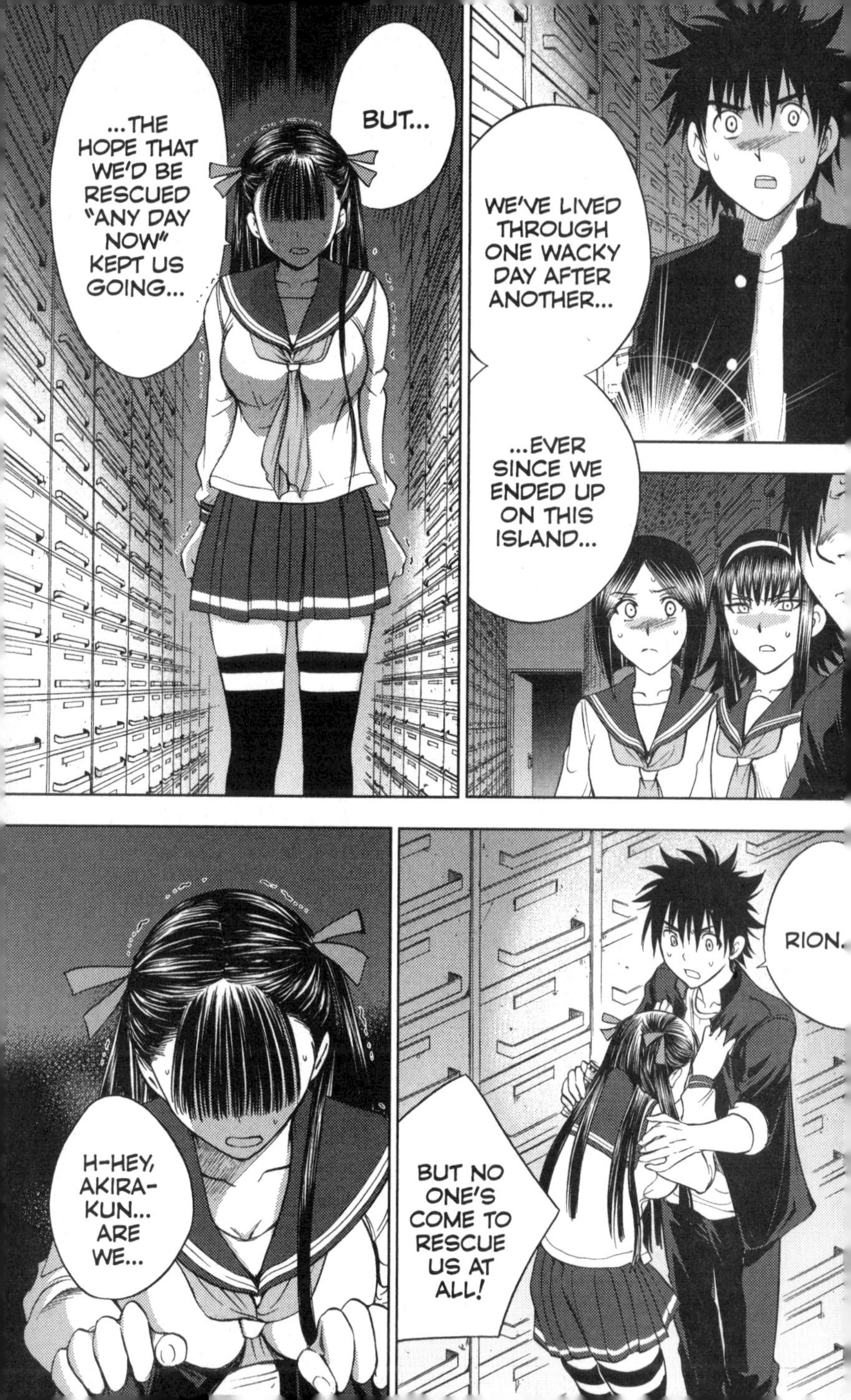
WE'VE LIVED THROUGH ONE WACKY DAY AFTER ANOTHER...
...EVER SINCE WE ENDED UP ON THIS ISLAND...
BUT...
...THE HOPE THAT WE'D BE RESCUED "ANY DAY NOW" KEPT US GOING...
RION.
BUT NO ONE'S COME TO RESCUE US AT ALL!
H-HEY, AKIRA-KUN... ARE WE...

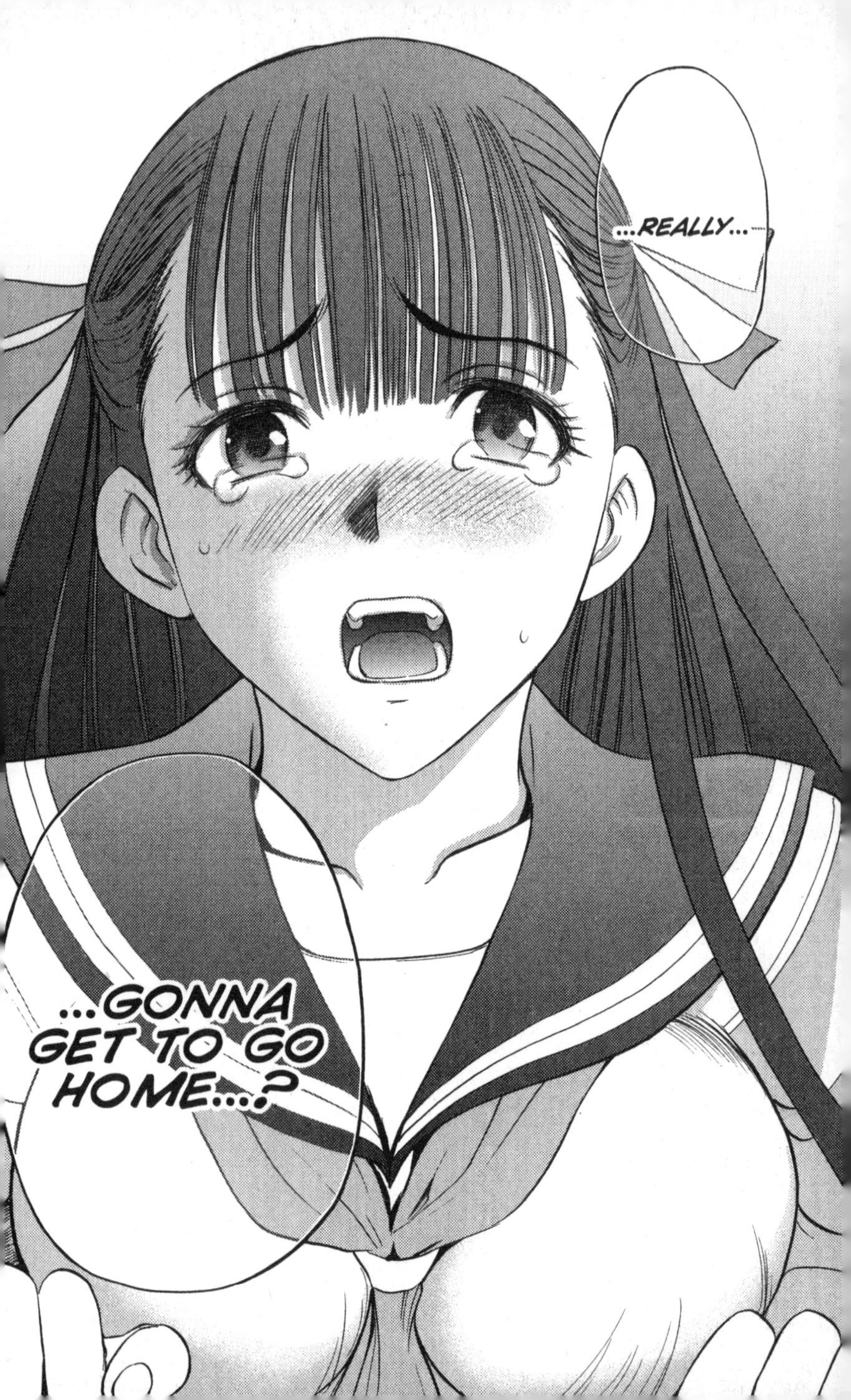
...REALLY...
...GONNA GET TO GO HOME...?

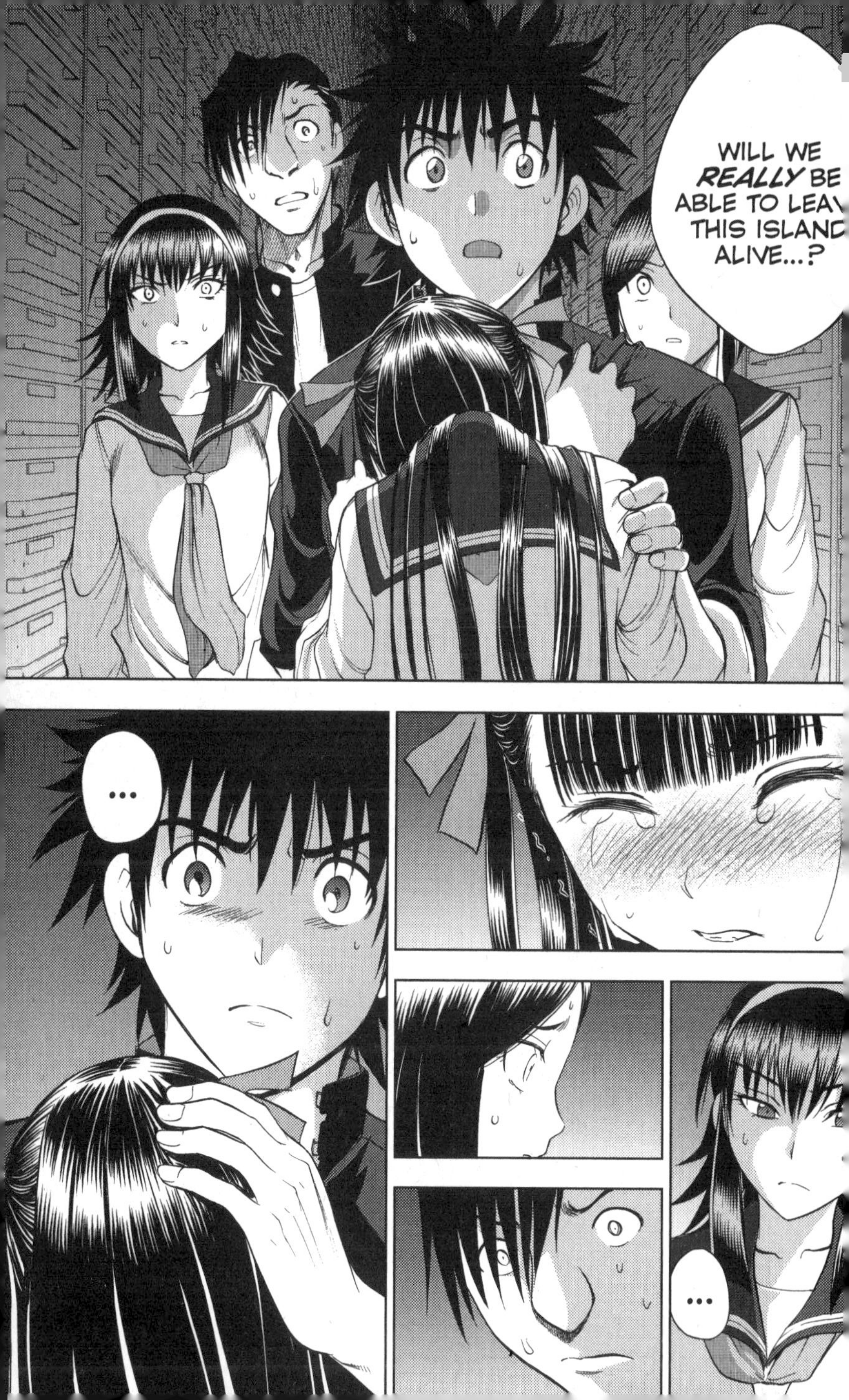
WILL WE *REALLY* BE ABLE TO LEAV THIS ISLAND ALIVE...?
...
...

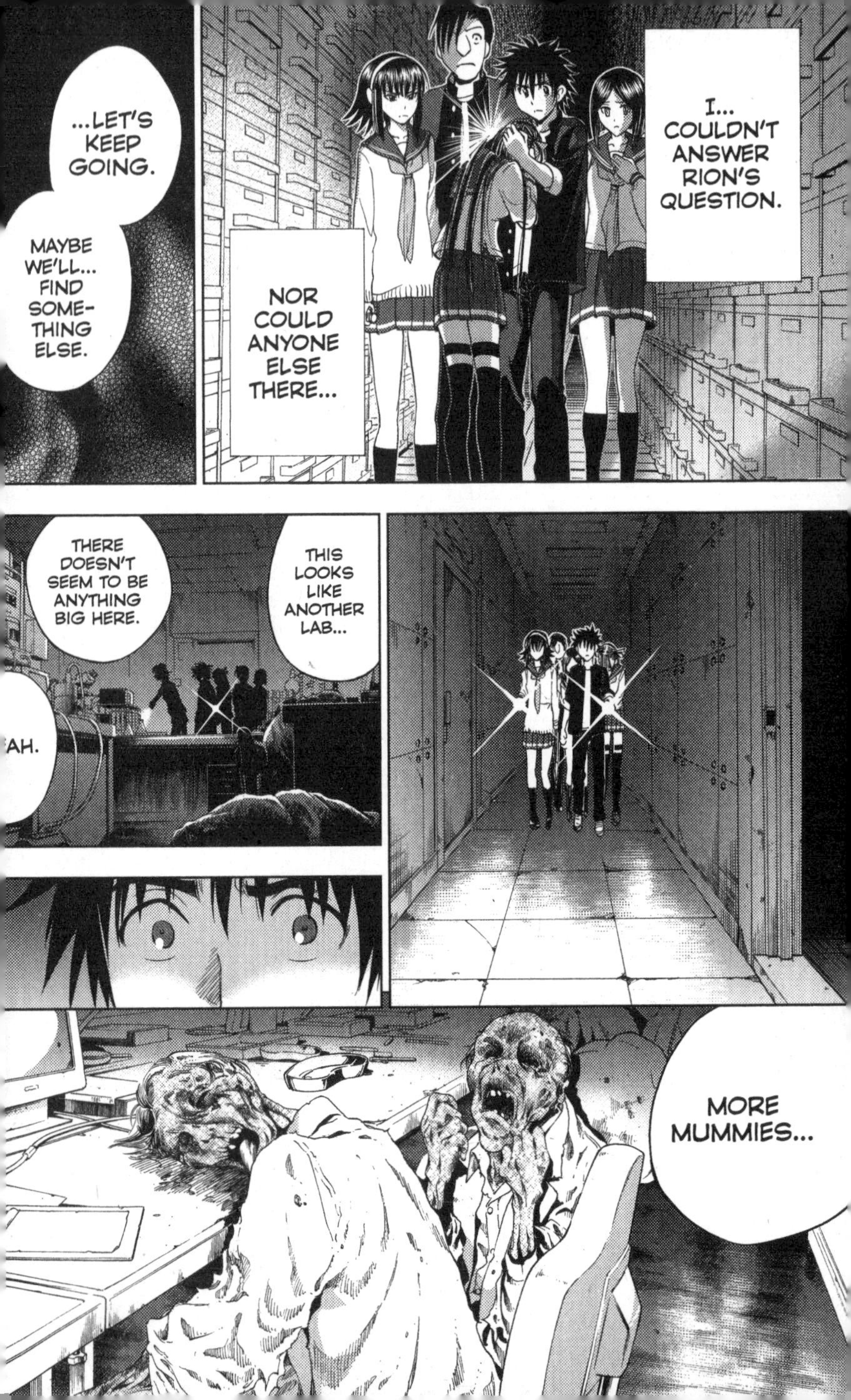
I... COULDN'T ANSWER RION'S QUESTION.
NOR COULD ANYONE ELSE THERE...
...LET'S KEEP GOING.
MAYBE WE'LL... FIND SOME-THING ELSE.
THIS LOOKS LIKE ANOTHER LAB...
THERE DOESN'T SEEM TO BE ANYTHING BIG HERE.
AH.
MORE MUMMIES...

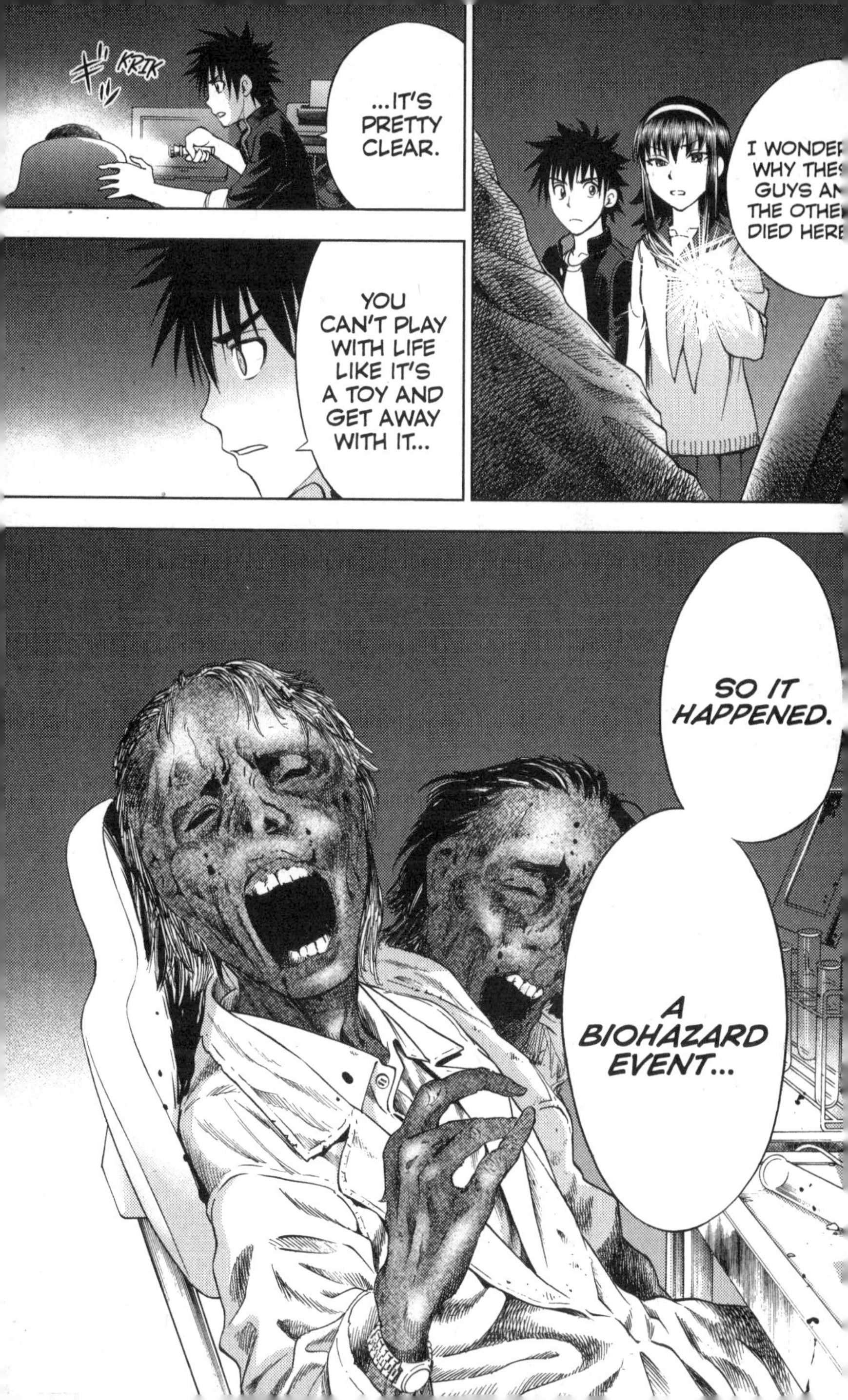
I WONDE
WHY THE
GUYS A
THE OTHE
DIED HER
ギッ
KRIK
...IT'S PRETTY CLEAR.
YOU CAN'T PLAY WITH LIFE LIKE IT'S A TOY AND GET AWAY WITH IT...
SO IT HAPPENED.
A BIOHAZARD EVENT...

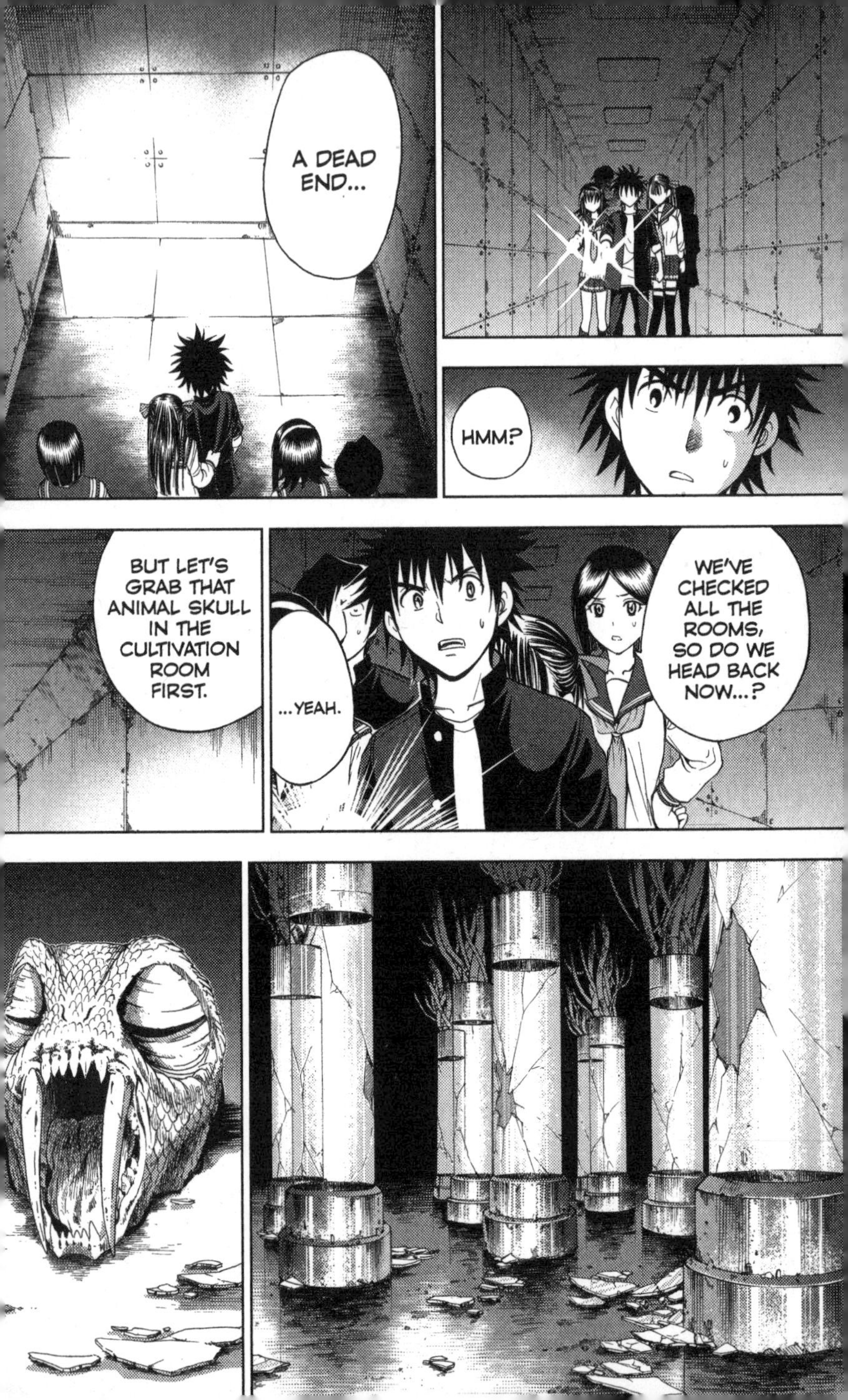
HMM?
A DEAD END...
WE'VE CHECKED ALL THE ROOMS, SO DO WE HEAD BACK NOW...?
...YEAH.
BUT LET'S GRAB THAT ANIMAL SKULL IN THE CULTIVATION ROOM FIRST.

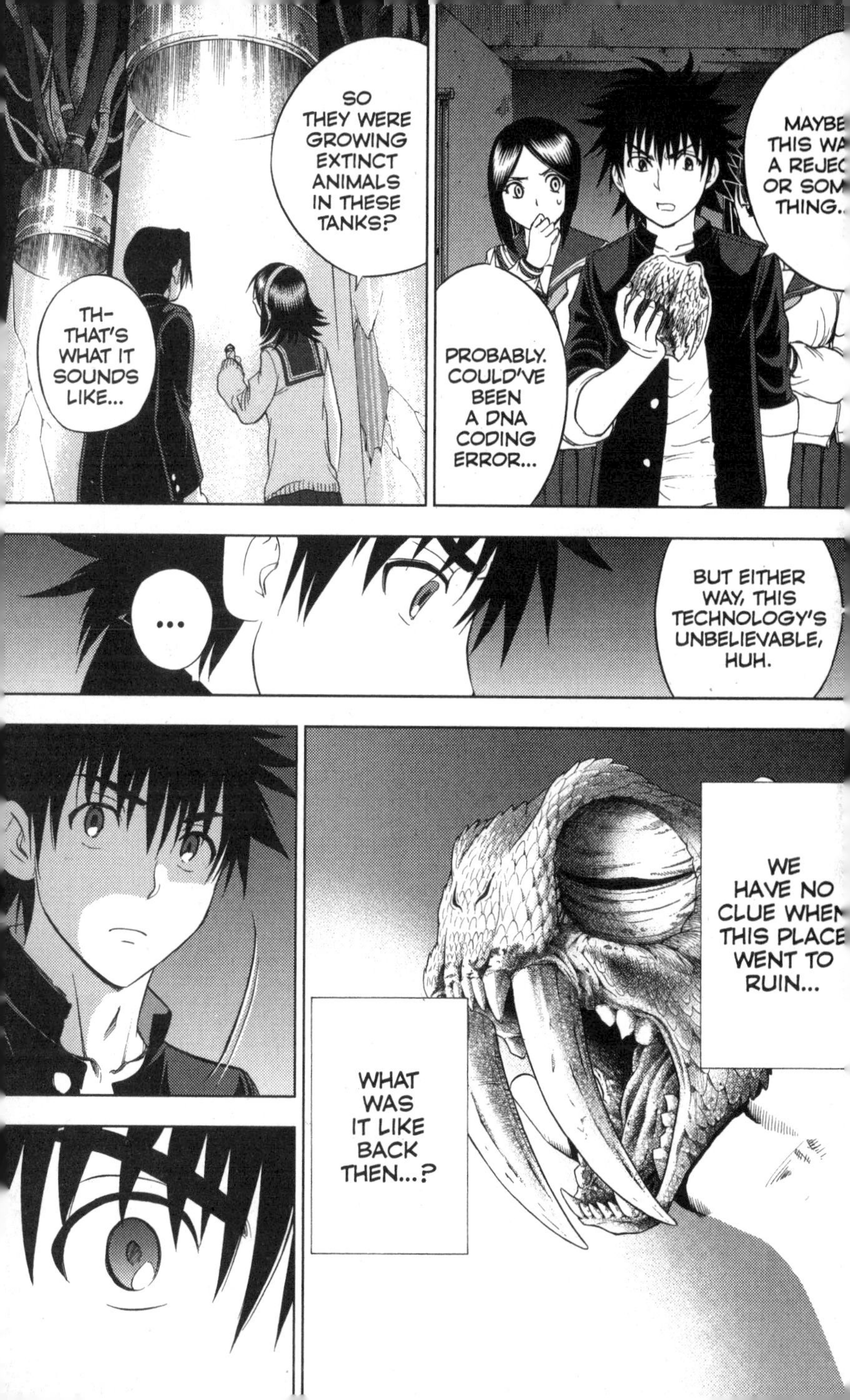
MAYBE THIS WA A REJEC OR SOM THING..
PROBABLY. COULD'VE BEEN A DNA CODING ERROR...
SO THEY WERE GROWING EXTINCT ANIMALS IN THESE TANKS?
TH- THAT'S WHAT IT SOUNDS LIKE...
BUT EITHER WAY, THIS TECHNOLOGY'S UNBELIEVABLE, HUH.
...
WE HAVE NO CLUE WHEN THIS PLACE WENT TO RUIN...
WHAT WAS IT LIKE BACK THEN...?

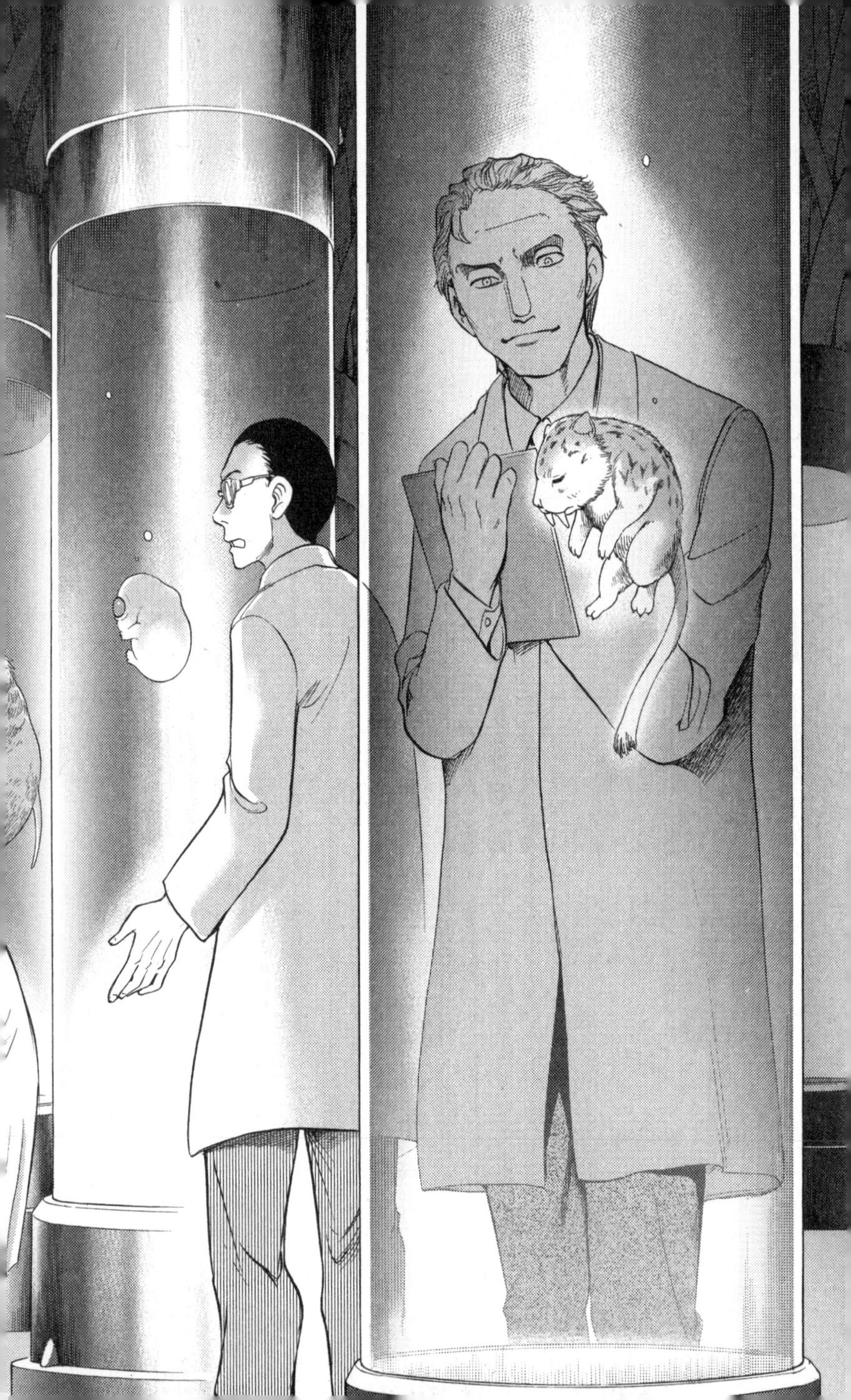

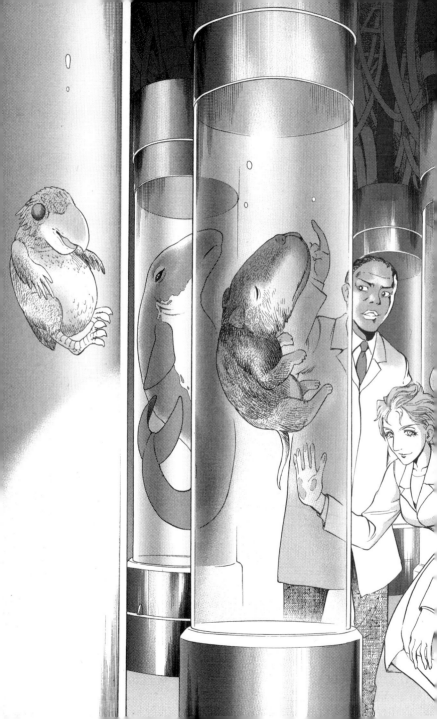

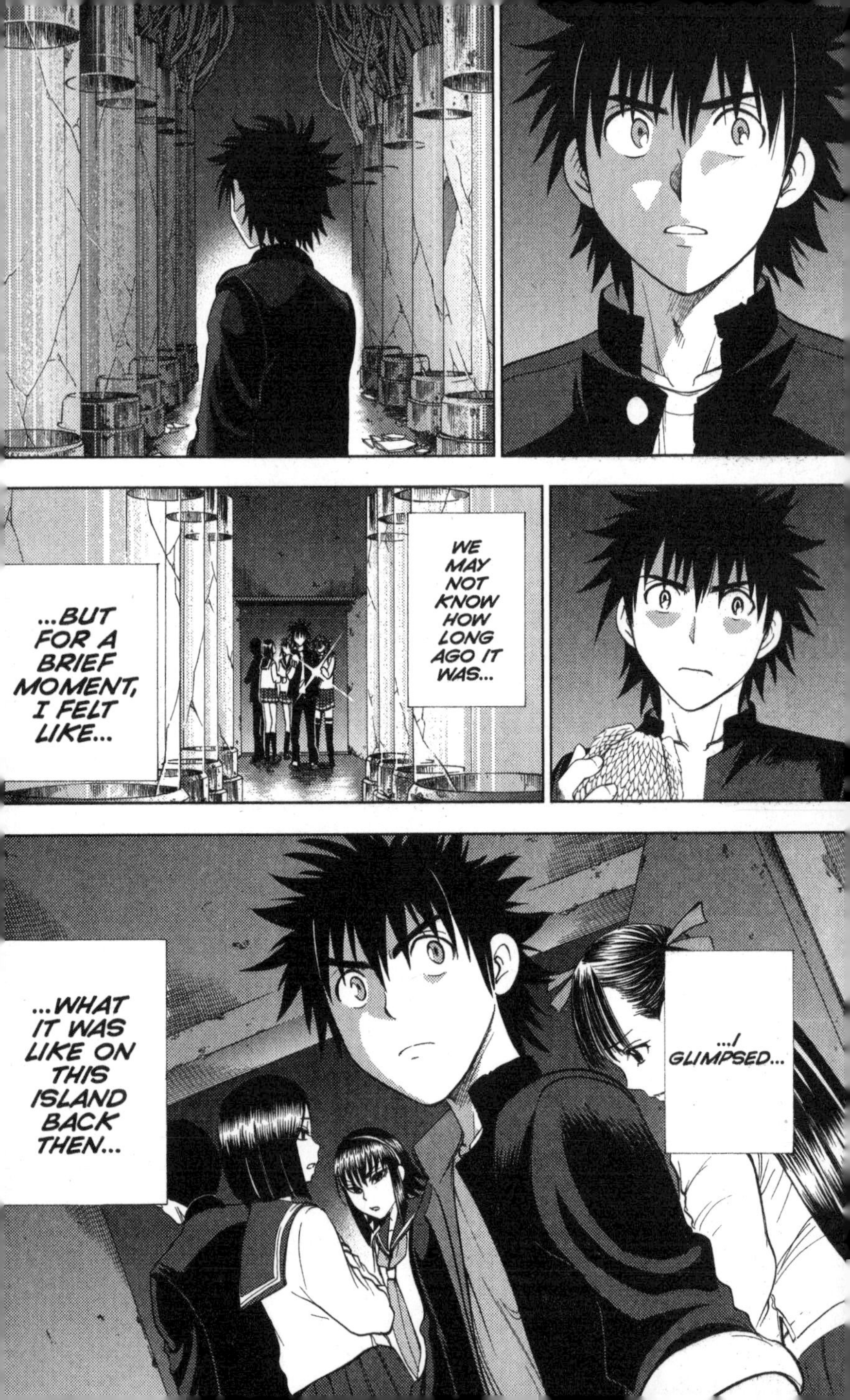
WE MAY NOT KNOW HOW LONG AGO IT WAS...
...BUT FOR A BRIEF MOMENT, I FELT LIKE...
...I GLIMPSED...
...WHAT IT WAS LIKE ON THIS ISLAND BACK THEN...

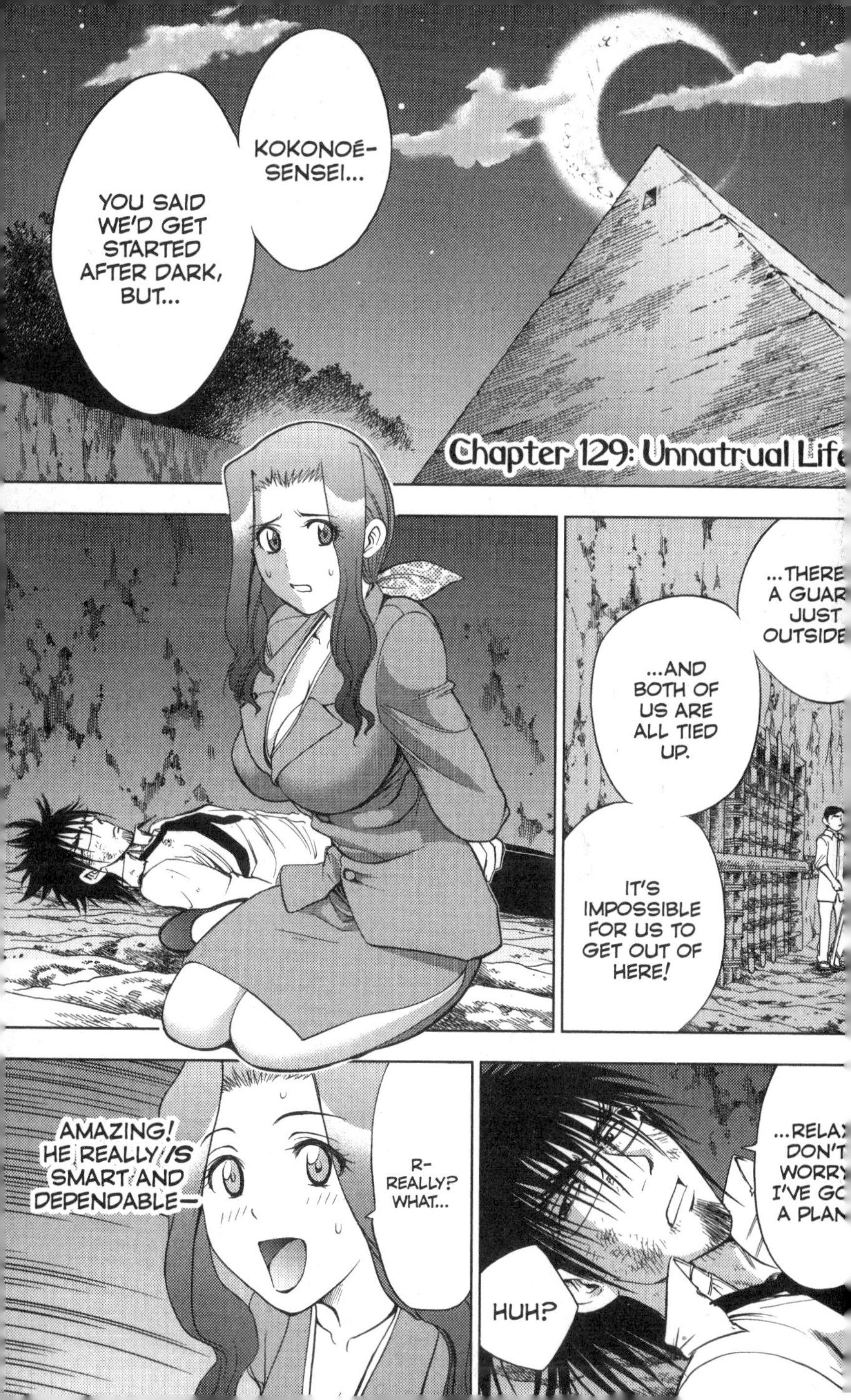
KOKONOE-SENSEI...
YOU SAID WE'D GET STARTED AFTER DARK, BUT...
Chapter 129: Unnatrual Life
...THERE A GUAR JUST OUTSIDE
...AND BOTH OF US ARE ALL TIED UP.
IT'S IMPOSSIBLE FOR US TO GET OUT OF HERE!
...RELAX DON'T WORRY I'VE GO A PLAN
HUH?
R- REALLY? WHAT...
AMAZING! HE REALLY IS SMART AND DEPENDABLE—

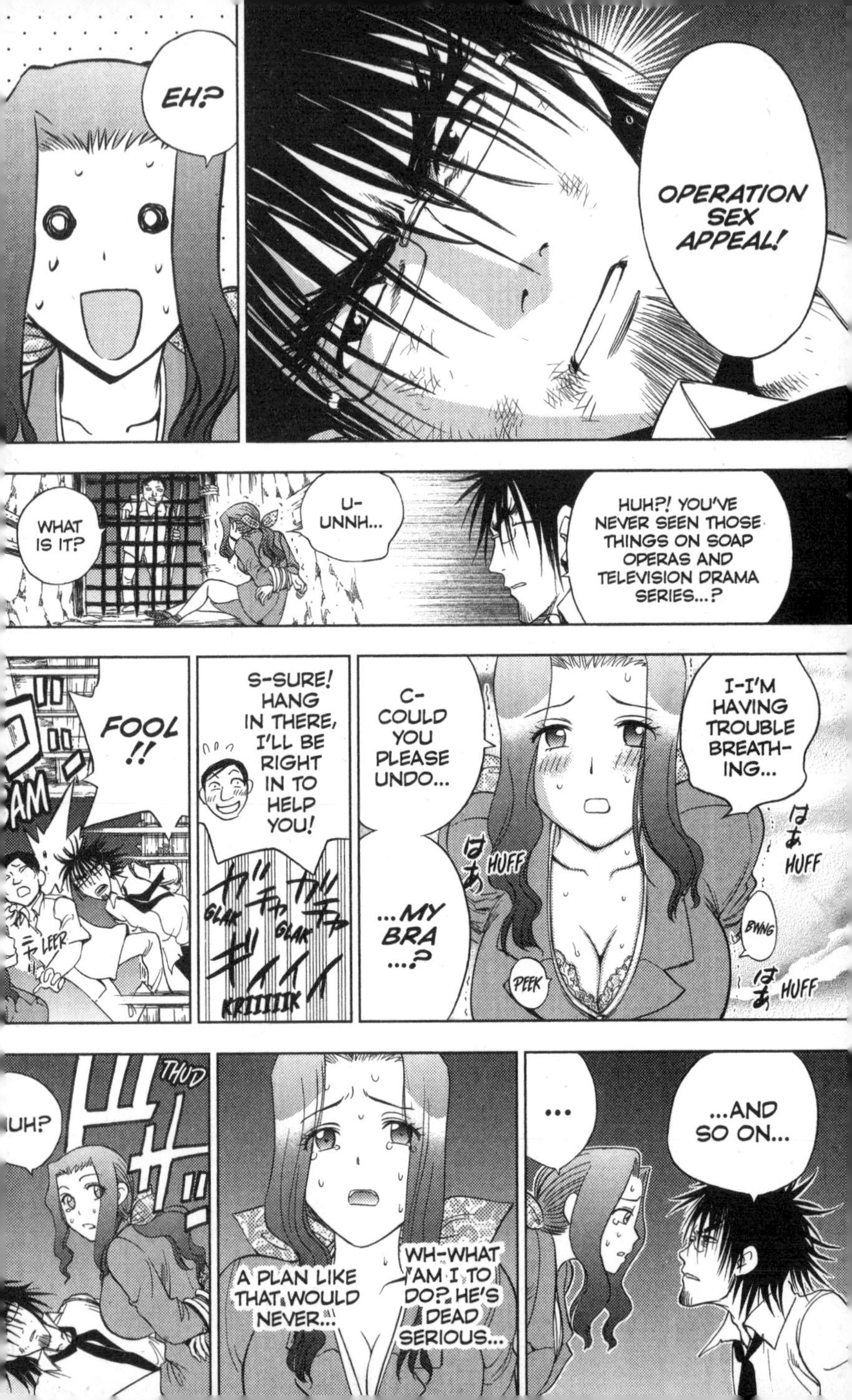
OPERATION SEX APPEAL!
EH?
HUH?! YOU'VE NEVER SEEN THOSE THINGS ON SOAP OPERAS AND TELEVISION DRAMA SERIES...?
U-UNNH...
WHAT IS IT?
I-I'M HAVING TROUBLE BREATHING...
はあ HUFF
BWNG
はあ HUFF
C-COULD YOU PLEASE UNDO...
...MY BRA...?
はあ HUFF
PEEK
S-SURE! HANG IN THERE, I'LL BE RIGHT IN TO HELP YOU!
GLAK GLAK
KRIIIIIK
FOOL!!
AM
LEER
...AND SO ON...
...
WH-WHAT AM I TO DO? HE'S DEAD SERIOUS...
A PLAN LIKE THAT WOULD NEVER...
THUD
UH?

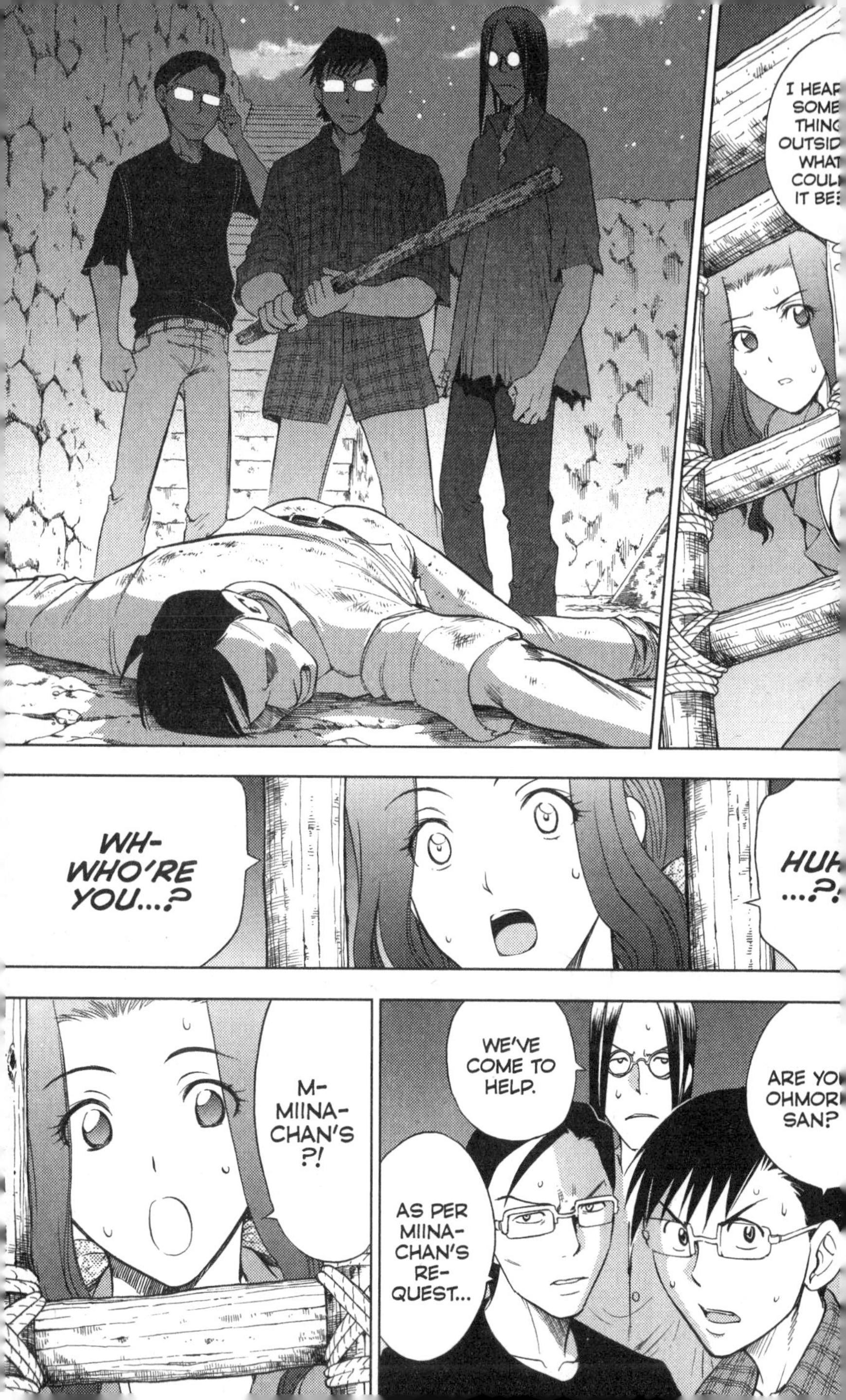
I HEAR SOME THING OUTSID WHAT COUL IT BE?
HUH ...?!
WH- WHO'RE YOU...?
ARE YO OHMOR SAN?
WE'VE COME TO HELP.
AS PER MIINA-CHAN'S RE-QUEST...
M- MIINA-CHAN'S ?!

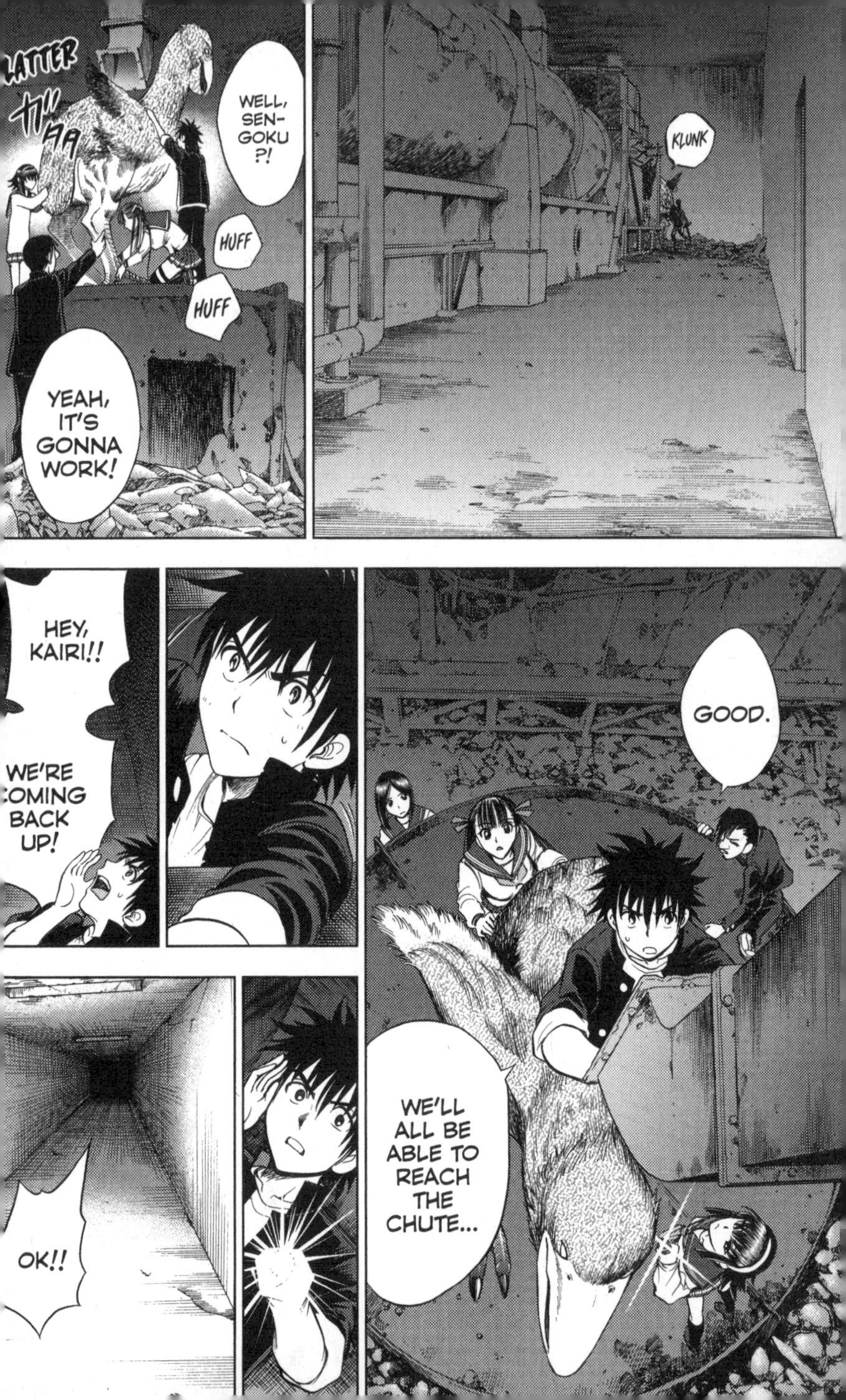
KLUNK
LATTER
WELL, SEN-GOKU?!
HUFF
HUFF
YEAH, IT'S GONNA WORK!
GOOD.
WE'LL ALL BE ABLE TO REACH THE CHUTE...
HEY, KAIRI!!
WE'RE OMING BACK UP!
OK!!

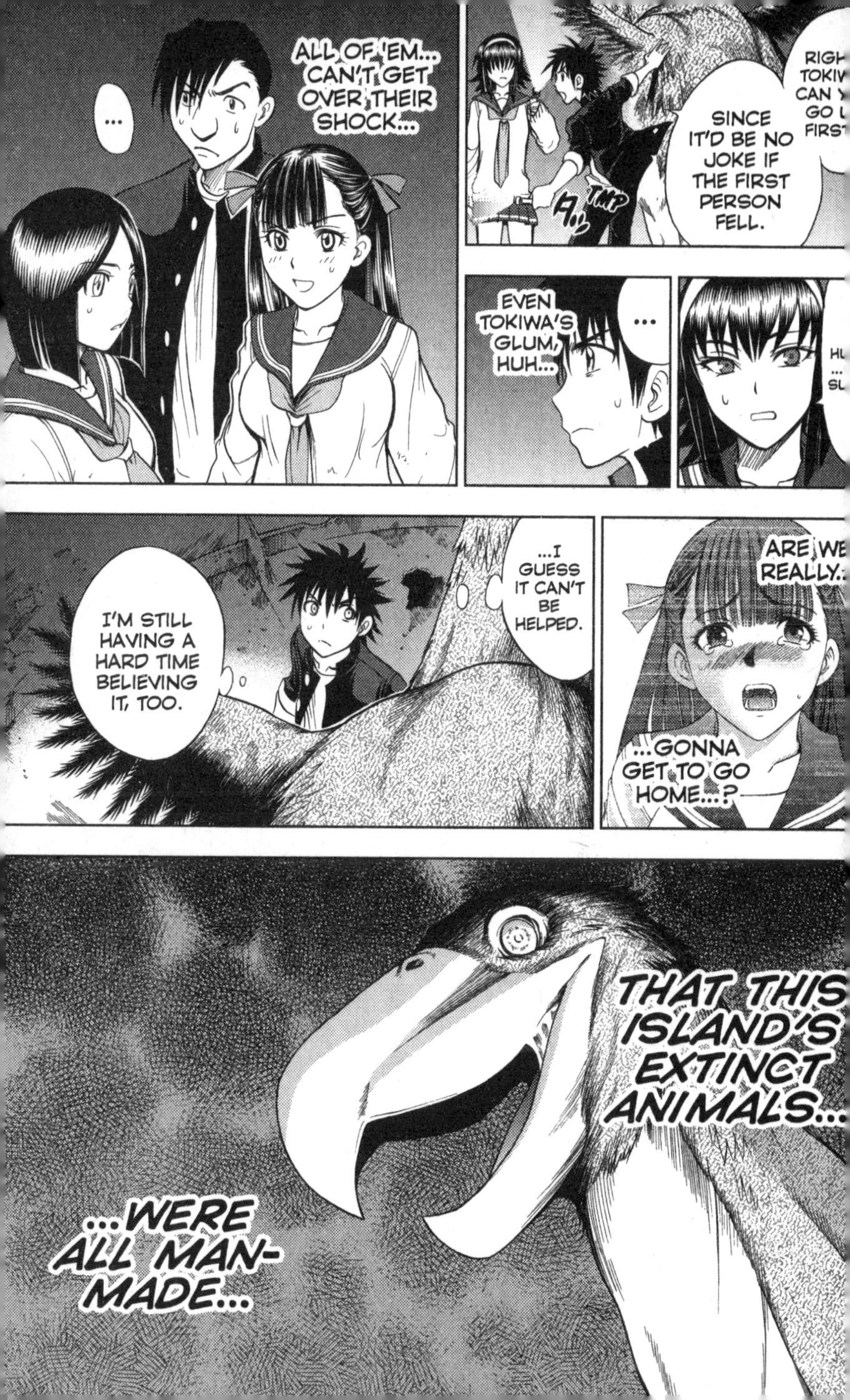
RIGH TOKIW CAN Y GO L FIRST
SINCE IT'D BE NO JOKE IF THE FIRST PERSON FELL.
TMP
HU ... SL
...
EVEN TOKIWA'S GLUM, HUH...
ALL OF 'EM... CAN'T GET OVER THEIR SHOCK...
...
ARE WE REALLY...
...GONNA GET TO GO HOME...?
...I GUESS IT CAN'T BE HELPED.
I'M STILL HAVING A HARD TIME BELIEVING IT, TOO.
THAT THIS ISLAND'S EXTINCT ANIMALS...
...WERE ALL MAN-MADE...

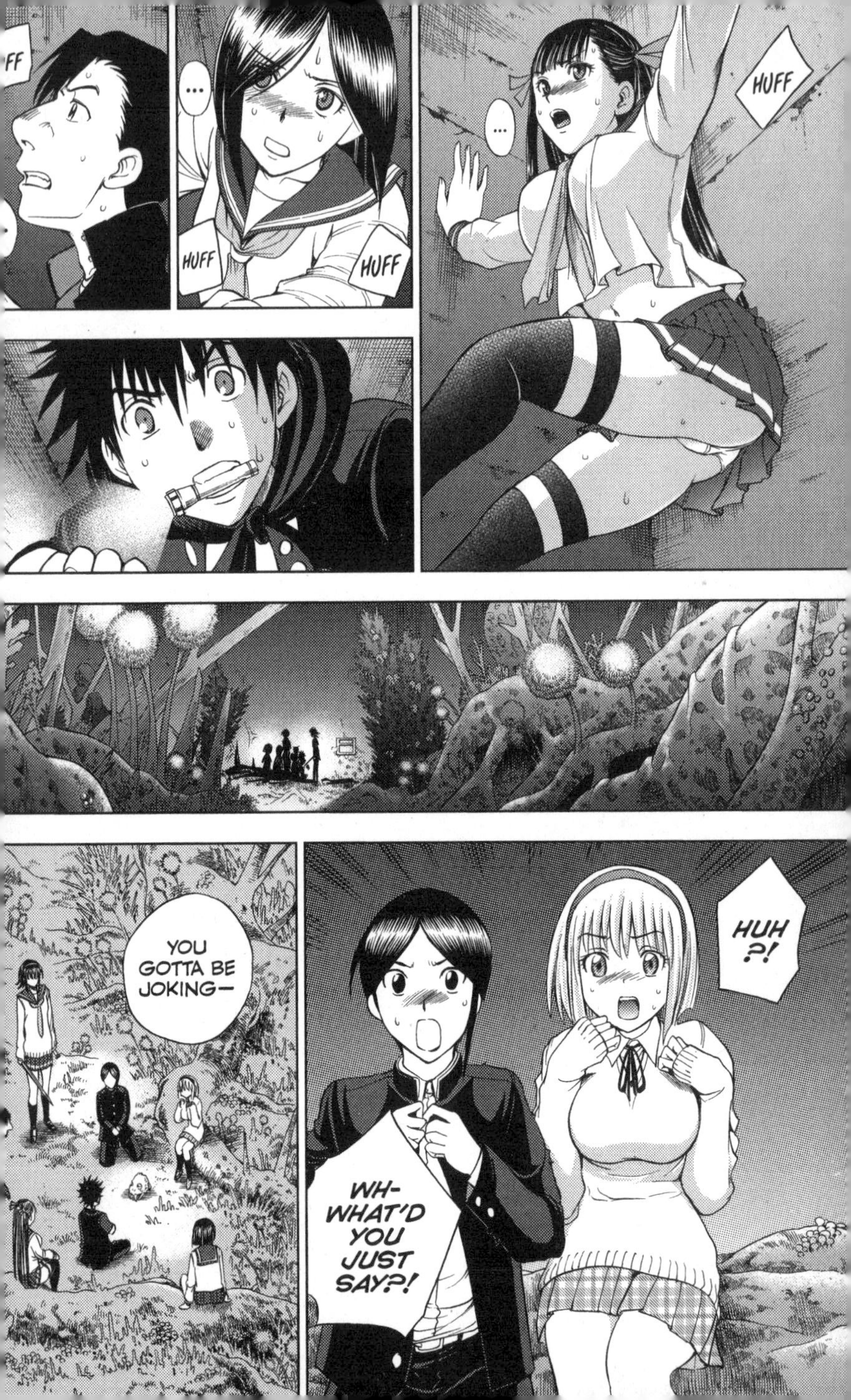

HUFF
...
...
HUFF
HUFF
FF
HUH?!
WH-WHAT'D YOU JUST SAY?!
YOU GOTTA BE JOKING—

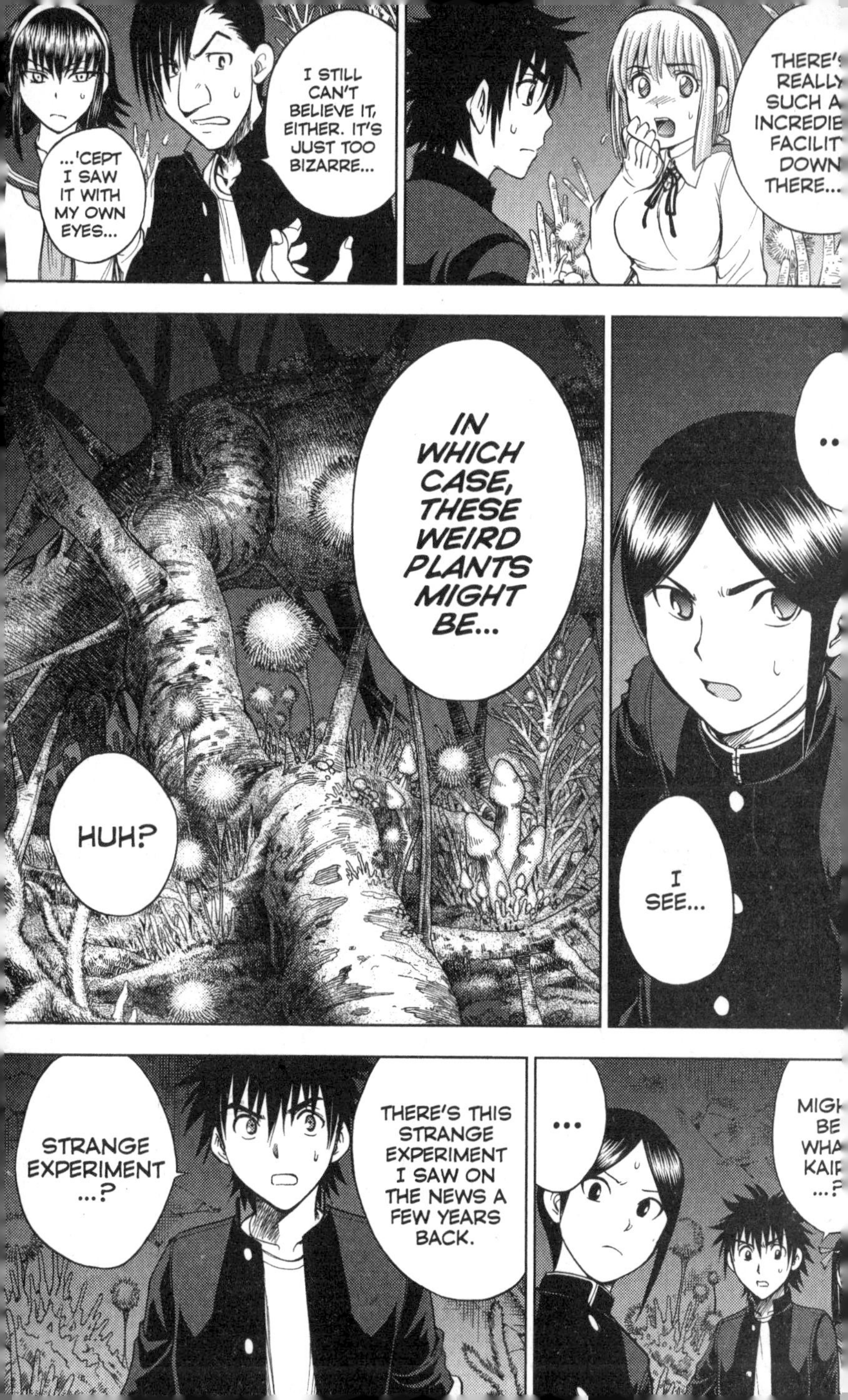
THERE'S REALLY SUCH A INCREDIB FACILIT DOWN THERE...
I STILL CAN'T BELIEVE IT, EITHER. IT'S JUST TOO BIZARRE...
...'CEPT I SAW IT WITH MY OWN EYES...
..
I SEE...
IN WHICH CASE, THESE WEIRD PLANTS MIGHT BE...
HUH?
MIGH BE WHA KAIR ...?
...
THERE'S THIS STRANGE EXPERIMENT I SAW ON THE NEWS A FEW YEARS BACK.
STRANGE EXPERIMENT ...?

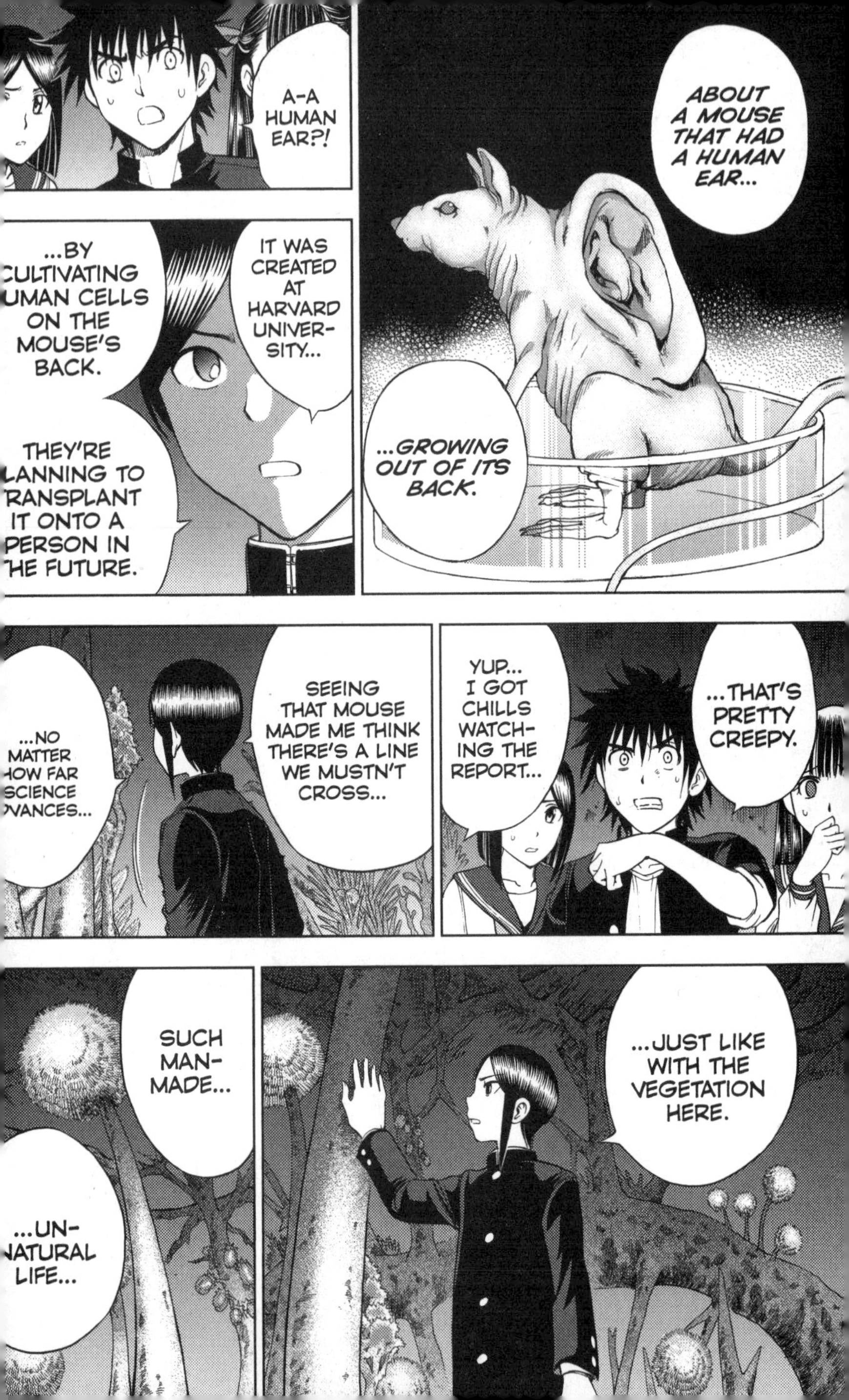
ABOUT A MOUSE THAT HAD A HUMAN EAR...
...GROWING OUT OF ITS BACK.
A-A HUMAN EAR?!
IT WAS CREATED AT HARVARD UNIVERSITY...
...BY ULTIVATING UMAN CELLS ON THE MOUSE'S BACK.
THEY'RE LANNING TO RANSPLANT IT ONTO A PERSON IN HE FUTURE.
...THAT'S PRETTY CREEPY.
YUP... I GOT CHILLS WATCHING THE REPORT...
SEEING THAT MOUSE MADE ME THINK THERE'S A LINE WE MUSTN'T CROSS...
...NO MATTER OW FAR CIENCE VANCES...
...JUST LIKE WITH THE VEGETATION HERE.
SUCH MAN-MADE...
...UN-ATURAL LIFE...

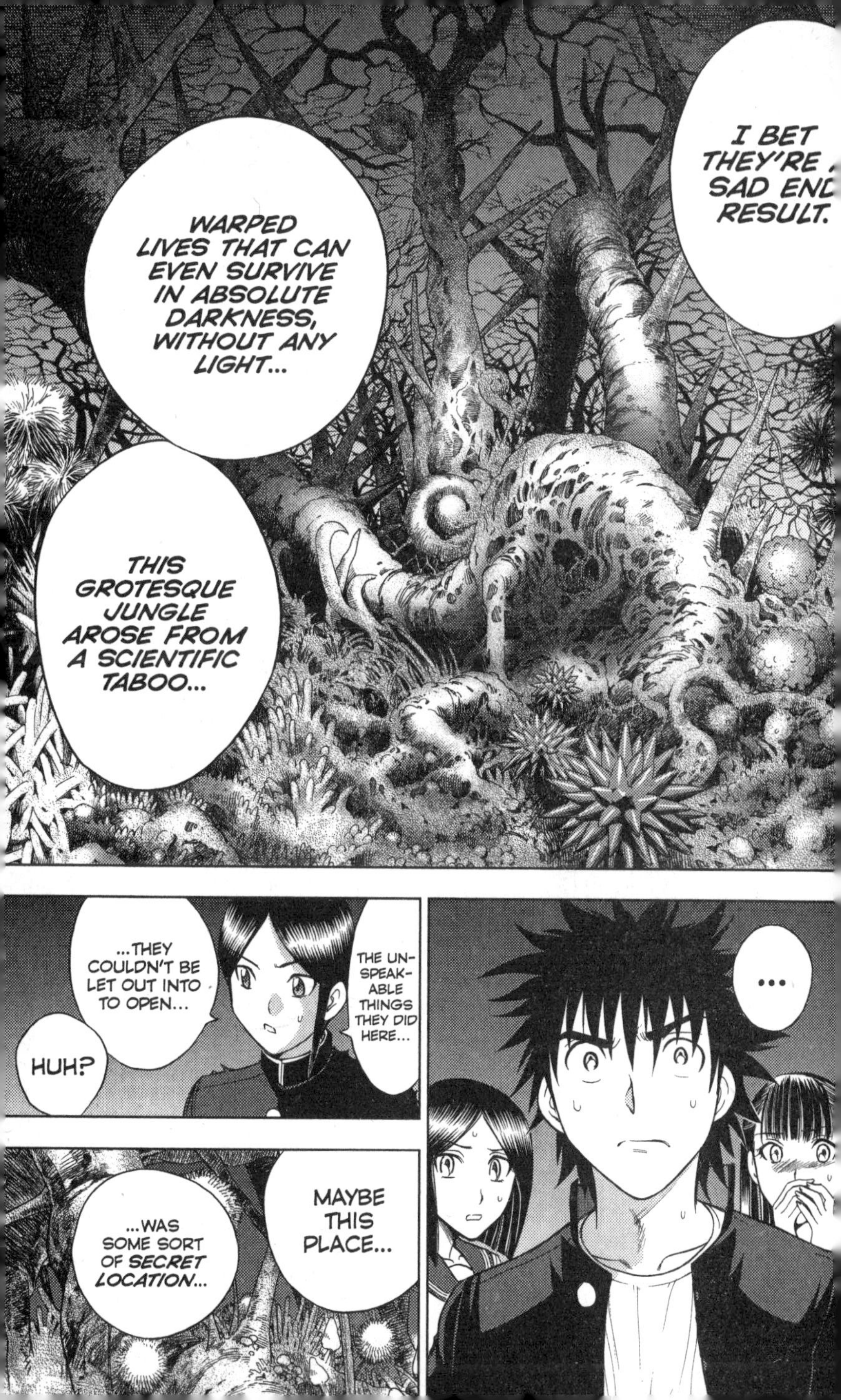

I BET THEY'RE SAD END RESULT.
WARPED LIVES THAT CAN EVEN SURVIVE IN ABSOLUTE DARKNESS, WITHOUT ANY LIGHT...
THIS GROTESQUE JUNGLE AROSE FROM A SCIENTIFIC TABOO...
...
THE UN-SPEAKABLE THINGS THEY DID HERE...
...THEY COULDN'T BE LET OUT INTO TO OPEN...
HUH?
MAYBE THIS PLACE...
...WAS SOME SORT OF *SECRET* LOCATION...

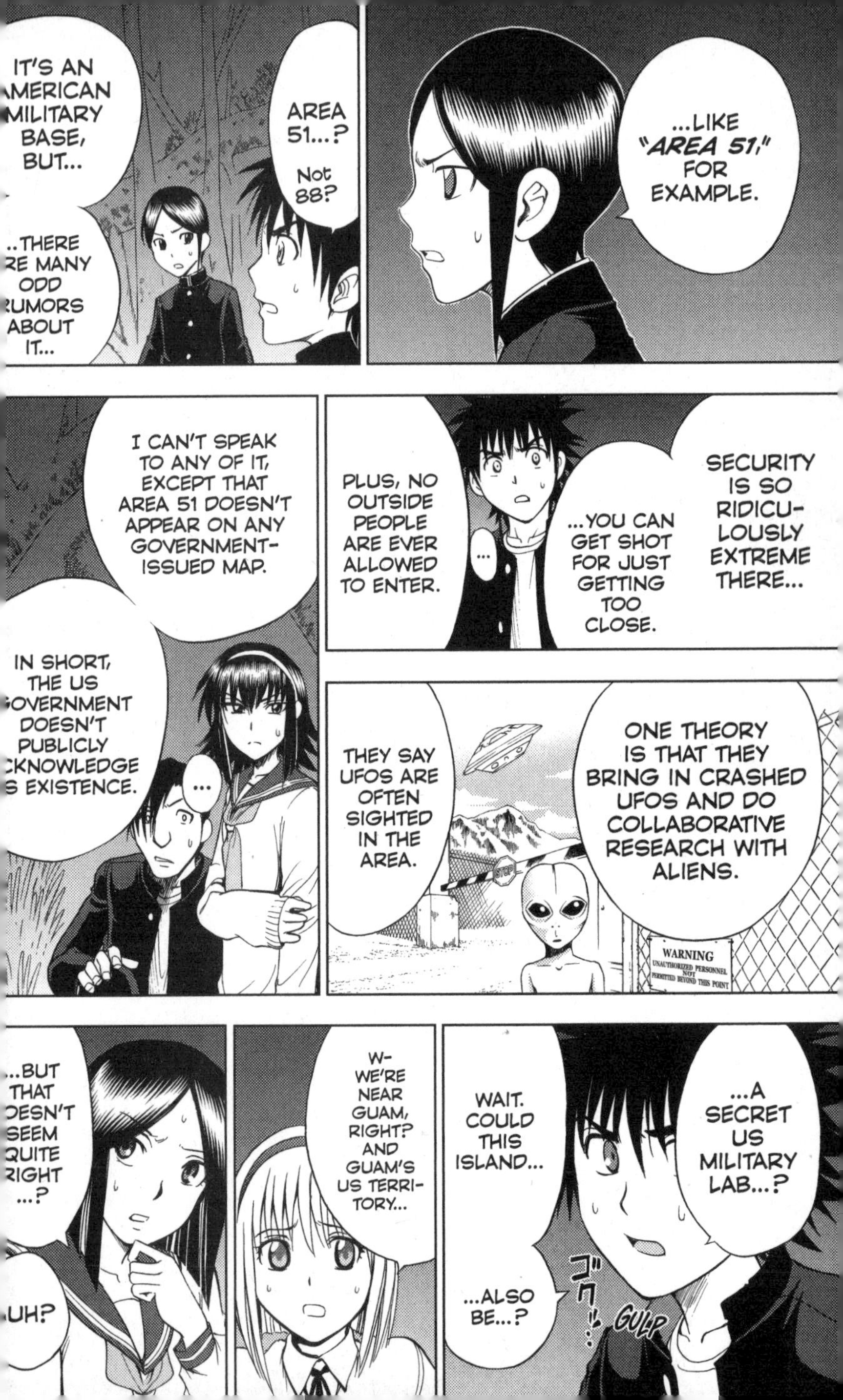

...LIKE "AREA 51," FOR EXAMPLE.
AREA 51...? Not 88?
IT'S AN MERICAN MILITARY BASE, BUT...
..THERE E MANY ODD UMORS ABOUT IT...
SECURITY IS SO RIDICU-LOUSLY EXTREME THERE...
...YOU CAN GET SHOT FOR JUST GETTING TOO CLOSE.
...
PLUS, NO OUTSIDE PEOPLE ARE EVER ALLOWED TO ENTER.
ONE THEORY IS THAT THEY BRING IN CRASHED UFOS AND DO COLLABORATIVE RESEARCH WITH ALIENS.
THEY SAY UFOS ARE OFTEN SIGHTED IN THE AREA.
STOP
WARNING
UNAUTHORIZED PERSONNEL NOT PERMITTED BEYOND THIS POINT
I CAN'T SPEAK TO ANY OF IT, EXCEPT THAT AREA 51 DOESN'T APPEAR ON ANY GOVERNMENT-ISSUED MAP.
IN SHORT, THE US OVERNMENT DOESN'T PUBLICLY CKNOWLEDGE S EXISTENCE.
...
...A SECRET US MILITARY LAB...?
WAIT. COULD THIS ISLAND...
...ALSO BE...?
ゴクッ
GULP
W-WE'RE NEAR GUAM, RIGHT? AND GUAM'S US TERRI-TORY...
..BUT THAT OESN'T SEEM QUITE IGHT ...?
UH?

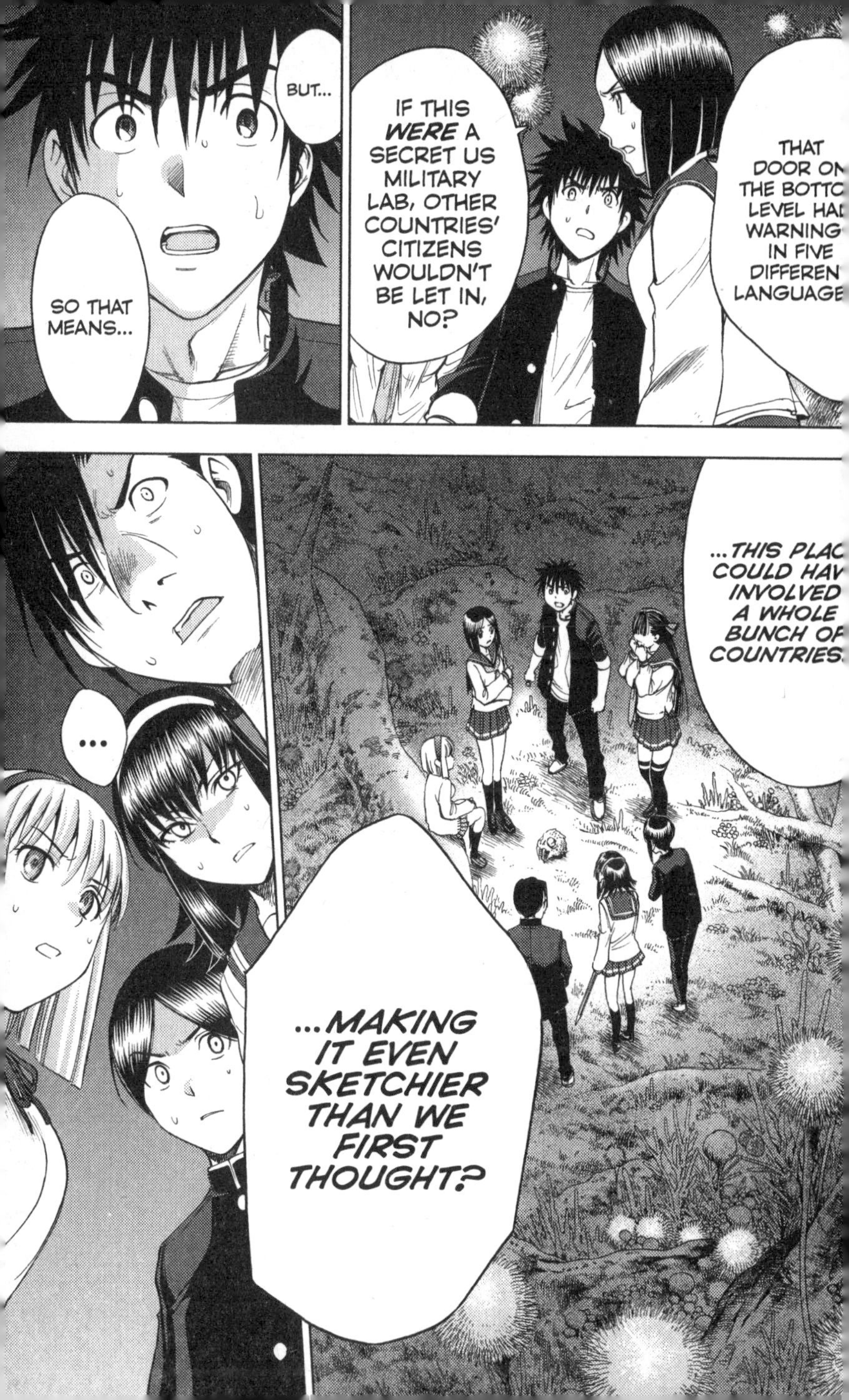
THAT DOOR ON THE BOTTO LEVEL HAD WARNING IN FIVE DIFFEREN LANGUAGE
IF THIS WERE A SECRET US MILITARY LAB, OTHER COUNTRIES' CITIZENS WOULDN'T BE LET IN, NO?
BUT...
SO THAT MEANS...
...THIS PLAC COULD HAV INVOLVED A WHOLE BUNCH OF COUNTRIES.
...
...MAKING IT EVEN SKETCHIER THAN WE FIRST THOUGHT?

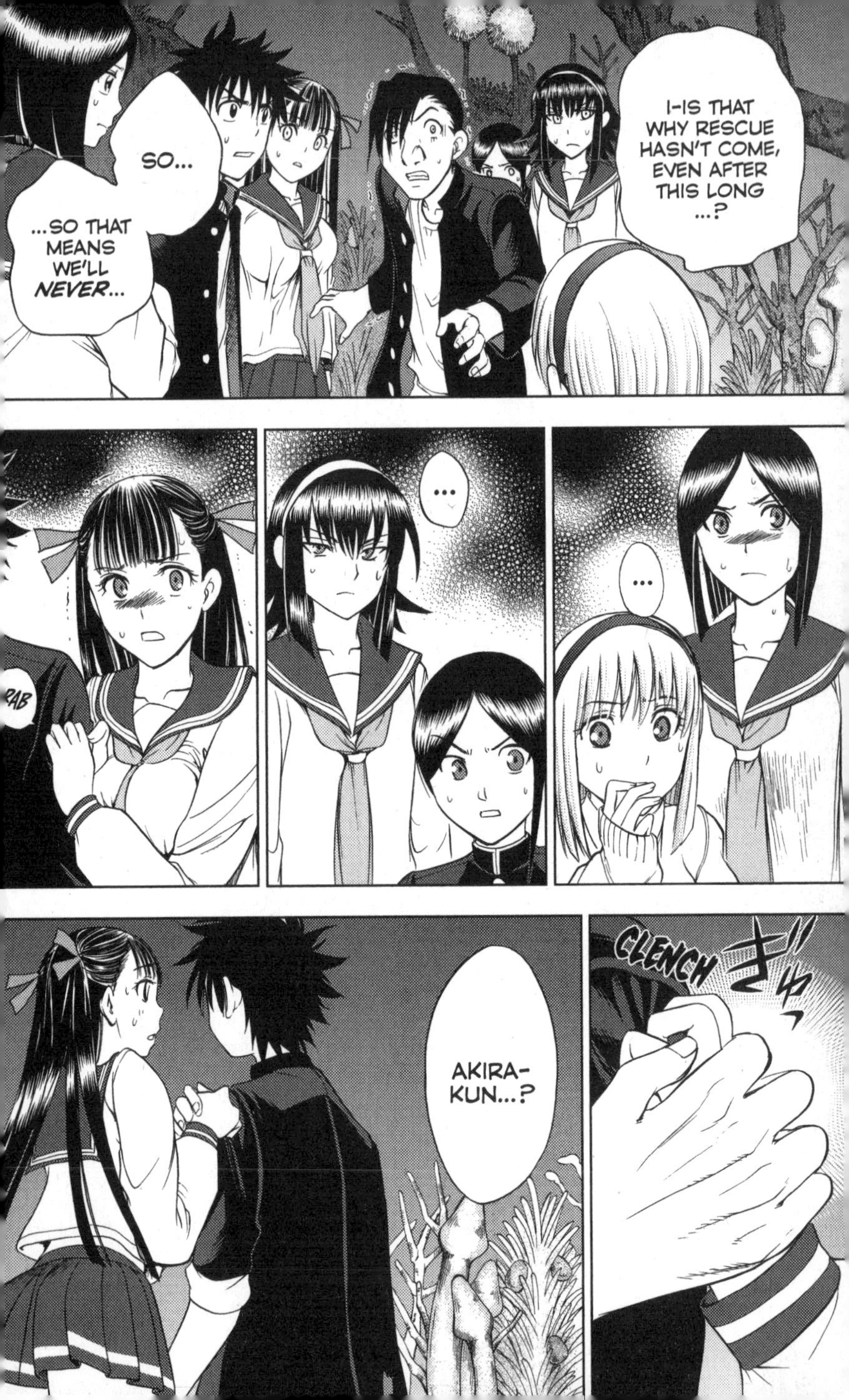

I-IS THAT WHY RESCUE HASN'T COME, EVEN AFTER THIS LONG ...?
SO...
...SO THAT MEANS WE'LL *NEVER*...
...
...
CLENCH
ぎゅっ
AKIRA-KUN...?

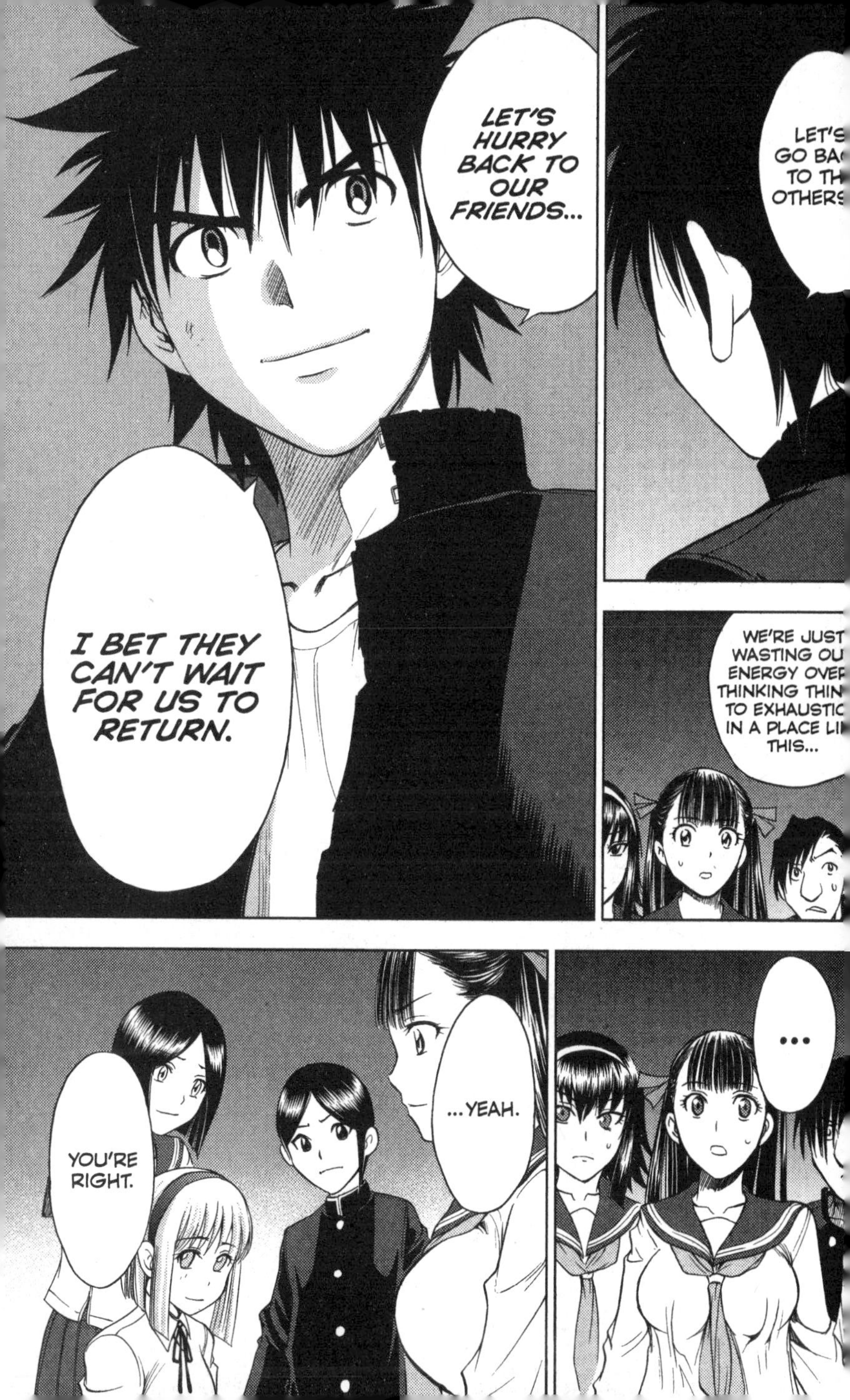
LET'S GO BA TO TH OTHERS
WE'RE JUST WASTING OU ENERGY OVE THINKING THIN TO EXHAUSTI IN A PLACE LI THIS...
LET'S HURRY BACK TO OUR FRIENDS...
I BET THEY CAN'T WAIT FOR US TO RETURN.
...
...YEAH.
YOU'RE RIGHT.

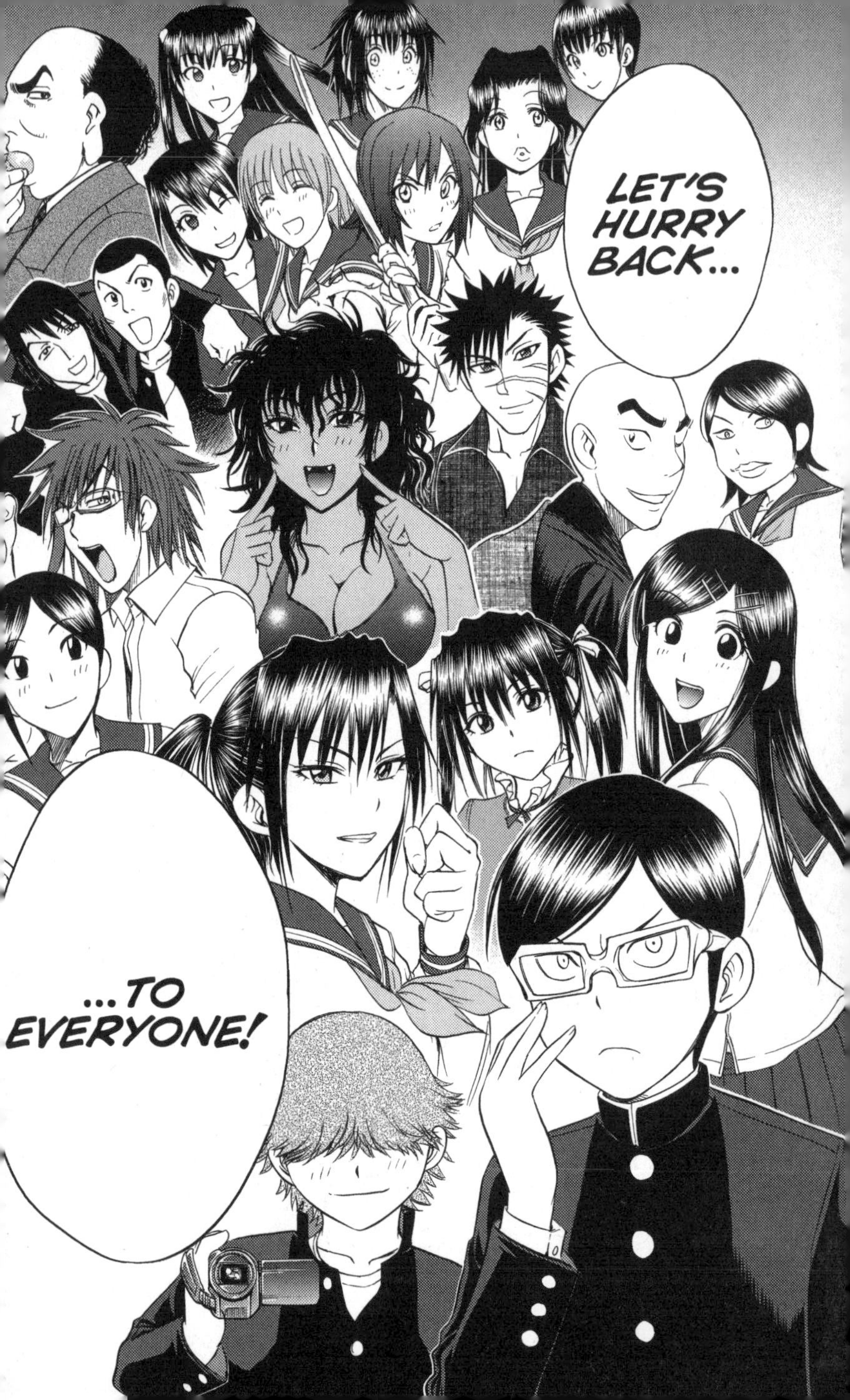
LET'S HURRY BACK...
...TO EVERYONE!

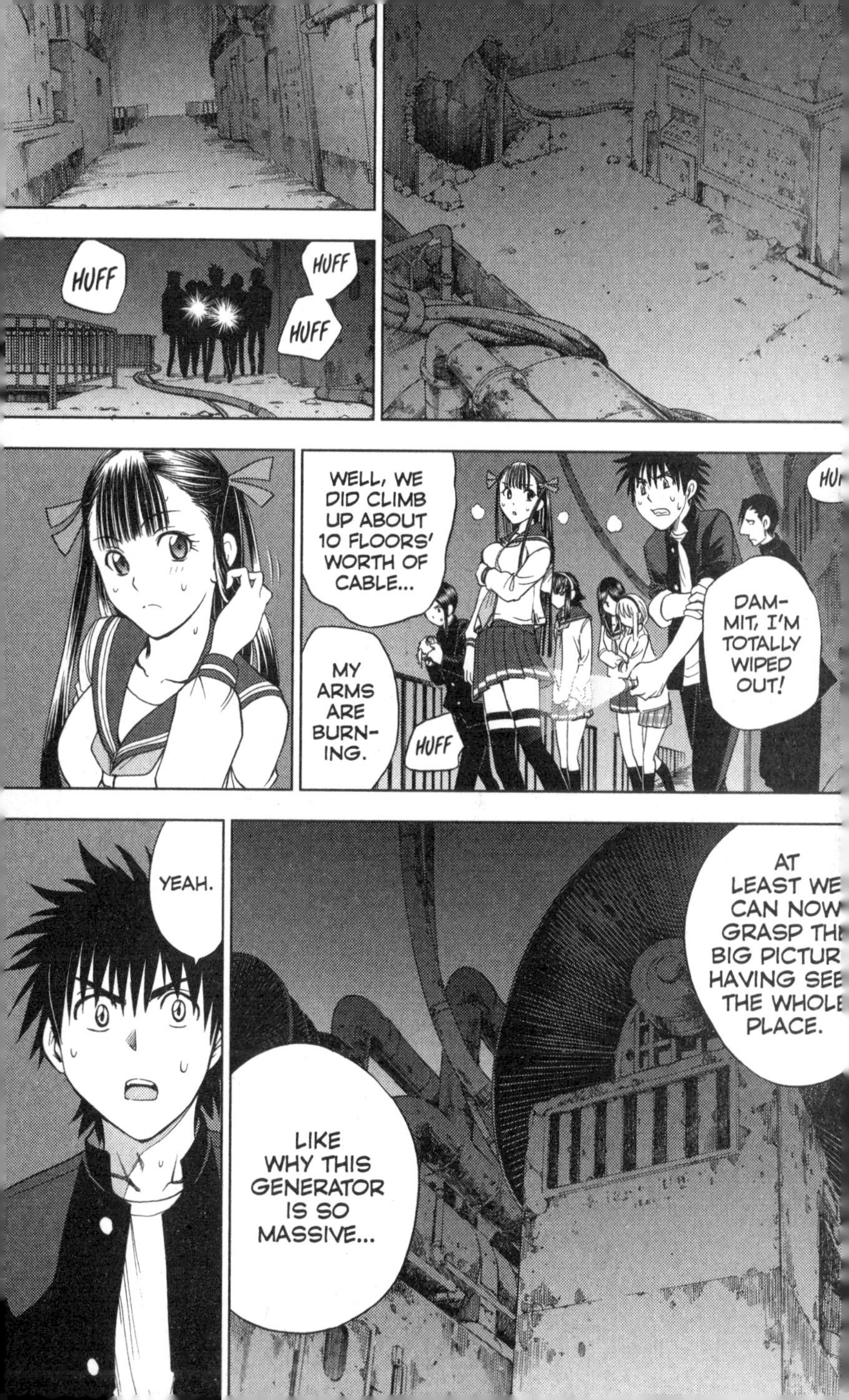
HUFF
HUFF
HUFF
HU
WELL, WE DID CLIMB UP ABOUT 10 FLOORS' WORTH OF CABLE...
DAM-MIT, I'M TOTALLY WIPED OUT!
MY ARMS ARE BURN-ING.
HUFF
AT LEAST WE CAN NOW GRASP TH BIG PICTUR HAVING SEE THE WHOLE PLACE.
LIKE WHY THIS GENERATOR IS SO MASSIVE...
YEAH.

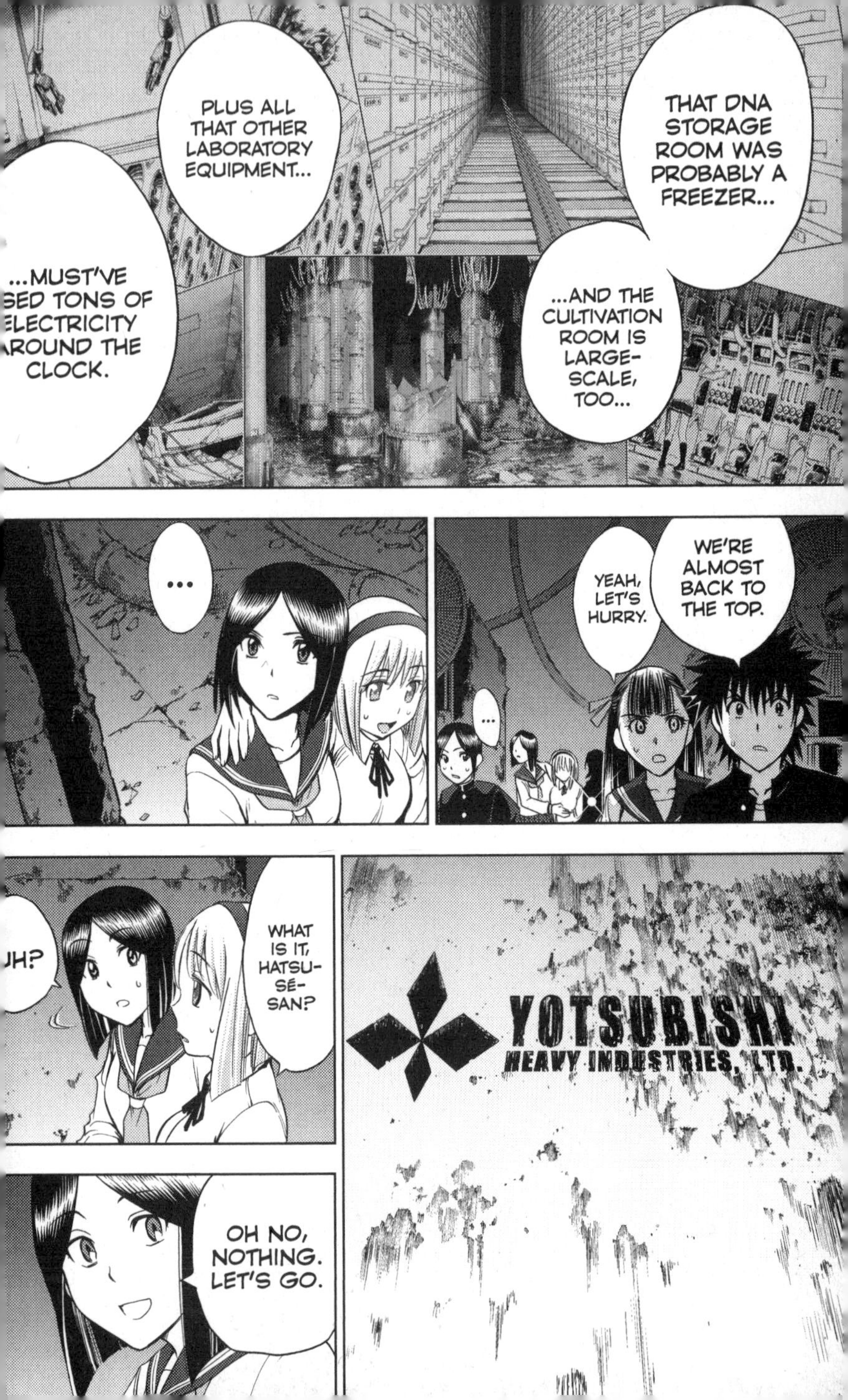
THAT DNA STORAGE ROOM WAS PROBABLY A FREEZER...
...AND THE CULTIVATION ROOM IS LARGE-SCALE, TOO...
PLUS ALL THAT OTHER LABORATORY EQUIPMENT...
...MUST'VE SED TONS OF LECTRICITY ROUND THE CLOCK.
WE'RE ALMOST BACK TO THE TOP.
YEAH, LET'S HURRY.
...
...
YOTSUBISHI
HEAVY INDUSTRIES, LTD.
WHAT IS IT, HATSUSÉ-SAN?
H?
OH NO, NOTHING. LET'S GO.

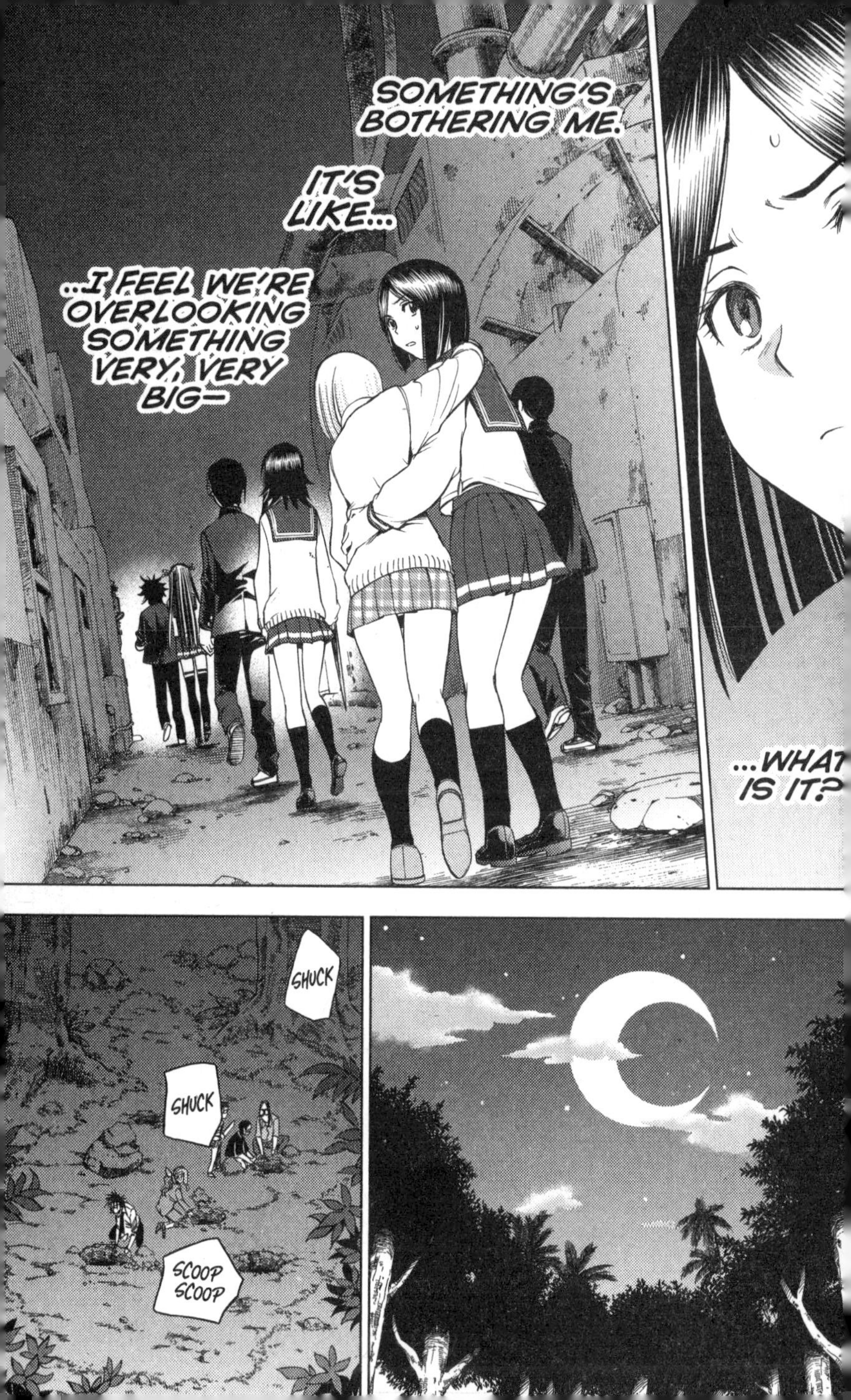
...WHAT IS IT?
SOMETHING'S BOTHERING ME.
IT'S LIKE...
...I FEEL WE'RE OVERLOOKING SOMETHING VERY, VERY BIG–
SHUCK
SHUCK
SCOOP SCOOP

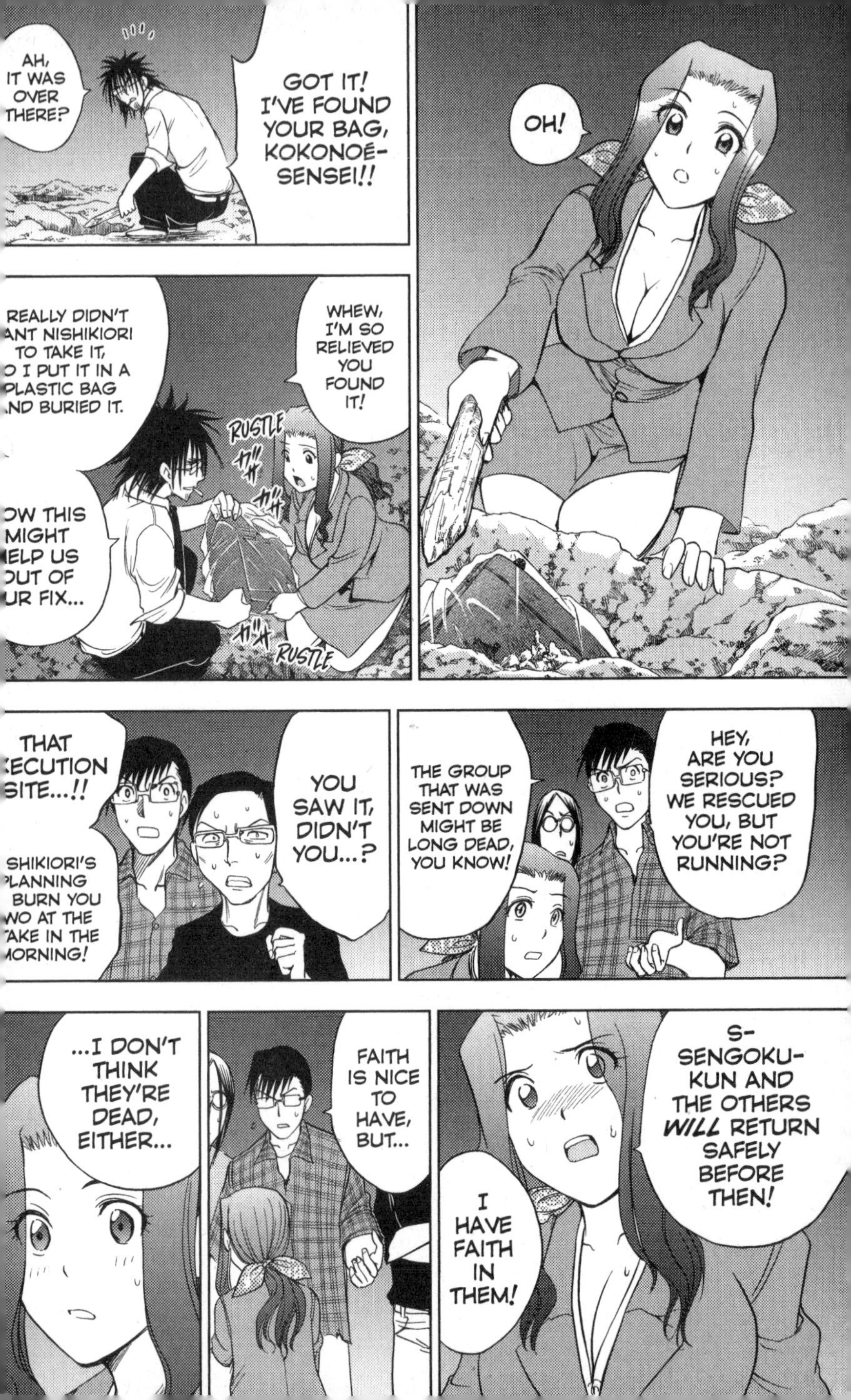
OH!
GOT IT! I'VE FOUND YOUR BAG, KOKONOÉ-SENSEI!!
AH, IT WAS OVER THERE?
WHEW, I'M SO RELIEVED YOU FOUND IT!
RUSTLE
REALLY DIDN'T
ANT NISHIKIORI TO TAKE IT,
O I PUT IT IN A PLASTIC BAG
ND BURIED IT.
OW THIS MIGHT
IELP US OUT OF
UR FIX...
RUSTLE
HEY, ARE YOU SERIOUS? WE RESCUED YOU, BUT YOU'RE NOT RUNNING?
THE GROUP THAT WAS SENT DOWN MIGHT BE LONG DEAD, YOU KNOW!
YOU SAW IT, DIDN'T YOU...?
THAT
ECUTION SITE...!!
SHIKIORI'S
LANNING
BURN YOU
WO AT THE
AKE IN THE
ORNING!
S-SENGOKU-KUN AND THE OTHERS *WILL* RETURN SAFELY BEFORE THEN!
I HAVE FAITH IN THEM!
FAITH IS NICE TO HAVE, BUT...
...I DON'T THINK THEY'RE DEAD, EITHER...

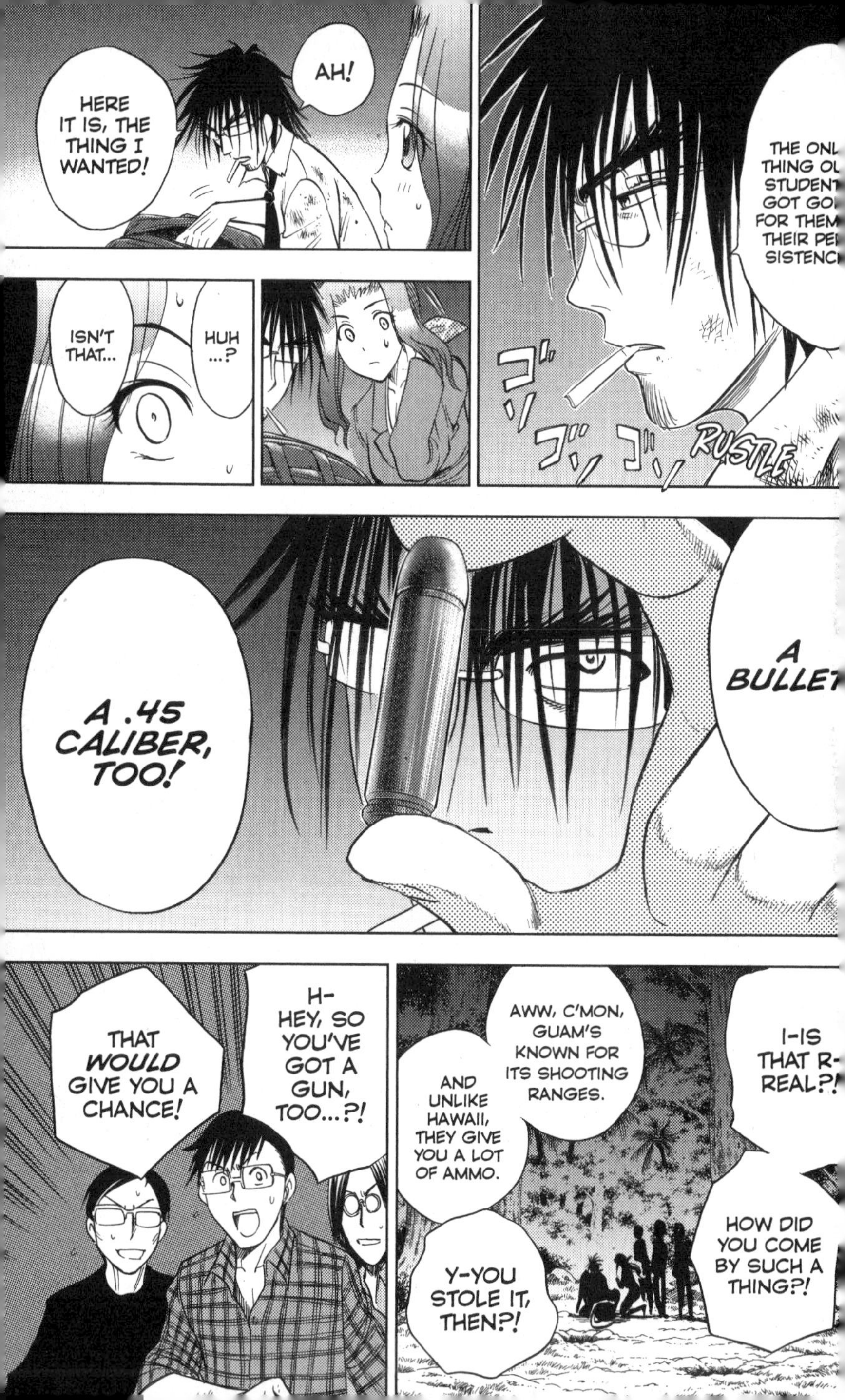
THE ONL THING OU STUDENT GOT GO FOR THEM THEIR PE SISTENC
ゴッ ゴッ ゴッ
RUSTLE
AH!
HERE IT IS, THE THING I WANTED!
HUH ...?
ISN'T THAT...
A BULLET
A .45 CALIBER, TOO!
I-IS THAT R-REAL?!
AWW, C'MON, GUAM'S KNOWN FOR ITS SHOOTING RANGES.
AND UNLIKE HAWAII, THEY GIVE YOU A LOT OF AMMO.
HOW DID YOU COME BY SUCH A THING?!
Y-YOU STOLE IT, THEN?!
H- HEY, SO YOU'VE GOT A GUN, TOO...?!
THAT *WOULD* GIVE YOU A CHANCE!

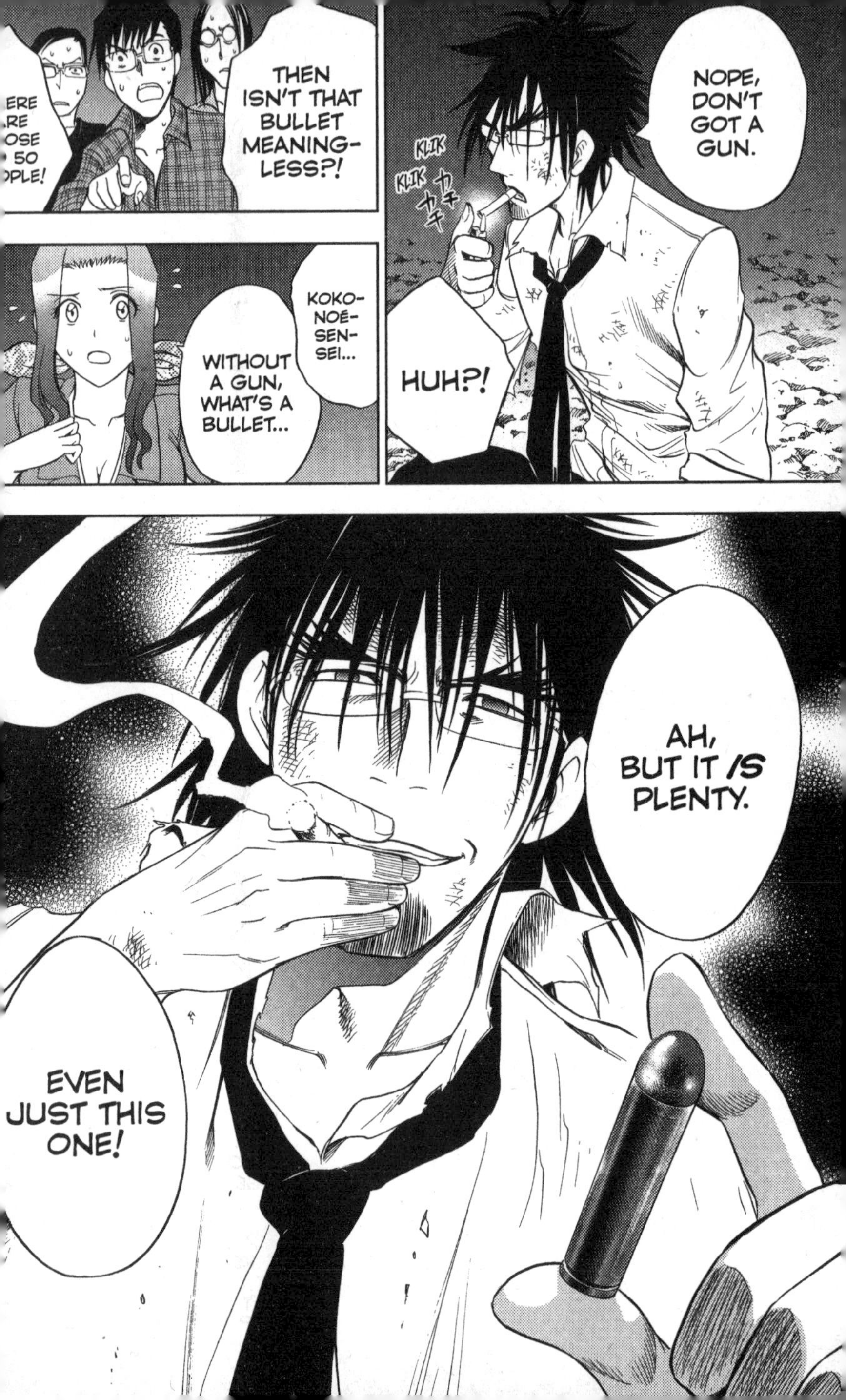
NOPE, DON'T GOT A GUN.
KLIK KLIK
カチカチ
HUH?!
THEN ISN'T THAT BULLET MEANING-LESS?!
ERE RE OSE 50 PLE!
KOKO-NOÉ-SEN-SEI...
WITHOUT A GUN, WHAT'S A BULLET...
AH, BUT IT IS PLENTY.
EVEN JUST THIS ONE!

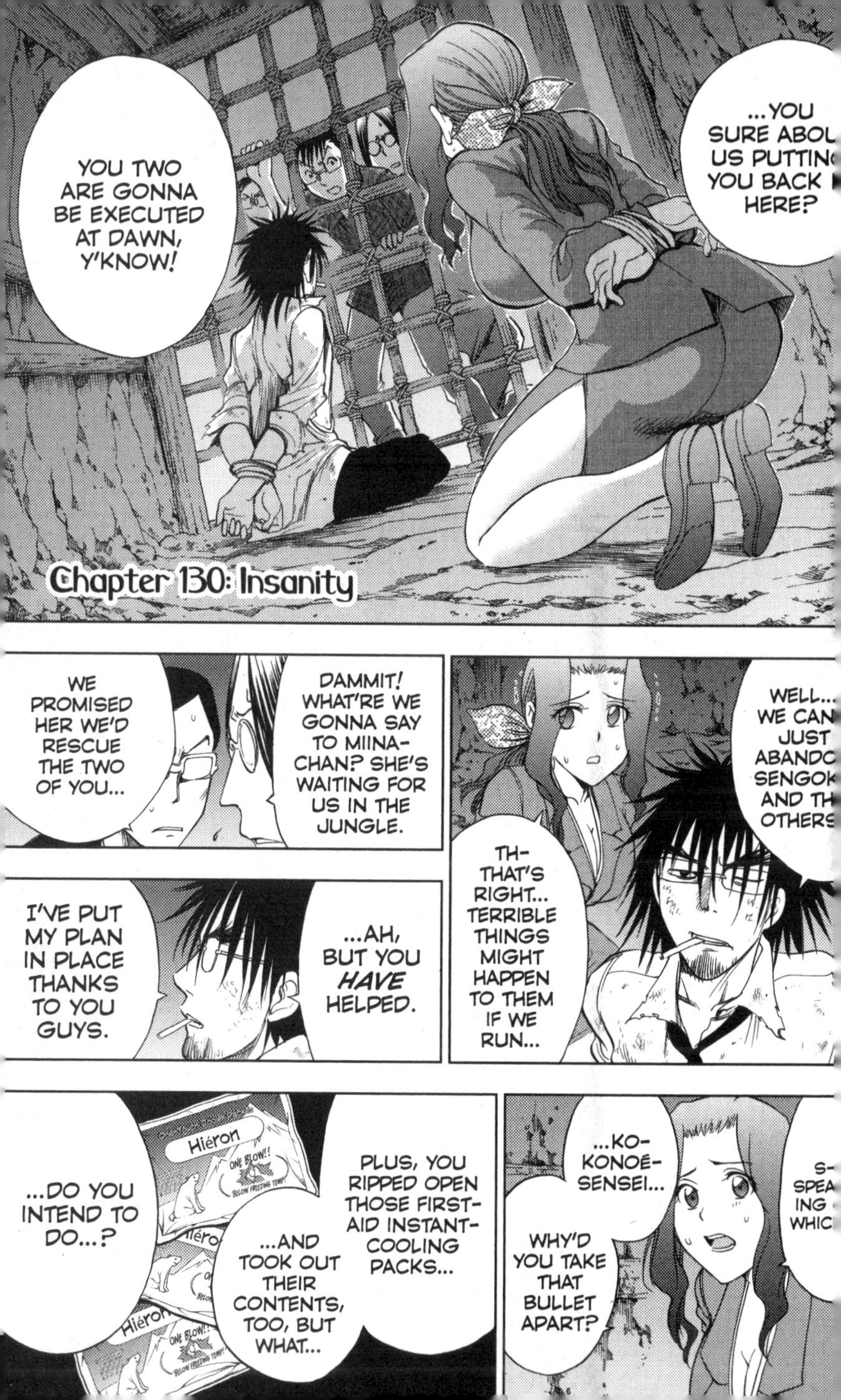
...YOU SURE ABOU US PUTTIN YOU BACK HERE?
YOU TWO ARE GONNA BE EXECUTED AT DAWN, Y'KNOW!
Chapter 130: Insanity
WELL... WE CAN JUST ABANDO SENGOK AND TH OTHERS
TH- THAT'S RIGHT... TERRIBLE THINGS MIGHT HAPPEN TO THEM IF WE RUN...
DAMMIT! WHAT'RE WE GONNA SAY TO MIINA-CHAN? SHE'S WAITING FOR US IN THE JUNGLE.
WE PROMISED HER WE'D RESCUE THE TWO OF YOU...
...AH, BUT YOU *HAVE* HELPED.
I'VE PUT MY PLAN IN PLACE THANKS TO YOU GUYS.
S- SPEA ING WHIC
...KO- KONOÉ- SENSEI...
WHY'D YOU TAKE THAT BULLET APART?
PLUS, YOU RIPPED OPEN THOSE FIRST-AID INSTANT-COOLING PACKS...
...AND TOOK OUT THEIR CONTENTS, TOO, BUT WHAT...
...DO YOU INTEND TO DO...?
Hiéron
ONE BLOW!!
BELOW FREEZING TEMP!

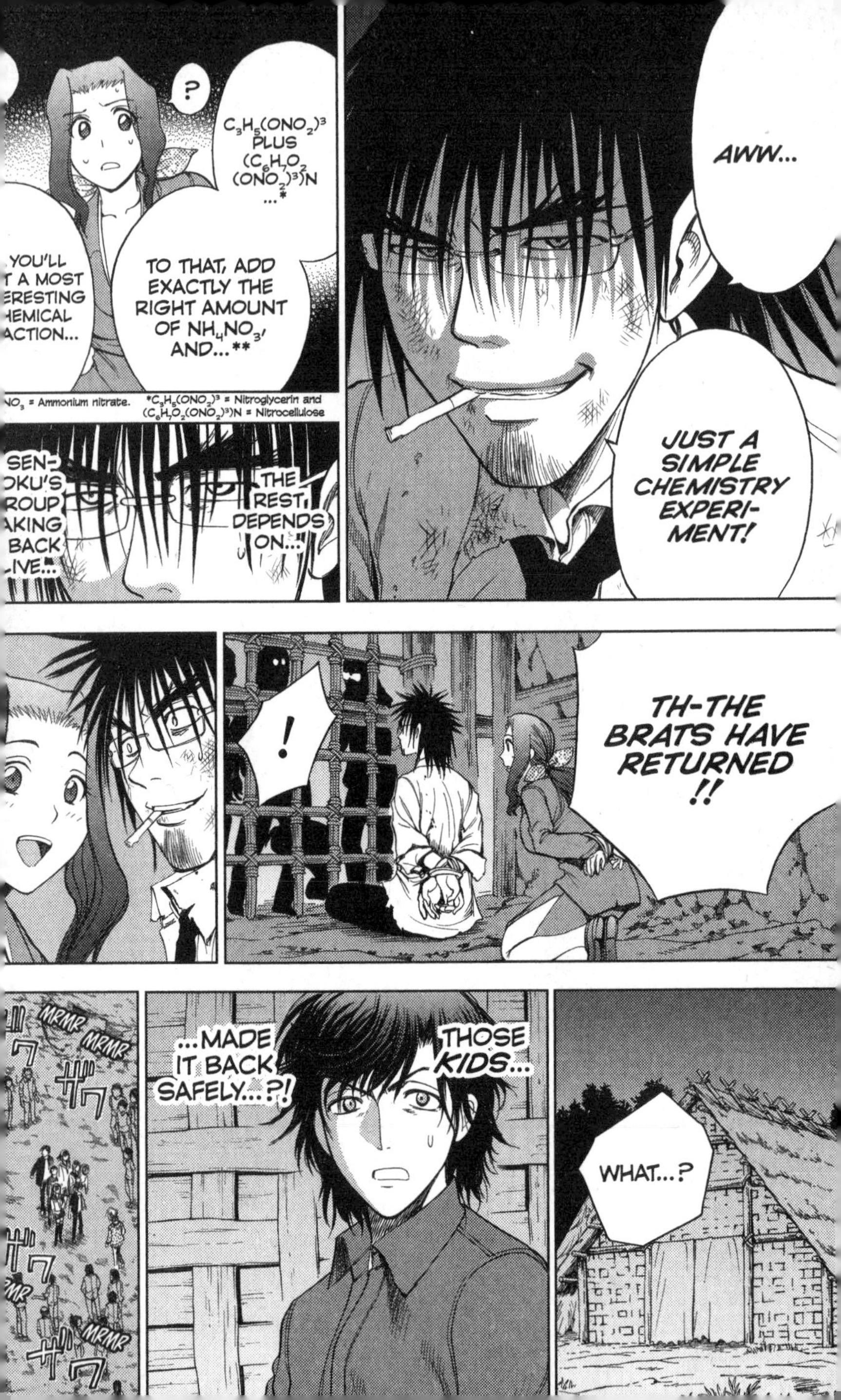
AWW...
JUST A SIMPLE CHEMISTRY EXPERI-MENT!
$C_3H_5(ONO_2)^3$ PLUS $(C_6H_7O_2(ONO_2)^3)N$ ...*
?
TO THAT, ADD EXACTLY THE RIGHT AMOUNT OF NH_4NO_3, AND...**
YOU'LL T A MOST ERESTING HEMICAL ACTION...
NO_3 = Ammonium nitrate.
*$C_3H_5(ONO_2)^3$ = Nitroglycerin and $(C_6H_7O_2(ONO_2)^3)N$ = Nitrocellulose
THE REST DEPENDS ON...
SEN-KU'S ROUP AKING BACK IVE...
TH-THE BRATS HAVE RETURNED!!
!
WHAT...?
THOSE KIDS...
...MADE IT BACK SAFELY...?!
MRMR
MRMR
ザワ
ザワ
ザワ
MR
MRMR
ザワ

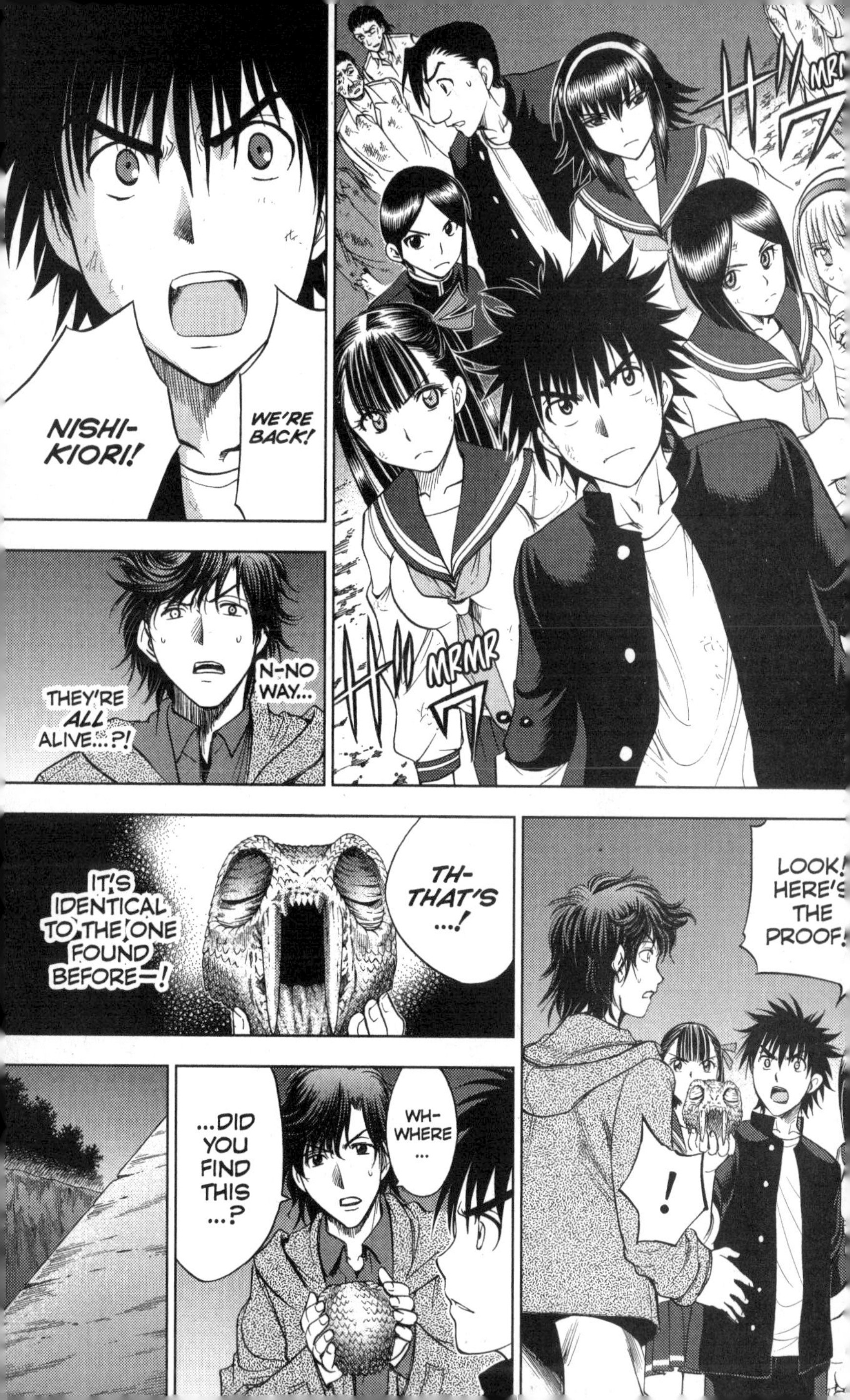
MRMR
MRMR
WE'RE BACK!
NISHI-KIORI!
N-NO WAY...
THEY'RE ALL ALIVE...?!
LOOK! HERE'S THE PROOF!
!
TH-THAT'S ...!
IT'S IDENTICAL TO THE ONE FOUND BEFORE—!
WH-WHERE ...
...DID YOU FIND THIS ...?

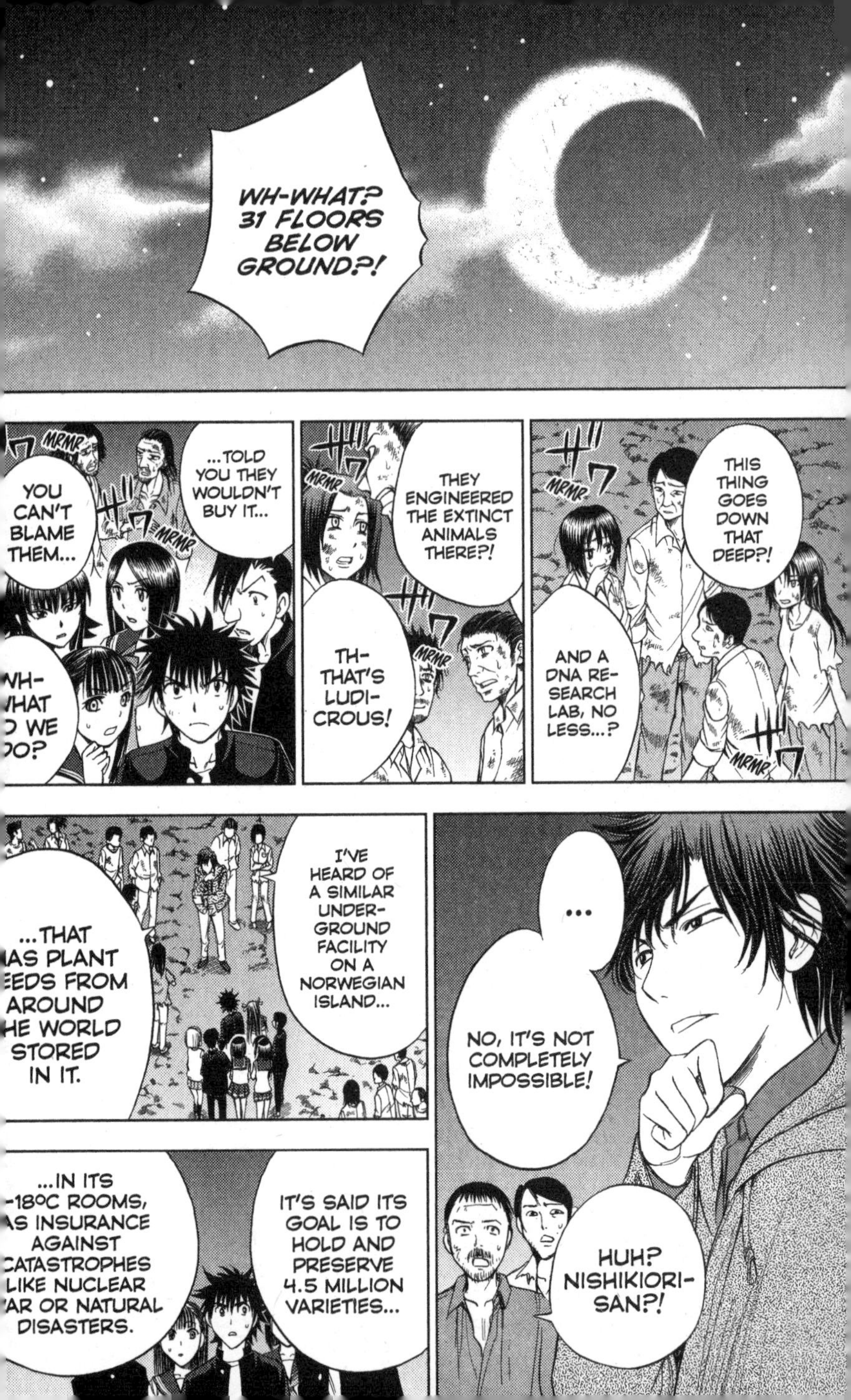
WH-WHAT? 31 FLOORS BELOW GROUND?!
THIS THING GOES DOWN THAT DEEP?!
MRMR
AND A DNA RE-SEARCH LAB, NO LESS...?
MRMR
THEY ENGINEERED THE EXTINCT ANIMALS THERE?!
MRMR
TH-THAT'S LUDI-CROUS!
MRMR
...TOLD YOU THEY WOULDN'T BUY IT...
MRMR
MRMR
YOU CAN'T BLAME THEM...
WH-
/HAT
D WE
OO?
...
NO, IT'S NOT COMPLETELY IMPOSSIBLE!
HUH? NISHIKIORI-SAN?!
I'VE HEARD OF A SIMILAR UNDER-GROUND FACILITY ON A NORWEGIAN ISLAND...
...THAT
AS PLANT
EEDS FROM
AROUND
HE WORLD
STORED
IN IT.
IT'S SAID ITS GOAL IS TO HOLD AND PRESERVE 4.5 MILLION VARIETIES...
...IN ITS
-18°C ROOMS,
AS INSURANCE
AGAINST
CATASTROPHES
LIKE NUCLEAR
AR OR NATURAL
DISASTERS.

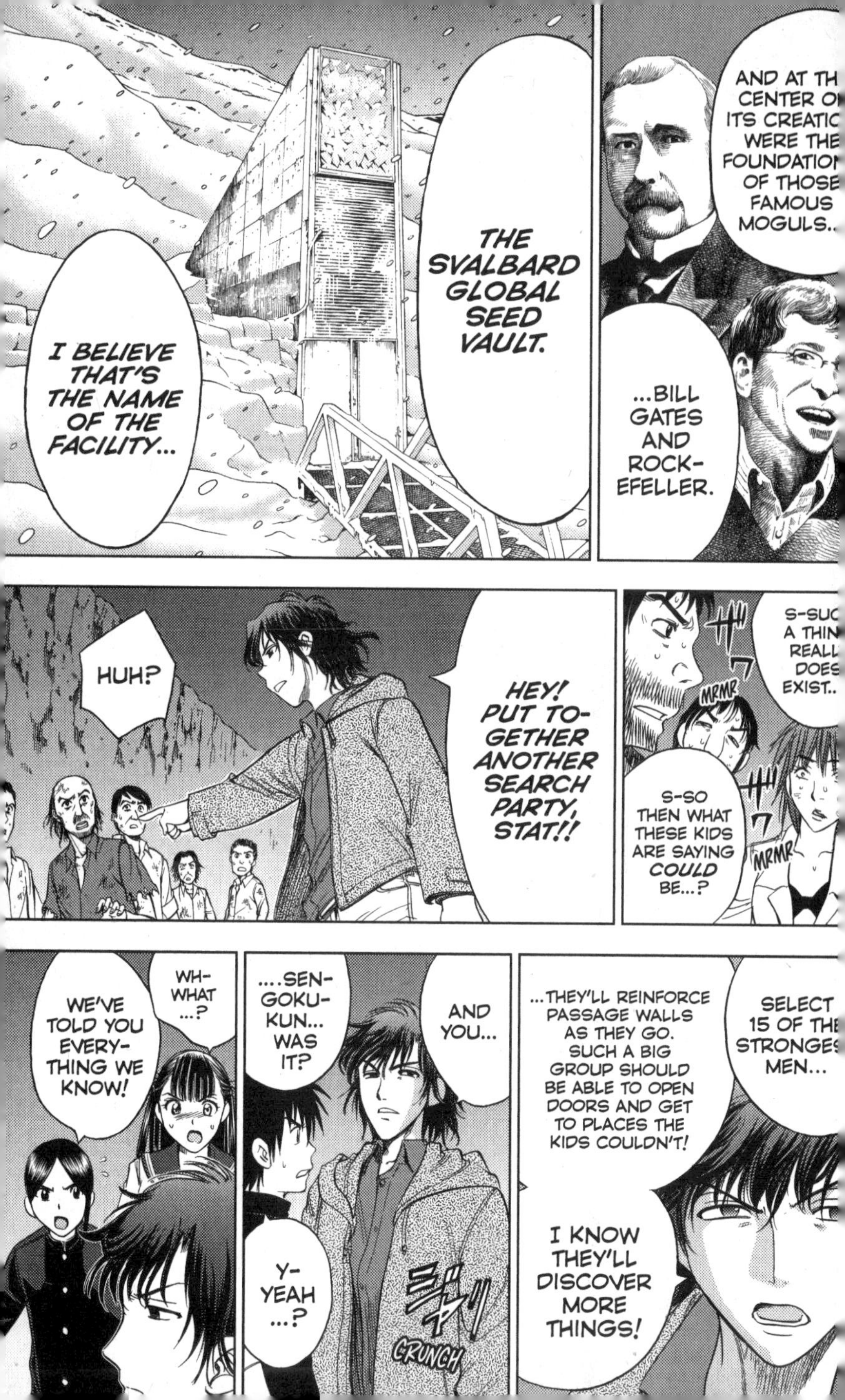
AND AT TH CENTER O ITS CREATIO WERE THE FOUNDATIO OF THOSE FAMOUS MOGULS..
...BILL GATES AND ROCK-EFELLER.
THE SVALBARD GLOBAL SEED VAULT.
I BELIEVE THAT'S THE NAME OF THE FACILITY...
S-SUC A THIN REALL DOES EXIST..
MRMR
S-SO THEN WHAT THESE KIDS ARE SAYING COULD BE...?
MRMR
HEY! PUT TO-GETHER ANOTHER SEARCH PARTY, STAT!!
HUH?
SELECT 15 OF THE STRONGES MEN...
...THEY'LL REINFORCE PASSAGE WALLS AS THEY GO. SUCH A BIG GROUP SHOULD BE ABLE TO OPEN DOORS AND GET TO PLACES THE KIDS COULDN'T!
I KNOW THEY'LL DISCOVER MORE THINGS!
AND YOU...
....SEN-GOKU-KUN... WAS IT?
Y-YEAH ...?
CRUNCH
WH-WHAT ...?
WE'VE TOLD YOU EVERY-THING WE KNOW!

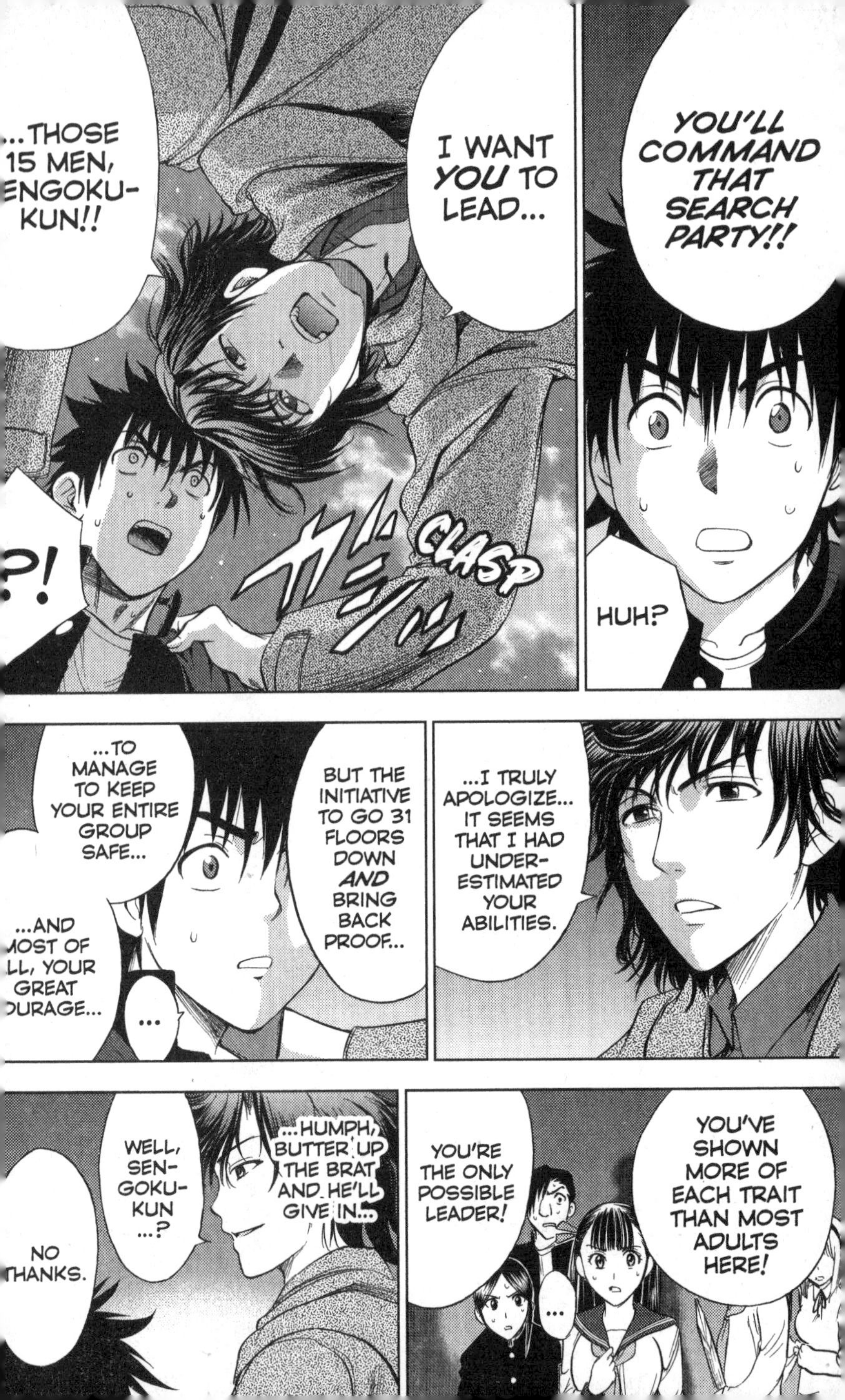
YOU'LL COMMAND THAT SEARCH PARTY!!
HUH?
I WANT *YOU* TO LEAD...
...THOSE 15 MEN, ENGOKU-KUN!!
CLASP
?!
...I TRULY APOLOGIZE... IT SEEMS THAT I HAD UNDER-ESTIMATED YOUR ABILITIES.
BUT THE INITIATIVE TO GO 31 FLOORS DOWN *AND* BRING BACK PROOF...
...TO MANAGE TO KEEP YOUR ENTIRE GROUP SAFE...
...AND MOST OF LL, YOUR GREAT OURAGE...
...
YOU'VE SHOWN MORE OF EACH TRAIT THAN MOST ADULTS HERE!
YOU'RE THE ONLY POSSIBLE LEADER!
...
...HUMPH, BUTTER UP THE BRAT AND HE'LL GIVE IN...
WELL, SEN-GOKU-KUN ...?
NO THANKS.

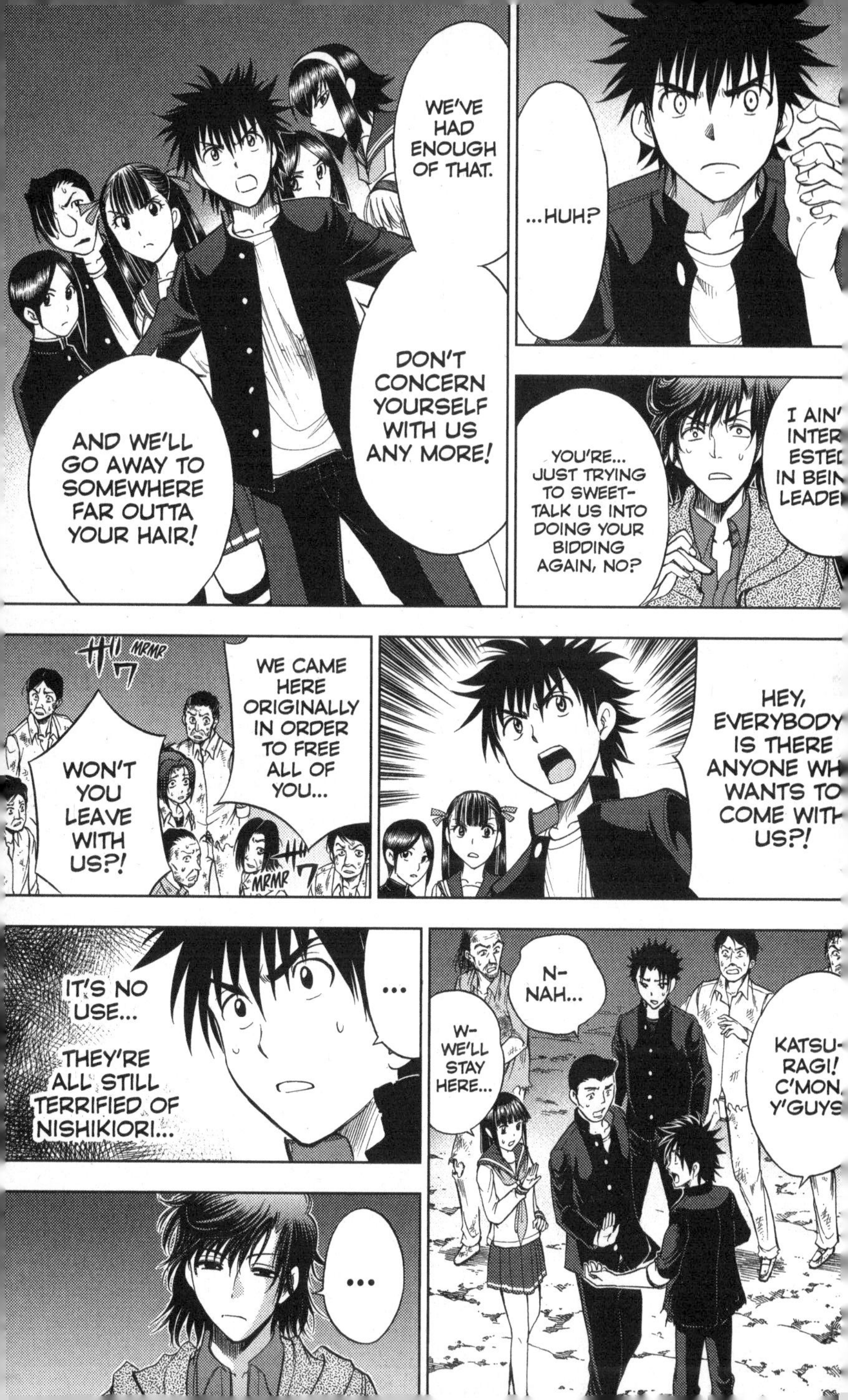
...HUH?
I AIN' INTER ESTED IN BEIN LEADE
YOU'RE... JUST TRYING TO SWEET-TALK US INTO DOING YOUR BIDDING AGAIN, NO?
WE'VE HAD ENOUGH OF THAT.
DON'T CONCERN YOURSELF WITH US ANY MORE!
AND WE'LL GO AWAY TO SOMEWHERE FAR OUTTA YOUR HAIR!
HEY, EVERYBODY IS THERE ANYONE WH WANTS TO COME WITH US?!
WE CAME HERE ORIGINALLY IN ORDER TO FREE ALL OF YOU...
MRMR
WON'T YOU LEAVE WITH US?!
MRMR
KATSU-RAGI! C'MON, Y'GUYS
N-NAH...
W-WE'LL STAY HERE...
...
IT'S NO USE...
THEY'RE ALL STILL TERRIFIED OF NISHIKIORI...
...

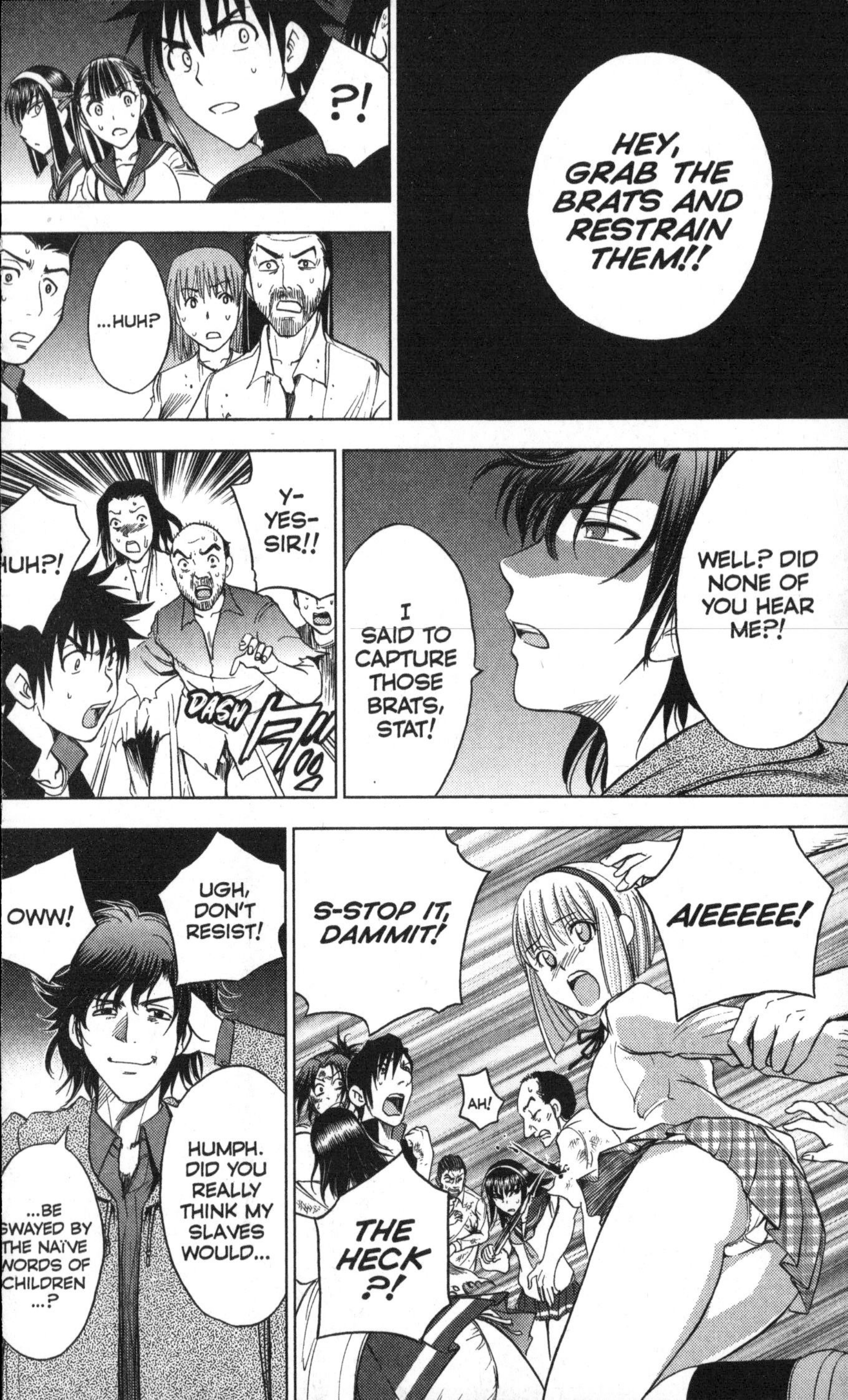
HEY, GRAB THE BRATS AND RESTRAIN THEM!!
?!
...HUH?
WELL? DID NONE OF YOU HEAR ME?!
I SAID TO CAPTURE THOSE BRATS, STAT!
Y-YES-SIR!!
HUH?!
DASH
AIEEEEE!
S-STOP IT, DAMMIT!
AH!
THE HECK ?!
UGH, DON'T RESIST!
OWW!
HUMPH. DID YOU REALLY THINK MY SLAVES WOULD...
...BE SWAYED BY THE NAÏVE WORDS OF CHILDREN ...?

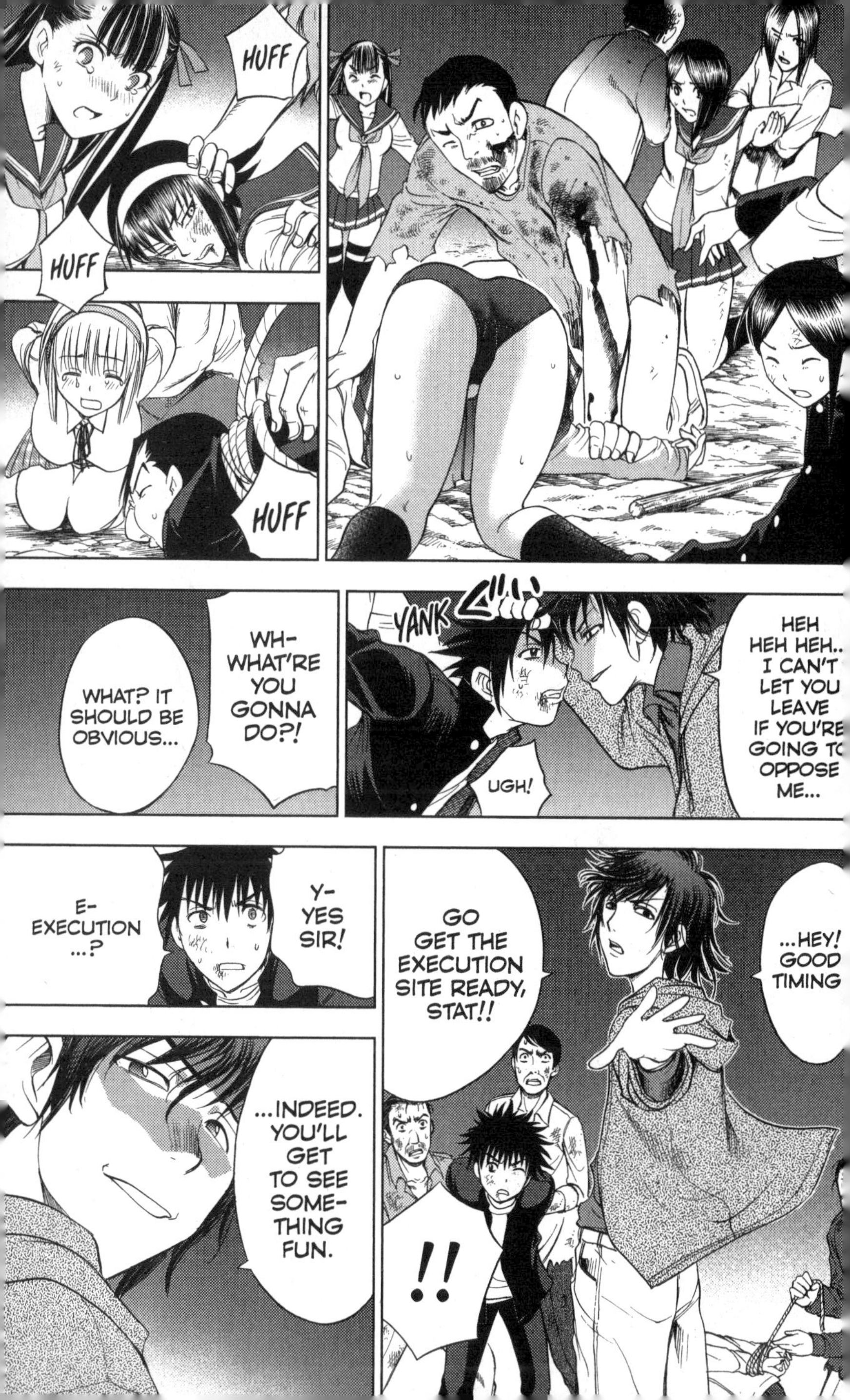
HUFF
HUFF
HUFF
YANK
HEH HEH HEH.. I CAN'T LET YOU LEAVE IF YOU'RE GOING TO OPPOSE ME...
UGH!
WH- WHAT'RE YOU GONNA DO?!
WHAT? IT SHOULD BE OBVIOUS...
...HEY! GOOD TIMING
GO GET THE EXECUTION SITE READY, STAT!!
!!
Y- YES SIR!
E- EXECUTION ...?
...INDEED. YOU'LL GET TO SEE SOME- THING FUN.

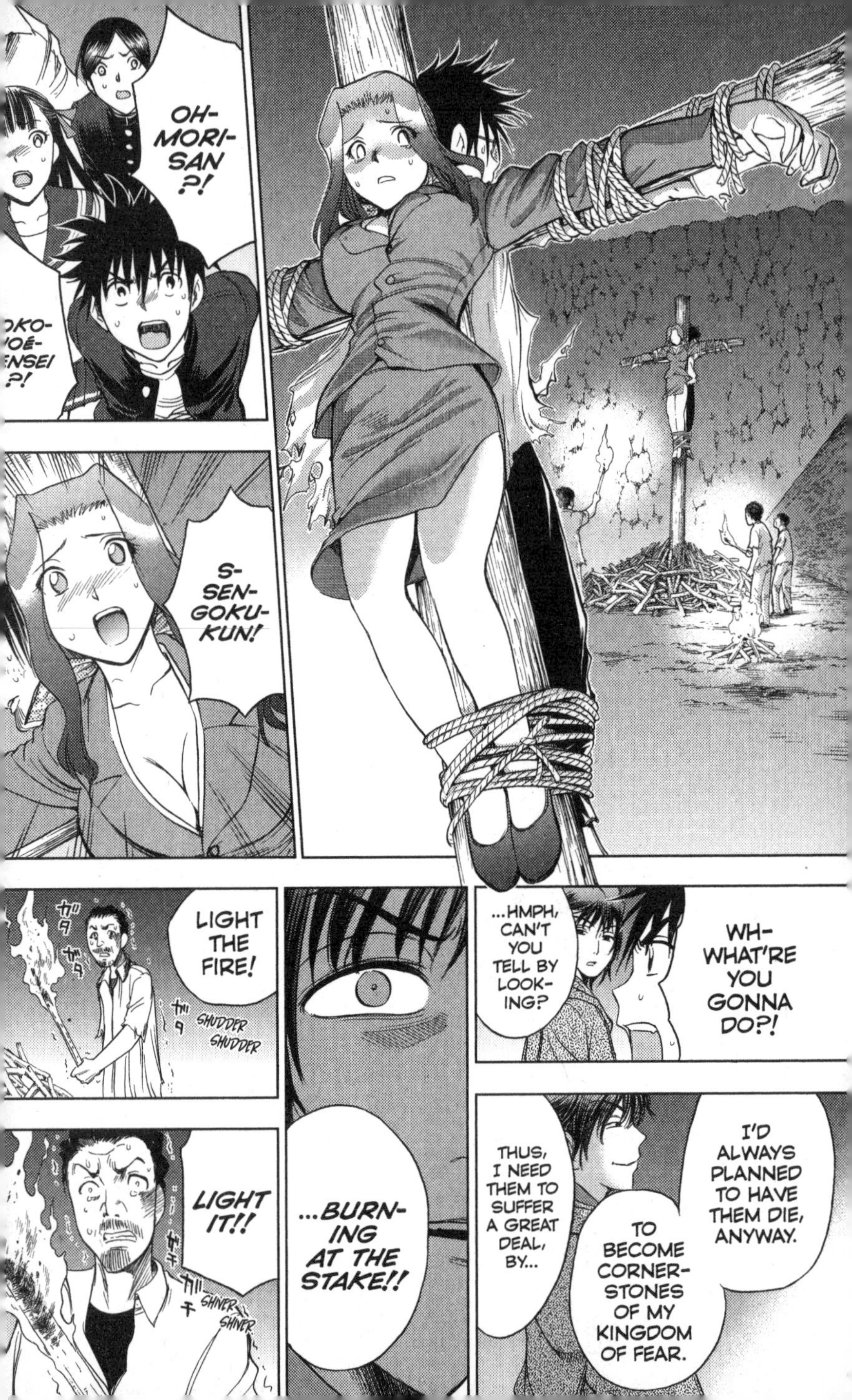
OH-MORI-SAN?!
OKO-OÉ-ENSEI?!
S-SENGOKU-KUN!
WH-WHAT'RE YOU GONNA DO?!
...HMPH, CAN'T YOU TELL BY LOOKING?
I'D ALWAYS PLANNED TO HAVE THEM DIE, ANYWAY.
TO BECOME CORNERSTONES OF MY KINGDOM OF FEAR.
THUS, I NEED THEM TO SUFFER A GREAT DEAL, BY...
...BURNING AT THE STAKE!!
LIGHT THE FIRE!
SHUDDER SHUDDER
LIGHT IT!!
SHIVER SHIVER

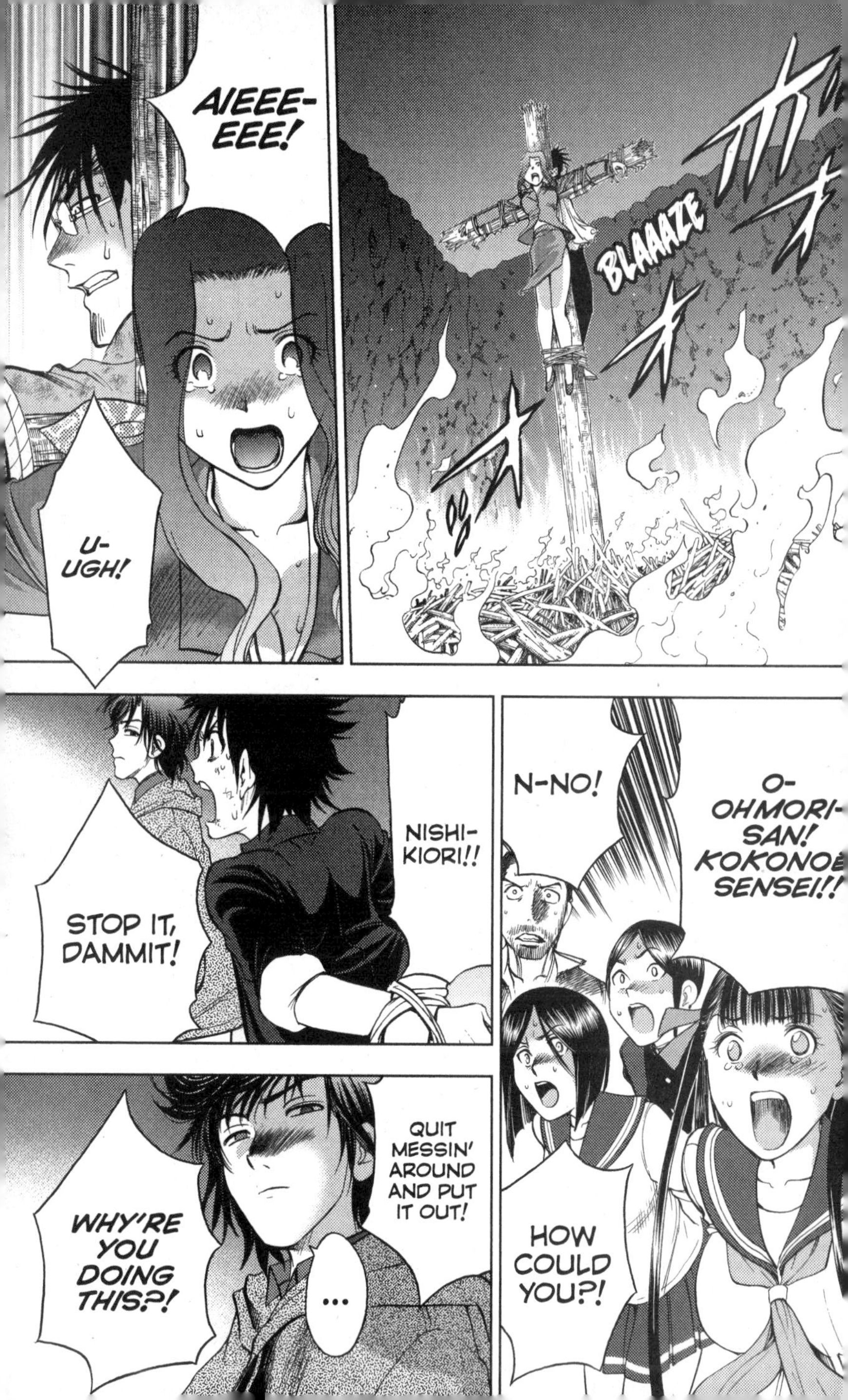
BLAAAZE
AIEEE-EEE!
U-UGH!
O-OHMORI-SAN! KOKONOE SENSEI!!
N-NO!
HOW COULD YOU?!
NISHI-KIORI!!
STOP IT, DAMMIT!
QUIT MESSIN' AROUND AND PUT IT OUT!
WHY'RE YOU DOING THIS?!
...

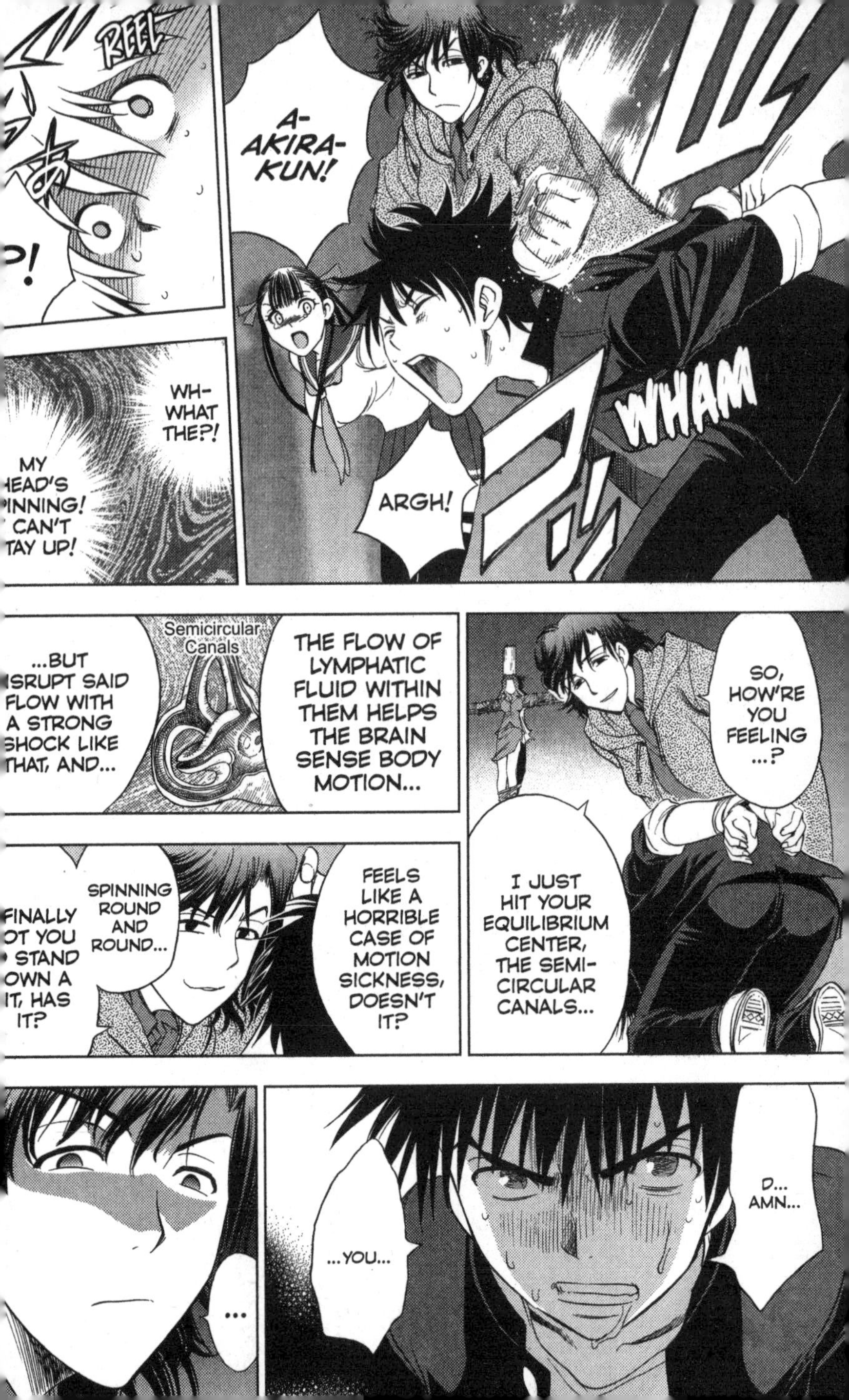

A-AKIRA-KUN!
WHAM
ARGH!
REEL
?!
WH-WHAT THE?!
MY HEAD'S PINNING! CAN'T TAY UP!
SO, HOW'RE YOU FEELING...?
I JUST HIT YOUR EQUILIBRIUM CENTER, THE SEMI-CIRCULAR CANALS...
THE FLOW OF LYMPHATIC FLUID WITHIN THEM HELPS THE BRAIN SENSE BODY MOTION...
Semicircular Canals
...BUT ISRUPT SAID FLOW WITH A STRONG SHOCK LIKE THAT, AND...
FEELS LIKE A HORRIBLE CASE OF MOTION SICKNESS, DOESN'T IT?
SPINNING ROUND AND ROUND...
FINALLY OT YOU STAND OWN A IT, HAS IT?
D... AMN...
...YOU...
...

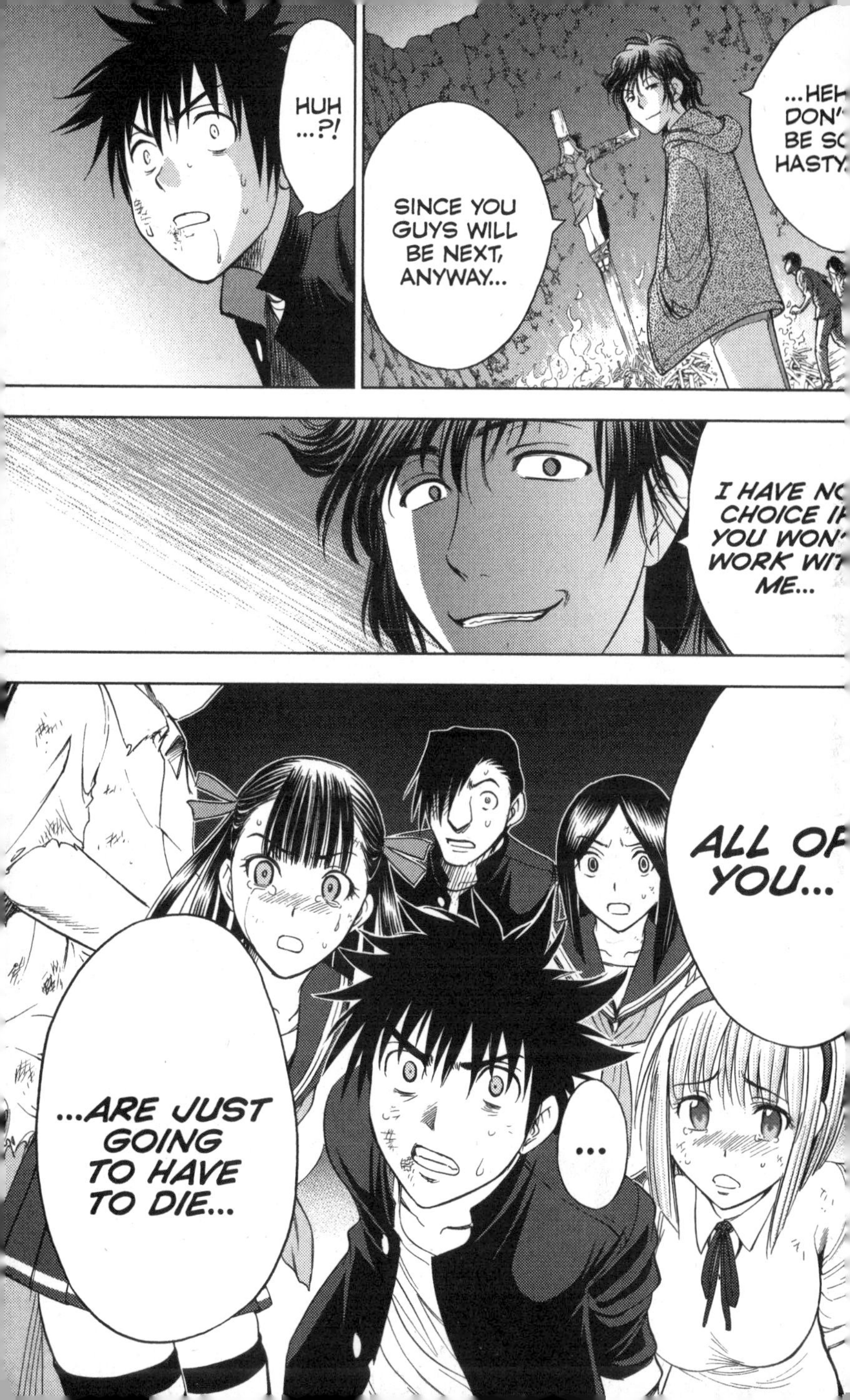
...HEH DON' BE SC HASTY.
SINCE YOU GUYS WILL BE NEXT, ANYWAY...
HUH ...?!
I HAVE NC CHOICE IF YOU WON' WORK WIT ME...
ALL OF YOU...
...
...ARE JUST GOING TO HAVE TO DIE...

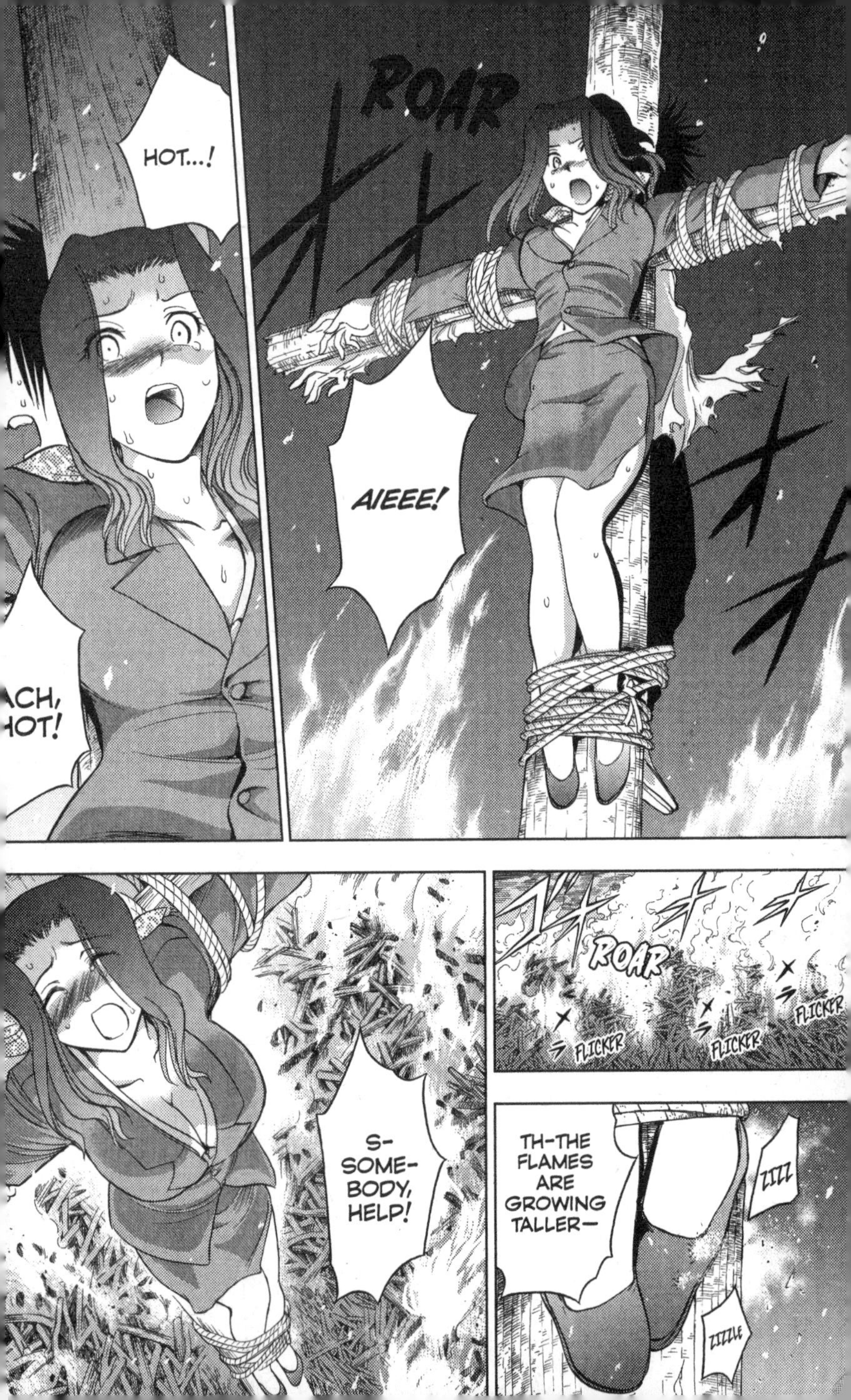
ROAR
AIEEE!
HOT...!
ACH, HOT!
ROAR
FLICKER
FLICKER
FLICKER
TH-THE FLAMES ARE GROWING TALLER—
ZIZZ
ZIZZLE
S-SOME-BODY, HELP!

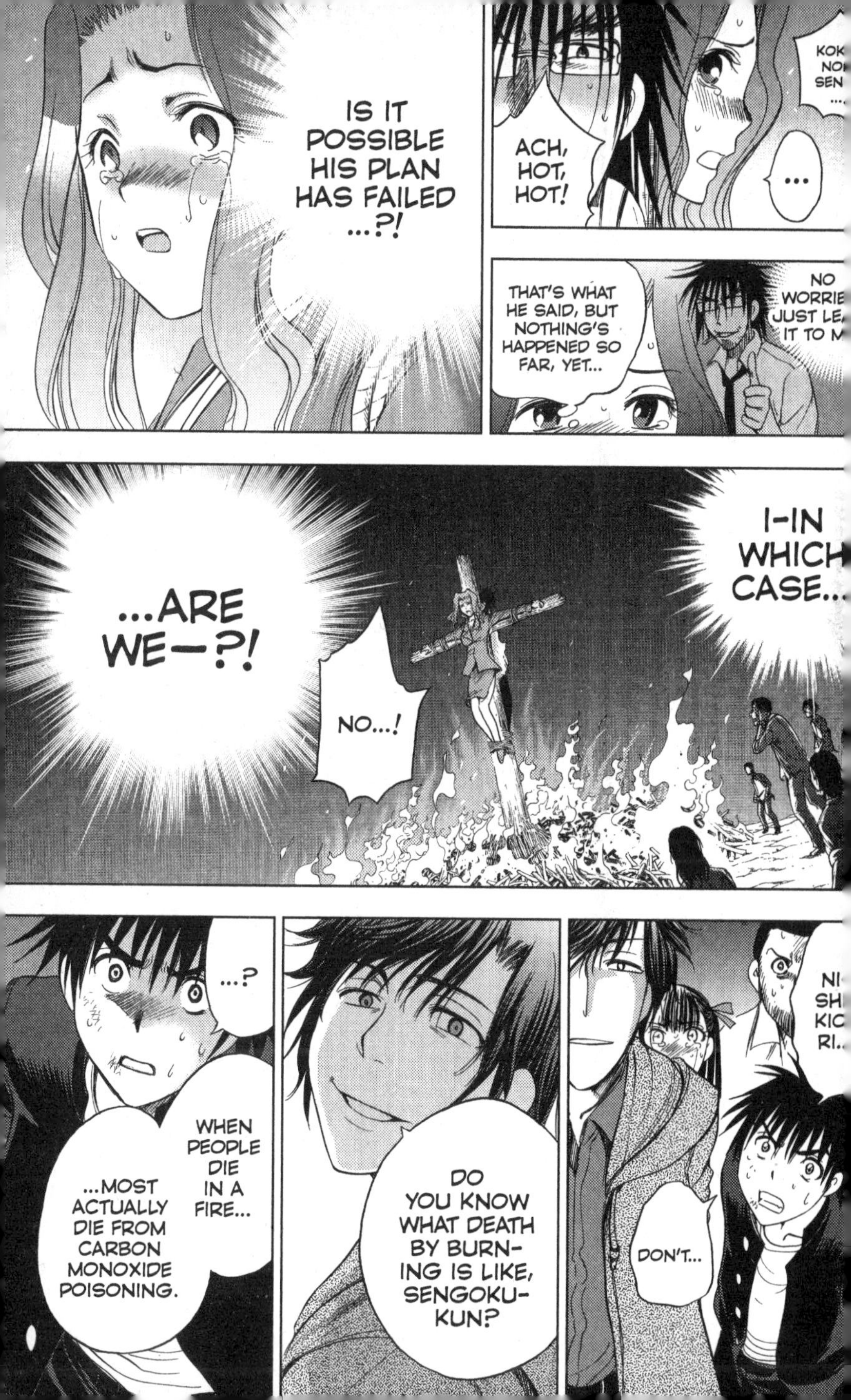
KOK NO SEN ...
...
ACH, HOT, HOT!
NO WORRIE JUST LE IT TO M
THAT'S WHAT HE SAID, BUT NOTHING'S HAPPENED SO FAR, YET...
IS IT POSSIBLE HIS PLAN HAS FAILED ...?!
I-IN WHICH CASE...
NO...!
...ARE WE—?!
NI SH KIC RI..
DON'T...
DO YOU KNOW WHAT DEATH BY BURNING IS LIKE, SENGOKU-KUN?
...?
WHEN PEOPLE DIE IN A FIRE...
...MOST ACTUALLY DIE FROM CARBON MONOXIDE POISONING.

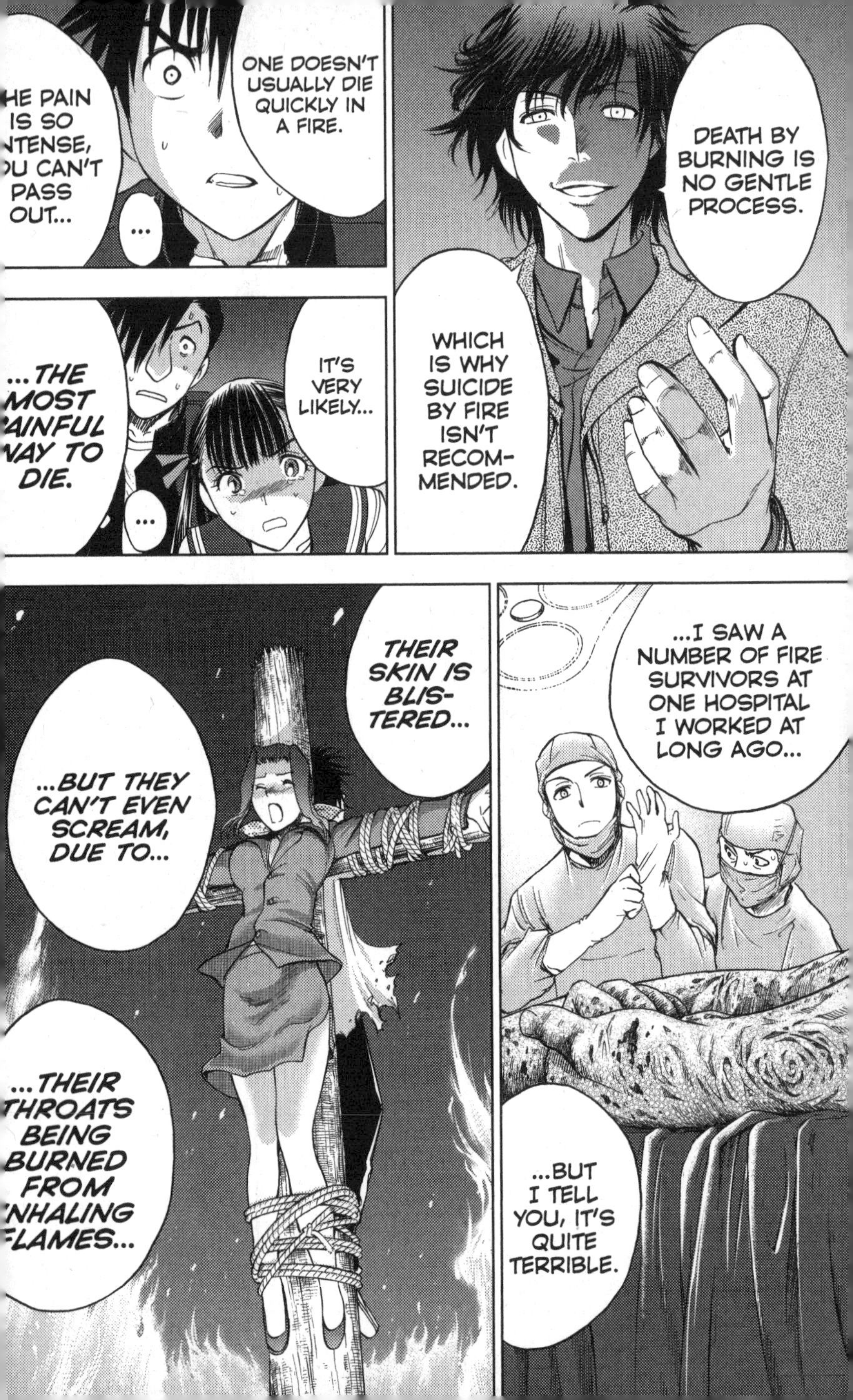
DEATH BY BURNING IS NO GENTLE PROCESS.
WHICH IS WHY SUICIDE BY FIRE ISN'T RECOMMENDED.
ONE DOESN'T USUALLY DIE QUICKLY IN A FIRE.
...
HE PAIN IS SO NTENSE, OU CAN'T PASS OUT...
IT'S VERY LIKELY...
...THE MOST AINFUL VAY TO DIE.
...
...I SAW A NUMBER OF FIRE SURVIVORS AT ONE HOSPITAL I WORKED AT LONG AGO...
...BUT I TELL YOU, IT'S QUITE TERRIBLE.
THEIR SKIN IS BLIS-TERED...
...BUT THEY CAN'T EVEN SCREAM, DUE TO...
...THEIR THROATS BEING BURNED FROM NHALING FLAMES...

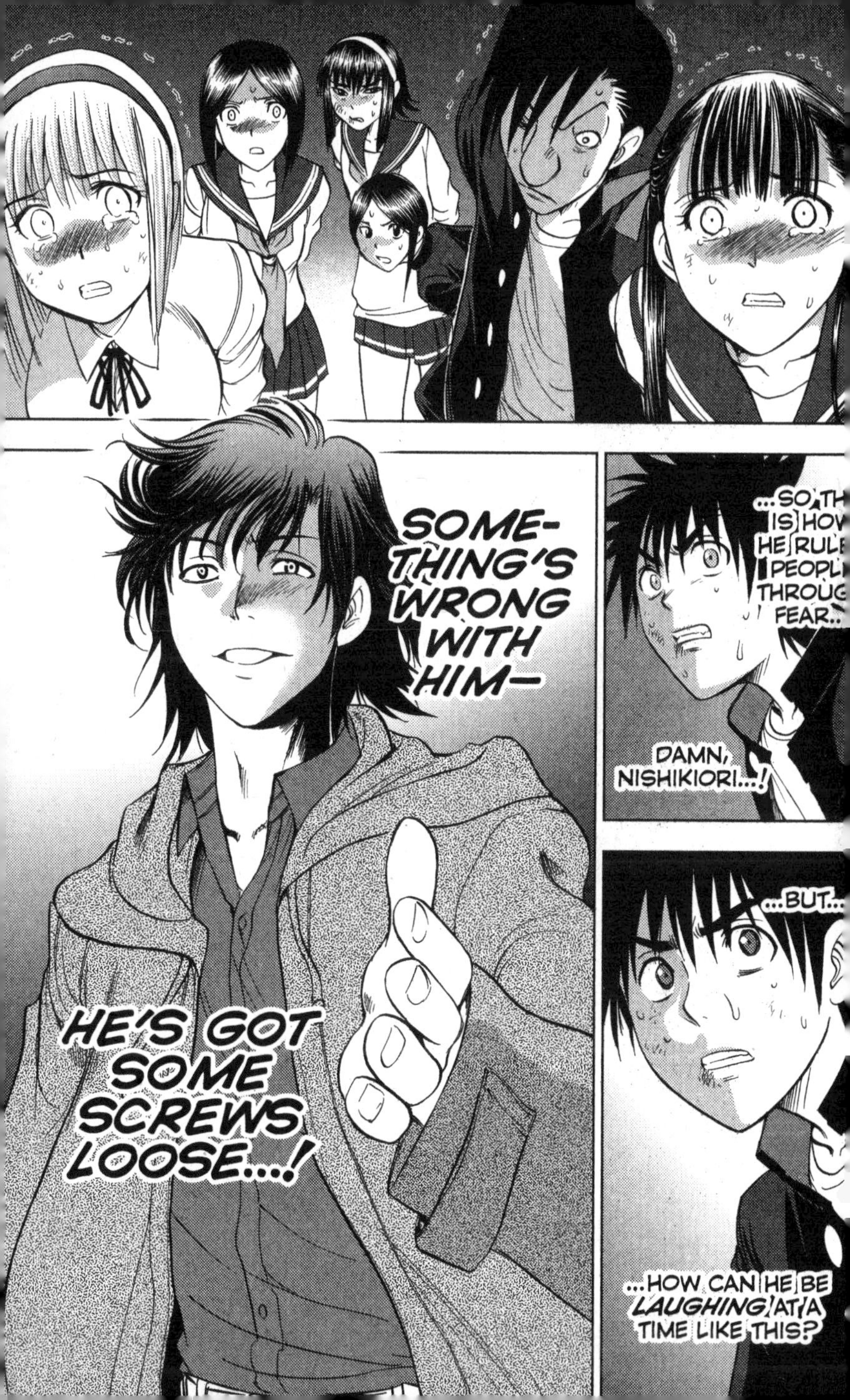
...SO TH IS HOW HE RULE PEOPL THROUG FEAR...
DAMN, NISHIKIORI...!
...BUT...
...HOW CAN HE BE *LAUGHING* AT A TIME LIKE THIS?
SOME-THING'S WRONG WITH HIM—
HE'S GOT SOME SCREWS LOOSE...!

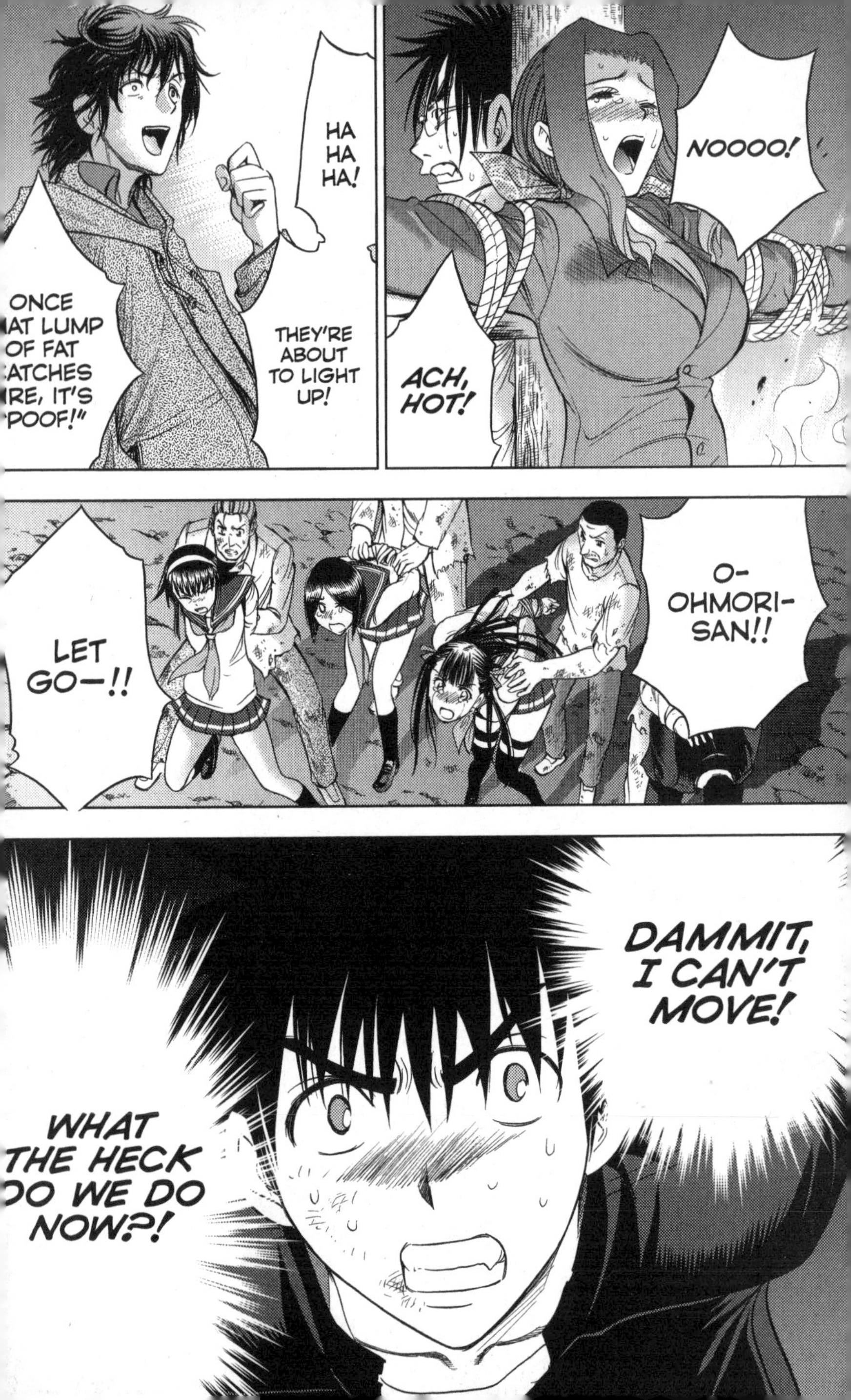
NOOOO!
ACH, HOT!
HA HA HA!
THEY'RE ABOUT TO LIGHT UP!
ONCE AT LUMP OF FAT ATCHES RE, IT'S POOF!"
O-OHMORI-SAN!!
LET GO—!!
DAMMIT, I CAN'T MOVE!
WHAT THE HECK O WE DO NOW?!

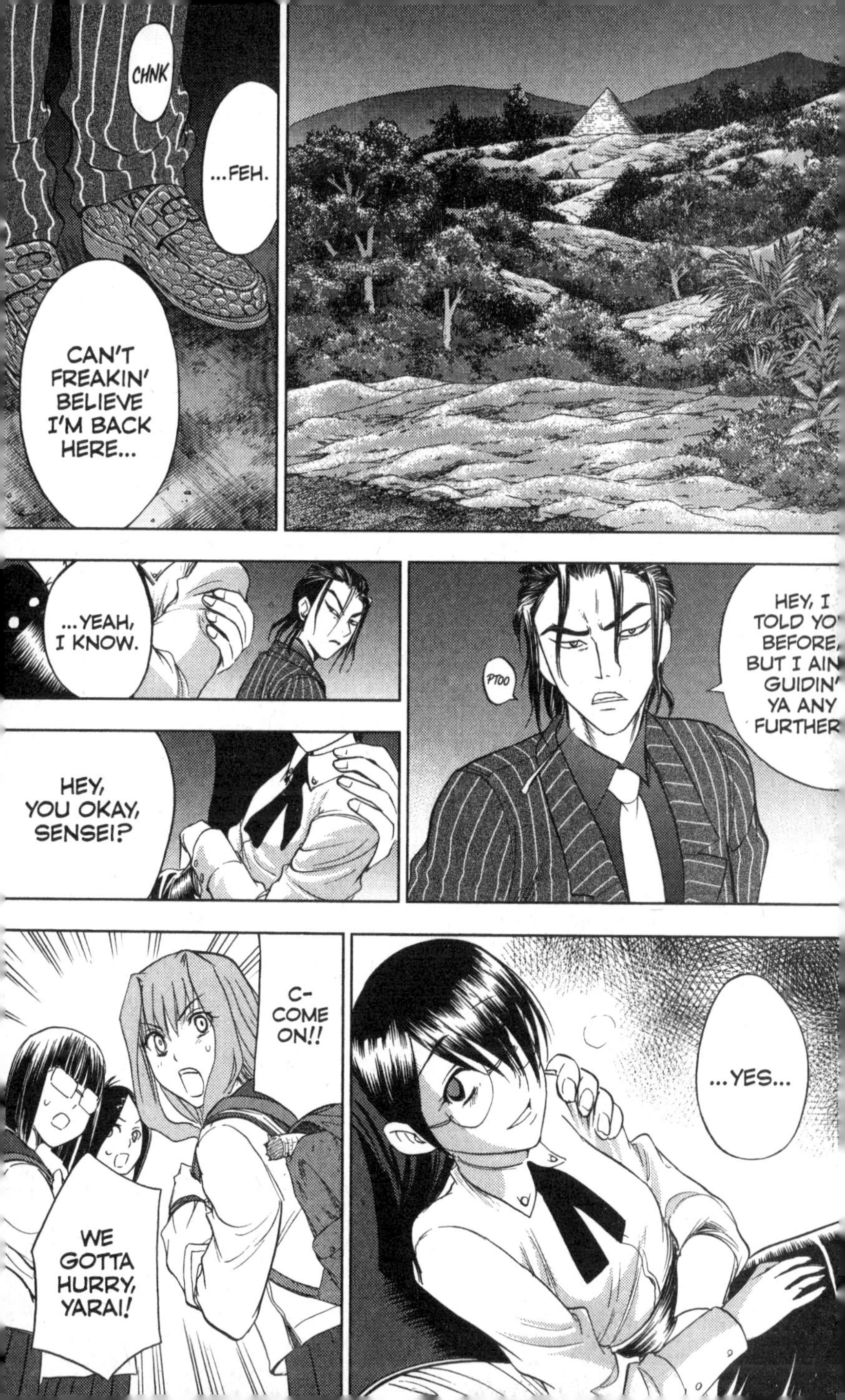
CHNK
...FEH.
CAN'T FREAKIN' BELIEVE I'M BACK HERE...
PTOO
HEY, I TOLD YO' BEFORE, BUT I AIN' GUIDIN' YA ANY FURTHER
...YEAH, I KNOW.
HEY, YOU OKAY, SENSEI?
...YES...
C- COME ON!!
WE GOTTA HURRY, YARAI!

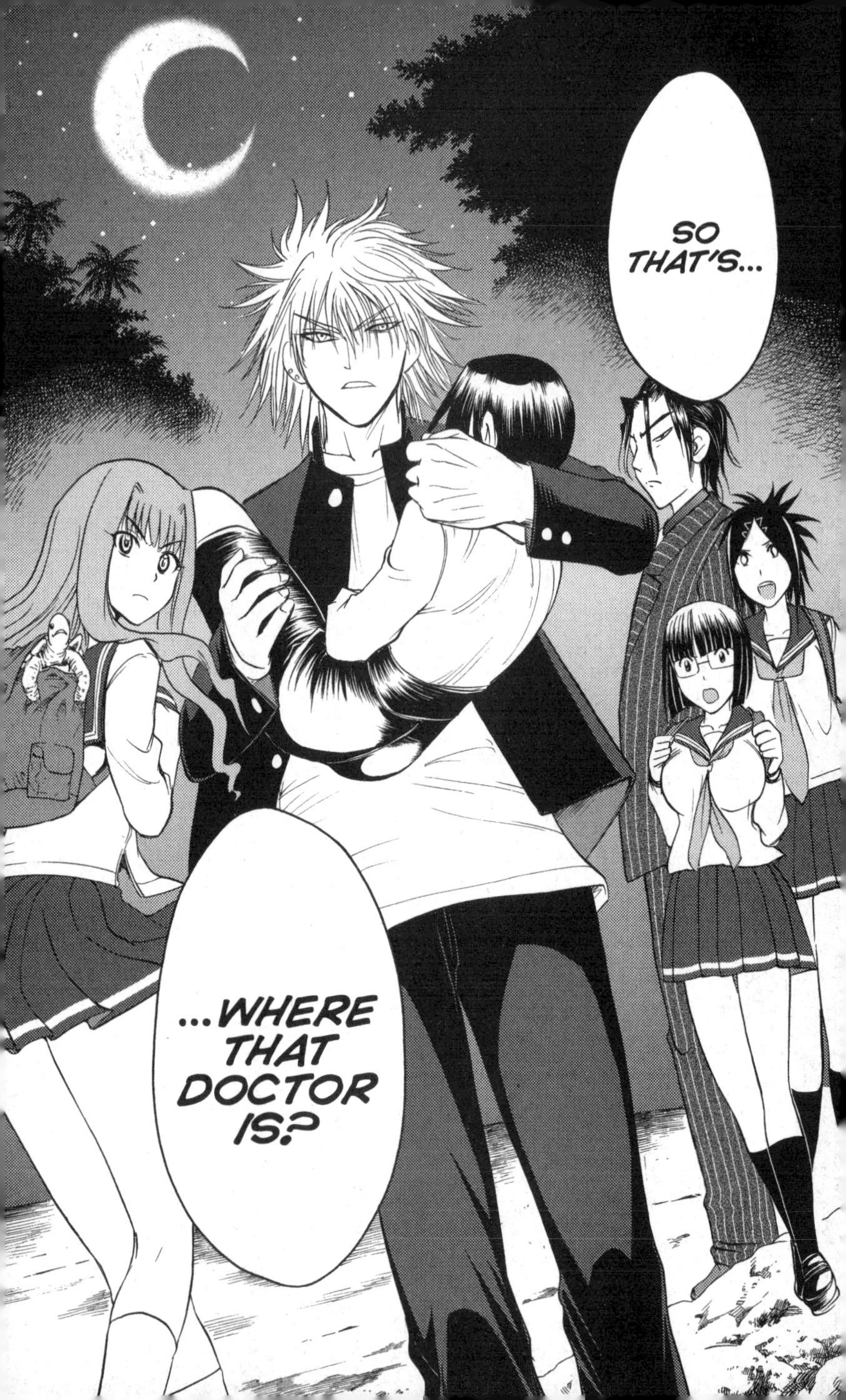
SO THAT'S...
...WHERE THAT DOCTOR IS?

To be continued...

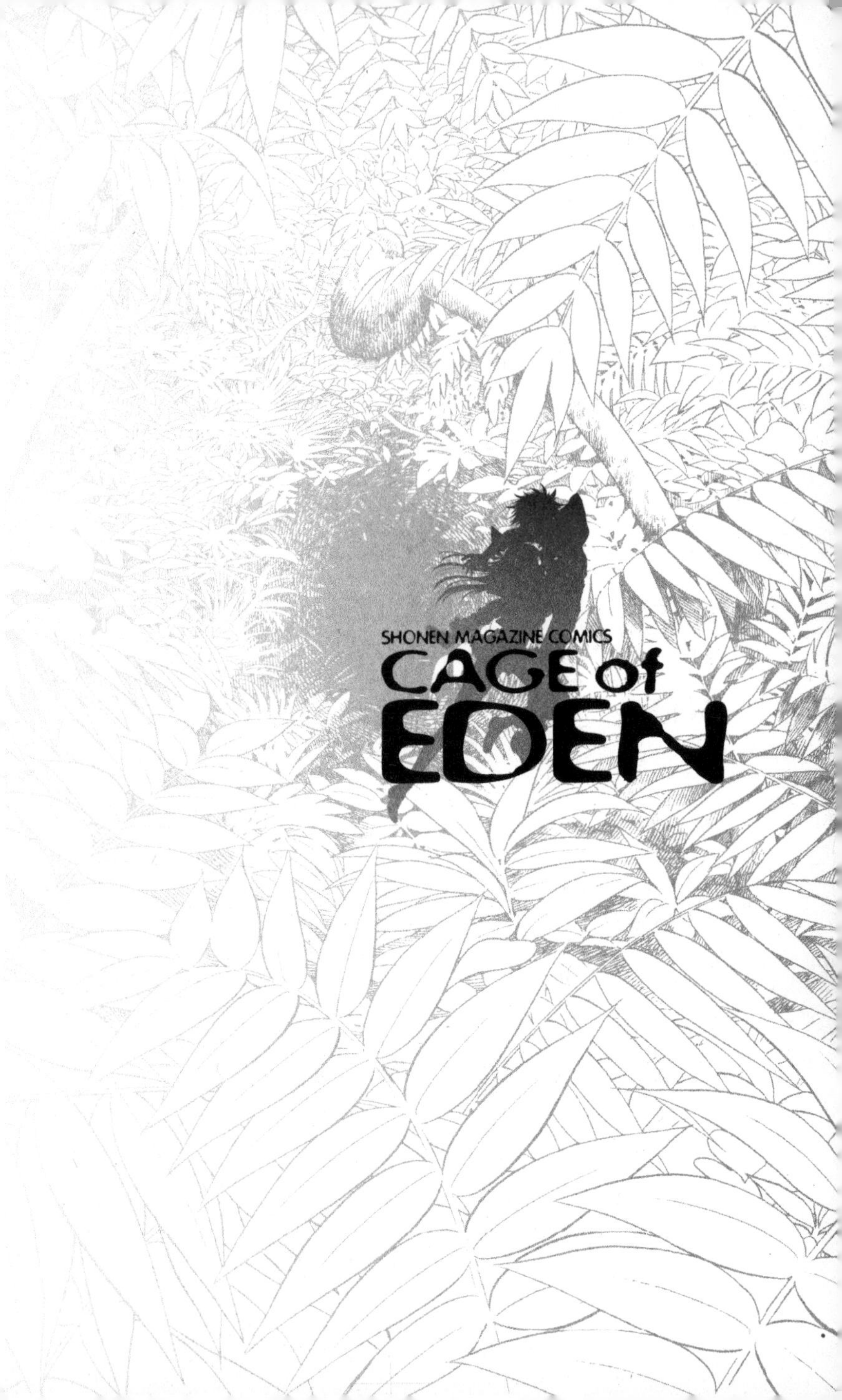
SHONEN MAGAZINE COMICS
CAGE of EDEN

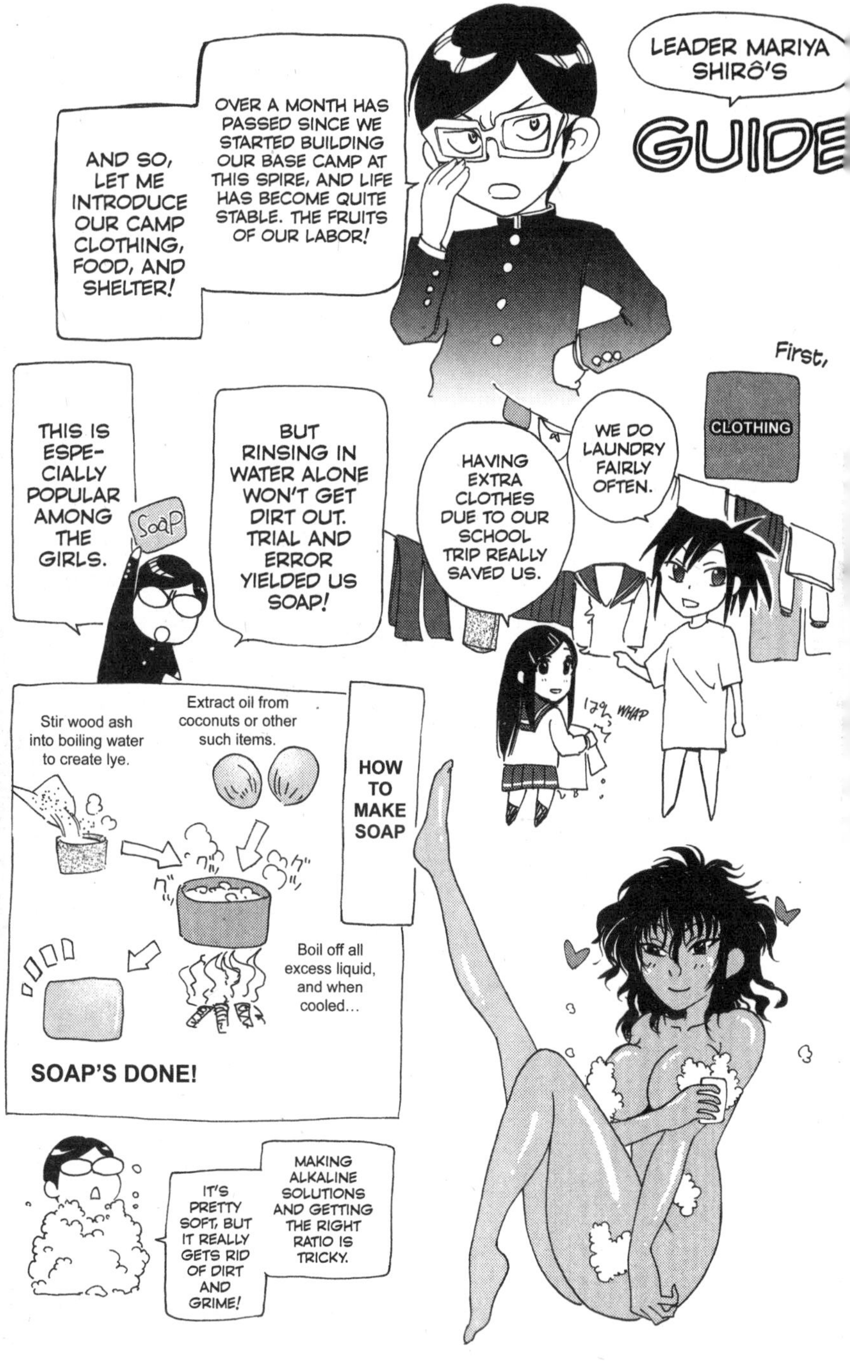
LEADER MARIYA SHIRÔ'S
GUIDE
OVER A MONTH HAS PASSED SINCE WE STARTED BUILDING OUR BASE CAMP AT THIS SPIRE, AND LIFE HAS BECOME QUITE STABLE. THE FRUITS OF OUR LABOR!
AND SO, LET ME INTRODUCE OUR CAMP CLOTHING, FOOD, AND SHELTER!
First,
CLOTHING
WE DO LAUNDRY FAIRLY OFTEN.
HAVING EXTRA CLOTHES DUE TO OUR SCHOOL TRIP REALLY SAVED US.
WHAP
BUT RINSING IN WATER ALONE WON'T GET DIRT OUT. TRIAL AND ERROR YIELDED US SOAP!
THIS IS ESPE-CIALLY POPULAR AMONG THE GIRLS.
Soap
HOW TO MAKE SOAP
Extract oil from coconuts or other such items.
Stir wood ash into boiling water to create lye.
Boil off all excess liquid, and when cooled…
SOAP'S DONE!
MAKING ALKALINE SOLUTIONS AND GETTING THE RIGHT RATIO IS TRICKY.
IT'S PRETTY SOFT, BUT IT REALLY GETS RID OF DIRT AND GRIME!

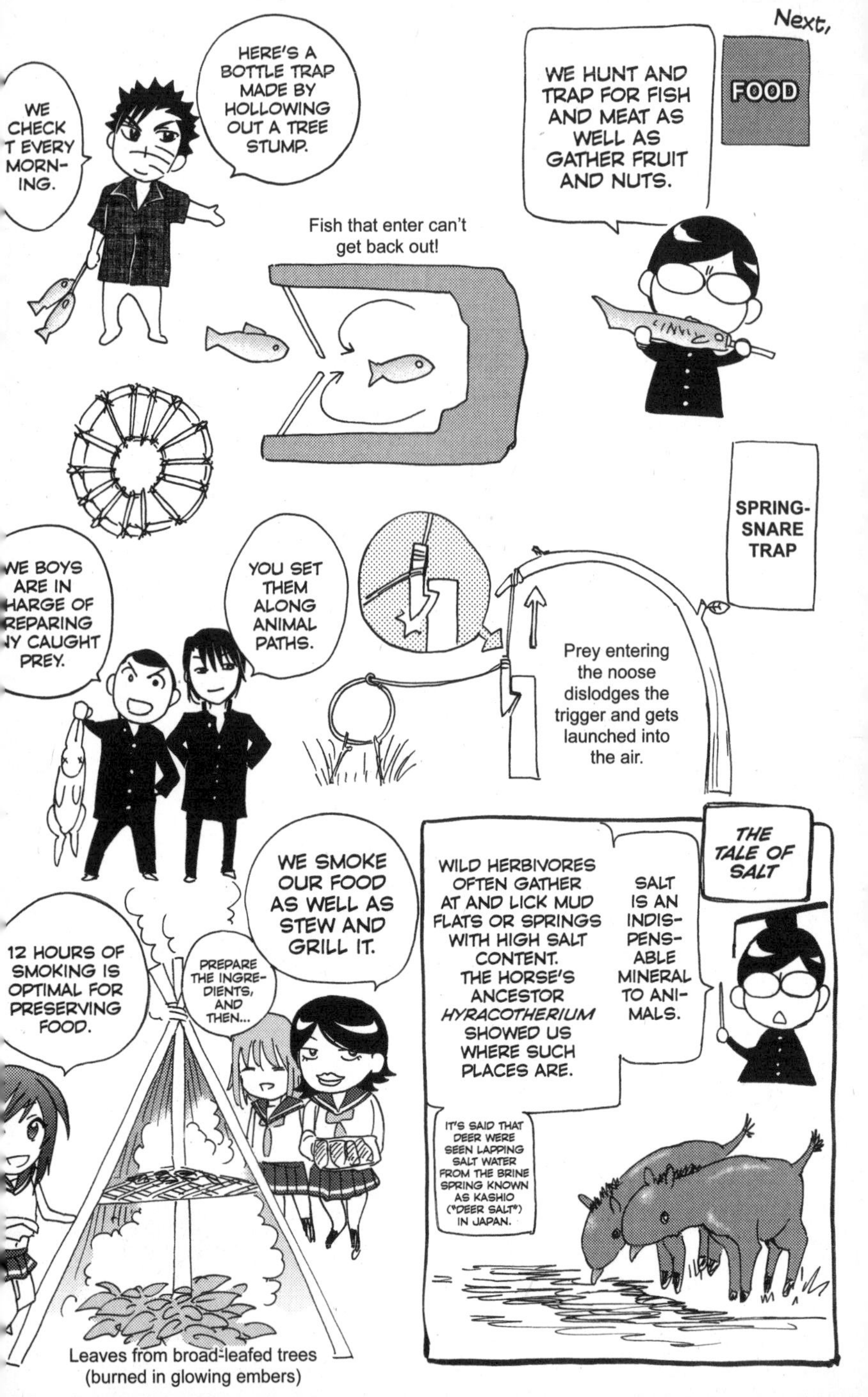
Next,
FOOD
WE HUNT AND TRAP FOR FISH AND MEAT AS WELL AS GATHER FRUIT AND NUTS.
HERE'S A BOTTLE TRAP MADE BY HOLLOWING OUT A TREE STUMP.
WE CHECK T EVERY MORN-ING.
Fish that enter can't get back out!
SPRING-SNARE TRAP
Prey entering the noose dislodges the trigger and gets launched into the air.
YOU SET THEM ALONG ANIMAL PATHS.
WE BOYS ARE IN HARGE OF REPARING NY CAUGHT PREY.
THE TALE OF SALT
SALT IS AN INDIS-PENS-ABLE MINERAL TO ANI-MALS.
WILD HERBIVORES OFTEN GATHER AT AND LICK MUD FLATS OR SPRINGS WITH HIGH SALT CONTENT. THE HORSE'S ANCESTOR HYRACOTHERIUM SHOWED US WHERE SUCH PLACES ARE.
IT'S SAID THAT DEER WERE SEEN LAPPING SALT WATER FROM THE BRINE SPRING KNOWN AS KASHIO ("DEER SALT") IN JAPAN.
WE SMOKE OUR FOOD AS WELL AS STEW AND GRILL IT.
PREPARE THE INGRE-DIENTS, AND THEN...
12 HOURS OF SMOKING IS OPTIMAL FOR PRESERVING FOOD.
Leaves from broad-leafed trees (burned in glowing embers)

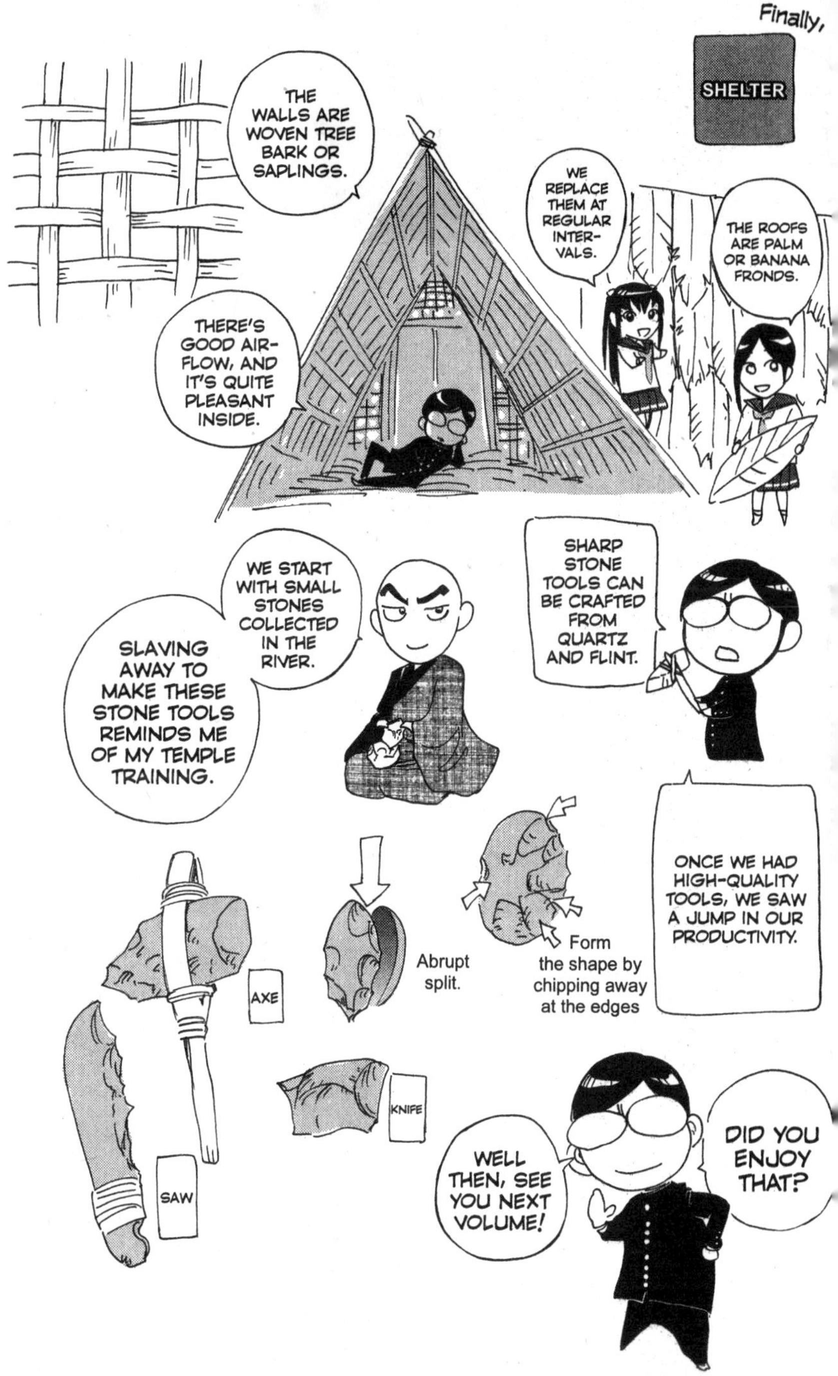
Finally,
SHELTER
THE ROOFS ARE PALM OR BANANA FRONDS.
WE REPLACE THEM AT REGULAR INTER-VALS.
THE WALLS ARE WOVEN TREE BARK OR SAPLINGS.
THERE'S GOOD AIR-FLOW, AND IT'S QUITE PLEASANT INSIDE.
SHARP STONE TOOLS CAN BE CRAFTED FROM QUARTZ AND FLINT.
WE START WITH SMALL STONES COLLECTED IN THE RIVER.
SLAVING AWAY TO MAKE THESE STONE TOOLS REMINDS ME OF MY TEMPLE TRAINING.
ONCE WE HAD HIGH-QUALITY TOOLS, WE SAW A JUMP IN OUR PRODUCTIVITY.
Form the shape by chipping away at the edges
Abrupt split.
AXE
KNIFE
SAW
DID YOU ENJOY THAT?
WELL THEN, SEE YOU NEXT VOLUME!

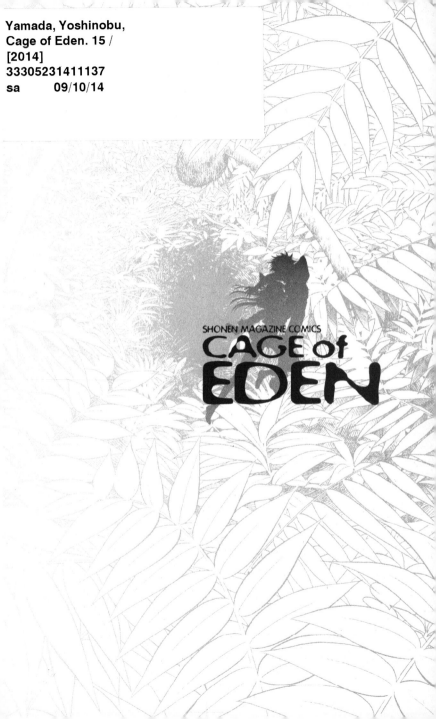

SHONEN MAGAZINE COMICS

CAGE of
EDEN

Translation Notes

"Sygdommen til Døden," pages 2, 69

The title of Chapter 125 refers to a book written by Danish philosopher Søren Kierkegaard, known in English as "The Sickness Unto Death," that is a treatise on despair.

NOW, NOW...
WHY DON'T WE USE JANKEN TO DECIDE!
JANKEN ...?!
THEN IT'D BE FAIR, NO? I WANNA BE USEFUL TOO, SO COUNT ME IN.

***Janken*, page 18**

Janken or *jankenpon* is the Japanese term for the popular hand game "rock-paper-scissors," also known as "roshambo." In Japan, it is used much more commonly to draw lots than flipping coins or throwing dice, and can involve any number of people to start.

Idol, page 29

While most commonly referring to young female media personalities, such as J-pop artists, actresses, and models (but occasionally also foreigners and young male stars), this Japanese phenomenon can extend to civilians as well, i.e. the prettiest student or junior employee.

Mammoth Resurrection Project, page 126

There are currently several such projects and research groups, some of which are seeking to bring back other extinct species, including ones such as the passenger pigeon that disappeared much more recently. Critics point out a number of ethical and practical concerns, such as the fact that with somatic cell transfer, these new de-extinct animals will not be exact replicas but genetically engineered chimeras, that it takes many more than one or two individuals to be a "species," that there may be tens if not hundreds of embryos who fail to develop to birth implanted in female surrogate wombs, and that, once born, there is the issue of how to restore their original social and ecological behavior patterns without true parents or groups to teach them. In addition, there are questions about the potential environmental impact if enough of a population can be raised for release into nature, whether attention, personnel, and funding ought to be diverted from efforts aimed at preserving extant species that are critically endangered, and even how or why certain species are selected for de-extinction over others.

IF SCIENTISTS CAN HARVEST MINIMALLY DAMAGED DNA-CONTAINING CELLS FROM ITS CARCASS...
...AND INJECT THAT DNA INTO DONOR OVA FROM MODERN ELEPHANTS...
...YOU CAN THEORETICALLY CREATE AN EMBRYO CONTAINING MAMMOTH GENES.
Modern Elephant
Remove nucleus
Ovum
Mammoth
Extract nucleus from cell
Transplant nucleus into empty ovum
Mammoth Clone Embryo

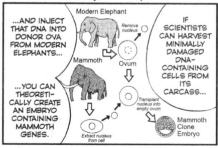

armouse, page 150

he "human" ear growing out of the ack of the first earmouse, also known s the Vacanti mouse after the Vacanti rothers who developed it, neither was n ear nor contained any human cells. It as a human ear-shaped structure that as formed from a biodegradable scaf-ld seeded with cow cartilage cells and ien implanted under the mouse's skin. was also developed at the University f Massachusetts Medical School, not arvard University. The Vacanti broth-rs are now considered the fathers of ssue engineering.

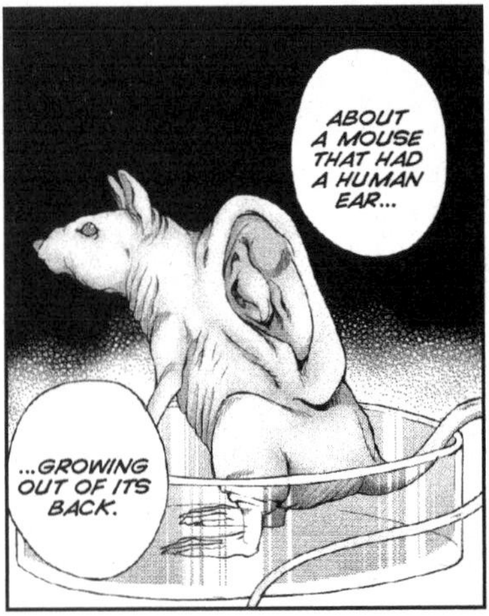
ABOUT A MOUSE THAT HAD A HUMAN EAR...
...GROWING OUT OF ITS BACK.

***rea 88,* page 152**

rea 88 is a seminal manga series from the early 1980s set in a fictional secret iercenary air force base of the same name. The story has also been adapted ito several anime works as well as a theatrical film.

rea 51 fact check, page 152

i July 2013 (two years after the original appearance of this chapter in both iagazine and graphic novel form), in response to a Freedom of Information Act equest, the CIA did finally release a document that officially acknowledged the xistence of Area 51.

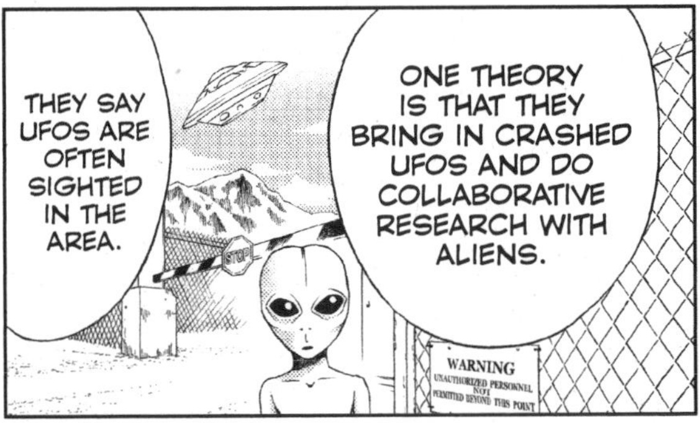
ONE THEORY IS THAT THEY BRING IN CRASHED UFOS AND DO COLLABORATIVE RESEARCH WITH ALIENS.
THEY SAY UFOS ARE OFTEN SIGHTED IN THE AREA.
STOP
WARNING
UNAUTHORIZED PERSONNEL NOT PERMITTED BEYOND THIS POINT

Yotsubishi Heavy Industries, page 158

Likely an homage to Mitsubishi Heavy Industries, which is part of the Mitsubishi Group conglomerate. "*Mitsubishi*" means "three diamonds (diamond-shapes)" and "*yotsubishi*" means "four diamonds." This is also reflected in the brand logo, which resembles Mitsubishi's except with the lower two diamonds moved upward to allow for an extra diamond at the bottom.

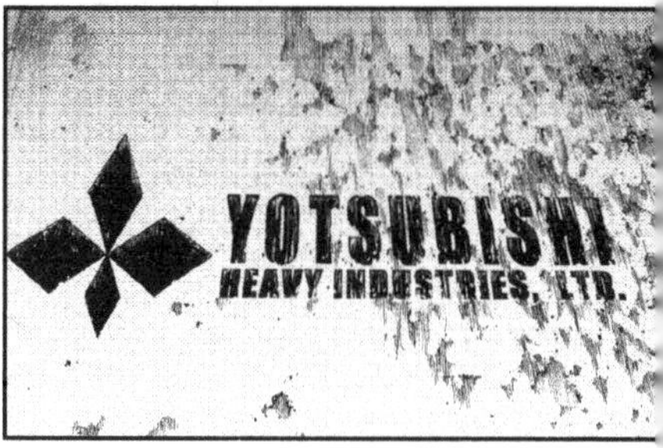
YOTSUBISHI
HEAVY INDUSTRIES, LTD.

***Hiéron*, page 163**

An homage to Lotte's *Hiyaron* instan cooling packs. "*Hié*" and "*hiya*" both mean "cold" or "cool" in Japanese. Lotte also manufactures a popular instant heat pack called "*Hokaron*" ("*hoka*" means "toasty").

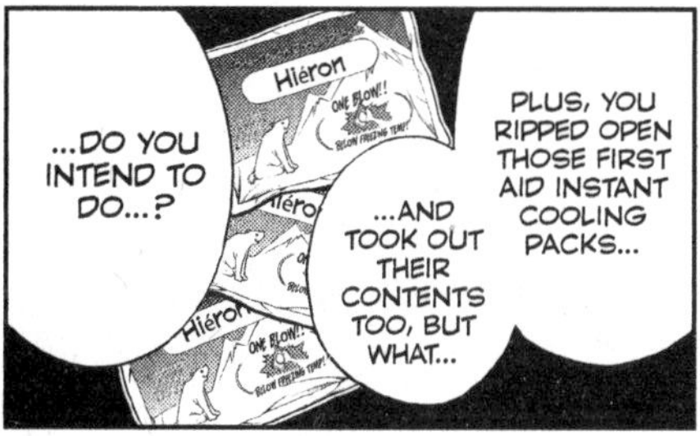
PLUS, YOU RIPPED OPEN THOSE FIRST AID INSTANT COOLING PACKS...
...AND TOOK OUT THEIR CONTENTS TOO, BUT WHAT...
...DO YOU INTEND TO DO...?
Hiéron
ONE BLOW!!

Svelbard Global Seed Vault, page 167

The Svelbard Global Seed Vault stores seed samples that are duplicates of thos contained in other seed vaults across the world. Its officially stated mission is to be a failsafe against the accidental loss of these other genebanks, many of whic are in politically or environmentally unstable regions, rather than to provide a "Noah's Ark" of plant life with which to launch repopulation efforts in the case of nuclear war or a natural disaster.

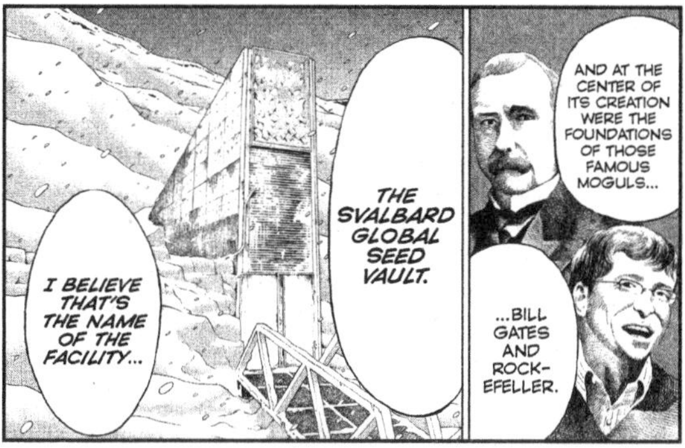
AND AT THE CENTER OF ITS CREATION WERE THE FOUNDATIONS OF THOSE FAMOUS MOGULS...
...BILL GATES AND ROCK-EFELLER.
THE SVALBARD GLOBAL SEED VAULT.
I BELIEVE THAT'S THE NAME OF THE FACILITY...

A Kodansha Comics Trade Paperback Original.

Cage of Eden volume 15 copyright © 2011 Yoshinobu Yamada
English translation copyright © 2014 Yoshinobu Yamada

Published in the United States by Kodansha Comics, an imprint of Kodansha USA Publishing, LLC, New York.

Publication rights for this English edition arranged through Kodansha Ltd., Tokyo.

First published in Japan in 2011 by Kodansha Ltd., Tokyo, as Eden no Ori 15

ISBN 978-1-61262-264-4

Printed in the United States of America.

www.kodanshacomics.com

9 8 7 6 5 4 3 2 1

Translator: Mari Morimoto
Lettering: Morgan Hart
Kodansha Comics edition cover design: Phil Balsman